THE POETICS
OF MANHOOD

Contest and Identity in a Cretan Mountain Village

MICHAEL HERZFELD

PRINCETON UNIVERSITY PRESS

Copyright © 1985 by Princeton University Press

Published by Princeton University Press, 41 William Street,
Princeton, New Jersey 08540
In the United Kingdom: Princeton University Press, Oxford

All Rights Reserved

Library of Congress Cataloging in Publication Data will be
found on the last printed page of this book

Paperback Edition, 1988

Publication of this book has been aided by grants from
the Bollingen Fund and the Paul Mellon Fund

This book has been composed in Linotron Bodoni

Princeton University Press books are printed on acid-free paper,
and meet the guidelines for permanence and durability
of the Committee on Production Guidelines for Book Longevity
of the Council on Library Resources

Printed in the United States of America

3   5   7   9   10   8   6   4

For Cornelia

CONTENTS

LIST OF ILLUSTRATIONS

Photographs by Cornelia Mayer Herzfeld

LIST OF FIGURES

PREFACE

Ethnographic work in Greece provides special challenges of its own. The country, though politically young in European terms, lays claim to a history said to be the very source of Europe itself, and the Greeks of today have derived both pride and discomfort from the intense preoccupation of their leaders with the status of this ancient heritage.

The several excellent ethnographic studies that have appeared so far recognize the importance of this aspect of Greek life (see especially Campbell 1964:1-6; Friedl 1962:105-106). Nevertheless, anthropologists have been taken to task for failing to relate rural concerns to the wider national and international contexts, and this complaint has been echoed at the broader level of Mediterranean studies in general (Mouzelis 1978:68-70; cf. Davis 1977:5-10). Such complaints, which reflect a widespread dissatisfaction with the contribution of Mediterranean ethnography to anthropological theory, have led in recent years to a greater understanding of the ways in which rural economy and political life are integrated with these larger structures. But they also pose a serious risk. While local-level ethnography demands a concomitant focus on the larger context of the nation-state, it also offers insight into the ways in which members of rural communities conceptualize the relationship between two levels. In the headlong rush to make our rural studies less exotic and more "relevant," we all too easily forget to give the villagers themselves a voice. Indeed, the very act of writing ethnography presupposes that the villagers' ideas belong to the level of description rather than of theory, and this obscures their ability to draw on a theoretical (or at least conceptual) capital of their own.

Take, for example, their understanding of political relations within the nation-state. The bureaucratic state endorses a pyramidal or hierarchical model of political relations. From the villagers' perspective, however, the relationship may instead be a segmentary one. In this model, rival kin groups unite in defense of their common village; feuding villages unite in their loyalty to a regional identity; and regions subordinate their competitive loyalties to the greater loyalty commanded by the all-encompassing nation. Although the segmentary model was initially developed by Evans-Pritchard (1940) for an agnatic idiom of social organization, and although the dominant idiom of political relations in Glendi, the community with which this book is concerned, is also an agnatic one, the idea of segmentation does not *require* any form of patriliny. In its simplest definition, it is a relativistic model of political relations, in which more localized allegiances and enmities are theoretically subordinated to the demands of larger ones. The villagers of Glendi fully recognize this aspect of their political vision, and talk about it. An essential component of the segmentary perspective is that the larger and smaller entities are all moral communities and so share essentially the same formal properties of inclusion and exclusion. Glendiots think of their community as a kind of small state, and thus assimilate the bureaucratic structures of statehood into an essentially segmentary view of the world.

Glendi may represent an extreme of explicitness in this direction. It is a predominantly pastoral community in a national society where pastoralism, and rural subsistence in general, have suffered a long and perhaps irreversible decline. Because the Glendiots have a long tradition of defiant independence, when under foreign occupation and more recently as citizens in the Greek state, their community has come to seem eccentric in comparative, national terms. Pause for a moment, however, and consider this apparent eccentricity. It is very largely a matter of the community's critical responses to bureaucratic domination and interference. Glendiots are politically aware; they are also proud of their identity as members of the Greek *ethnos*. What they do not accept so readily is the bureaucratic assumption that the state necessarily constitutes the best representative of the *ethnos*. Many a word or deed in Glendi probes the bureaucratic system, and finds it wanting. The sense of criticism is all the stronger because every such action exemplifies what the Glendiots take to be characteristic expressions of Greekness in themselves. These actions not only express Greekness, but also Cretan, regional (Rethimniot), and village identity, and so pit the Glendiots against other claimants to an idealized, ultimate excellence. A strong sense of distinctive identity does not constitute political separatism as such. On the contrary, the Glendiot experience shows that concentric loyalties are embarrassing to the bureaucratic state, not because they represent a secessionist threat, but because they offer an alternative ideological vision of the nation itself.

In the process of exploring their own attitudes, and the problems created by the evident disparity of the latter with the official ideology, the Glendiots talk a great deal about "meaning." They entertain an idiosyncratic, often dissident concept of social value, which allows them to comment critically on the social values of the official world that surrounds them. Rather than attempt to use some generalized notion of meaning, anthropological or otherwise, I have tried in this book to follow their own definitions and uses of *simasia*—their own term for "meaning"—and to show how and when they recognize this property in the actions and speech of others—their covillagers, the members of rival communities, and the officials and politicians with whom they come into frequent contact.

This raises a fundamental issue of methodology. *Simasia* is a complex idea, with theoretical underpinnings that deserve to be taken at least as seriously as our own technical apparatus. Some may object that I am attributing the status of abstract theory to largely inchoate notions that more properly belong to the level of mere description. What should perhaps come under challenge instead, however, is the largely implicit distinction that we conventionally draw between theory and ethnography—a "folk theory" of our own discourse, as it were. The Glendiots taught me a great deal about semantics and semiotics through their fascination with their own etymological cognate, *simasia*. Consequently, I feel that I am not dishonoring the several major academic authorities I cite by putting their ideas into a common analytical framework with the Glendiots' own social and semiotic theories and concepts. I have learned from them all.

What is it that makes the Glendiots so preoccupied with questions of meaning? Part of the answer seems to lie in the tensions peculiar to their relationships with the bureaucratic state. This conflict is most evident in their dealings with the political establishment over the endemic practice of animal theft. The villagers raid each others' herds systematically and in accordance with a well-understood set of norms: there are right and wrong ways to steal—clearly a distinction that has nothing to do with a legally minded bureaucratic ideology. They do this, they say, "in order to make friends." In other words, a raiding cycle, successfully completed, creates a new alliance. At the same time, however, it also pits the participants against the law. Here then lies the crux of their special identity: how to remain good Cretan men, which includes being good raiders, while also being good Greek citizens. For them, the choice is not difficult: their actions express the devil-may-care love of independence that wrung freedom from the Turkish oppressor, and that to this day treats the pettiness of bureaucratic "pen-pushers" with proud contempt. It is the *state* that experiences an irresolvable contradiction here. But, as we shall see, the entire system of animal raiding could not have survived intact without at least some political interest at high levels. Thus, the Glendiots who still raid—and the number seems finally to be decreasing significantly—bring to the fore some crucial questions of national identity. Those who condemn animal raiding as an outmoded "barbarism" have accepted the rule of bureaucratic law more willingly, perhaps, but they, too, are involved in a continuing exploration of what the relationship between national and local levels of identity should be. An anthropology that seeks to make sense of the role of the nation-state in social experience can perhaps learn something from the actions and, still more, from the more reflexive musings of the Glendiots—from their attribution of *simasia* to deeds that support or defy the bureaucratic definition of identity.

As will rapidly become clear, *simasia* is not a lexicographical abstraction. On the contrary, it is something that Glendiots recognize in *action*, a term that includes speech but does not necessarily give linguistic meaning any special priority. It is an essentially *poetic* notion, in the technical sense that it concerns the means in which significance is conveyed through actual performance. Moreover, since it cuts across the boundary between speech and other forms of action, we can also let it dissolve for us the entirely artificial distinction between linguistic or symbolic and political concerns. Meaning is found in all spheres of social action, the commonplace as much as the ritualistic or artistic. At the same time, the key concept here is *action*. The Glendiot concept of meaning gives short shrift to any text, be it a song, a raid, or a malicious remark, unless it is drawn from specific and lived experience. Glendiots have no interest in formal taxonomies as such, but they do have an acute understanding of the ways in which formal properties can be gleaned *by actors* from *all* forms of social experience as a means of investing that experience with a shared significance.

This does not mean that we should recognize only those aspects of meaning that the Glendiots have already explicitly identified for us. On the contrary, the formal interrelationship between different areas of experience is not something on which the villagers have any particular reason to dwell. But their recognition of meaning in so many domains of social life does point the way to structural analogies that may be of comparative interest. A crucial example here is the close analogy between social events and narrative structure: the latter provides the principal means by which we can explore the significance attributed by the actors themselves to the former. This study as a whole concerns itself with the poetics of social interaction and of the self; it is an attempt to understand how individuals negotiate the tensions between the congruent but potentially conflicting levels of social identity that are implied by the segmentary model. It is itself the process and product of my own negotiation of meaning with the villagers.

The idea of a social poetics has already had a productive effect on the study of specific problems of analysis.[1] In this book I suggest that it is capable of a highly integrative application, since poetic principles guide all *effective* social interaction. Such a poetics must also correspond intelligibly with local social theory, with indigenous ideas about meaning, and with criteria of style, relevance, and importance. A poetics of any kind is concerned with the constitution of meaning. We cannot hope to understand how Glendiots find and make meaning in their lives unless we can discover something of the principles by which they are able to recognize meaning. Embedded ideas about meaning are both a cause and an effect of the actions that ethnographers are trained to observe. Some ethnographies of rural Greek society have implicitly recognized this; my aim here is to build on their rich sensitivity to indigenous social theory, using the generously shared and profoundly conceived insights of the Glendiots themselves to develop an ethnographic poetics that corresponds, as far as I am able to make it do so, to their experiences and understandings.

While the emphasis on meaning and discourse builds on some of the insights of earlier ethnographers of Greek society, it also leads the present work in a somewhat different direction. Many of the themes developed here—social organization, the political and social uses of friendship, moral values (especially concepts of sin and responsibility), and the relationship between the village and the rest of the world—bear clear marks of my indebtedness to the work already done in other communities. At the same time, I have deformed the conventional ethnographic layout in order to do justice to a conviction that social relations themselves constitute a kind of discourse—the poetics described here—that parallels and converges with the discourse of narrative, jest, and song. Two kinds of structure, social and narrative, are thus approached within a single framework.

Some may object that much of the narrative material is best left to narratologists and folklorists. In my view, however, that is an entirely invidious and artificial distinction. Admittedly, the main function of narrative material in local-level ethnographies of Greek society has so far been primarily illustrative. But the sensitive embedding of narrative materials in discussions of social relations (e.g., Campbell 1964:118-121, 135, 314-315; du Boulay 1974:38-39, 82) recommends a more thorough examination of structural links between the two categories of material—an aspect of ethnographic research that is already well represented by Danforth's (1982) study of Greek death rituals.

In this book, I retain the convention of working with a single, relatively small community. At the same time, I focus heavily on the ideological, political, and historical relationship between the local community on the one hand, and the state and other encompassing entities on the other. In developing this focus, I have derived great benefit from the example suggested by my predecessors, notably Campbell (1964), Friedl (1962), and Loizos (1975). Here too, however, I have placed less emphasis on the mechanisms of social organization as such, and have tried instead to illuminate the ways in which rhetoric and discourse mediate the integration of the local community into the larger entities. This approach makes it easier to see what the grand political and historical circumstances of their existence mean to the villagers themselves. For it is clear that they do not regard the national capital as the center of their moral universe. That exalted position is taken by their own community, and the deployment of their relations with the outside world stems from that fact.

A common criticism of anthropological research in Greece and elsewhere is that it rests too heavily on the examination of obscure, peripheral communities. One could easily counter that charge by pointing out that these communities, or others much like them, have played a vital role in the formation of national self-stereotypes, and that they lie at the very core of the self-image that Greeks collectively present to the outside world. To understand Greece's relationship to the world at large, it is necessary to understand the relationship of such "eccentric" communities to the administrative center; and it seems likely, on the face of it, that the same holds true for most other countries. In that sense, the villagers' view of the matter, rather than that of the critics of anthropological research, offers a better prospect of understanding. And this, in turn, strenghtens the case for an ethnographic focus on the rhetoric or discourse of local identity.

The name "Glendi" is fictitious and an index of my respect for the villagers' privacy. It does not ensure an impenetrable disguise—no detailed description can also be entirely cryptic—but I hope that readers of this book will agree to share the ethical responsibility that my use of an invented place-name implies. The Glendiots' generosity calls for no less. They allowed me to penetrate matters that could have proved highly embarrassing for them, knowing full well that I intended to use this material in a book. Most were happy with the explicit understanding that their personal anonymity would similarly be protected by pseudonyms. I have been strictly systematic where necessary in my use of personal as well as topographical pseudonyms, so that the ethnographic saliency of such matters as naming patterns should not be lost. Glendiots differed in their views of what should be included, or how it should be presented; and many of them might be uncomfortable with the analysis itself, especially since unfavorable press treatment has led them to expect the worst. Yet nothing in this book is written out of anything but the profoundest respect for them; and my insistence on recognizing their own contribution, at a theoretical level rather than grandly treating them as "ethnographic subjects," is the best evidence of this. If this book can influence others to share my respect for the Glendiots, I should be well satisfied. Especially with respect to animal theft, I hope that what I have written may help to counterbalance some of the more sensationalistic caricatures that the customs and institutions of highland Crete have so often evoked in other parts of Greek society as well as abroad.

I have called the village "Glendi" after the local (and standard Greek) term for a festive occasion. Few excuses are needed by the villagers for a social gathering with all the merriment, music, dancing, food, and drink that constitute a true *ghlendi*. There is nothing flippant about this pseudonym: *ghlendia* are major contexts for the structuring of social experience. An important subjective dimension of my field experience, moreover, was the appreciation of Glendiot humor. It is not that other people do not laugh and joke, but that the Glendiots joke in ways that highlight their oxymoronic sensibilities. Their collective experience has proved so bitter and so full of danger and contradiction that their only salvation lies in defiant laughter. Here, in confrontation after uproarious confrontation with a rival thief, with the assassin of a loved brother, with the might of the law, even with the very moment of death, the Glendiots act out amused contempt for the fear within them and the dangers around them. It is in joking with the terrible, above all else, that the Glendiots—poets of social experience—draw meaning from their tension-ridden lives.

To the Glendiots themselves, of course, my debt is enormous. Through their lively exegetical concerns, their imaginative interest in my work, their constant offers to help me in my task, and their willingness to record on tape an enormous range of narratives and other texts, they can claim a remarkable degree of involvement in the authorship of this book.

In the course of my research, other friends and colleagues also supported and advised me. I should particularly mention John Campbell, who, when I was still a doctoral student, encouraged me in my decision to work on Crete from December 1974 through May 1975 as a supplement to my unexpectedly brief period of work on Rhodes and thereby provided me with a research focus that I was able to develop much further once I had put my doctoral work behind me. It was the inspiration of this early visit that led to my return in July 1976, and again from August 1977 through June 1978. Richard Bauman, Loring M. Danforth, Mary Douglas, James W. Fernandez, Roger Joseph, Nennie Panourgia (who also provided valuable archival assistance), Akis Papataxiarchis, and Nora Skouteri-Didaskalou all subsequently read versions of this manuscript and offered me the benefits of their critical insight. John M. Hollingsworth turned my eccentric scrawls into elegant line drawings, and Peter J. Nebergall did a fine job of preparing the photographs for publication. I am warmly grateful for the patience and skilled guidance of Alice Calaprice and Gail Ullman at Princeton University Press. I should also like to express my appreciation of a summer research grant from the American Council of Learned Societies (partly supported by the National Endowment for the Humanities), which allowed a useful visit to Glendi in 1981, during the crucial pre-election period. I returned again for a few days in 1984 with manuscript in hand, in the course of wider research on disemia (see chapter 1, note 5) that was supported by grants-in-aid from Indiana University's Office of Graduate and Research Development, Russian and East European Institute, and West European National Resource Center. It was invaluable both to observe the 1981 political campaigns, and then, some three years later, to discuss my findings with villagers before sending the final manuscript back to Princeton. Needless to say, the responsibility for the final form and content of the text is entirely my own, but this should in no way conceal the very real gratitude I feel for all the professional, personal, and institutional support that I have received.

Unquestionably, my greatest debt is to Cornelia Mayer Herzfeld, my wife. She shared with me the vicissitudes as well as the delights of village life; provided, through her careful but open demeanor, a fine road into the intimate company of both women and men in Glendi; and advanced the research itself in innumerable practical ways and with seemingly limitless acuity. Her perceptive eye becomes a notable presence in this book through a selection from the rich archive of photographs that she created. In them, the reader can see the Glendiots' warm response to her interest in them; and to her I dedicate this product of our triune exchanges of understanding.

NOTE ON TRANSLITERATION

Modern Greek presents notorious transliterational problems. In the system I have adopted for this book, I have opted to maintain the distinctions between *d* and *dh*, and *g* and *gh*, as these are phonemic in the Cretan dialect. I do not use them in proper names, including pseudonyms, as this would have resulted in the unfamiliar presentation of the names of some well-known Greek people and places. I believe that the increase in clarity justifies any consequent sense of inconsistency.

The Greek is given as it occurred, which often means a mixture of local and standard forms. This extends to a high degree of both lexical and phonological inconsistency, not all of which is haphazard.

In the specimen texts given in Greek characters in the Appendix, I have used the Latin characters *b*, *d*, and *g* to indicate the sounds that correspond to them in English; these are phonetically distinct from the Greek ντ, μπ and γκ.

Palatalization is indicated by a diacritical mark (ˇ) in both Latin and Greek character transcriptions (e.g., č = k̆).

For the Cretan dialect and demotic Greek (but not for *katharevousa* in the References) I have adopted the monotonic accentuation convention. Especially when mixed dialect and "standard demotic" forms occur, this convention obviates the necessity of dealing with transcriptional questions of dubious significance.

NOTE ON KINSHIP ABBREVIATIONS

I have adopted the following conventions:

B	= brother	M	= mother
D	= daughter	S	= son
F	= father	W	= wife
H	= husband	Z	= sister

and combinations thereof (e.g., MBS = mother's brother's son).

In the bibliography, all *katharevousa* titles are given with all accents; elsewhere I use the monotonic convention.

THE POETICS OF MANHOOD

CHAPTER ONE

THE POETICS OF MANHOOD

Obscurity and Pride

In 1671, just a few years after the Turkish invasion of Crete, Ottoman documents made the first mention of the hamlet of Glendi.[1] The small village, then the home of some 230 people, lay half-hidden in a rocky valley that broke the treeline of the Mount Ida foothills at about six hundred meters above sea level. Of whatever families may have resided here during the preceding Byzantine and Venetian periods, all that remains is a single questionably Byzantine family name and a ruined Veneto-Byzantine chapel well outside the presently inhabited zone—a sharp contrast indeed to the rich testimonies of these and still older periods in nearby communities. In Glendi itself, the oldest building in the presently inhabited area dates from the late nineteenth century, when the end of Turkish rule was already in sight.

Glendi's foundation legend, moreover, offers no clue to chronology. In part, its timeless quality springs from its celebration of something that the Glendiots of today still applaud in word and deed: the serendipitous response to hardship and poverty, the ability to turn the meager gifts of chance to advantage. When an errant goat chanced upon a rare water hole, its owner decided to settle on the spot. Later settlers consisted of men who had fled from their home villages further west to escape certain vengeance for deaths committed by their own hands. Again, the few oral records of these individuals are stereotypically uninformative.

Such obscurity seems thoroughly in character. Exposed by its sparse vegetation to the burning sun and gritty Saharan winds of summer, and chilled in midwinter by a dreary alternation of snow and drizzling rain, Glendi hides behind a reputation as opaque and uncertain as the *katsifara*—the cloud cover that often drifts through the village during the winter months and brings both risk and concealment to those who have furtive business in the surrounding foothills. Despite the frequent rain and fog, and the chill winter snows that occasionally render the local roads impassable, there are few safe natural sources of drinking water. A dried-up river bed, bisecting the village's main road at its lowest point, exposes some of the houses built alongside it to the risk of flooding after a heavy rain, but offers no reliable source of water. Concentric curls of terracing fade into the winter mist or summer haze above the village, attesting to a meager agricultural activity now abandoned for two decades. Rock and scrub cover almost the entire landscape beyond the village, except where a few fields—each divided into small shares and often an equal number of different kinds of crops—bear witness to a system of equal partible inheritance that discourages large holdings. Not a place, one would think, to encourage new settlers, except perhaps those who might prefer that their whereabouts remain unknown. Today, the creation of a gleaming new silo, a sports ground, and winter animal shelters in and around the village suggests an accelerated level of activity. But the overall impression, reinforced by the villagers' deprecating commentary, remains one of adaptation to harsh circumstances, rather than of an enthusiastically chosen location. People have rarely been expected to take up residence here voluntarily; the tradition of a refuge from authority and revenge is still an active focus of the villagers' collective self-image.

Whatever that self-image may be—and it is the purpose of this book to explore and define it—the obscurity of the village's situation has certainly played a major part in forming it. This obscurity protected the Glendiots from the more onerous attentions of the Turkish administration, and apparently gave them a sound refuge in which to live according to their own ideals and values. Even this freedom was ambiguous, since the local *aghas* (Turkish administrator) allegedly forced the local Christian maidens to dance barefoot on dried peas for his pleasure. However incomplete it may actually have been, the Glendiots' concealment became an important aspect of their collective self-view in its own right; it expressed both their isolation from, and their contempt for, the world of farmers, merchants, and bureaucrats.

Glendi's relationship to the rest of Crete resembles that of the island as a whole to the Greek nation-state. Glendiots regard their wealthier fellow-Cretans with marked disfavor, resenting their access to the generously watered lowland vineyards and olive groves and to the comforts of urban life in the major coastal towns (see map, fig. 1). The group of villages to which Glendi belongs, and through which it is enmeshed in a nexus of reciprocal animal raiding, is starkly marked off from the richer lowland zone by a series of severely depopulated and crumbling hamlets along the Rethimno road, while the Iraklio road is straddled by a large

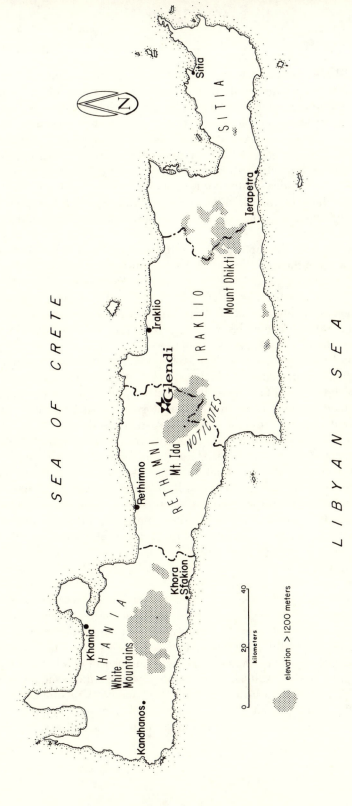

Fig. 1. Sketch-map of Crete showing approximate location of Glendi.

village whose two sections, upper and lower, seem to mark the end of the wild zone and the beginning of domesticity, respectively. Few trees grow in the upper reaches of this wilder area, although Glendi's location in a relatively sheltered valley has permitted the planting of a few stunted olive and fruit trees, as well, it is said, as the development of a relatively mild-tempered personality type that allegedly contrasts strongly with the comparatively uncontrolled, violent tempers of the inhabitants of more exposed communities. Natural differences define cultural ones; and the social ideology of the Glendiots—the central topic of this book—is "naturally" defined by the circumstances of physical isolation and a hard life.

By standing at the top of the road that sweeps down into Glendi after tracing a circuitous and laborious route uphill from Rethimno, the regional capital on the coast, the visitor can get a good sense of the village's sheltered yet isolated character. Above the road, distant yet looming, rears the snowcapped peak of Mount Ida. Closer to hand come the vast areas of scrub, rock, and deserted terracing. Only in the inhabited valley itself are there many signs of cultivation—mostly small vegetable gardens, and an occasional fig tree. When tracing this road through the long, outstretched satellite cluster down to the dry river bed and on through the main village area, then gently uphill again at right angles out to a modern church on a small promontory, the visitor then encounters a different picture. Straight ahead, a road leads down to some well-watered villages known for their extensive orange groves. Slightly to the right, another valley boasts olive trees and some straggling vines. And at right angles to the first road, a longer, straighter one leads gently upwards, away from cultivation and back up to the bare rocks on which Psila, the highest village, perches out of sight. A few smaller hamlets can be discerned in the middle distance. Suffused with bluish and violet tints, a circle of misty crags defines the horizon, and hides the sea that both protected and exposed Crete over the many centuries of a long recorded history.

Crete, by far the largest island at the outer, southern edge of the national territory of present-day Greece, regards itself as an idiosyncratic and proudly independent part of the national entity, distinct from it, physically separated from it, but yet endowed with qualities that have made Crete the birthplace of many national leaders in politics, war, and the arts. Glendiots see their village as a microcosm of what the island should have been—as, in short, one of the few communities that rebuffed any truck with foreign invaders and that preserved the moral and social values that modernity has since corrupted in the plains. While the coastal towns were open to all manner of foreign influences in dress, language, manners, and ideas, the highlanders fiercely preserved their sense of separate identity. As Greece was ideologically represented as the victim of Great Power duplicity, and Crete the victim of Greek political machinations,[2] so Glendiots saw their own lot as determined by unscrupulous local operators who had no concern for the Glendiots' condition except insofar as it could be exploited for their own political ends. At the same time, as Greece claimed to have "given the light to Europe," and Crete set an example of heroism to the rest of Greece through the islanders' incessant resistance to the Turks, so the Glendiots and their immediate neighbors could claim to have preserved the essence of Cretan identity in their inaccessible mountain fastnesses. For example, in 1866, when Cretan monks and civilians were trapped by the Turks in the monastery of Arkadi during one of the island's periodic insurrections, the Greek defenders preferred to blow themselves up rather than surrender. The Greek and foreign press upheld this as a true instance of *Greek* heroism; island historians still recall it as a mark of the isolated heroism of a *Crete* battling the Turks long after the beginnings of continental Greek independence in 1821; and the villagers of Glendi, while proud of both these levels of achievement, find special meaning in the fact that several *Glendiots* perished in the flames. Political repression and isolation are thus combined with moral purity at all three levels of a hierarchy in which Glendi stands to Crete as Crete stands to Greece.

In 1898, when Crete became an autonomous state under Greek supervision, little of this changed. Independence was short-lived, but even the incorporation of Crete into the Greek State in 1913 made little difference to the local sense of isolation. To this day there are Glendiots who remember the single village grocer laboriously driving his donkey, laden with sacks of produce that the poor soil of Glendi could not sustain, returning along barely visible tracks from the nearest market town a full day's trek away. Even by the time the Germans invaded Crete in 1941, conditions had not changed appreciably, and indeed the continued isolation of the highland villages sustained the underground resistance during the four harsh years, full of vicious reprisals and forced labor, of German control. Glendiots played an active role in the resistance movement, and profited from the Allies' gratitude at the end of the war. Then, and only then, did the economic and political isolation of the village begin slowly to dissipate.

Only in 1956, however, did a highland road network finally start to draw Glendi into the economic and administrative nexus of the state to any radical degree. Today, Glendiots ride down frequently to the towns by bus or private car—to arrange bank loans, buy consumer goods not brought to the village by the constant flow of vending trunks, or deal with bureaucrats and lawyers. Glendi is a mere ninety-minute bus ride away from the busy tourist center at Iraklio (a port town and point of departure for the great archaeological sites at Knossos and Phaestos), and an only slightly longer one from the regional capital of Rethimno. Even so, however, the relics of isolation are hard to overcome. Mention of the village still elicits a curious blend of indifference and alarm from urban Cretans. Irakliots wonder openly, if perhaps hyperbolically, how one can live there without getting killed or wounded; one man even expressed amazement that the Glendiots really did have municipal elections just like everyone else. In the village, new buildings, made for the most part of large cement blocks and decorated with wrought-iron railings and modern electrical fittings, are springing up everywhere, in contrast to the desolate stone ruins one encounters in so many of the lower-lying communities; but this, too, is an almost invisible development from the perspective of the urban centers. To the townsfolk, the Glendiots and their immediate neighbors are still fearsome mountain people, admired for their preservation of idealized ancient virtues as much as they are despised and feared for their supposed violence and lawlessness.

A Poetics of the Self

This study may seem to exemplify the obsession with remote and atypical communities that some have attributed to ethnographic research. Anthropologists, however, do not characteristically insist that the communities they study necessarily exemplify national or other encompassing entities (see the discussion in Dimen and Friedl 1976:286). On the other hand, scholarly nationalists of the country itself often take such apparently marginal communities as typical in an extreme sense: often, their location at the territorial edges of the country is sufficient reason to insist on their typicality in defiance of counterclaims from across the border. In the case of Greece, which is far from unique in this respect, the problem is nicely illustrated by Campbell's (1964) study of the Epirot Sarakatsani, a transhumant pastoral community. On the one hand, the *social* marginality of the Sarakatsani is amply illustrated by vignettes in which they are humiliated and mocked by farmers, lawyers, and officials; on the other hand, as Campbell's opening pages (pp. 1-6) make clear, the question of their Greekness was (and is) a burning issue, since it forms the crux of territorial disagreements with Greece's neighbors. Much the same can be said of all the *akritikes periokhes* (border areas), whose very name conjures up the ambiguous status of the Byzantine heroes known as *akrites*—men who defended the outer reaches of Greek culture, yet represented in their own persons its adulteration by foreign influences. In the border areas, national identity confronts regional difference. The prevalence of animal theft in many such societies throughout southern Europe (see Di Bella 1983) suggests, moreover, that from a comparative perspective the choice of a community in which it is prevalent may lead us right to the heart of the paradox.

Crete certainly occupies a position at once eccentric within the wider framework of Greek society, yet one that is also central to its self-image. Its people are often despised and feared outside the island, yet its role in the development and defense of the modern Greek nation-state is widely acknowledged. Within Crete, highland villages such as Glendi have long elevated this paradoxical status to a further extreme. Even under Turkish rule (1645-1898), Glendiots were directly involved in the major events of island (and therefore also national) history, despite their physical isolation and the deep cultural and social contrasts that made them so much an object of fear and contempt to the lowlanders and townsfolk. This isolation was clearly sufficient to permit the persistence of what, by present-day Greek standards, seems a highly idiosyncratic way of life. On the other hand, it did not prevent the villagers from participating in some of the most significant events in recent national history, in ways where their fierce opposition to authority gave them a distinct advantage. In the Greek War of Independence, which began in 1821, a band of Glendiots was led by the descendant of one of the early fugitives from another village's revenge. Their patrigroup, though depleted in numbers, is still in existence, and the fighter's name survives as the collective designation of a sub-patrigroup consisting of his own descendants.

In 1866, again, seventeen Glendiots perished in the burning of the Arkadi Monastery at the end of a fierce but unsuccessful revolt against Turkish rule. This event so dramatized the Cretans' plight in the context of both Greek and international politics that it hastened the emancipation of the island from Turkish rule. Their involvement cost the Glendiots dearly: the Turks, in retaliation, burned the village to the ground. The visceral meaning of this event was demonstrated to me over a century later by an octogenarian Glendiot, self-consciously dressed for the occasion in the white boots and formal waistcoat of the older local costume, who declaimed his own verses about the heroism and tragedy of his ancestors' role in the defense of Arkadi. His usually robust voice cracked and faltered, and tears streamed down his cheeks, as he reached the point where his own relationship to the main protagonist—his grandfather—became explicit. This was not a response that could be explained away by reference to the intrusion of nationalistic rhetoric in village life; indeed, such an explanation could only succeed in sounding hollow and cheap.

Instead, what we see here is a complete *identification*. The narrator, imbued with a notion of selfhood that defines identity in terms of continuity in the male line, lamented an encapsulating death—one in which he, his father, his grandfather (the actual protagonist), and indeed all possible ancestors in the same line, are fused into a single identity. He never knew his grandfather, who was slain almost two decades before his own birth, just as another Glendiot who took the life of his brother's killer had never known his brother. In the case of vengeance killing, one might argue that social pressure would make such direct contact with the deceased irrelevant: the shame of failing to "take the blood back" would be sufficient incentive to do so. But this misses the point of a patrilineal ideology in which the inheritance of selfhood in the male line means that the deaths of one's agnates are wounds of the self. The old man who so profusely lamented his grandfather's heroic demise had also inherited his grandfather's baptismal name, and the fact that the grandfather had died fighting for an independence that was at once Glendiot, Cretan, and Greek gave special poignancy to the identification. In his own day, the grandson had acquired a fearsome reputation as an animal thief, and had then also fought against the German invaders and served as village president. In reciting the story of his grandfather's death, he brought together the various strands of the poetics of Glendiot manhood.

The term "poetics" needs some elaboration. Although the concept of poetics has never lost its intimate Aristotelian association with dramatic criticism, it does not seem to have played a great part in the metaphorical extensions of drama into the realm of social relations and their performance. There has been a surprising lack of connection between treatments of "social drama" on the one hand (e.g., Turner 1974) and the orientation toward code decipherment and manipulation that we find in discussions of self-presentation (especially Goffman 1959). Yet it is clear that the successful performance of selfhood depends upon an ability to identify the self with larger categories of identity. In any encounter, the skilled actor alludes to ideological propositions and historical antecedents, but takes care to suppress the sense of incongruity inevitably created by such grandiose implications; as with virtually any trope, the projection of the self as a metonymical encapsulation of some more inclusive entity rests on the violation of ordinariness (cf. Burke 1954:90). A successful performance of personal identity concentrates the audience's attention on the performance itself: the implicit claims are accepted because their very outrageousness carries a revelatory kind of conviction. It is in this self-allusiveness of social performances, and in the concomitant back-grounding of everyday considerations, that we can discern a poetics of social interaction. The self is not presented within everyday life so much as in front of it (illus. 1).

This temporary suspension of context is characteristic of poetic discourse in even the narrowest sense. Poeticity is a "Set (*Einstellung*) toward the *message* as such, focus on the message for its own sake" (Jakobson 1960:356; Waugh 1980:58). There is no intrinsic reason to restrict this insight to the purely verbal manifestations of poetic discourse. Moreover, a poetics of social interaction does not ignore the wider context; but it does attempt to explain how and why the conventions of that context may be violated without injuring the perpetrator's standing. Since the performance of male Glendiots is predicated on a celebration of self—the statement that "I am [the one who matters], and no one else [*Egho ime, če čanis alos*]"—the set toward the message is effectively synonymous with *eghoismos*, self-regard. To the extent that a man's performance successfully announces his personal excellence, it fits the poetic canon of Glendiot social life. Glendiot men engage in a constant struggle to gain a precarious and transitory advantage over each other. Each performance is an incident in that struggle, and the success or failure of each performance marks its progress. Since *eghoismos* is paradoxically a *canon of being different*—whether as a person, or as a representative of kin group, village, or island—its projection is necessarily poetic: it is the projection of difference for its own sake.

The multiplicity of specific meanings attached to *eghoismos* strengthens this argument, too. Whereas the cognate English word "egoism" suggests a pure focus on the self, the Greek term can only be understood as a *social* category. The fierce mustache and insouciant cigarette of the truly successful *eghoistis* are recognizable precisely because they fit a pattern (illus. 2-4). One has *eghoismos* on behalf of a collectivity, be it kin group, patriline, village, region, island, or country. In social performance, it is not always clear which level of identification, if any, is intended as primary. When Glendiots deride the lowlanders, for example, they may hint indirectly at parallels between the comforts of life in the plains and the comparable ease enjoyed by the Turks in their day. When a shepherd attacks the flocks of a powerful rival, his stance is presented as a protection of the good name of household, patriline, and village, and all these entities are likened through a series of narrative expressions to the nation-state itself. A good performance is one that conveys at least a hint of *all* these levels of the hierarchy of social difference. Denotative precision produces a thin performance, and one

1. Evocative poses: "The self is not so much presented within everyday life as in front of it."

2. Mustache and *sariči*: signs of Cretan male identity.

3. Two generations of Glendiot men: pride in unity.

4. A thoughtful smoke: *eghoismos* includes both aggression and reflection.

that can be challenged too directly. As with all poetic utterances, "[t]he breaking of the tie between sign and object/idea . . . means that a particular contextual variant may be correlated with a variety of different referents" (Waugh 1980:72). In a social universe which is organized conceptually on segmentary principles and articulated by a single dominant opposition between insiders (*edhiči*) and outsiders (*kseni*), the performance that captures the greatest number of levels of social bounding at once will be taken the most seriously.

Throughout this book, we will meet Glendiot men in a variety of rhetorical poses. We will see under what circumstances these poses work, and when they are more likely to fail. They are interactional strategies in a markedly agonistic mode; but they are far from mechanistic. Indeed, predictability is a deficiency in Glendiot eyes, and a genuinely poetic strategy always entails elements of surprise, ingenuity, shock, perhaps even repulsion. The conventions are not rejected so much as creatively redefined, and each actor's performance is critically and unceasingly evaluated as the only tangible index of his intrinsic social worth. Insofar as he can foreground the quality of his "doing," Glendiots are enabled to appreciate what he "is." They have no other means of doing so, since they consider personal qualities to be ultimately opaque.

The poetics of social interaction proposed here thus has its roots in a combination of semiotic theory and Glendiot cosmology. In Glendiot idiom, there is less focus on "being a good man" than on "being *good at* being a man"—a stance that stresses *performative excellence*, the ability to foreground manhood by means of deeds that strikingly "speak for themselves." Actions that occur at a conventional pace are not noticeable: everyone works hard, most adult males dance elegantly enough, any shepherd can steal a sheep on some occasion or other. What counts is, to use Fernandez's expressive terminology (1976-77:472-476), effective *movement*—a sense of shifting the ordinary and everyday into a context where the very change of context itself serves to invest it with sudden significance. Thus, instead of noticing *what* men do, Glendiots focus their attention on *how* the act is performed. There must be an *acceleration* or *stylistic transfiguration* of action: the work must be done with flair; the dance executed with new embellishments that do not disrupt the basic step of the other dancers (illus. 5); and the theft must be performed in such a manner that it serves immediate notice on the victim of the perpetrator's skill: as he is good at stealing, so, too, he will be good at being your enemy or your ally—so choose! Both the act of theft and the narration that follows it focus on the act itself. They announce the quality of the theft, the skill with which it has been

5. "If the billy-goat is strong, the sheepfold can't hold him in; a man makes his patrigroup, not the patrigroup the man!" (*mandinadha*) Women observe while men perform: a nearby village.

performed and recounted, as primary components of the actor's claim to a manly selfhood that captures the essence of Glendiot, Cretan, and Greek identity all at the same time. To the extent that they succeed, they are said to have *simasia*, meaning.

Simasia is an indigenous concept that further enriches our ability to understand the poetics of social interaction in this society, since it constitutes the yardstick by which villagers attribute success or failure to individual actions. It is not a purely verbal concept, although the metaphor of speech is important in all Glendiot attributions of significance; a deed that fails to achieve the appropriate impact—a pointless quarrel, for instance—is said "not to say anything" (*dhe lei prama*). Even as a verbal concept, however, it pays far closer attention to the vagaries of context and usage than do the traditional lexicographies of philological scholarship. Although it may be identified in other, more peaceful communities (e.g., Herzfeld 1981), moreover, the frequency with which *simasia* is mentioned in Glendi acts as a constant reminder that, in the Glendiot view of life, *nothing*—and least of all the meaning of the immediately experienced world—can be regarded as subject to fixed definition; nothing, in short, is certain.

Careful attention to this local concept of meaning reminds us of the pervasion of everyday experience by the same processes of ordering and ranking that we more easily recognize in formal acts such as ritual; it tells us that we should not seek meaning only in verbal texts such as songs and proverbs, for example, but also in the commonplace occurrences that shape ordinary experience (cf. also Rosaldo 1980:23-24). This transcendence of the division between the symbolic and the ordinary is consistent with recent critiques of the absolute categorical distinction between "poetic" and "ordinary" language (and, we might add, of all other modes of human action) without reference to the actors' own concepts of discourse and performance (e.g., Bauman 1977:22-24). It also has the virtue of fitting the indigenous category closest to our own concept of "meaning."

The Glendiot raids to give meaning to his social life: the greater the risk, the more *simasia* he experiences (cf. also Meeker 1979:32). This *simasia* is associated with the qualities of heroism and bravery, as well as of insubordination, which Glendiots associate with being a true Greek. And if it seems curiously inconsistent to an outsider that a Glendiot should foreground his loyalty to the national ideal by defying the laws of the state, the Glendiot does not share this sense of incongruity. For him, the physical isolation of his village and the inevitable hardship of the pastoral life make all hostility to the complacent camp of the bureaucrats seem entirely natural. The tension between local and national ethics gives added spice to each adventure: a man is only a man if he welcomes such tensions and bends them to the demands of his public self.

The Argument of Hunger

There can be little doubt of Glendiot loyalty to the conceptual unity of the Greek nation (*ethnos*). But this has never meant acceptance of the right of the central bureaucracy, the administrative state (*kratos*), to dictate moral and legal principles. Removed from the urban centers of power, resentful of what they see as their systematic neglect at the hands of politicians, Glendiots express hostility to *any* source of authority outside the local community. They bring to their dealings with officialdom a consistent mode of self-exoneration: they are neglected and oppressed by turns; they have no effective means of redress against the excesses of patron-landowners (on whom they depend for grazing rights); they have no alternative but to meet spoliation with spoliation. In short, they use the argument of inequality to represent their rebellious actions as a redressive form of reciprocity.

Far from compromising their loyalty to the principle of national identity (as opposed to loyalty to the bureaucratic state), their stand allows them to claim moral excellence above all other Greeks. Elsewhere, Greek citizens may be willing to tolerate the intrusive exercise of bureaucratic authority. Glendiots, however, make their own rules, regardless of the disapproval of state or church: "We here are the free Greece!" The apparent contradiction is resolved rhetorically by means of a conflation of bureaucratic authority with the aura of Turkish misrule. At least until the 1981 victory of Andreas Papandreou's Panhellenic Socialist Movement (PA.SO.K.) in the national elections, Glendiots could point a derisive finger at the generally conservative and patronage-ridden administrative establishment in Athens and say, "It's time we got rid of them; we've had them for four hundred years!" Actually, only *four* years had elapsed since the previous elections, and seven since the collapse of the colonels' junta; but "four hundred years" is the symbolic duration of Turkish rule. (The Turks actually ruled most of Crete for the period 1645-1898, but such formulaic inflations are common in connection with Turkish rule [cf. also Halpern 1956:13, on Serbia].) Here is the very core of the Glendiots' quarrel with officialdom: it concerns the relationship between national and political identity. Whether PA.SO.K., a party born in reaction to the military regimes that ruled Greece from 1967 to 1974, has genuinely escaped the taint of elitism that the Glendiots associate with virtually all other mainstream political parties still remains to be seen. Some cynical voices were heard to comment that it was no different from all the rest, but its newness and its explicit rejection of the patronage network cultivated by the older politicians gave it a certain appeal to younger and poorer Glendiots.

Glendiots, like many other Greeks, generally express pessimism about *all* politicians' motives. The military had promised to clean up corruption, then fell prey to the same temptations themselves. Then, in 1974, many of the old politicians came back, and started baptizing huge numbers of children in order, it was said, to secure the parents' votes; yet when the parents asked for help in getting other offspring relocated to more convenient military camps or placed in lucrative government office jobs, the politicians stalled just as in the old days. Would the Socialists prove to be any better? Their supporters enthusiastically proclaimed a new order; other villagers simply thought that it might be worth a try, but that one should not expect big surprises. Past history thus justifies taking the fullest possible advantage of the politicians' need for votes. What makes the Glendiots different, however, is the extent to which they use their connections to break the law.

Without a doubt, Glendiots do many things that contravene the official code. They steal sheep and goats, abduct brides, illegally own cherished machine guns and pistols, which can—just as illegally—be fired off at weddings and baptisms. They speak a distinctive local dialect that defies nationwide attempts at language standardization, though they are also adept at manipulating the officially recognized forms of the Greek language when they deal with the official world. They fight democratic elections according to principles of agnatic kinship solidarity. These peculiarities change slowly, and only within the framework of a rhetoric of traditionalism. Animal theft, for example, only becomes negative because its penetration by commercial values and practices has gradually eroded its social significance as a mark of true manhood and increased its scope to the point where it attracts the censorious attention of outsiders. The prospect of ridicule is indeed a powerful deterrent. When Glendiots talk about such matters as animal theft to outsiders, they oscillate between acute embarrassment (since every outsider is a potential representative of official values) and defiantly self-conscious assertions about what makes Cretans different from—and better than—all other Greeks.

The tension between these introspective and extroverted self-images reproduces a similar tension at the national level. Against the familiar self-view of the Glendiot as a lawbreaker must be set statements to the effect that "animal theft doesn't happen around here any more," and that "animal theft was because of the Turks," in much the same way as the idealized official self-image of the Greeks as heirs to the Classical tradition may be contrasted with the far more self-critical stereotypes that characterize more introverted discourse. The middle ground is occupied by a similar contrast between stereotypes of Cretans in general as fiercely independent and incurably violent. Again we see here that hierarchy of tensions which, conceptually and rhetorically, creates analogies between the respective situations of Glendi, Crete, and Greece.

Glendiot men manipulate these tensions constantly in their everyday discourse. Theirs is a rhetoric of self-justification balanced against self-recognition. On the one hand, they are well aware that their activities excite official disapproval and punitive action. On the other, they maintain that animal theft, in particular, will survive as long as Mount Ida continues to tower over the region; and their cheerful insubordination emphasizes their identity as Cretan mountain dwellers through the poetics of theft and narration. The repression which they have experienced through the centuries, and which they see as continuing under an unsympathetic national government, provides their favorite argument in favor of maintaining the old values and practices. Greece, Crete, Glendi— at every level, suffering has always justified practices which conflict with the idealized, extroverted self-image, but which have come to define in their poeticity the very essence of collective identity. The Glendiot shepherds' rhetoric is an expression of this condition.

Above all, they insist, they are hungry. They were hungry under the Turks, so they stole livestock in order to have something to eat. During the German Occupation, again, the skills necessary to the successful conduct of a raid became a valuable asset to guerrilla fighters. Even when (as often happened) they raided the flocks of other Cretans, rather than the flocks that the enemy had sequestered, they could argue that conditions made it inconceivable that they should do otherwise. Perhaps they are less hungry today; but a young shepherd may still plausibly cite hunger as his motive for stealing several sheep in a night's work, while another will complain that systematic, large-scale raiding represents his only hope of repaying bank loans and thereby ultimately establishing himself in a respectable business.

Such hunger is of a special order, not to be confused with trivial stomach rumblings. It is a key element in the discourse of Glendiot identity, and as such should be interpreted ideologically rather than literally. Above all, its use as the justification for animal theft underscores its peculiar significance. Glendiots seem in fact to have experienced truly devastating famine only rarely, if at all. Even under Turkish and German rule, moreover, meat was one form of sustenance that villagers could apparently rely on finding in plenty.³ Other foodstuffs might run low; grain crops, for example, were cultivated on the meager terraces high above the village and their yield was very much at the mercy of climatic vagaries. Farmers, a small minority of the population until the mid-1960s and mostly of low status, may have come a good deal closer to destitution, especially as they were normatively debarred from raiding; even they, however, would occasionally steal the odd watermelon or, if greatly daring, a house-tethered sheep or goat. But it was the shepherds who raided systematically, and it is still the shepherds who plead "hunger" in defense of their exploits.

In the light of what we know about other rural Greek communities (e.g., Friedl 1962; Campbell 1964; du Boulay 1974), it may seem surprising that the shepherds should have so much greater status than farmers. This status, however, is internally defined: shepherds are exposed to greater danger; they have more opportunities for experiencing a larger world through their annual migrations to winter pastures on the coast and in the east; once (before the last war), they constituted approximately 90 percent of the adult male population; and they may, in exceptional cases, amass exceptionally large flocks with which to feed both their families and their prestige. To achieve this status, they raid the flocks of other communities—not to turn their gains into cash, which traditionalists contend subverts the local code, but instead in order to gain their victims' admiration and, eventually, alliance. Their *excuse* for doing so is "hunger," but their *explanation* is a more overtly political one.

Rather than trying to deny or confirm the truth of their claims, we should instead view the idiom of "hunger" and "eating" as an integral part of the ideological discourse of oppression and deprivation. Claims of hunger are used to contrast the condition of Glendi with that of the towns and agricultural lowland villages. Those who "eat" are the wealthy, and they do so, it is automatically assumed, at the expense of the poor— among whom the Glendiots categorize themselves. A talented Glendiot versifier complained to his powerful political patron about the latter's cynical vote catching:

When the elections draw near, you come to our village,
and tell us lies and promise that you'll be at our side.

And when the elections go by, and it'll be fine for you to *eat*,
this poor place of ours—you won't remember it at all!

Hunger is a condition inherited, it is said, from the terrible days of Turkish dominion. This is the usual explanation of the *present* prevalence of livestock rustling; and, although it is often said that it was the flocks owned by Turkish landowners or commandeered by the German troops that the Glendiots attacked, stories of personal exploits soon give the lie to that amiable generalization. But the claim to personal "hunger" that sometimes opens a raiding narrative recalls the larger ideology: the hunger of the moment is, metonymically, that of the oppressed Cretan mountain people. The poetic effect of introducing a narrative with allusions to hunger or some other conventionalized form of deprivation is precisely to identify the thief's condition with that of the larger society, and so to focus attention on the manly qualities of the act itself. In this fashion, an apparent contradiction between idealized history and personal experience is resolved in performance, the message being made to carry both levels of meaning at once.

The appeal to hunger under foreign occupation, which ironically has more literal force in respect of the towns and lowland villages, becomes still more strikingly at variance with economic conditions in the context of Glendi's present prosperity. In a village whose population is still expanding,[4] and where some households have bank balances of close to a million drachmas (about $18,000 [1981]), one easily feels the contrast with the depopulation and economic disintegration to be found elsewhere in rural Greece (cf. Allen 1976; du Boulay 1974). Glendiots are not simply lying when they talk about their "hunger"; on the contrary, they are openly proud of the economic success attained by so many of them, even though they feel that without constant bureaucratic interference they would have done much better still. But it is precisely this interference, this imbalance between center and periphery, that engenders the symbolism of "hunger." Perhaps a better word would be "dissatisfaction"—the dissatisfaction that both creates insubordination and becomes its most characteristic expression.

The tension between national and political identity forms a dominant theme of this book; it guides many of the actions in which Glendiot men delight, and which they consider to be distinctively their own. To them, one of the true marks of manhood is the ability to hold one's head high in the face of government repression. This entails a high level of awareness of the implications of official rhetoric, and a striking ability to mock and parody it.

Indeed, if authoritarian discourse is characterized by such totalizing equivalences as nation and state, or religion and church (cf. Goldschläger 1982:13-16), then by the same token the Glendiot response is a constant, irreverent deconstruction of that discourse. Glendiot male humor is forthrightly anticlerical and antistatist to a degree unusual in Greece; much of it consists of word plays that make fun of official discourse by revealing its internal contradictions or by turning it against itself: of priests, for example, a disgruntled villager remarked that *they* were the (only true) "sinners" (*amartoli*). Glendiot men's physical actions often serve the same ironical goal. A sheep rustler may, for example, represent his independence and courage as "national" values, but he inevitably directs them *against* the bureaucratic polity even while deriding the politicians whose protection enables him to escape punishment.

Glendiot men glory in the tension which their actions highlight in the relationship between local and official values. At the same time, their glee is for strictly local consumption. They regard their reputation among other Greeks as "goat thieves" (*katsikokleftes*) with considerable ambivalence, and clearly dislike being called by this sobriquet to their faces. One young man, who otherwise denied that he had ever rustled livestock, proudly claimed that the one occasion when he did so was in response to a non-Cretan shepherd's sneer that he was a "Cretan goat thief." Obviously he was not trying, unrealistically, to prove that Cretans did *not* steal goats; rather, he was simply not prepared to tolerate derision on this score. What invests his particular experience with piquancy, moreover, is the fact that it happened when he was on military service! Such ironies are the real grist of Glendiot humor.

As their sensitivity toward insults shows, the Cretans' distinctiveness can be a two-edged sword. A linguistic example will illustrate the complexity and ambiguity of the stereotypical attitudes in question. A villager once complained to me, with some bitterness, that Athenians would always show how much they despised a Cretan by calling him *kritikatse katsikoklefti*, "little Cretan goat thief." The taint of being categorically described as a goat thief seemed bad enough; but the term *kritikatse* conveyed many additional layers of mutual dislike. *Kritikos* is the standard term for "Cretan." The diminutive *kritikaki(s)* is at least mildly offensive, and perhaps conveys a mocking awareness that most Cretan surnames end in the same suffix (*-akis*)—a feature Glendiots attribute to a Turkish administrative decision designed to humiliate the Cretans, but from which the inhabitants of Glendi and surrounding villages largely escaped. Implicitly, at least, the Athenians seem to be behaving as unpleasantly as the Turks; shades, again, of those "four hundred years"!

But the irony goes still further. Most Cretans palatalize the suffix as /-*ači*/. My Glendiot friend, however, knew that Athenians found /č/ extremely difficult to pronounce, and found this way of mocking his tormentors in his own way. Dialect finally reasserted itself, however, since the terminal /e/ of *kritikatse* is a possible local variant for the more standardized /i/ in this position. Without overemphasizing the importance of a single linguistic example, we can see very clearly that the complaint against being called *kritikatse* encapsulates a whole series of deep mutual antagonisms.

Their uneasy relationship with the urban, mainland middle class cannot easily be separated from the Glendiots' feelings about the national bureaucracy, since the latter represents, to them, the political and economic triumph of that class. While there is little to be done about this imbalance in the larger arena, however, the Glendiots are free to think of themselves as *morally* superior, and to enact that superiority on the domestic stage.

Thus, each agonistic display—whether in song, dance, swearing, drinking, raiding, bride theft, or feuding—does several things at once. It embodies a local conflict; it claims a higher order of wit and courage; and it mocks officialdom's claims to the absolute right of arbitration. It is at once a medium and a message: it takes a sentiment of local rivalry and turns it into an expression of disregard for the bureaucratic and legal establishment.

It does not do so at the level of extroverted, idealized images of Greek and Cretan. Rather, it takes a dimension of the more introspective self-image of the Greeks,[5] the notion of low cunning or *poniria*. This is an attitude of insubordination widely claimed by Greeks as a national trait, and furnishes an appropriate response to perceived oppression; a source of amusement at the Turks' expense, it also signifies the conventionally disrespectful attitude that Greeks bring to their dealings with those in power (Danforth 1976:91, 105-107; cf. also Friedl 1962:80). *Poniria* is illustrated by the stereotypical case of the Glendiot shepherd who sells a cheese at 90 drx. on the grounds that in a certain other village it would cost 130 drx., when in fact the cost there was actually only 80 drx.! Such behavior, seen as typifying Cretan highlanders in relation to other Greeks, and shepherds in relation to farmers, is at once an emblematic attribute of manhood and, because quintessentially *Greek*, a source of aggressive pride. Here, then, is an area in which Cretans can claim a special kind of excellence through their personal performances.

Role performance in the sense I am using the term here is not just a matter of fulfilling stereotypical expectations. On the contrary, the conventionalized unconventionality of Glendiot male behavior provides virtually limitless opportunities for the display of inventive rebellion against stylistic norms—a rebellion that effectively reproduces the political rebellion of which it is also an index. Effective performance in any domain can gain from judicious rule breaking, since this foregrounds the performer's skill at manipulating the conventions (see Bauman 1977:34-35). Since Glendiots believe that the greatest achievements are those that entail seizing some quite unexpected chance, their improvisational skills in dance, song, and banter signify the very excellence *as Glendiots* that they also demonstrate at the immediate level of the performance itself. Self-regard, *eghoismos*, is a social value, not an individual trait. Personal idiosyncrasies only score if they serve that ultimate identification between the self and the collectivity, by foregrounding the performer's ability to project the Glendiot character of his idiosyncrasies. Such, then, is the basis of the poetics of Glendiot manhood:

> *Fronimi če nikočiri dhe zoun stom Bziloriti.*
> Lawful people and landowners do not live on Mt.
>   Ida.
>
> *I kouzouli tin gamane athanati tin Griti.*
> [It was] the crazy people [who] made Crete immortal.

Good Patriots, Rebellious Citizens

The official response to all but the most flagrant infractions of the law by Glendiots is often surprisingly muted. This is not to say that the police and other official functionaries fail to do their jobs properly according to their own criteria. On the contrary, they demonstrate a high degree of commitment to establishing a greater amount of conformity to the law in this region; but their efforts are tempered by restraint and diplomacy, and especially by painstaking respect for the unwritten local rules for dispute management. They recognize fully that any strategy that contravened these rules would eventually backfire: for example, jailing a man for theft or attempted murder would only increase the latter's thirst for revenge against his intended victim, who, he supposes, must be responsible for the law's punitive intervention. For this reason, local police may even try to persuade the victim *not* to prosecute, on the grounds that a formal reconciliation in traditional style would more effectively terminate the quarrel.

The police also know that an attitude of respect for local norms constitutes a far greater asset than their status as the representatives of a resented legal system. Occasionally, they learn the hard way. A non-Cretan police officer obstinately insisted on going up into the foothills alone to arrest a suspected sheep thief, ignoring the Glendiots' advice to take a couple of local mediators with him. As he approached the *mitato* (stone-built shepherds' hut) where the suspect was hiding, the latter dashed out and started to run away at great speed. The officer drew his service revolver and took aim. The suspect's elderly crippled father, fearing for the life of his son, suddenly hurled himself at the officer and beat him senseless with his stick, snatched up the officer's uniform cap and revolver, and hastily disappeared. The officer eventually regained consciousness and crawled painfully back down to the village, where he was given first aid as well as a stern homily on the importance of listening to local advice and custom. After a suitably admonitory delay, his cap and revolver were restored to him. Upon recovery, he applied for a transfer, and at the same time lodged a formal complaint with the local court. When the case finally came up for adjudication, the judge asked the suspected sheep thief's father to stand up. The old man did so. Was *this* the Glendiot who had so badly mauled the healthy young police officer? Assured that indeed it was, he dismissed the case amidst derisive laughter.

This incident shows why it generally makes better sense for officials to use local forms of mediation rather than imposing bureaucratic or legal sanctions. The Glendiots' delighted reaction to it also demonstrates their solidary independence. The elderly father was neither popular nor of high status. When confronted with outside interference, however, the Glendiots close ranks; they consider complaining to the police about theft or injury to be an act of "betrayal" (*prodhosia*).

Apart from its immediate, practical benefits, a policy of compromise also suits the interests of the state. It reduces the risk of political disaffection, and, in particular, of large-scale conversions to communism. So far, in fact, Glendi has never produced more than eighteen voting communists in any one election (1984); most villagers seem to share the official sentiment that communism is categorically incompatible with being genuinely Greek.[6] The police, however, according to their own comments as well as those of the villagers, fear that widespread and repressive law enforcement might provoke massive conversions to the communist cause—not so much for reasons of political doctrine, as because communism has always been represented to them as the antithesis of law and order as defined by the hitherto dominant, conservative strain in Greek political life. The police are thus placed in a curious position: they must deal more or less sympathetically with those who violate national *law* in order to retain their loyalty to the national *ideology*. Whether in practice such large-scale disaffection would ever occur is an open question; but the doubt is sufficient to demand circumspection of the police, who are consequently forced to affirm the rebellious Glendiots' fundamental loyalty to the national ideals.

This curious official reluctance to confront animal theft repressively has another, complementary source. However little officials may be willing to concede the point, the Glendiots' insubordination reproduces certain diagnostic features of the struggle against the Turks: the rejection of authority, the contempt for the settled life of the towns, the emphasis on personal risk, even some of the terminology associated with the particular life style called *kleftouria* ("thieves' way of life").[7] The Glendiots' own rhetorical conjunction of today's government with the Turkocracy reinforces the identification of yesterday's national struggle with their own current battle against centralized authority. No discussion of the poetics of Glendiot manhood can ignore the reproduction, in the modern context, of features more usually associated with the national struggle for independence. The unexpectedly meek police response to animal raiding is not one of compliance; the police are extremely active at trying to dissuade the local shepherds from the practice, mounting frequent meetings and forming local committees in the hope of breaking its hold. But they are also aware that a more violent response on their part would pit them against a virtually national tradition, and that it would be so regarded by the local shepherds. Herein lies the greatest danger: that in suppressing animal theft, *externally* defined as un-Greek, they would in fact be viewed *internally* as oppressing the last exponents of true Greek virtue. From this point to a massive political defection is perhaps not an unimaginable progression, especially given the Glendiots' view of the central bureaucracy as a virtual replay of foreign misrule.

The sense of replay in the current relationship between Glendi and the Greek State further strengthens the signifying impact of Glendiot men's agonistic behavior. Glendiot resistance to the law alludes, in part, to the history of "kleftic" resistance to the foreign oppressors, and the successful performance of a Glendiot animal thief—whether judged in the action itself or in its subsequent narration—may well be guaranteed by foregrounding this image of center-periphery relations as a replay of the past. The particular rhetorical device by which this goal is achieved is principally the theme of *hunger*. A truly poetic theft, or an equally poetic narration, must emphasize that bureaucratic indifference is the root cause of all such behavior, and of the specific deed in particular. In this way, successful performance alludes to history in a manner that can hardly fail to embarrass officialdom.

The beginnings of Greek independence were achieved early in the nineteenth century by a disparate and uneasy alliance. On the one side were the largely Western-educated intellectuals and politicians, along with their foreign admirers (the philhellenes). And on the other side were the bands of largely uneducated local guerrillas, often puzzled by and dismayed at the cause they were asked to serve, who provided a ragged but eventually effective military support.[8]

These guerrillas became known collectively as "klefts" (Greek *kleftes*), a term that thus became transformed in meaning from "thieves" to a category of patriotic heroes. Through a process of reclassification, the term *kleftes* was rapidly detached from its less reputable meaning, while at the same time coming into categorical opposition to *listes* ("brigands"). The latter, meanwhile, was held in reserve for those who fought on after the establishment of a Greek central administration and thereby, at least implicitly, threatened the statist assumption that all Greeks would necessarily prove to be loyal to the state as such (see Politis 1973:xii-xviii; Herzfeld 1982a:66-69). What these people called themselves is no longer known, although the example of Glendi at least suggests the likelihood that it was *kleftes*; nationalist writers, understandably, were not anxious to dwell on this use of the term. A similar terminological tug-of-war is currently being played out in and around Glendi, as officialdom tries to persuade the self-styled *kleftes* that their activities are really more representative of *listes*.

In a sense, as some studies of Italian banditry have demonstrated, the concept of banditry is itself a product of statism (e.g., Molfese 1964; Moss 1979). Any definition of outlawry invokes some principle of moral boundary formation, with a concomitant suppression of the outlaws' own view of their relationship with the state (cf. also Kevelson 1977). In Greece, where academic scholarship was long dominated by various degrees of commitment to statist ideology, it is only in comparatively recent work that the klefts' activities have come to be viewed as the expression of an alternative social ideology to that of the state (e.g., Kondoyoryis 1980). This insight is extremely important, since it challenges the artificial chronological distinction between pre-Independence klefts and post-Independence brigands, and thereby allows us to appreciate more fully the analogies which the Glendiots draw between the fight against Turkish rule and their present resentment of bureaucratic domination.

Hobsbawm's (1959:23) insistence that social bandits lack a distinctive ideology thus ironically echoes statist and nationalist formulations, since it represents banditry as an undirected rejection of state law rather than as the expression of an alternative ideology (see also Mintz 1982:271-276). This perspective apparently derives from a view that ideology is necessarily the product of an organized literate tradition. Yet if ideologies are "highly figurative" attempts "to render otherwise incomprehensible social situations meaningful, to so construe them as to make it possible to act purposefully within them" (Geertz 1973:220), then the very uncertainty of Glendiots' experiences of the bureaucratic state might well be expected to generate a distinctively local, antistatist ideology. Glendiot "hunger," as we have seen, is a strikingly metaphorical expression by which villagers organize their responses to any kind of domination.

That it is not articulated in terms of the grand political theories of our time does not mean that it is not ideology; on the contrary, we shall see that it represents something to which the political party platforms constantly have to adjust.

Whether it reproduces the ideological concerns of early nineteenth-century kleftism is unclear. It is in any case important not to push the historical analogy too far. Crete is not the Greek mainland, and this is another century. Furthermore, the common awareness of similarities between themselves and the nineteenth-century heroes imparts a measure of artifice to the Glendiots' occasional pronouncements on the subject. Above all, there are few Glendiots who would tolerate being described as professional brigands; rather, some of them are known to be "good at stealing" (*kala kleftes*) under appropriate circumstances.

Here, in fact, is one lesson that Glendi may be able to teach history: that perhaps the concept of a dedicated class of brigands, occupationally defined as such, may be something of an illusion. The notion of a chronologically and definitionally bounded category of klefts belongs more to official ideology than it does to local discourse. Professionally, Glendiots may be shepherds (*vosčí*), not thieves. *Kleftis* is a performative term: it is only when a shepherd has pulled off a series of particularly daring or retributive thefts that he is known for a while as *kala kleftis*— a man who knows how and when to steal. Glendiot men may become thieves in Kenneth Burke's (1954:237) sense of an "occupation": they are known for their daring in particular kinds of circumstances, and these become generalized to an ethical structure that categorically justifies the activity of rustling—in short, to an ideology.

There are two complementary dimensions to the ideological status of animal theft in Glendi. On the one hand, Glendiots justify this activity as a continued aftereffect of Turkish oppression. On the other, their embarrassment when it is mentioned in the presence of foreigners or non-Cretans springs from their awareness that, in the official view, it is definitively un-Greek. As a result, in some situations, Glendiots can end up sounding more nationalistic than even the police. They insist on its Turkish origins:

> Animal theft, Mikhalis, arose in Crete from the following circumstance, when the Turks were here. When the Turks were here, they had gathered together all the sheep of Crete and had made harems of them! For example, here in Thalassa [the coastal village where the speaker now resided], in the Thalassa area, there were a thousand sheep. The Turks had taken them away from the shepherd and had put them there and watched over them. Well, animal theft

in Crete began as a result of great perturbation, of people's hunger (*pina*). Eh, the Turks gathered the sheep together in the lowlands. . . . Well, and the *Katsiaounidhes* [i.e., the Greeks] . . . swept down and stole them from the plain. . . . Because they were hungry! In other words, [they did it] with every right (*dičiomatikos*)—the Turks had stolen them from *them*!

Note how the speaker appeals to the rhetoric of "hunger," as well as the notion that raiding the Turks was an act of reciprocity; the term "harems" plays on a popular Glendiot analogy between sheep and women, both objects of male capture, but here deployed to suggest the bestiality and unmanliness of the hated enemy. There is also at least some slight equivalence implied between plainsfolk and Turks, and this kind of categorical slippage is extended in the speaker's closing observations:

And then [after the Turks' departure] came the refugees [*prosfiyes*], from Asia Minor. And after that there was unrest here in Crete, and hatreds had been created between Cretans again. Because then, there was a revival [i.e., of wealth among people], and they cast envious eyes on fields, properties, houses.

Such insistence on the role of the *Tourkokratia* in the genesis of animal theft ignores the considerable local evidence—mostly in the form of fourteenth- and fifteenth-century church wall paintings depicting the sheep thief descending into hell[9]—that it was endemic at least as early as the Venetian period, and probably long before that. Of course, even the ancient evidence for animal theft or other forms of brigandage among the Greeks could be attributed to some form of foreign influence, and this was the usual tactic among nationalistic historians and folklorists (e.g., Xenos 1865). But at least one police officer with whom I discussed the phenomenon insisted that it was the survival of an ancient *Greek* tradition, evidenced in Homeric descriptions of cattle theft. Thus, even at an official level, what Glendiots see as commendable *poniria* can be put to the service of the concepts of national unity and continuity with the most ancient past.

All such claims must be seen as rhetorical strategies, entailing the constant renegotiation of stereotypical categories. In this context, raiding becomes a peculiarly salient expression of the tensions inherent in local identity. As villagers struggle with the problem of being simultaneously Glendiot, Cretan, Greek, and Christian, the mercurial significance of raiding reproduces the ambiguities and uncertainties of their situation.

Glendi's recent prosperity has, if anything, underscored these internal tensions. Wealth alone does not necessarily mean integration or conformity. On the asphalt road winding down into the village, irregular rows of modern concrete houses bear witness to the stretching of a former cluster pattern along the contours of the main mountain road. A dull explosion, followed by a slowly rising cloud of dust, marks the construction of a new road in the foothills rising up toward Mount Ida. Here, you think, is a busily expanding community that fits squarely into the modern, bureaucratically organized world. Up to a point, certainly, you would be right: Glendi is undoubtedly reaping the benefits that come with increased access to public services and economic opportunity.

But then other snippets of half-whispered knowledge start to redraw the image. A pig, wandering bulkily across the main village street, has been left unattended, but no petulant official comes on the scene to scold its owner or levy a fine; too many people remember what happened to the last policeman who tried to do that—he was the officer who ended up being ridiculed in court. A large house down by the dried-up riverbed belongs to someone who, you eventually hear, has a fine reputation for sheep stealing: is *that* how he got the means to build it? Even the new foothill roads that snake up into the hills have contributed to the curbing of livestock theft: since shepherds can no longer convincingly plead convenience as a reason for staying away from home overnight, small-scale rustling has become more difficult to carry out, and the roads themselves assist police surveillance. As to the innocent-looking commercial trucks that grind through the village, some of them owned by Glendiots, well-informed rumor has it that some regularly carry stolen livestock and are driven by desperadoes armed with guns and hand grenades.[10] Seeing some imposing strangers in almost exaggeratedly Cretan garb, with high leather boots and carefully arranged black turbans, you ask a local friend whether these men are *arotikhtadhes*, shepherds come to investigate the location of stolen animals. "Probably," comes the cautious reply; if you knew enough to ask the question, what is the point of telling you a straight lie? But it might have been less embarrassing not to ask at all, or to make a meaningful jest about visiting "tourists."

Glendiots must constantly balance their rebellious values against the pragmatics of interaction with the official world, and the care they take to present a reasonably law-abiding external face is some indication of their awareness of this necessity. Without such a compromise, official restraint would be correspondingly harder to maintain: the discrepancies between Glendiot and statist ideologies would force an open confrontation.

The state does not control the situation entirely on its own terms. Were that the case, one could surmise that animal theft and other systematic violations of the official code would have disappeared long ago. But the functionaries of law and order are constrained by both ideological and pragmatic concerns at least as much as the villagers. Two key factors have emerged so far: the fear of turning "Hellenes" into "communists," and a tendency to see in the Glendiots' insubordination some of the pride and courage conventionally associated with both the Homeric and the Revolutionary heroes of Greece's idealized past. A third consideration, to which we shall return later in the book, is the alleged role of influential politicians in subverting or modifying official attempts to suppress livestock rustling.

All three factors show how inaccurate it would be to treat Glendi as marginal to the wider study of Greek society. They make it clear that, eccentric though the Glendiot experience may be in many respects, it does focus on the abiding problematic of modern Greek identity—the relationship between nationhood and the bureaucratic structures of the state. The villagers' distrust of bureaucracy and authority is far from unique, even though it is sometimes translated into acts of defiance that one would not ordinarily encounter in other regions of Greece. Centralization is not necessarily control, except in a trivially bureaucratic sense. The Glendiots' boast that "the law doesn't reach here" (*edho o nomos dhe ftani*) thus offsets the conventional view of a rigidly controlled, centralized Greek nation-state with a radically insubordinate alternative perspective.

Of Scholars and Shepherds

A recent criticism leveled at Mediterranean ethnographies concerns their failure to situate particularistic village analyses in larger national contexts (Davis 1977:8-10). A major difficulty has been that of establishing criteria of typicality (see, e.g., Friedl 1962:3), and the consequent perception of high risk in generalizations based on particularistic ethnographies. While these issues have gradually been addressed, much of the resultant work has dealt primarily with administrative, political, economic, and to some extent religious issues, in terms of directly observable influences between state structures and local societies. Little has been said about possible relationships between local scholarship and villagers' self-perceptions, perhaps because this represents a less tangible area for investigation, and perhaps also because of a disturbing reluctance on the part of anthropologists to acquaint themselves with local scholarly traditions in detail.

Yet it is abundantly evident that these traditions do represent a sig-

nificant part of the "larger context." Even though most villagers may not
have directly read the works of their learned fellow-Cretans, they express
some of the same sentiments, even to the point of demonstrating marked
similarities in the ways in which they handle the tension between local
and national identity. While these writers may seem to have more in
common with the statist cause than with that of the villagers, they do
confront analogous problems in reconciling the concentric national and
local loyalties to each other, and their work provides a useful complement
to our examination of Glendiot identity. At the very least, they illustrate
the sources of some of the rhetoric to which the Glendiots have recourse
in dealing with the official world.

An important aspect of Greek ethnological writing in the past was its
insistence, through the demonstration of continuity with the Classical
past, upon the essential homogeneity of Greek culture.[11] Local scholars
would argue that their home areas presented the most formidable evidence of such continuity. This common device allowed them to be both
patriotic and localist at once, in a manner that reproduced the nesting-
box model of allegiance which also characterizes village discourse: all
Greeks are hospitable, yet the people of the next village are not hospitable
in comparison to us (see Friedl 1962:103-106). It is important to recognize this essentially segmentary mode of conceptualizing cultural and
political relations for what it is: despite the stereotypical view of Crete
as a hotbed of separatism (e.g., Papamanousakis 1979), local pride is
conceived *within* the idiom of national patriotism by urban intellectuals
and village lawbreakers alike. Aligning the nesting-box model to the
anthropological concept of segmentation, moreover, will make it much
easier to understand how the Glendiots manage to reconcile their internal
organization based on agnatic segmentation to the demands of a very
different set of encompassing national models.

Most Cretan scholars, then, followed the usual pattern of claiming a
special measure of local continuity with the ancient past. They departed
significantly from standard rhetoric, however, in their definition of that
past. Whereas writers from other areas were generally content to award
primacy to ancient Athens, Cretan scholars claimed an "older" past as
well as a distinctive Byzantine phase. Thus, while some nineteenth-
century Greek folklorists rewrote folksong texts to include Classical
references, the only comparable reference in a Cretan folksong is to
King Minos (Romanias 1965:110).[12]

Indeed, some Cretan ethnology seems to represent the Classical period
as a virtual irrelevancy: "They say that human civilization started from
ancient Assyria, passed to Egypt, and afterwards leaped to this beautiful
island, five thousand years ago, and thereafter clasped the shores of

Europe" (Romanias 1965:7). Another writer, having dutifully insisted that "Hellas is one unity," then argues that the influence of Classical Greece on modern Cretan folksongs was small, whereas that of Byzantium resuscitated the Homeric virtues in the Cretan singers' repertoire; but that little could be gleaned about the music of Crete during the Classical era save that it was "Dorian"—in other words, not Attic (Hadjidakis 1968:26, 30). One of the most prominent of all Cretan scholars, the eminent historian and folklorist Pavlos Vlastos (1909), did try to show that the Digenes of folk legend was not so much a Byzantine hero as a version of the ancient Herakles; but this was specifically a *Cretan* Herakles, the "son of Zeus,"[13] whose own birth was believed to have taken place on Mount Ida.

All this may seem tangential to the concerns of today's Glendiots. Few of them, if any, are likely to have read any of the philological literature for themselves. They seem unaware that the term *samia*, used for the property-mark cut into a flock animal's ear to discourage theft, is probably derived from a Doric form of *sēmeion*, "sign, mark." But they do talk of the birth of Zeus on Mount Ida as though it were historical fact, and they do rehearse scholarly arguments linking local toponyms to ancient names, including that of Zeus himself. Their strategic interests in so doing come disconcertingly close to those of the scholars; both groups are concerned with the place of Cretans in the larger Greek entity, and with the maintenance within it of a distinctive identity that will nevertheless permit full access to the benefits of citizenship.

The segmentary idiom provides an ideal medium for the purpose:

> In our land, called Greece, all is beautiful, sweet, calm, measured. Equally beautiful, simple, and calm are our folkloric treasures, too.
>
> In our Crete, things are still more beautiful. From every mountain, peak, hill, hillside, from every gorge, valley, or plain, swells a song, a legend, a phrase. . . .
>
> Our grandfathers . . . passed on from generation to generation the diamantine wealth of Greek traditions that became the unquenchable hearth that held in its core the flame of our National traditions and the proof of our continuous descent from our glorious Ancient ancestors. (Lambithianaki-Papadaki 1972:5)

The earlier work from which this passage was apparently copied sought to demonstrate "the ethnic unity of the Greeks" (Frangaki 1949:4), by showing that it was brought about by massive emigration from Crete: Athens stands displaced from the center of Greek history.

It is of course difficult to assess the impact of such writings on village attitudes. Nevertheless, the striking compatibility between these two domains of discourse suggests that schoolteacher-scholars and highland shepherds do not inhabit entirely separate symbolic universes. On the contrary, the apparent eccentricity of Glendiot values may be more accurately seen as the extreme expression of a more widespread localism, and this may in turn help to explain the consistency of official restraint in dealing with Glendiot violations of the law.

Hierarchy and Opposition: The Rhetoric of Identity

The kind of scholarly discourse that I have briefly reviewed in the preceding section is not usually concerned with local differences *between* the various parts of Crete, although some folklore collections by authors of local origin focus on a particular district, or even a single village. For the Glendiots, on the other hand, finer discriminations of identity are extremely important, and provide the necessary intermediate bridge for us to relate their concerns with Greek and Cretan identity to the specialized quarrels internal to Glendi itself. As in English, so also in Greek "differences" (*dhiafores*) may be qualitative or political, and in the Glendiots' segmentary view of the social universe that distinction is not always relevant: in any given context, enemies are inferiors.

Crucial to this discussion is the homology that exists between all levels of Glendiot response to outsiders. *Any* outsider—whether foreigner, non-Cretan, East Cretan, non-Rethimniot, lowlander, non-covillager (*ksenokhorianos*), non-kin, or more or less distant kin—is definitionally inferior. These discriminations are hierarchically ranked: the further removed the outsider, the fewer the mutual obligations, and the greater the display of voluntary hospitality. It goes without saying that one should offer hospitality to those closest to oneself; but what a Glendiot foregrounds in offering his home to strangers is the voluntary character of the act. "As in your own house" is a conventional hyperbole which underscores the poetic properties of the performance: the point is precisely that the visitor is *not* at home, but is indeed highly dependent upon the host. For many Glendiots, indeed, the height of *eghoismos*, self-regard, is a lavish display of hospitality, since it speaks volumes about the social importance of the actor. In the fluid social world of the Glendiots, however, it also gives the guest some leeway to perform, since the guest-host relationship is ultimately idealized as a reciprocal one. As an outsider in several, layered senses, I was able to experience these dimensions of Glendiot social life. At an early stage in my fieldwork, I apparently gained a measure of acceptance by insisting on standing my fair share of coffeehouse treats; if the villagers did not allow me to do so, I argued, they would be denying my right to call myself a Glendiot. Since that right was metaphorical at best, analogous in its implications to the injunction to "feel at home," the gesture worked mainly, I suspect, because it appealed to poetic principles of social behavior that I had not yet appreciated. At the same time, it established a degree of autonomy for me in my interaction with the villagers, since it proved that I could joust with the best of them in at least one important arena.

Such rearrangements of social relationships, however, do not alter the basic hierarchy of stereotypes; they merely illustrate the tension, never fully resolved, between personal experience and stereotypical attribution—a tension nicely illustrated by the explicit distinction villagers make between foreign friends and their hateful governments. The underlying dichotomy between insiders and outsiders is automatically assumed to dictate attitudes and even emotions, at every level at which it is realized: one will always "love" one's own people more than the corresponding outsiders. So strong is the analogy between the levels at which this categorical distinction is made, moreover, that Glendiots constantly draw illustrative parallels—for example, between intercommunal conflicts and international problems. Speaking of a boundary dispute between Glendi and the neighboring village of Psila, one villager mentioned the "Greek mountain [territory]"—in other words, that of his own village. Then he caught himself; but meanwhile his slip of the tongue had revealed a strong sense of analogy.

What is it that ties these various levels of discrimination together? Above all, the rhetoric of deprivation, or "hunger," constantly recurs. The specific basis on which the boundaries are drawn is highly variable: nations are separated by language, religion, and political claims to territory; regions are given their distinguishing features as much by ecological differences as by cultural ones; villages may have "differences" of a more ostensibly political order. But the assumption is always that the outsiders have more to "eat." Foreign states are wealthier, and so are in a position to tyrannize Greece; Crete has been victimized by Athens and does not have the wealth to fight back; the lowland zones of the island are endowed with flowing water and high-grade soil; the largest neighboring mountain village can get special privileges because so many of its leaders did well in regional and national politics and can now exercise their influence on behalf of their own people. This does not make the insiders, in each of these classifications, in any sense inferior. The possession of wealth may confer political power; but it also suggests moral corruption. Thus, at whatever level they happen to be speaking, Glendiots can always represent their own position as one of moral advantage, a position that both sanctifies their ramified illegalities and at the same time allows them to despise those who represent the law or have recourse to it.

These arguments are especially well developed in their stereotypical treatment of other Cretans. For east Cretans, especially those of the Sitia nome, Glendiots express only profound distaste, calling them "law-court types" (*anthropi tou dhikastiriou*)—a real insult, coming from people who regard any truck with the law as treason. Many Glendiot shepherds rent winter pasture land from Sitians. The rich pasturage of the eastern coastal plains, coupled with a low rainfall and relatively high temperatures, makes the region an especially tempting one for the transhumant Glendiot shepherds; but it also leads them into conflict with the local population, whose jealously enclosed orchards and wheatfields are often damaged by passing flocks. As an indication of the Sitians' total lack of social worth, Glendiots accuse them of practicing an inverted form of coffeehouse etiquette, saying that, contrary to west Cretan practice, a Sitian who enters a coffeehouse may take it upon himself to treat those already seated. Just how bizarre this behavior must seem to any Glendiot will become apparent shortly.[14]

Within the area of western and central Crete, the Glendiots also find plenty to deride in their fellow-islanders. They regard the townsfolk as corrupt but possibly rather clever for having made a good situation for themselves. Those who live to the south of Mount Ida (the *notičotes*) are thought of as slightly ridiculous: Glendiots sneer that the south wind (*nothias*) blows in their eyes, preventing them from seeing the adventurous Glendiots come over the mountain paths to raid their flocks. The inhabitants of the lowland villages all around the base of Mount Ida— the *katomerites*, or "people of the low places"—are considered effete and unambitious by the Glendiots. And those who inhabit the plains around Iraklio, the *kambites* ("plainsfolk") may be wealthier, because of their fortune in having good, well-watered land, but they also lack spine. To each of these groups, Glendiots conceptually oppose themselves as *aorites*, "mountain people." This proud name confers on its bearers the right to represent themselves as the best among those best of Greeks, the Cretans, and thereby extends the segmentary logic that conjoins the interests of villagers and scholars at the broader levels of inclusion.

Glendi is one of the highest villages on Mount Ida, and the usual idiom for "go up, ascend" is "go out" (*vyeno*). Thus, the village is, as it were, *outside* the locus of power; it is "up," where the air and men's souls alike are purer. Iraklio, by contrast, is always called *mesa*, "[the place further] inside." (Rethimno, the much smaller and poorer regional

administrative capital, is merely "down.") Thus, the politically exterior
is both geographically and morally superior from the Glendiots' point of
view—an attitude, moreover, that they willingly amplify with tale after
tale to illustrate the cowardice, greed, venality, and stupidity of those
who inhabit the urban centers.

The most distinctive act of the highlanders in this context is the
livestock raid. All shepherds who expect to maintain their flocks at a
reasonable level feel obliged to raid, since by doing so they establish a
reputation as men whose own property is well and ferociously protected
and who would be worth having as allies. The younger shepherds, those
who are below the age of about thirty and are still building up their
flocks to maximum size (rarely over six hundred animals), are especially
active; after marriage and procreation, a shepherd may feel constrained
by the demands of domestic life and civic responsibility, although he
will continue to retaliate against younger raiders who attack him first.
The exact frequency of raiding is hard to establish. Some shepherds who
clearly had been out stealing from neighboring villages were understandably reluctant to tell me the details of time, location, or size of the raid,
or whether others were implicated, and much of the information that I
was able to gather concerned events now regarded as "old." It seems,
however, that even today scarcely a moonless night goes by without at
least one Glendiot shepherd taking full advantage of the cover of darkness
to steal a few animals. Shepherds, in particular, hold up these acts as
emblematic of Glendiot pride, a pride in which unquenchable youth,
daring, independence, and strength are combined.

It is no coincidence that stolen meat (*klepsimeiko kreas*) is considered
"tastier," and that this is also the quality of meat eaten in the foothills
above the inhabited area of the village. The moral superiority of the
aorites is not of a kind that lowlanders would claim for themselves, still
less the members of the educated urban classes. According to a Glendiot
"jest" (*kalambouri*) that clearly follows the local joking idiom in that it
plays with matters of symbolically weighty import, the ideal food of the
thief is the hard belly fat (*knisari*[15]) eaten raw. As Kapsomenos has
observed (1980:228-229), in part on the basis of song texts recording a
way of life much like that of the Glendiots, the nature/culture opposition
may be reversed wherever the standpoint is that of the bandit standing
against the representatives of an official order. To many Glendiots,
especially to those who are shepherds, the bourgeois culture of the towns
may be desirable; but it is also corrupt. The man who is good at raiding,
the *kala kleftis*, should be closer to nature than to so despicable a form
of culture, and the token consumption of raw fat symbolizes that stance.
Adept sheep thieves always prefer to boil rather than roast meat, since

the latter process gives off telltale smoke; and this, too, means that the serving of massive amounts of boiled meat at wedding feasts—where much of the meat is traditionally assumed to be stolen—comes to signify, again, a relative degree of moral closeness to nature.[16] Stolen meat is also called *aziyasto*, "unweighed," since it usually has to be consumed in haste and without the domestication of social life symbolized by the "cultural" act of weighing.

The act of eating also conveys another important message. To be wealthy, as we have already seen, is to "eat," and this is always thought to be possible only at others' expense. But "eating" is also a standard metaphor for "stealing." In the narratives about animal theft I will discuss below, its use creates both ambiguity about what actually happened and a sense of the moral equivalence between theft and consumption. In any description of a raid on the wealthy, however, its principal importance is that it fits the act to an ideal model of reciprocity: *aorites* are able to "eat" in the sense of taking their wealth away from them. The use of this metaphor also brackets the despised lowlanders with the Turks, who, until their departure from the island, were always considered legitimate targets and possibly profitable ones as well. Such reciprocity is of course not the same as that which occurs between approximately well-matched *aorites* from neighboring villages, but represents a structural transformation of the same ideological principle.

The following story illustrates the moral superiority of those who live closer to nature (symbolized by "rocks") as well as the Glendiots' dislike and jealousy of the people of the fertile plains. It also provides a further demonstration of the Glendiots' claim to quintessential Greekness on the basis of *poniria*:

> Once upon a time, the shepherd was at [the locality of Glendi called] Korakinia. And Christ was coming down the hillside wearing Cretan boots. Well, He says to him, "Your health, *koumbare!*"
>
> "Welcome, *koumbare!*" says the shepherd to Him.
>
> So they got to meet there, and Christ told him who He was. And Christ asks him, "Do you have any complaints, my lad, hereabouts? What complaints do you have? Do you live well? do things go well for you?"
>
> Says he [i.e., the shepherd], "What! do I have any satisfaction? You gave us here all the rocks and we can't make a living and we're in difficulty. And you gave all the soil to the plain." (In Messaria, that is, Iraklio!)
>
> Says He, "I, my lad, put the soil there and the rocks here, so that the plainsfolk should work and you should eat!"

This triumphant conclusion to a tale explicitly explained to me as being about animal theft shows how the central metaphor of "eating" works. The plainsfolk are ordinarily those who "eat," in the sense of enjoying their easily won wealth; but the Glendiot Christ reverses all that, by providing the mountain shepherds with a symbolic justification for raiding them.[17]

A second story translates the rather specialized, local variety of *poniria* exemplified here on to a national plane:

> When they captured Christ and put him in jail—since you want to collect all that stuff—the Englishman went [to visit Him] first. The *Inglis*!
>
> And he says to Him, "My dear Christ, what are you doing in here, shut up in jail here?"
>
> (Listen, and you'll get a good one!) And so he says to Him, this Englishman, "I, my dear Christ, will get you out of this here dungeon."
>
> "How will you get me out?"
>
> "I'll put up some gold to get you out of the dungeon."
>
> "May you have my blessing, and forever have gold!"
>
> After a feast [*sic*], the Russian went, and says to Him, "My Christ, what are you doing here in jail?"
>
> "Look, I'm locked up here, I can't [do anything], I'm in jail."
>
> "I'll bring out an army to abduct you from prison."
>
> Says He, "May you have my blessing and always have an army!"
>
> The Greek went. The *Greek*! The Greek—that's me, that's what that means, eh? "My Christ, what are you doing in here?"
>
> "Look, I'm locked up here in jail."
>
> "Oh, my dear Christ, I'll get you out of here."
>
> "How will you get me out?"
>
> "I'll pierce a hole in these walls and *steal* you out of here!"
>
> "May you have my blessing, and ever [be] a thief!"
>
> Well, there it is, that's where we got the blessing from. And we Greeks are . . . [*then, after interruption:*] . . . thieves!

This is a far cry from that nationalist rhetoric which treats all forms of "brigandage" as foreign importations. At the same time, it partially explains how—despite that rhetoric—Glendiots' raids can convey identification with a Greekness that, it is implied, only other Greeks could really understand.

Yet the nationalistic rhetoric has also made its local inroads. Glendiots are not all equally amused by the prevalence of animal rustling among the village shepherds. Those who are no longer shepherds themselves are increasingly embarrassed by the problem, and handle the discourse to express their dissenting view. In response to the tale about Christ and the Cretan shepherd, told to me by a self-styled traditionalist and experienced shepherd and rustler, another Glendiot raised vociferous complaints about its implications. The conversation is worth reproducing here, since it illustrates the process whereby local identity is negotiated:

> *Stelios (the shepherd)*: . . . [It's] an old story, of course, from Glendi.
> *MH*: And it's about animal theft, of course?
> *Stelios*: But of course! Because He was coming down from here. So draw your own conclusion about where we've got to and how much progress we've made. That is: do we have progress or not? In money, in property, in whatever each Glendiot has created, he's done it through his personal worth. One man through his work, the next—that is, whoever can't [work], whoever doesn't want to work, steals! He goes down and steals from the plainsfolk, and lives!

Note that the local prosperity is not denied; on the contrary, it forms the basis of Stelios' argument for living according to the old ways. Here is yet another indication of the metaphorical character of that ever-present "hunger" to which Glendiots so easily resort for the explanation of their social values.

Stelios then went on to explain:

> How can animal theft cease? All of us who go to winter pastures don't have [any land of our own for the purpose]. . . . That's why I told you about Christ going up there. So, we too go down to winter pastures.
> *Eftikhis (a farmer, recently returned from an extensive spell of work in Germany, and presenting an urbane contrast to Stelios' deliberate traditionalism)*: No!
> *Stelios*: Eftikhis, if we don't go to winter pastures and all of us end up together right here, how are we going to live?
> *Eftikhis*: But we *aren't* living! No!
> *Stelios (ironically)*: We aren't living?
> *Eftikhis*: This is a mountainous place. . . .
> *Stelios*: This story I told Mikhalis [i.e., MH] has meaning [*noima*, a term that closely glosses *simasia* but also suggests that the meaning in question is *consciously* created]. If there were no animal theft, all the plainsfolk would have their own animals! Do *you* know that?

Eftikhis: They wouldn't have.

Stelios: They all would, Eftikhis. They do now! I'll tell you actual cases. *I* will! Don't I live through all that? Why, I'm telling you, the moment animal theft stops for just one hour, everything will be turned inside-out, fences will go up [to enclose scarce grazing land], there'll be sheep behind them, those folks'll buy up sheep. Well, how are *we* going to live after that, Eftikhis? Where will *we* go after that? That's what has meaning (*simasia*), in other words.

The problem with which Stelios is concerned is a frequently voiced concern in Glendi. If the lowlanders were to engage intensively in sheep farming, they would effectively close off all the available winter pastures, and would also eventually create such large flocks that the transhumant highlanders would find the competition too great for them. Such a defeat at the hands of the despised lowlanders is not to be contemplated; yet the fear intrudes explicitly into most Glendiot discussions about the future of shepherding in the area.

The argument became increasingly passionate, the protagonists' voices rising in pitch and volume. A sensitive issue emerged, that of the lowlanders' active hostility toward the presence of mountain shepherds in their villages:

Eftikhis: There're so many properties, so many things, so much land. . . .

Stelios: Nothing, nothing, for us there's nothing!

Eftikhis: You're wrong!

Stelios: Look here, Eftikhis, anyone who wants to buy a field, the locals go and intervene with the owner and take hold of him, and tell him, "Don't sell it to him, he mustn't get a foothold here! He mustn't so much as approach!" Do you hear me? What I mean is, it isn't an easy matter for us mountain folk to make peace with the *kambites* [plainsfolk]. And I'm telling you, it [animal theft] is our biggest weapon, for us who have no other means of fighting. Our biggest weapon! In this case, it's this [i.e., animal theft].

Eftikhis: You're wr—

Stelios: What I'm afraid of is, if they do things their way, all the people from these villages [i.e., in the vicinity of Glendi] will be excluded, won't be allowed a single step in that direction.

Eftikhis: I know just one thing, that—leave the sheep out of it!—I know just this one thing: if our village is at a certain level, not

a *high* level but anyway a relatively good level, let's say, economically . . .

Stelios: Yes.

Eftikhis: . . . the cause is local development.

"Local development" sounds good to Glendiots as a general principle;
it suggests infusions of government money, new wealth brought back by
returned migrants from Germany, the gradual increase in the availability
of urban-style comforts in these mountain villages. But what Eftikhis
wants is that shepherding should decrease in importance, and he suggests
that shepherds who really cannot obtain winter pasturage should change
their line of work. Stelios, however, responded with all the pride of a
profession that treats farming as an essentially feminine occupation:

> *Eftikhis*: If you don't have the means to keep up your flock, friend,
> there's other work! Just keep a hundred animals! [In other words,
> there is no need to be solely dependent upon animal husbandry.]
>
> *Stelios*: A shepherd, Eftikhis, who's used to herding, can't just
> become a wage laborer.

After a good deal more in the same vein, Eftikhis finally threw the
question of local pride in Stelios' face:

> *Eftikhis*: I neither steal nor "eat" [here probably in the sense of
> eating stolen meat], nor do I have any [animals] for others to eat
> [i.e., steal] from my property! The only thing I have to tell you
> is, go and *eat each other up*, so you'll all die, that'll simplify
> things for us! *(Here Eftikhis is reversing the "eating" formula as
> well, perhaps, as unconsciously borrowing from the common charm
> formula whereby an evil spirit is destroyed by eating something
> specially prescribed for the purpose; see, e.g., Herzfeld 1977:38-
> 40.)* I've heard, I have—I've been to Germany, I've been to
> Athens, I've been everywhere [and heard people say]: shame on
> the Cretans!
>
> *Stelios*: But it isn't only in Crete, Eftikhis, that people steal!
>
> *Eftikhis*: Here they *do* steal!
>
> *Stelios*: Here they steal sheep. Elsewhere they steal other things.
> I'm not in favor of animal theft. I condemn it! In the present day
> and age, in other words, people shouldn't steal. But they steal
> everywhere. In one place they steal sheep, in another they burgle
> shop stalls, elsewhere they burn stores, yet elsewhere banks. In
> other words, it exists everywhere, in each place according to
> what's possible!

I have recounted this conversation in detail because it illustrates the extent to which local identity, with its tensions between the various levels of inclusiveness (Glendi, *aorites*, Crete, Greece), is invested in the problem of animal theft. At stake also is the inevitable tension between the internally legitimate admiration of *poniria* and the very different self-images that many Glendiots feel should be displayed to the external world. Both modes are ways in which a villager may, in the Glendiot idiom, "hold up his head." Which is more appropriate, and under what circumstances, are questions that demand ceaseless renegotiation. The conversation between Stelios and Eftikhis illustrates the terms in which this happens. Throughout their exchange, the richly ambiguous "eating" idiom allows them to treat a wide range of violent acts as essentially analogous forms of reciprocity. "Eating," which in a positive sense is the key theme of reciprocity, is also the key metaphor for the insubordinate violence that Glendiots recognize as being equally characteristic of their society.

A Theft of Meaning

This constant uncertainty about his exact place in the world is what gives "meaning" (*simasia*) to a Glendiot male's actions and words. The argument between Stelios and Eftikhis reflects another level of debate, in which the authorities are trying to convince the Glendiots that animal theft, far from being a manly activity, is cowardly and demeaning. This is one of several ways in which official rhetoric has come to mesh more effectively with local sentiment in the last few years, with the result that animal theft may finally be on the verge of decline. These changes can only be understood against the background of the durable nexus provided by the concepts of *simasia* (meaning) and *andrismos* (manliness) and the experience of uncertainty in Glendiot society. These are the chief organizing principles of the villagers' social ideology, and furnish an advance key for deciphering the texts of Glendiot life.

It is through risk that a Glendiot shepherd discovers the meaning of his existence. Risk exposes him to internal tension and anxiety, and tests his skill and determination. As the mother of a man jailed for killing his brother's murderer remarked, "If a man doesn't suffer torment, he doesn't find peace" (*ama dhe tirannisti čanis, dhen isikhazi*). This lapidary observation makes very good sense to Glendiots. Life is regarded as a barren stretch of time, a blank page on which the genuine poet of his own manhood must write as engaging an account as he can. Time, say the Glendiots, is something to be "passed"; the more outrageous the diversion, the more successful the transcendance of mundane existence and the more pleasing aesthetically the resulting memory. "Passing the time" is a frequently cited reason for youths to go off raiding. Through such initiations they learn what most of this book is about—the poetics of being a true Glendiot man.

That phrase needs some elaboration. Anthropological concern with the meaning of cultural phenomena has not always brought with it much interest in indigenous abstractions about meaning. This is a serious problem, since such concepts are likely to prove both a cause and a consequence of much of what the ethnographer tries to interpret. Common sense will not suffice as a basis for interpretation, since it is precisely the common sense of the culture being studied that the anthropologist wants to disentangle from the data (see also Crick 1976; Douglas 1975; Geertz 1973).

This is the strongest argument for a semiotic perspective on ethnography (see also Herzfeld 1983a). Such a perspective rejects the artificial distinction between symbolic discourse and objective data, and instead treats the ethnographic text—which is no less empirical as a result— as a construction resulting from the fusion of the ethnographer's conceptual framework with that of the local informants. In this approach, informants' presuppositions, whether consciously articulated or not, acquire pivotal importance. They constitute, in effect, the indigenous semiotic without which the ethnographer's claim to be dealing with meaning would have little basis.

We should also beware of our own verbocentrism. While it is fashionable to attribute meaning to all sorts of nonverbal cultural phenomena, the usual model by which anthropologists address the topic is at least derivatively linguistic. In trying to identify an indigenous semiotic, by contrast, the ethnographer may discover that other dimensions than language are equally or more significant.

This is not to say that language cannot provide the best means of access. Indeed, a start can perhaps best be made by trying to juxtapose our own concepts of meaning, relevance, importance, and explanation with the nearest local glosses. Often, a seemingly bizarre response to basic questions will serve this purpose well. When I asked Glendiots why they habitually stole livestock, they often replied, "To make friends!" Even when I realized that raiding was the first step toward contracting an essentially political alliance with the victim by forcing him to acknowledge one's daring and skill, I found it hard at first to see why a man should expect his victims to turn into particularly trustworthy allies. But as my attention began to focus on the importance of a raider's possessing style and flair rather than purely technical skills alone, the answer "to make friends" began to make sense—Glendiot sense—as the encapsulation of ideas about performance, significance, and social worth.

Effective performance uses form to draw attention to a set of messages. When Glendiots reject a particular action as "without meaning," they generally imply that it lacks performative flair or distinctiveness. It is not enough just to be a man; even the lowest ones of all were born male. One must be good *at being* a man.

This is the burden of the grammatically peculiar construction *kala 'ndras* or *kala eghoistis* ("well man" and "well self-assertive man," respectively; both constructions thus qualify the noun with an adverb instead of the more canonical adjective ["good man"] in order to create the resultant ellipsis). The distinctive usage does two things at once. It emphasizes the performative aspect of an individual's social standing; and it foregrounds the Cretans' claim to distinctiveness through the use of a dialectological characteristic that violates the syntactical norms of standard Greek speech—an illustration, in itself, of the poetic qualities of Glendiot discourse.

It also evokes an unambiguously active condition: the *kala 'ndras* is not one who rests on his laurels, but one who continues to earn them. Thus, performance is essential to the maintenance of a worthwhile reputation among Glendiot men. A truly gifted performer may win kudos for sheer nerve, as when he invites policemen to sit down with him to a meal of the meat of the animals that he has just stolen. On other occasions, a sudden reversal may call for admiration: a man whose anger is backed by real influence (*kozi*, "knuckle") drops his voice to one of bored reproach, thereby humiliating his lesser rival all the more effectively. Improvisation is at a premium, and a good performer will make sure that his audience realizes that he is indeed improvising, or—in a sheep-theft narrative, for example—did so in the actions of which he now boasts. The ability to play with the conventions in aesthetically intriguing ways, and above all to seize opportunity from unpromising materials, is what generates *simasia* in particular contexts. Much of this book is an extended illustration of that principle.

Glendiots do talk about meaning, usually in connection with specific situations or texts. Their contemptuous comment that something "doesn't say anything" (*dhe lei prama*) may be filled out with more particular objections. They devote considerable attention to the significance of gesture, dress, and linguistic behavior, and to the etymology of their own lexicon. They explicitly attribute the use of the retroflex in place of /l/, for example, to "tough talk" in imitation of the speech of a village with a still more ferocious reputation than Glendi's. Politicians who wear Cretan costume or speak in a strongly local accent are mocked, especially if their "village speech" seems to come from the wrong village; one Glendiot remarked that a certain politician's affectation of Cretan high boots reminded him of the fish vendors who advertised their presence by playing *rebetika* in the lowland villages but hastily switched to Xylouris when they passed through the defile leading to the highland villages.[18]

Such semiotic sensitivity deserves explicit mention in any ethnographic study. *Simasia* is a concept that Glendiots use to judge and order all social experience, and is firmly grounded in observation. The term is rarely used in the abstract; instead, it is applied evaluatively to particular performances. An action that fails, or a verbal jest that falls flat, lacks *simasia*. Glendiots recognize, moreover, what ethnographers all too often overlook: that signs, far from representing eternal verities, undergo constant renegotiation with shifts in social context, principals' interests, or personal mood. Their perspective in this regard is essential to any attempt at semiotic ethnography (cf. also Meeker 1979:30).

I have chosen to focus on the poetics of *manhood* because I had far fuller access to male than to female society during my fieldwork. Nevertheless, the women's view of male actions does not always harmonize with that of the men, and provides a necessary counterpart to the androcentric discourse with which this study is primarily concerned. Generally speaking, the women's vigorous disapproval of male excesses was directed at the avoidance of dangerous conflict, and was usually reserved for occasions when it would not undermine the public dignity of a son, brother, or husband, and provided a revealing counterweight to male scorn for "women's matters." It also served to underscore the moral analogy between women in general and men who had passed their prime: like women, old men avoid strong drink, attend religious services, and avoid eating meat during the Lenten fast, allegedly out of fear that their sins (*amarties*) would return to haunt them in the rapidly approaching afterlife.

Like old men, too, women always seem to close ranks with their wilder menfolk in the face of an external threat. They may, for example, help conceal stolen meat; it would do them no good if their husbands ended up in jail. In one case, when a policeman came searching for stolen meat, the suspect's sister hurled herself at the helpless investigator just as he was about to open her dower-chest (where the meat was hidden under a layer of her underclothes). If the policeman opened the chest, she screamed, she would kill him; his action would have been tantamount to violating her virginity by peering through her underclothes. The policeman backed off hastily.

Such actions evoke admiration from the men, who argue that *eghoismos* (aggressive self-regard) is not so much a male prerogative as defined in relation to male concerns. It may, for example, characterize the actions of a woman who takes it upon herself to speak up for her husband's agnates during a neighborhood confrontation, or to bring honor on her household through especially hospitable behavior. Thus, women's actions are not seen as lacking *simasia*, even by the men; there are moments, however, when women actively disagree with men of their households as to what actions do in fact deserve to be taken seriously.[19]

Glendiot fascination with *simasia* is appropriate to a society which lives largely in suspicion of the official world of fixed rules, prescribed history, and legalistic definitions. Men experience that world more than women because men represent the village to it in virtually all official contexts. But all Glendiots, women and men alike, encounter the tensions that exist between the two sets of values, and turn these tensions into the materials out of which they must fashion and refashion their identities.

Their exuberance makes Glendiot men a particularly apt subject for a study of the poetics of social interaction. In other Greek villages, everyday demeanor seems to conform much more predictably to both local and national conventions.[20] In Glendi, too, there are certainly men whose actions rarely if ever challenge their covillagers' sensibilities. Whereas such diffidence may count as a virtue elsewhere, in Glendi it is incontestably regarded as a major disadvantage. Thus, the Glendiots may be said to have more aggressively poetic expectations of social life. In verbal art, not all texts are equally poetic, and those that were never intended to be so at all usually make bad poetry (Jakobson 1980:96-97). This does not necessarily mean that they are totally lacking in poetic qualities, only that these qualities cannot be said to predominate. Thus it is with social interaction: the Glendiots, because of their determined nonconformism, can teach us where to look for poetic elements in the performances of identity that we meet in other, less obtrusively insubordinate communities. If other communities subject themselves more willingly to the dictates of officially sanctioned convention, they surely lead more *prosaic* lives. Because of—rather than despite—its idiosyncrasies, Glendi can point the way to a better understanding of the principles of agonistic interaction in Greece and elsewhere.

In a social world marked more by poetic than by definitional concerns, meaning is evanescent and indeterminate. It has to be seized as opportunity offers, as the Glendiots taught me to realize. One day, chuckling amiably, a villager teased me for taking my chance to "steal" a snippet of conversation. Although I would not have volunteered this metaphor first, I encountered it often enough in the village; returned migrants, especially, would recall how they had "stolen" bits of the German language. Note that they did not *master* the language, any more than an animal thief would normatively steal a whole flock. Instead, they displayed skill and cunning by exploiting the chance of a moment to abstract a few usable items. This, apparently, was what I was thought to be doing with the conversation. In Glendi, where men steal animals "to make friends," it was not considered unreasonable for me to "steal" a conversation in order to render my own experiences intelligible. On the contrary, this was an early sign of acceptance, later explicitly confirmed to me as such. It was also an early source of insight, conferred by villagers with a very lively sense of the search for significance in social life.

CHAPTER TWO

LINES OF CONTEST

Idiosyncrasies: Personal and Collective Selfhood

Glendiot distinctiveness quickly strikes the new visitor to the village. Perhaps the most immediate sign is in the villagers' unusually open expression of hospitality, which leads householders and coffeehouse proprietors to call from their doorways, "Come so we may treat you (*elate na sas čerasoumene*)!" or, in winter, "Come and get warm (*elate na pirothite*)!" Such exuberant generosity, as well as the sheer proliferation of coffeehouses, is attributed to male pride. In 1981 there were twenty-nine of them, an enormous number which, in a community of just over fourteen hundred people, reflects both a high degree of competitiveness and a desire for generous arenas of social interaction.[1] As if these gathering places were not sufficient, moreover, homeowners lounging on their balconies over a glass of wine and the midday meal are apt to insist that passers-by take a *podhariko*—"something taken on foot"—even if they cannot find the time to sit down to the feast at leisure. Private hospitality is a matter for public performance. Still more remarkable is the frequent appearance in this context of huge quantities of meat—a relatively rare everyday food in other rural Greek communities, even pastoral ones (e.g., Campbell 1964:207).

Other surprises soon follow. Coffeehouse patrons, for example, do not seem to be distinguished on the basis of age. Moreover, contrary to what has been reported for the northern Greek Sarakatsani (Campbell 1964:160), fathers and sons may often be found sipping coffee together in public here. As elsewhere in Greece, the coffeehouses as well as the streets may become settings for violent quarrels, in which bystanders become advocates of restraint as well as the means whereby hatred can be safely displayed—because, as one Glendiot remarked, "if you hold someone back, he can afford to be brave (*ama kratizis ton allo perni aera*)." When closely related men quarrel, it is said that "they've spilled the curds [*ekhisan to khouma*]," an allusion to the cooperative group of close agnates who make cheese together, and against whom the greatest insult is to damage their cheese-making cauldrons.

All these superficially disparate sources of distinctiveness are articulated by a strongly androcentric public ideology. Meat is definitively a male food, as the discussion of narrative materials will demonstrate; even though women do eat it, the cutting and roasting, as well as the public consumption of conspicuously large quantities of it, are all acknowledged in word and deed as male activities. Quarrels are said to occur chiefly over women and animals—a far from accidental bracketing of the passive objects of male competition, as the allusion to the Turks' making "harems" of their flocks has already suggested, and as the use of a single term (*klepsa*) for animal theft and bride abduction also indicates. Coffeehouses are exclusively male preserves.[2] Public fights quickly bring out demonstrations of agnatic solidarity, in which it is absolutely imperative that fathers and sons demonstrate mutual loyalty: not for them the fragmentation into households that is so common among the Sarakatsani, for example. In this respect, coffeehouse etiquette parallels the more dangerous context of the pastures: close agnates who stand together are better able to defend their flocks and their own persons, and it is far from uncommon for an eldest son to signify his identification with his father by retaining the same property-mark on his own sheep.

The agonistic pattern of Greek male interaction is in no sense necessarily dependent upon agnatic relationships. Indeed, in Cyprus and more especially among the Sarakatsani, it has been associated with the defense of interests defined by the nuclear household alone (Peristiany 1965:180; Campbell 1964:38). Vague generalizations about "residual patriliny" in the Mediterranean (e.g., Davis 1977:197; but cf. Herzfeld 1983c) have never been linked to this interactional pattern in the existing literature. Agnatic ties, however, play an important role in Glendiot social life, and this despite the fact that the Glendiots use a cognatic kinship terminology closely resembling standard Greek usage.[3] Glendiots do, however, use several terms for agnatic groupings, and of these at least two are known to have been used by the pre-Independence guerrillas of mainland Greece—a further point of similarity between that phase of Greek history and the current Glendiot experience.[4]

But even this terminology partially disguises the importance of agnation in Glendi: *soi*, the term which, for convenience, I translate here as "patrigroup,"[5] elsewhere signifies the bilateral kindred, while the term which ordinarily means "household" (*ikoyenia*) is sometimes used as an official-sounding synonym for *soi*. For Glendiots, there is something faintly embarrassing about admitting to a nonnormative kinship system: it sets them apart from other Greeks, and—through a popular association of Cretan family values with the blood feud—portrays them as wild outlaws. By calling the agnatic group *ikoyenia*, they are able to offset this negative image somewhat. The use of the term suggests adherence to the official system of reckoning relationships: the members of a household constitute the minimum unit within the surname group, and its implied extension to the entire surname group, or *soi*, is only accessible to insiders. This might well stand as an instance of the poetic use of kinship terminology, given both the delicate ambiguity of the exact range of kin and the use of the term as a shibboleth to negotiate the ever indeterminate boundary between insider and outsider. When Glendiots used the term instead of *soi* in speaking to me, they were treating me as an outsider while still leaving open the possibility that I might know enough to be able to bridge the gap. The apparent interchangeability of the two terms provides a poetic device that Glendiots use to explore and manipulate the uncertain contours of their relationship with the outside world.

Entailed in this tension in Glendi between two kinship ideologies are two contrasted definitions of the social self. On the one hand, the official system foregrounds principles of "European" and "Christian" identity, in which the personality of each individual is thought to derive in equal measure from both sides of the family. In this view, too, the individual is restrained from political violence by obligations to a nexus of interrelated groups: no single descent group stands out as claiming his allegiance against all comers. On the other hand, the Glendiot system of agnation identifies the male self with a whole line of patrilineal ancestors. In this, the Glendiots differ even from the highly agonistic Sarakatsani. It may be significant that the Sarakatsani rarely eat meat except on festive occasions such as Easter, whereas the Glendiots regard—and apparently have long regarded—the consumption of meat as an essential component of male self-definition: meat and wine are seen as essential to the procreation of brave sons.

The entailment of self in the agnatic ideology means that any insult to the patriline becomes an insult to the person as well. Character traits are assumed to be transmitted, in the main, through the male line. An elderly Khloros, for example, sourly attributed his chronic diarrhea to a general, patrigroup-wide tendency! There are many more violent implications. A dispute involving a group of Diakakis brothers and a Khloros family was triggered when an exasperated Khloros, tactlessly alluding to the recent death of one of the Diakakis group in a road accident, yelled, "I screw your dead as [the worthless representatives of] a patrigroup (*ghamo ts' apothamenous sas ya soi*)." This was the signal for the Diakakis knives to come whipping out, pointing their embittered rage at the Khloros group, who immediately responded in kind.

Glendiots do not actually deny the significance of uterine kinship altogether, although they do regard it as a weaker bond—"kinship through women creates a distance (*to athiliko sinjenio alaryeni*)"—and this is attributed to the polluting power of sexual contact with women. This androcentrism is further enhanced by a preference for agnatic endogamy, provided that it does not conflict with incest restrictions.[6] A peculiarity of the local kinship terminology replaces the usual wife-giver/wife-taker distinction with reciprocal terms of address and reference: since it is assumed that in-laws will ideally be of the same patrigroup, no distinction of status should be made (see fig. 2).

Interestingly, the term for "brothers-in-law" (*kouniadhi*) also used to be applied to close cousins, and the same was true of the female equivalents. Among men, all those who could be designated by this term were categorically defined as appropriate raiding companions—unlike brothers and fathers, be it noted, since there is some fear that a whole male line could be eliminated if a raid culminated in the wholesale killing of the offenders, leaving the women unprotected from insult and abuse.

This is a system that very much favors the large patrigroups, and it also suggests a reason for the maintenance of emphasis on kinship in the male line. It is probably significant that here in the western highlands of Crete, where shepherding is still an important occupation even though the attrition rate seems to increase year by year, the emphasis on agnatic kinship remains strong. Elsewhere, both shepherding and collective violence seem to have dwindled together, and the desire for large families is replaced by a conviction that civilized human beings should not breed

---

Fig. 2. Terminology for affines in two generations.

STANDARD GREEK

kouniadhos	=	WB	*kouniadha*	=	HZ
ghambros	=	ZH, DH	*nifi*	=	BW, SW
badzanakis	=	WZH	*sinifadha*	=	HBW

GLENDIOT

kouniadhos	=	WB, ZH, WZH	*kouniadha*	=	HZ, BW, HBW
ghambros	=	DH	*nifi*	=	SW

---

like animals—a view that those Glendiots who have turned away from pastoralism also increasingly espouse.

The connection between pastoralism and family size is clearly understood by the villagers themselves. Members of the principal patrigroups can call on a large number of agnatic cousins when planning serious retaliation against raiders: one villager recalled an expedition in which as many as eighteen agnatic kinsmen were involved! As long as raiding continues, therefore, there is good reason to maintain extensive agnatic ties. The proverb that "many children are wealth" thus takes on greater significance in this context. A father who sires many sons may expect his flock to continue on after his death, even if the patrimony is eventually divided; the sons will continue to help each other, taking turns at guarding their sheep all together, and thereby ensuring the improved protection that allows a flock to maintain a size worthy of others' respect. Experience shows that those without brothers find it hard to maintain a reasonably sized flock (that is, above about a hundred animals); anything under about fifty animals ceases to be economically viable, and also provides a humiliating public index of failure.

Many of those whose flocks have approached or even fallen below this critical level in recent years have found it expedient to turn to farming— a less demeaning, because vastly more profitable, enterprise than it was before the early sixties. One disgruntled shepherd, whose only brother was either uninterested in helping him or simply incapable of doing so, complained bitterly of the hardship he was forced to endure. Eventually, his flock decimated by endless raids to which he could not respond without leaving his small flock unguarded against still other depredations, he became a farmer. While such men do not immediately forget about the priority of agnatic over uterine ties as soon as they leave pastoralism behind them, it is clear that their more fortunate kinsmen do depend very heavily upon the solidarity of close agnatic kin in order to maintain and increase their flocks; and they also try to plan for the future, and for the survival of their names as well, by siring as many sons as they can. In this way, practical considerations regarding the security of flocks reinforce the symbolic identification of a large progeny with a large flock of animals—both sources of an *eghoismos* at once collective and individual. Once the shepherd has become a farmer, on the other hand, his labor needs are more intermittent, and his progeny will not inherit an infinitely expandable estate: over a period of several generations, the principle of undifferentiated partible inheritance favors small families.

Similar differences in motivation affect the choice of allies. Shepherds tend to make intensive use of baptism to create political alliances outside the village; they argue that it is pointless to make such alliances with covillagers, since the latter are already committed to respecting their property. It is only after a shepherd has turned to farming instead that he *may* decide to invite covillagers to baptize his children. With land boundaries a constant source of mutual irritation, farmers have more interest in creating such ties *within* the village.

Reading Village Spaces

The concern with agnatic groupings and the limitations upon it are also reflected in the physical plan of the village. Patrigroup endogamy (see fig. 3a) is theoretically justified on the grounds that this keeps the various family properties within at least the nominal possession of the *soi*. Most (though not all) of the village neighborhoods are named for patrigroups. Not all presently existing patrigroups are so represented, however, and the pattern is further confused by the common practice of "alienating" (*apoksenononde*) patrigroup territory through the sale of house plots to the fathers of in-marrying grooms, who then build their new homes there.

A partial sketch-map of the village in 1907 shows how far this process had already gone by that date (fig. 3b); it was subsequently advanced still further by sales of house plots to uterine kin. Whenever a house plot is to be sold, the relative claims of agnatic and uterine kin and affines have to be weighed, and every effort is made to avoid the embarrassment—for so it is regarded—of selling to complete outsiders (*kseni*). In a moral sense, land remains eternally the conceptual property of the patrigroup to which it historically belonged. Thus, even though patrigroups do not own land corporately for any practical purposes, villagers do recognize corporate *identity* as a serious factor in decisions regarding the sale of land.

A specific case will illustrate how such factors are gauged. A Koumbis inherited a plot of land from his mother, who was born a Khloros. When he was about to sell it, he first "preferred" (*protimise*[7]) his son-in-law, a small-patrigroup member, but the latter preferred to buy a vineyard instead. Then the Koumbis tried to sell it to his first cousin, another Koumbis, but was turned down for similar reasons. Finally, he sold it to a Khloros, so that it reverted to its original patrigroup (as the informant, himself a Khloros, proudly remarked). At this point, a Skoufas family offered to buy it for 15,000 drx. (as opposed to the 12,000 drx. agreed upon for the sale to the Khloros). Rather than "alienate" the plot from Khloros control again, however, the old and new owners agreed on a mutually acceptable price of 14,000 drx., thereby preserving the original

Fig. 3a. Patterns of marriage in Glendi.

Year	Weddings		Surname Endog.	Skoufas	Potamitis	Khloros	Other
				m/f	m/f	m/f	m/f
1933	5	[0m/0f][a]	1	1-1/1[b]	0-0/0	0-1/1	0-3/3
1934	2	[0m/1f]	0	0-1/0	0-1/0	0-0/0	0-0/2
1935	7	[1m/0f]	1	1-3/3	0-1/0	0-0/2	0-3/2
1936	1	[0m/0f]	1	0-0/0	0-0/0	1-1/1	0-0/0
1937	2	[0m/0f]	1	0-1/0	0-0/0	1-1/1	0-0/1
1938	7	[2m/0f]	3	3-3/4	0-2/0	0-0/1	0-2/2
1939	4	[0m/0f]	0	0-1/2	0-1/0	0-1/1	0-1/1
1940	5	[1m/0f]	1	1-1/1	0-1/1	0-0/1	0-3/2
1941	2	[0m/0f]	1	0-1/0	1-1/1	0-0/0	0-0/1
1942	10	[1m/0f]	0	0-1/3	0-2/0	0-0/3	0-7/4
1943	4	[0m/1f]	0	0-1/0	0-2/0	0-1/0	0-0/4
1944	3	[0m/0f]	0	0-1/1	0-0/1	0-0/0	0-2/1
1945	5	[0m/0f]	1	0-1/1	1-1/3	0-1/0	0-2/1
1946	5	[0m/0f]	1	0-0/2	1-1/2	0-1/0	0-3/1
1947	6	[0m/0f]	2	2-3/3	0-2/0	0-1/0	0-0/3
1948	3	[0m/0f]	0	0-0/0	0-0/1	0-0/1	0-3/1
1949	10	[0m/1f]	0	0-6/1	0-2/1	0-0/1	0-2/7
1950	8	[0m/0f]	2	0-1/1	1-1/1	0-2/1	1-4/5
1951	6	[1m/1f][c]	2	1-2/2	1-1/2	0-1/0	0-2/2
1952	5	[1m/0f]	1	1-2/1	0-1/1	0-0/1	0-2/2
1953	7	[1m/1f]	0	0-0/1	0-2/0	0-0/1	0-5/5
1954	6	[1m/1f]	0	0-0/1	0-2/0	0-1/1	0-3/4
1955	7	[0m/1f]	3	1-3/3	0-0/1	1-1/1	0-4/2
1956	8	[1m/1f]	1	0-0/1	0-0/1	0-0/1	1-8/5
1957	5	[0m/0f]	2	1-1/3	1-1/1	0-1/1	0-2/0
1958	13	[2m/1f][c]	2	1-5/1	0-1/1	0-2/1	1-5/10
1959	5	[0m/1f]	1	0-1/2	0-0/0	1-1/1	0-3/2
1960	9	[3m/0f]	2	0-0/2	1-2/3	1-3/1	0-4/3
1961	12	[1m/0f]	3	2-5/2	1-1/4	0-0/2	0-6/4
1962	9	[1m/0f]	3	0-0/2	0-1/2	2-4/2	1-4/3
1963	5	[0m/1f]	2	2-2/2	0-0/1	0-2/0	0-1/2
1964	12	[3m/0f]	5	2-4/3	1-2/3	1-1/1	1-5/5
1965	20	[2m/0f]	5	1-5/4	2-2/4	1-2/2	1-10/8
1966	11	[3m/2f][c]	1	1-1/4	0-0/2	0-2/1	0-8/4
1967	8	[1m/0f]	0	0-4/1	0-1/2	0-0-1	0-3/4
1968	8	[1m/0f]	2	1-2/3	0-0/3	0-1/0	1-5/2
1969	10	[1m/0f]	5	5-6/6	0-0/0	0-0/0	0-4/4

Fig. 3a. (*cont.*)

Year	Weddings		Surname Endog.	Skoufas	Potamitis	Khloros	Other
				m/f	m/f	m/f	m/f
1970	5	[0m/0f]	0	0-1/1	0-2/1	0-0/1	0-2/2
1971	7	[1m/0f]	1	0-1/0	1-3/1	0-0/0	0-3/6
1972	10	[2m/0f]	4	1-2/2	3-4/5	0-0/1	0-4/2
1973	8	[4m/0f]	1	1-2/3	0-2/1	0-0/2	0-4/2
1974	12	[4m/0f]	4	4-5/6	0-1/3	0-0/0	0-6/4

NOTES: Note that both village exogamy and patrigroup endogamy begin to increase after 1960, suggesting increasing external contacts as well as local intensification of patrigroup interests; also, the growth of both the Skoufas and Potamitis patrigroups encouraged the increased frequency of patrigroup endogamy at that period. Both of these trends are still continuing.

ᵃ The figures given inside the square brackets indicate village-exogamous marriages, with the first figure standing for the number of inmarrying men and the second for the number of inmarrying women.

ᵇ The figures given under each of these patrigroup headings indicate, before the hyphen, the number of marriages endogamous to the patrigroup for the given year; after the hyphen are the respective numbers of men and women of each patrigroup who married in that year.

ᶜ In these years, the figure is augmented by one case each of an elopement or abduction from elsewhere.

deal with its sentimental implications but at the same time partially recompensing the old owner for the profit he had turned down.

As this incident shows, both economic and ethical factors are taken into account in negotiating a deal of this sort. Glendiots do not object to sales between close agnates. It is felt that, in an economic sense, each household must look to its own interests. Ideologically, however, a man should be willing to accept at least a small financial loss in order to enable his agnates to purchase his land at a reasonably advantageous price; he may also sustain a still smaller reduction of income in order to sell to a uterine kinsman or affine. Perhaps because of the good terms he must give, perhaps as a bow in the direction of agnatic solidarity, moreover, a man is always said to be "giving" (rather than "selling") to his brother.

The physical layout of the village certainly does not suggest corporate patrigroup activity. Businesses are owned by individuals, and run on a household basis; even the small cement-block and thread factories are barely larger than private houses, and the old threshing floors on the outskirts of the village were similarly owned by single households. The

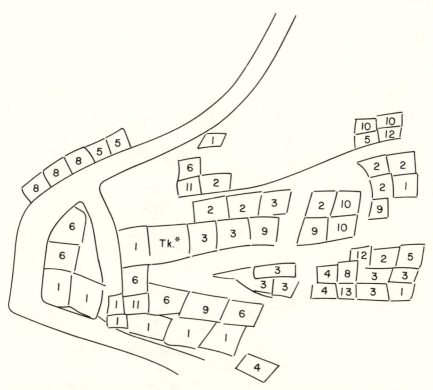

Fig. 3b. Part of a sketch-map of Glendi as it was in 1907. Numbers indicate patrigroups. KEY: 1, Skoufas; 2, Potamitis; 3, Khloros; 4, Diakakis; 5, Zonaras; 6, Koumbis; 7, Arapakis; 8, Kondos; 9, Kozalis; 10, Peristeris; 11, Peponis; 12, Florakis; 13, Dendrinos.
*House inhabited by the last Turk to dwell in Glendi.

coffeehouses are similarly small establishments, and their clientele is usually drawn from more than one patrigroup; a man will try to visit his affines' and uterine kinsmen's *kafenia* as well as those of his agnates, and some coffeehouse patronage is simply a matter of neighborliness.

But it is in the coffeehouses that the importance of agnatic loyalties becomes most obvious. Take, for example, the group of men sitting in a Khloros establishment discussing a murder committed by the proprietor's sister's son in another village (fig. 4). Although the miscreant was not of the same patrigroup as his uncle, the latter was visibly upset, as the whole affair promised to bring out some disreputable stories about his close kin. Note that every single one of the men with whom the proprietor was discussing the affair belonged to the Khloros patrigroup;

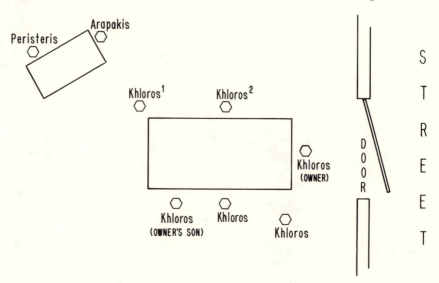

Fig. 4. Coffeehouse discussion of a Khloros family problem. Khloros¹ is the son of Khloros².

those seated nearby were close affines, but it is unlikely that the proprietor, a normally rather circumspect individual, would have been quite so open had his immediate hearers included non-Khloros men. Another non-Khloros (not marked on fig. 4, but sitting fairly near the door) was again an affine, an elderly man whose restrained counsel made him an acceptable if slightly removed audience. The proprietor's own posture, with his back to the door in contravention of village etiquette, well expressed the conversion of this public arena into a temporarily private space for the mulling over of an internal patrigroup problem.

Such conversions intensify during times of heightened inter-patrigroup competition. For several weeks before municipal elections, certain coffeehouses become informal patrigroup council chambers in the evenings. Since they thus become the setting for discussions of such strictly internal matters as patrigroup leadership and election strategy, their public character is severely redefined so as to exclude all non-patrigroup members. The point of this is well understood, and gives no offense. At other times, a man may have private business to discuss, perhaps an animal theft or a family quarrel, matters that do not concern the entire patrigroup directly; in that case, he will step outside into the street with his companions, and in the evenings it is quite common to find little clusters of slightly furtive-looking men talking quietly just outside the entrances of coffeehouses. But any matter that concerns the whole patrigroup directly can provide a signal for a sudden gathering of its members, and outsiders are expected to melt away tactfully.

Coffeehouses can serve to focus agnatic allegiances in other ways as well. Especially when a patrigroup member has become embroiled in a dangerous feud, they provide an apt and practical setting for the expression of solidarity. One coffeehouse, down on the central street, is almost exclusively frequented by Skoufas regulars, especially by shepherds. Its owner was jailed for killing his brother's murderer, and the daily gathering of turbanned, whiskered patrigroup stalwarts is seen explicitly as both a statement of loyalty and a deterrent against would-be avengers driving wildly through the village. One of these regulars killed the father-in-law of the Zonaras owner of another coffeehouse just across the street. Studied avoidance sets a barrier between the two establishments, but that is all: the Zonaras is not an agnate of the dead man, who died without male issue, and is therefore under no obligation to avenge his death as a son or brother would have been. Such tensions are not sufficient to deter many customers from frequenting both places, and so demonstrating the limits as well as the lines of solidarity.

While individual households may not often be drawn into full-scale inter-patrigroup conflict, agnatic clustering can produce violence on occasion, and it may then spill over into the street. Once, a Diakakis fired his pistol into the house of a Khloros living directly opposite, across the main road. When the fight flared anew, groups from both patrigroups converged and clashed in midstreet, only to be separated by a crowd of mostly black-clad women from both sides. The wife of one of the Diakakis protagonists flung a towel to a young Koumbis man, so that he in turn could wrap it around his hand and snatch away her husband's knife by the blade, thereby defusing the confrontation almost immediately. The women, who spend much of their time visiting one another in the neighborhood but still technically belong to their husbands' respective patrigroups, were able to play this mediatory role because the quarrel took place in an open space that appropriately conveyed their own conflicting allegiances; and the appeal to a neutral third party similarly made use of the public character of the street. This was not a *domestic* dispute as such. In fact, it concerned property rights: the Diakakis segment (actually a group of brothers) owned most of the houses on both sides of the street, but at the end of their two rows came small pieces of Khloros property, and it was over one of these that the dispute had arisen. Since it was physically localized in this way, and since both parties to the dispute were groups of brothers, most other agnates of both sides were reluctant to get involved with anything fiercer than words. The fact that the step-mother of the principal Khloros disputant had been born a Diakakis, albeit only connected to the other side by family name, perhaps also limited the actual conflict; she herself sat close to her house on a stone outcrop high above the street hurling curses and entreaties in frenzied alternation as her neighborhood erupted before her.

As this account shows, the village layout accurately reflects some of the loci of tension. There is no village square in the more usual Greek sense in which coffeehouses surround an open space. Instead, the village expresses a more abstract kind of unity and is certainly far less likely to erupt in immediate confrontation: it has a small square in front of the main church that is bounded on its other sides by the village's administrative offices, a disused school building, and the village war memorial abutting the central street. The absence of a square of more conventional type may partly be due to the construction of the main mountain highway through the center of the village. As a result of this, some of the largest and politically most active coffeehouses line the highway—a particularly desirable location because it brings more activity and customers. But whatever the practical reasons for it, the displacement of a main square by a more obviously symbolic space avoids direct public confrontations between large agnatic blocs operating out of "their" coffeehouses. When quarrels occur in public, they take place in spaces defined by the households and agnatic clusters that engender them; the communal square is, in a quite literal sense, *outside* such localized but potentially catastrophic disputes.

Despite the absence of a central square in the conventional sense, the centripetal effect of coffeehouse interaction has affected the village ground plan. Each of the two ribbonlike, satellite house clusters at the extreme ends of the village has only two coffeehouses: these areas are relatively isolated, and the inhabitants tend to gravitate to the main part of the village when matters of any importance need to be discussed with people outside the immediate neighborhood. The two satellite clusters contain some of the oldest, partially ruined stone houses in the village, as well as some modern two-floor buildings painted in pastel shades and ornamented with iron railings and aluminum window and door frames. This resettlement of the village peripheries reflects sudden demographic growth, but it has not immediately created new social foci. The main cluster of coffeehouses, in the central stretch of the main street, gives villagers a good view of all comings and goings, since it is here that the buses from Iraklio and Rethimno stop the longest. Here, too, the most powerful men in the village, including the two village presidents who served during my major periods of fieldwork, have their establishments. Some of the newest coffeehouses have been created out of houses in this zone, showing that the real locus of power remains, literally, in the center of the village.

This concentration of social activity releases the church square for a more obviously symbolic role as the locus of collective identity. The church square is where all formal celebrations, such as those that mark national Independence Day (March 25), take place. On this solemn occasion, the schoolchildren line up in stiff parade, many of them clad in mainland Greek costumes intended to recall the kleftic heroes of the struggle for independence; a few wear traditional Cretan costume, including the baggy pants (*vraka*) that are hardly ever seen any more in everyday use in the region. Here, too, the villagers congregate to celebrate marriages and to express their solidarity in the face of death; while the wedding and funeral services take place within the church, all but the most intimate friends and kin gather in the square. Indeed, during weddings this focus on unity is stronger now than in pre-World War II days, when only those who had received an invitation (*kalesma*) would move on to the feast; nowadays, everyone is automatically considered a guest, and public wedding processions insure that all are duly alerted (illus. 6). Another change may also have intensified the emphasis on the square's symbolic character: the solemn Good Friday procession with the icon of Christ's bier (the *Epitafios*), which used to wind around the entire village and consequently provoked outrage whenever some small side street was omitted, now takes place within the church square (including the narrow band around the back of the church itself). As a result, the church and square together have developed into an increasingly evocative microcosm.

One social division is emphasized rather than suppressed here (see fig. 5). This is the separation of women and men; the two sexes may only mingle as they dance in a chaste circle around the seated musicians or stroll *en famille* through the center of the square. During most events calling for communal participation, more men sit outside than within the church. At weddings they enter only long enough to pay their respects to the bridal couple and make a monetary gift (*kharisma*, in 1981 about 500 drx.); at funerals they do not enter at all. Women are also often more numerous outside than in, although there is an expectation that they will be in the majority in the actual congregation.

The ground plan of the square both reproduces and yet also contradicts that of the church. In both, men are to the right of the priest, women to his left, as he faces the crowd. But the placing of the church along the ritually prescribed west-east axis places the inner sanctum (*ieron*), a place ritually forbidden to females, on the "female" side of the square. Whether by accident or by design, the relationship between church and

6. Wedding processions are public announcements.

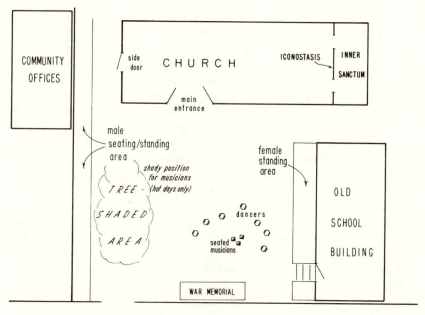

Fig. 5. The arrangement of space in the church square.

square thus spatially reproduces the internal strain between respect for ritual values and secular distrust of the institutional church. During services, this tension is repeatedly emphasized by the shepherds, whose collective dislike of the formal church is perhaps the most marked of any group in Glendi: they unwind their turbans to enter at the last possible moment, near the end of the service. They then hastily wrap their turbans back around their heads as soon as, blinking in the sunlight, they step back into secular space through the exit door well over on the "male" side.

This spatial arrangement dramatizes the symbolic contrast between male and female stereotypes in Glendiot society.[8] The square is a public space, and as such is controlled by male-defined conventions. Thus, when women join in the dances that take place there at the conclusion of a wedding ceremony, they do so with conspicuously chaste steps, avoiding the self-preening acrobatics of the young males. Older women walk sedately up and down, minding their children or chatting in small groups. Other, mostly young women line the wall on the "female" side, watching the general activity but avoiding direct personal contact with individual young men. To a very large extent the women of Glendi, much as their counterparts elsewhere in rural Greece, are typecast as passive, indecisive, and unable to control either their sexuality or their tempers; and they are similarly supposed to transcend these frailties by a devotion to religious matters that both excites the respect of the men but yet arouses the suspicion that perhaps such piety is simply another form of gullibility—the deceivers, in this case, being the priests. In the church square, their demeanor appropriately reflects the formal stereotype: both the sanctity of the church and the temptations of sin—the young men dancing out their masculinity to its utmost—are near at hand. In other, less unequivocally defined settings, they may stage idiosyncratic performances of their own: a woman who can manage to "pull off" what would normally be regarded as a male performance—for example, by defeating a man at bantering wordplay—can bring credit to herself and her family. Even when women do breach the conventions in some poetically effective way, the male reaction is usually one of rather condescending approval. Here, in the church square, the women have few opportunities for such self-projection, even as the representatives of husband and agnates: the setting is too formally public.

Glendiot spatial symbolism, and more especially the idiom of movement, can be approached most effectively through its various embodiments in language. To "enter" has implications of social control or invasion (as when a man of different patrigroup buys land), and of rights to intimacy and respect (as when one "enters" a spiritual kinship tie). These implications also strongly affect daily etiquette, since leaving and entering houses and coffee shops entail contextual readjustments of relationships. Entering the church square is thus a symbolic affirmation of one's membership in the community, with all that this entails.

Perhaps coincidentally, the arrangement of buildings around the square also reinforces normative ideas about male and female roles. On the "male" side stands the community office, the epicenter of all administrative matters, and the formal sign of the village's political integration into the national bureaucratic structure. Opposite, behind where the women stand, the old school building served for several years as a weaving factory, and was thus regarded as a good place for keeping unmarried daughters out of mischief. During elections, to be sure, it also served as a polling booth; but the military guard mounted outside served notice that this "male" use was an arrangement of convenience organized cooperatively with state officialdom. The war memorial, around which a rare flowerbed is kept in good condition, occupies center space both in relation to the square and through its visibility from the road. Those whose patrigroups were decimated by war can point to its inscription as evidence of the past glory associated with their surnames, and as an explanation of their present numerical decline. Since the dead are recorded in surname clusters, local agnatic ideology is well served.

Here in the church square, the contrasts and tensions as well as the congruences between official and Glendiot values come into sharp focus. The imposing church front and the small but dignified memorial obelisk, the community office, and the respect shown by men's removal of their headgear as they enter the church—these are testimonies to the official values. Pervading the same space, however, are the less obtrusive evidences of a contrary symbolic order: the surname clusters, the men's reluctance to enter the church at all, the agile male dancing with its implications of aggressive masculinity and, by extension, of the skills of the good raider.

Five Hundred Cartridge Cases

Only once did I witness a scene overtly suggestive of discord here in the square. In this case, however, the situation was one in which the actors tried to *use* the harmonious implications of the square for their own ends. During the 1975 municipal elections, which were locally fought according to agnatic principles, the members of the smaller patrigroups convened here to discuss the possibility of forming a third-party coalition to displace the two major patrigroups (Skoufades and Potamitides). Calling themselves *ta mikra valkania* ("the little Balkans") as an evocative metaphor of collective resistance to Great Power hegemony, they were ultimately unsuccessful: the Diakakis leader made such an impassioned bid for the leadership of this potential coalition that the members of other patrigroups realized that they would merely be exchanging one form of domination for another, perhaps less advantageous one; the relatively numerous Diakakides' claim to "little Balkan" status was always potentially open to debate, and its leader's apparent opportunism dismayed any would-be allies. I never saw any other political meetings in this space. The 1975 incident occurred because the small-patrigroup leaders hoped to imply a collective ability to transcend the division of the village into Skoufas and Potamitis camps, but the unmistakable contrast between the Diakakis leader's bombast and the symbolic associations of the church square soon overcame that project.

Patrigroup disputes conflict with national ideology at two levels. First, they challenge the role of the state as ultimate legal arbiter; and second, their emphasis on agnatic loyalties—exemplified by bloc voting in municipal elections—contradicts the official ideals of electoral process. Moreover, the strong agnatic bias contradicts the ecclesiastical endorsement of the bilateral kindred (see Alivizatos 1949:99-100) as well as the basic provisions of civil law. For these reasons, interpatrigroup tensions do not belong in the church square. They may more appropriately be expressed in the coffeehouses, in the streets, and in the wild foothills above the village—all legitimate domains of competitive behavior, and relatively free from the restraint of official intervention.

While the village plan as such may at best only partially reflect agnatic groupings, Glendiots use the village spaces to express both unity and discord. A Diakakis had been engaged for over a year to a Skoufas woman when their respective patrigroups became embroiled in a bitter feud. Since they were already betrothed, there was no way of avoiding the suddenly unwelcome alliance; had the Diakakis groom suddenly rejected his bride, the Skoufades would probably have felt compelled to avenge the insult. Instead, therefore, the wedding took place. Members of both patrigroups who were less directly involved in the feud showed up in the church square. Immediately afterwards, however, the two groups repaired to their separate celebrations, described as "two weddings" (*dhio ghami*[9]); festivity itself was, as it were, segmented. The bride, now a Diakakis, went to her husband's agnates' party. The two celebrations were conspicuously apart from each other, thanks to the location of the respective household clusters: the Skoufades made merry in a centrally situated house fronting the main street, while the Diakakides all gathered in a house in the older satellite cluster—thereby inadvertently expressing their collective removal from the central locus of village power. In order to reinforce the message, the Skoufades allegedly fired off five hundred cartridges into the air in the course of a noisy night, and in the morning the street was strewn with the empty cases.

Gunfire at weddings and baptisms emphasizes the close relationship between feuding and resistance to the law. In the years after the Civil War, when the police were afraid that whole areas would become disaffected, gun control was much more severely enforced, and people avoided firing weapons at weddings because they thought it a "sin" (*amartia*) to involve the groom in something he had not initiated and for which he—being unable to betray the real culprits—would have to pay the penalty. This secular and markedly antiestablishment sense of "sin" is common in Glendiot discourse.

Displays of firepower at weddings and baptisms are among the activities that Glendiots specifically recognize as distinctive of their mountain zone and as a mark of their insubordination. Remarking on this association between festive shooting and local independence, a shepherd went on to say that the Turks had never succeeded in conquering the district; nor, he implied, would any government at all. In the same way, the Skoufades' noisy demonstration suggested their collective identification with the heroism of yore. That some members of other patrigroups decried it as typical Skoufas bombast shows only that claims of moral paramountcy may be, and often are, contested.

Weapons abound in the village. Some have been brought in illegally by returning migrants; many are left over from World War II, including the British-made machine gun that was used to announce the start of at least one wedding procession. One young man was so delighted with his acquisition of a new pistol that he spent the evening carousing around the village, mostly with patrigroup mates of various ages, firing the pistol repeatedly into the air, and at one point joining his friends in a rousing rendition of a *rizitiko*—a kind of west Cretan song long associated with rebellion against the foreign oppressor, and hence an apt symbol to mark a new flouting of the law.[10] Another Glendiot who reportedly went through the security check in the airport with a knife hidden in his sock reflected a common attitude of amused contempt for the mechanisms of official control. In a neighboring village, to give a somewhat more extreme example, a man who was wanted for murder, but who had managed to use political connections to avoid arrest, drunkenly shot through the windows of the police station, as "a demonstration of strength" (as a Glendiot described it). The callow and very frightened policeman who was alone inside phoned the regional superintendent for advice, and was told to do nothing unless the villager actually broke into the building. Such extreme restraint, while undoubtedly politic, reinforces many *aorites'* conviction that they are substantially free from official restraint.

Any act of retributive violence, and by extension any symbolic demonstration of armed strength, challenges the state's authority. Threats against another patrigroup at any level of segmentation are also necessarily threats against official control. But there is also another level at which the Glendiots, unlike the police, justify their hoarding of arms. No one knows "how much stuff [i.e., weaponry] lies sleeping" in the village; but it is certainly ready in case the Turks should ever attack. In short, while the village may be a "little state" (*kratidhio*) in its own right, as the villagers claim, it is also ready to go to war in the service of the encompassing political state. Official restraint thus resembles a practical anthropology: it recognizes that the segmentary proclivities of the agnatic structure are also extended by the Glendiots to the broader levels, and therefore serves to identify local with national interests instead of pitting the one against the other. Above all, it recognizes that a greater risk of political disaffection arises from suppressing those activities that Glendiots regard as peculiarly their own, than from allowing them a certain latitude in at least the symbolic demonstrations of their independence. Only actual violence brings a tough response: the shedding of blood—Greek blood—is a direct affront to the rule of law, and as such cannot be tolerated.

The Shape of Violence

Within six days of each other, a young Skoufas told me that the villagers had been more affectionate with each other in the old days, and an elderly Peristeris remarked that people used to be far more violent. Statements of the past are often idealized in some way. What these two apparently contradictory remarks reveal, however, is that both speakers felt that Glendiot social relations had moved toward a greater degree of disengagement: the Skoufas based his view on the observation that people would no longer intervene so willingly in a quarrel, while the Peristeris based his on the recollection of violent fights between the two major patrigroups in his youth.

The two accounts also share another feature. This is their embodiment of agnatic concerns. The Skoufas illustrated his point by indicating two of his agnates and remarking that, in the old days, if one had threatened the other, everyone else would have broken up the fight. Note that the Skoufas used his own agnates as examples; an intrapatrigroup knifing was still very fresh in the mind of every Skoufas, and my informant's choice does not seem to have been entirely coincidental.

The Peristeris, on the other hand, did not represent a major *soi*. His memory of the bad old days was associated with a dilemma that faced all patrigroups too small to be politically independent: that of choosing sides. The Peristerides had in fact thrown in their lot with the Potamitides, because they had more affinal links with the latter than with the Skoufades. But the remembrance of incessant and tiresome disputes that forced involvement upon the unwilling client patrigroups gave this informant a more negative view of social relations in the past.

Within the village, almost all violence is channeled by agnatic allegiances. Outside it, participation in a feud may be restricted to a few closely related agnates, but these individuals act as *village* representatives. While there is a good deal of diversity among the case histories that follow, the one common feature is the guiding belief that violence is for men, and that men should therefore unite according to their agnatic bonds.

THE ILL-TEMPERED BOY

On two occasions, Stelios, a Potamitis boy of about fourteen, got into fights that threatened to engulf both his parents and his closer agnates. In the first incident, the son of a Khloros coffeehouse proprietor told him off for playing cards in the coffeehouse, as this was illegal for a minor and might involve the owner in an unnecessary argument with the police. When Stelios refused to desist, the owner's son punched him. The next day, Stelios' mother entered and, after formally greeting the company, began to complain about what had happened. The owner, Panos Khloros, pointed out that Stelios had acted illegally. Both announced that they did not want to quarrel, and both then proceeded to argue about whether the dispute would grow. "Like fire!" remarked Panos, ironically. Stelios' mother, fuming with rage, retorted that Stelios spent a hundred drachmas every day in Panos' coffeehouse; she rushed out, returned to scream further insults, and then disappeared. Another Khloros now offered his comments: that there would be "war," that whoever took on the Khlorides should have weapons, and that Stelios' mother was a "male woman"—a remark presumably prompted by her noisy invasion of a definitively male space, and by her none too successful adoption of an essentially male stance as defender of the family name. The next day he again remarked that she was a "female-male woman" (*athilikarsernikia*). All of these comments constitute an ironic challenge, less perhaps to the boy's mother than to his father and other close agnates. The reference to "war" is an inscrutable hint: would a family whose women can be called "men" *really* relish a fight? Or are they just playing "war games"? It is true that women sometimes get the better of men in a competitive arena, notably in singing bouts,[11] but these are exceptional cases which then redound to the collective glory of the victorious women and the humiliation of the opposing men. But just as a low-status man who brags is all but certain to provoke his peers into calling his bluff, the married woman who takes on a male role not only dishonors herself but also brings ridicule to her husband's agnates (see also Campbell 1964:275; Danforth 1983:207-209).

Although Panos Khloros remarked that "a child's [quarrel] doesn't mean anything"—a good illustration of the sense in which Glendiots associate meaning with social action—there clearly was some danger of its spreading to the adults; such things have apparently happened in the past. His ironical refusal to take Stelios' mother very seriously challenged her "male" behavior successfully, however, and little more was heard of the matter. Young Stelios was in any case known as an extremely belligerent youth. On another occasion, he shot a Skoufas child in the foot with an airgun, allegedly in retaliation for a blow on the temple. His father and father's brother chanced to meet the Skoufas child's father's brother in a third-party coffeehouse; the latter demanded to know whether the Stelios' father realized that his children were worthless (*atima*). In the ensuing fray, the Potamitis uncle hit the Skoufas uncle over the head with a piece of firewood. As a result, agnates of both these protagonists had to intervene, and the two sides sat down and "clinked glasses" (*skourdiksane*)—a formal act of reconciliation that nevertheless failed to get them back on speaking terms.

DANGEROUS BOUNDARIES

It is the ease with which seemingly trivial quarrels spread that dismays Glendiots, and provokes rapid intervention. Agnates of the principals often adopt a conciliatory role, rather than automatically take up arms. Again, this does not belie agnatic loyalty as a guiding principle. Mediation is regarded as a *defense* of agnatic interests since, if it succeeds, it protects the patrigroup from further harm and from ridicule: why should grown men do battle on account of a child's temper, for example? What is more, any internal quarrel is seen as exposing the patrigroup or even the whole village to ridicule (*rezili*) by outsiders, so that mediators can always present themselves as acting in the interests of all concerned. Their role is difficult, since it involves getting both parties to back down from a stance of implacable enmity, and it is also sometimes dangerous: a Skoufas recalls restraining a Koumbis from using his dagger against a Zonaras, when the latter, apparently still acting in self-defense, hurled a stone at his foe but only succeeded in wounding the mediator instead. "Sometimes," I was told, "the mediator (*kseberdhetis*) gets more [wounds than anyone else]" (cf. also Mavrakakis 1983:379). But the defense of patrigroup and village pride is thought to be worth the risk.

The very notion of agnatic and village solidarity contains an inherent source of strain. Those who are most closely related are the most likely to share common field and house-plot boundaries, as land is subject to equal partible inheritance (see Herzfeld 1980c). Within the village proper, moreover, the virilocal residence rule means that—again in theory—close agnates are more likely to be close neighbors also; we have already seen, however, that other constraints operate here. Before 1964, when government-subsidized grain made it unnecessary for Glendiots to continue the unrewarding cultivation of the foothill terraces for wheat and barley, disputes over field boundaries appear to have been common between kin, and could turn into quarrels between agnatic groups with occasionally fatal results.

Discussing the disappearance of those bad old days, villagers interpreted the change as a move from a period of "barbarism" (a word closely associated with the *Tourkokratia*) to one of "letters": today, they have teachers of their own, and even a Glendiot lawyer living in Iraklio. At the same time, the villagers also pointed out that they had formerly not enjoyed the benefits of viticulture, whereas now they were producing three hundred tons of raisins annually. All of this was summarized in the symbolic contrast between the "hunger" of the old days and the "ease" of the present: locally produced barley was once used to make black bread, whereas today special flour is brought from Iraklio to make white bread in a commercial electric bakery; and the days when oil was so scarce that a housewife would only be able to wipe an oiled feather across the flat stone (*blaka*) that did duty as a frying pan are only a memory. Not one of those speaking, however, was a shepherd. For the farmers of Glendi, the symbolism of "hunger" is reversed, though it is still important as a means of expressing their own emergent ideology. Moreover, their association of hunger with a predominantly pastoral economy allows them to explain the disappearance of serious boundary disputes by contrasting the past with the new freedom from "barbarism"—a freedom marked by *agricultural* wealth, peaceful interaction, and education. This contrast also permits the remaining shepherds to continue the use of "hunger" as an explanation of their own stance—while the segmentary organization of Glendiot social theory still allows the agriculturalists to resort to that symbolic condition whenever they wish to stress their continuing identity *as Glendiots*.

Despite their claims, however, nonshepherds do quarrel over boundary violations. A Zonaras goat chewed an overhanging Potamitis olive tree; the aggrieved owner of the tree told the field warden that if the Zonaras refused to do anything about it, he would let his sheep into the Zonaras' crops to graze. Whether or not this retaliatory message was ever actually conveyed to the offender, nothing further was heard of the matter. When a Kondos turned his animals loose into a field where another Potamitis was cultivating animal fodder, on the other hand, an agnate of the latter advised him to kill the offender. This was clearly a rhetorical response, expressing solidarity; but when I asked whether the victim should not go and discuss the matter with the offender first, I was told that the offender would simply refuse to make any concessions. Again, despite the considerable anger expressed, the dispute eventually fizzled out.

On the other hand, the one field dispute that erupted into violence involved two shepherds; they were also agnates, and second cousins at that. To complicate matters still further, the dispute grew out of a question of stolen sheep. Dimitris Skoufas was asked by a shepherd from the neighboring village of Psila to check with one Eftikhis Skoufas, a senior member of the patrigroup, whether he knew anything about the missing animals. Eftikhis, who years before had quarreled violently with the Psila shepherd's patrigroup after killing another of its members in a hunting accident, exploded with anger. Dimitris' brother (another Eftikhis) intervened; Nikos, the son of the irate first Eftikhis, spoke up for his father, accusing the others of allowing their animals to graze in their olive groves and eat up the young tree shoots. In the fray that followed, the second Eftikhis stabbed Nikos seriously enough to necessitate a long and expensive period of hospital care.

This quarrel presented the Skoufades with a serious threat. The mockery to which their collective name was now exposed offered tactical advantages to its electoral foes within Glendi, as well as to at least one additional Psila patrigroup whose members sought revenge on the Skoufades for earlier killings. To make matters still worse, both the stabbed man and his assailant were members of the Dimitriani, a distinct segment of the Skoufas group. Their quarrel thus entailed a loss of standing to at least three concentric social groups—segment, patrigroup, and village. As a result, most Skoufas males of any prestige tried to mediate.

The need to do something became more urgent still when the first Eftikhis encountered the other one on the hillside beyond the village and shot at him—evidently aiming to miss, but still increasing the pressure on other agnates to intervene urgently. Eventually, and with great reluctance, the two cousins named Eftikhis Skoufas and the wounded son Nikos were prevailed upon to accept the customary resolution: the assailant baptized a son of his victim, placing the two families in the collective relationship of *sindeknia* (spiritual kinship through baptism)— a relationship more commonly used to resolve disputes between unrelated groups from different villages, but in this case the only means of averting further bloodshed. Even thereafter, however, the principals refused to speak to each other. Their mutual avoidance—fortunately they lived at opposite ends of the village—was generally interpreted as a sign of respect for the community in which they lived, since they would not be able to avoid clashing again if ever they met. One of the mediators was a Grigorianos (see fig. 6) whose sister had married another brother of the assailant; his genealogically equidistant relationship to the two quarreling families, and his affinal connection to the one, put him in an especially good position to work toward a resolution, and in fact when his daughter married a Diakakis—in the tense and divided wedding

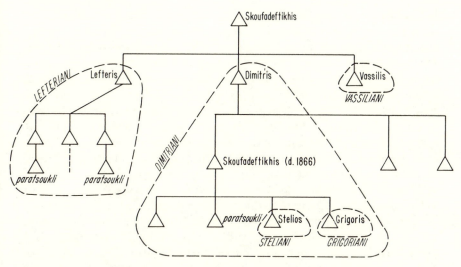

Fig. 6. The principal patrigroup segments of the Skoufades.

already described—a brother of the victim was present at the Skoufas celebration. In this case, the paramount concern was to express patrigroup solidarity; the brother went instead in order to preserve a fragile and provisional intra-patrigroup peace. Patrigroup solidarity is part of Glendiot social experience, but so is the potentially disruptive effect of personal hatred; consequently, for one member of a small segment to stand for the segment as a whole is regarded as an acceptable and even as a laudable form of compromise.[12] Glendiots, with a fine sense of ethnographic nuance, consequently take care to note who is present and who stays away.

One of the sources of confusion in the literature about segmentation results from the common assumption that this social phenomenon is only observable in physical actions. The intervention of agnates to prevent an internal feud may be taken, as in the above example, as a desire to preserve the ideal of agnatic solidarity. But the same can also be said when patrigroup members intervene to prevent quarrels with outsiders. Here the rationale is essentially that true self-regard (*eghoismos*) is best demonstrated through restraint. In the next case to be examined, involving a poor Khloros family, the protagonists' willingness to take violent action was regarded by covillagers as absurd. To be a *pseftoeghoistis* ("faker of self-regard") is worse than humility, since it exposes the braggart as a fraud. A Peristeris recounted with some admiration how, when an agnate of his had wounded a Psila shepherd, the victim's father had prevented their own agnatic kin from rushing off to take violent revenge. The father, who could speak with greater force because of his relationship to the victim, dissuaded the would-be avengers on the grounds that the Glendiot had not gone with *intent* to kill but had merely been defending himself in the course of raiding the victim's flock. Lack of intent is not necessarily treated as a mitigating factor, although here much depends on the strategic interests and political skill of those directly involved. In this case, however, the father evidently felt that his patrigroup would be made to look foolish, and perhaps evil as well, if its members killed for a mere wounding, and one which could have happened to any shepherd.

Thus, the strategic considerations that lead agnates to intervene in both intra- and interpatrigroup disputes do not contradict the implications of the segmentary model. On the contrary, given that the distinction between insiders and outsiders is always a matter for negotiation and debate, their efforts often represent contextual understandings of where their patrigroup's best interests lie. This is an inevitable consequence of a situation in which villagers consequently have to strike a balance between their own idea of what makes a good person and the very different public ideology encouraged by the official authorities of church and state. An exceptionally devout elder woman once remarked of vengeance killings that men should look to the example of God, who told *His* son to resist the temptation to avenge his humiliation by humankind, as God alone had the right to punish. This furnishes a model directly opposed to that followed by men bent on vengeance, and it may be significant that it was relayed to me by a woman, especially as she was also proud of her daughter's marriage to one of the village teachers and of her own affinal relationship to the village priest. But restraint, however para- doxical this may seem, *is* a legitimate alternative to force as a claim to collective superiority; this makes the segmentary model harder to "read" in the everyday actions of Glendiot men, but does not thereby invalidate it. One only has to watch a large-patrigroup member calmly refusing to accept the bait offered by a furious covillager of obviously low status to realize that restraint itself can be the ultimate violation of another's claim to manhood.

AN INCESTUOUS DISPUTE

Fighting one's close agnates, by contrast, represents an *abandonment* of true manhood. In striking ways, it bears a structural resemblance to incest. It entails social reciprocities (*sinallayes*) of kinds thought to be especially immoral between close kin; it consequently besmirches the reputation of the village as a whole, as well as that of the patrigroup concerned; and it leaves its wounds open: the incestuous couple cannot marry, and the estranged agnates, especially if brothers, are unlikely to become ritual kin (*sindekni*) as well. The theoretical expectation that a father will take the lives of both a daughter and a son caught in incestuous union lends force to the analogy between incest and internecine violence: Glendiots call revenge "taking the blood back" (*na yirisi to ema piso*) and incest "blood mixing" (*emomiksia*).

The public reaction was very similar when a violent dispute over a plot of land led Frangias Khloros to hit his half-brother Mikhalis in the stomach and arm with an ax; Mikhalis retaliated the very next day by stabbing Frangias in the belly. The police, who had happened to be in town in force the previous evening for a shepherds' meeting to discuss animal theft, had intervened rapidly on that occasion. On the second evening, Mikhalis, after stabbing Frangias, phoned the police and told them that Frangias had threatened him; Frangias, when arrested, said nothing about Mikhalis' attack on him. Coffeehouse conversation generally condemned the Khloros brothers and their father, who—as the main protagonists in the fight with the Diakakis brothers—had already tried their covillagers' patience excessively. Even other Khlorides turned against the family, saying that all three of them should go to jail, and that the police should just let them get on with the job of slaughtering each other. Such hostility is a good measure of the embarrassment generally felt over internecine violence.

Much of the anger was directed at the father, who had originally promised the disputed plot to Frangias (the older of the two half-brothers) and now wanted to turn it over to Mikhalis instead. An incensed Skoufas remarked that anyone who set his children to quarreling was a *poustis* ("passive homosexual")—note again the analogy with what is seen as a socially unproductive sexual relationship (cf. also Loizos 1975:286). In a revealingly inconsistent reaction, another Skoufas first declared that "it doesn't concern us"—that is, as outsiders—but then corrected himself: "It *does* concern us" because "he's a bad parent." At one level, there was no reason for a self-respecting Skoufas to get involved in a Khloros dispute by which even the Khloros leaders were themselves manifestly disgusted. But there was another level at which the father's misbehavior concerned him very much indeed: it threatened to disrupt the communal peace over a trivial matter, and to bring shame upon the village as a whole. For these reasons alone, it was everyone's business to correct the old man's morally objectionable stance. Others may have had more specialized motives. Since Mikhalis was the son of his father's present wife, *her* brother sought to blame the father without criticizing his own nephew (ZS), on the grounds that a parent's behavior was what counted in such matters. As a Diakakis, of course, he may also have welcomed the opportunity of putting some distance between himself and his embarrassing Khloros brother-in-law.

To put an end to the potentially explosive situation that had been created, two senior Khlorides who also happened to hold village office traveled to police headquarters with Mikhalis and arranged for Frangias' release. The local deputy police chief was relieved: had Frangias been put on trial, he would have been under considerable moral pressure to kill Mikhalis when he finally got out of jail. The quarrel did flare up again verbally when the father informed Frangias that he intended to shoot him; but nothing further happened, and eventually others managed to prevail on the family to accept a compromise.

The bitterness of this quarrel prompted many deprecating remarks about the family's low status, and especially about its failure to provide its daughters with good marriages. Every time he had a chance, remarked one critic, the father always held out for a still better son-in-law. Others commented equally sourly on his habitual refusal to accept well-meant intervention. When, as an outsider, I was encouraged to offer my services as a peacemaker, he refused to talk until suddenly he blurted out that I should leave him alone—"I screw my Virgin Mary!" This exclamation reveals his acute discomfort: usually hurled at the holy figures of *others*, its unusual form ("my" for "your") suggests a man deeply unhappy with a situation that he had made impossible for himself.

Although they eventually succeeded in reaching a compromise, the half-brothers and their father had succeeded in bringing the already low status of their family to an absolute nadir. Another son by the first wife attempted, early on, to get the three aggrieved family members to "clink glasses," but was rebuffed. Ranking Khloros worthies were quick to dissociate themselves from this aberrant family. Two Khloros leaders, however, used their official status to force a quick solution. Such public discord was embarrassing in the extreme to them, both as patrigroup members and because their public positions made it impossible for them to tolerate such illegal acts of violence. The disputants alienated their covillagers in a way quite at odds with what might have happened if, for example, they had become embroiled in a dispute with shepherds from Psila. The father was dismissed as *vromos* ("stinker"), a term with strongly negative sexual (and, more specifically, female) implications. While there is a place for violence in Glendiot social ideology, it is as a defense of legitimate interests. Incestuous violence, by contrast, represents an inversion of true manhood.

An Acceptable Vengeance

To illustrate the opposite extreme, we now turn to a killing of clearly "exogamous" import. It is no coincidence that the only possible solution envisaged by Glendiots for the vendetta of which it is part is through a marriage alliance. The Glendiot response to the jailing of the Skoufas protagonist, moreover, was a forty-day period of village-wide mourning. Clearly, he had done the right thing.

Some time before the war, a Psila shepherd came to Glendi to settle a dispute over stolen sheep with a Skoufas. The Skoufas would have none of it. Instead, encountering his foe in Iraklio, he shot and wounded him, whereupon the Psiliot waited for his chance and killed the unrelenting Skoufas. At this time, the Skoufas' younger brother Stamatis was a young boy. Years later, he had business in the district courthouse on the same day as his brother's killer. When the latter was pointed out to him, anger suddenly flared in him: he leaped upon him with drawn knife and slit his throat as though slaughtering an animal, right there in the courtroom.

Although Stamatis went to jail, his victim's agnates were not appeased. Unfortunately for the Glendiots, this patrigroup was an extensive one, with segments outside Psila proper. On several occasions, Glendiots have been ambushed on the road through Psila and its outcrops. A senior Skoufas who was thought to have pointed out Stamatis' victim to him, and another Skoufas who is Stamatis' patrilateral first cousin, were in the greatest danger; but a Kozalis who was wrongly supposed to have brought Stamatis to the courtroom in his van has also been attacked, and bitterly observed that his patrigroup was therefore evidently held to have "almost the same guilt as the Skoufades."

This last remark shows that more peripheral actors who would prefer not to be involved may represent the dispute as being between patrigroups rather than whole villages. Those who are at the center, on the other hand, view their struggle as taking place at the broader level. Of an older dispute between the Potamitis patrigroup and a group of Psiliots, for example, a villager known for his skill in making up rhyming couplets had this to say:

> Psiliots and Glendiots went forth to do battle;
> No one was killed, or suffered any harm. . . .

In the present case, where blood had actually been shed, and where the attempt on Stamatis' cousin's life served particularly fierce notice on the Skoufades that they were still in real danger, non-Skoufades were less than anxious to be bracketed with the principal patrigroup in this way.

The Kozalis had a special reason for being resentful. He owned the largest bakery in the district, and used to take a cinema show regularly to Psila as well. His rival, a Psiliot baker, saw this as an excellent way of getting rid of such unwelcome competition. The level of segmentation at which rivalries are expressed depends, then, on the actors' strategic interests. Once again, the segmentary model is not so much an accurate or inaccurate representation of social reality as a trope expressing the possibilities and difficulties of making the appropriate choice between possible levels of opposition.

This becomes clearer when we examine current relations between the two villages. Stereotypically, a Glendiot may claim that no Psiliot will tolerate a Glendiot in his village: "He'll tell you, 'You're a Glendiot? Get out of here!' " But Glendiots other than those most directly concerned do visit Psila often enough; many, including the majority of Skoufades, have spiritual kin there, and may visit the latter when searching for stolen animals or passing through on other business. Damianos Skoufas explained that if he went into a Psila coffee shop where agnates of the dead man's were sitting, they would be obliged to make a show of belligerence, demanding to know what a Skoufas could be looking for there; if they did not make such a move, their covillagers would deride them as worthless. Their stance would force the Skoufas to take up an aggressive posture in response, and the ensuing quarrel would automatically lead to the forcible expulsion of the Skoufas from the coffeehouse. On the mountainside, by contrast, with no critical eyes watching them, some members of the dead man's patrigroup regularly share food and drink with Skoufas shepherds—an amiable reciprocity that leaves the fighting to those most immediately involved.

Damianos Skoufas' observations underscore the importance of treating each confrontation in terms of its *audience*. Every fight is in some sense a performance of roles. At what level of the segmentary model these roles are defined is not simply a matter of the structural distance between the main actors, but depends on how they perceive their respective relationships to the bystanders. Consequently, although there are always certain expectations about how individuals ought to behave in situations of this kind, each actor must evaluate the probable social consequences of each act. For Skoufades and their foes to sit down convivially in the foothills, far from any audience likely to take umbrage, is a very different matter from doing the same thing in either village.

Violence does not arise only from the urging of agnates. In the coffeehouse situation just described, it is the *outsiders* whose presence forces the patrigroup members to act belligerently, so as to avoid bringing a reputation for weakness upon their name. Outsiders both provoke and restrain violence. They provoke it implicitly, since they provide the audience in front of which the patrigroup's reputation is at stake. They also restrain that same violence, usually through physical intervention—whether by expelling the "offending" visitors, or by holding back their furious covillagers. When the the Kozalis baker and the "guilty" Skoufas elder drove through Psila just as a funeral procession was wending its way to the cemetery—always a flashpoint because of intensified emotions—a brother of the dead man attacked. Other Psiliots restrained him and told the Glendiots to leave immediately, thereby at once showing their sense of decorum and demonstrating their solidary dislike of the Glendiots.

Audience reaction was probably also an important factor in the killing itself. Here we must think of the audience not as a specific group of people gathered in a single place (although the district courthouse certainly served that role, too), but as a constituency of covillagers and fellow-*aorites* generally. In refusing to heed warnings that Stamatis was present, the Psiliot was essentially issuing a contemptuous challenge, which Stamatis could only refuse at the price of his covillagers' discomfiture and the derision of the whole region. Apparently, too, others told Stamatis that he, alone among his brothers, was the right man to "take the blood back," since he was childless and therefore did not have to worry about making a good patrimony for his heirs. If he could not prove his manhood by siring many sons, so the implicit logic went, then vengeance gave him another way of doing so. Drinking red wine is a symbol of manhood, since it is thought to produce the blood that creates sons; "taking back the blood" through an act of vengeance is thus a structural analogue.

Goaded by these insistent urgings, and perhaps genuinely ashamed of his failure to produce heirs, he performed his manhood in full accordance with the principle of seizing a rare and dramatic chance. The courtroom killing, in the district capital, defended self, sibling group, patrigroup, and village.

The aftermath still haunts Glendi. Fears are frequently expressed that the Psiliots will attempt to take revenge in turn, especially now that Stamatis is out of jail. But other counsels are also heard. Right from the very beginning, there were those who attempted to set up an arranged marriage (*sinikesio*) between the two patrigroups; this is generally thought to be the only effective way of bringing a cycle of vengeance to a close, and represents the equivalent at the level of vengeance resolution to the use of spiritual (baptismal) kinship for the resolution of raiding cycles. The analogy goes even further. In a raiding cycle, the property violation of theft is converted into a form of friendship; the erstwhile foes come to see each other as worthy allies. So, too, with vengeance killing, the ultimate aim is to establish a sense of parity. At this point, with one man killed on each side, it ought to be slightly easier to achieve an end to the reciprocal killing. Against the obvious arguments in favor of peace, however, the simultaneous need to satisfy their constituency of covillagers faces the last victim's kinsmen with a dilemma that only time will answer. In the end, what makes the whole case so characteristically uncertain is that no one can read the actual emotions—and therefore the likely reactions—of the actors. Villagers recognize the structural principles of the vendetta. But they also recognize that these principles are negotiated by individual actors, who may choose to interpret them in favor of either restraint or further violence.

Despite obvious differences between them, all these case histories show that restraint as much as violence represents political action on behalf of the social group. Restraint can be expressed in a number of ways, from verbal cautions, through forcibly holding a fellow-villager back and disarming him, to actively seeking a reconciliation.

The most effective form of reconciliation, at least in the short term, is the *sasmos*.[13] A *sasmos* is considered to be taking place when the principals are brought together by interested third parties and "clink glasses" in a formal display of amity. They are supposed to toast each other with the phrase *nero č'alatsi* ("water and salt," meaning that their mutual enmity should now dissolve as salt in water), and to eat meat together; it is well understood, however, that wounded dignity will make it difficult for them to speak to each other for a while thereafter, and every effort is made in serious cases to arrange a baptism so that the two mutually antagonistic groups enter into a relationship of *sindeknia*. This theoretically precludes any further active hostility between them— possibly the greatest advantage, in a general sense, that the relationship of *sindeknia* can bestow.

Those who mediate successfully in arranging a *sasmos* gain immensely in stature. For this reason, anyone who thinks he has a chance of achieving some good will make the attempt, and those concerned are usually a mixture of kin of both parties, affines, and *sindekni*. Particular efficacy is attributed to the intervention of "those who come from outside" (*i ap' okso*)—men whose prestige makes it extremely embarrassing for the principals to refuse them the "favor" (*khatiri*) of making peace.

On one occasion, a Kozalis stole a goat from Kostas Skoufas—a violation of the rule that one should never steal from a covillager. When Kostas finally identified the culprit, hard words were exchanged, words led to blows, and Kostas eventually struck the thief down with a stick.

After a period of mutual hostility, they finally made up (*ta saksame*) when a Psiliot, an old friend of both, asked to baptize Kostas' daughter and suggested that Kostas should also invite his enemy. As a third *sindeknos*, the Psiliot suggested a *sindeknos* of his own, to act as a further guarantor of good faith. Faced with the choice of swallowing their anger or *both* insulting their mutual friend, the two foes accepted the mediation.

In another case, Eftikhis Diakakis got his sheep mixed up with those of Kostas Potamitis. When they finally managed to sort the animals out, one of Diakakis' remained with the other flock, whose owner tossed it over the sheepfold wall and half killed it in the process. When Diakakis found it, he was beside himself with anger, but was somewhat mollified when Kostas Potamitis' brother Yoryis spoke "like a man" (*andristika*), offering to give Diakakis one of his own sheep in compensation (the two brothers kept their flocks jointly). Even so, when they together encountered Kostas, Eftikhis Diakakis again lost his temper and struck the offender with his shepherd's crook. Since it was the shearing season, there were many shepherds present, and they soon managed to separate the two antagonists and sent Eftikhis on his way. By the evening, however, a reconciliation had been effected, thanks to the mediation of a powerful Skoufas who was also an uncle of Eftikhis, Eftikhis' own father-in-law, and at least two of his agnates. In this case, the quarrel had been on a sufficiently small scale as to permit a rapid resolution. Here too, however, we can see the same anxiety to dampen a conflict before it could lead to bloodshed. In more serious cases, outsiders from relatively far away are asked to come and mediate, in the hope that their request for the *khatiri* of a peaceful resolution will be respected; when Eftikhis Skoufas knifed his second cousin Nikos, for example, those involved included some of Nikos' father's spiritual kin from as far away as the Sfakia district to the southwest.

I was involved in a *sasmos* only once, when a Skoufas took umbrage at our interest in a massive garbage-collecting effort, apparently on the grounds that it showed the village in an undignified light.[14] By the same evening, his brothers and other agnates had managed to calm him down, and a *sasmos* was duly arranged. Making a gracefully conciliatory gesture, my erstwhile foe addressed me as *koumbare* ("ritual kinsman through marriage"). Few *sasmi* end so amicably; most are concerned with much more serious quarrels, and are best seen as provisional agreements needing reinforcement through marriage or baptism at the first opportunity. In my case, however, some of the villagers were pleased that I should see the other face of violence, the rush to intercede in the cause of peace. Truly, while anthropologists have written a great deal about

social discord and violence, the Glendiots seemed to welcome opportunities of competing to create peace.

Negotiating Blame

The incidents just described show that while the segmentary model is
in itself quite unambiguous, selective interpretations of it guide each
actor's choices and thereby influence the outcome. A villager can choose
between violence and restraint, between verbal and physical defense of
the patrigroup, between public bombast and private diplomacy. He may
decide to represent a wounding as intentional, to accept it as an accident,
or to treat the question of intention as irrelevant to the attribution of
responsibility. The segmentary model does not furnish a means of prediction. On the contrary, it is a conceptual and rhetorical tool for defending one's actions, and—like all seemingly fixed moral verities (cf.
Meeker 1979:39; Herzfeld 1983b)—it is subject to negotiation and manipulation for individual purposes.

The incident to which we now turn exemplifies the process of negotiating loyalties, in this case through the idiom of blame. To "read" the
event effectively, note that "fate" provides a negotiable counterweight
to personal responsibility. Cosmology itself is grist to the political mill.

Some background is needed. As a young man, Vassilis Skoufas com-
peted with Mikhalis Diakakis for the hand of the same girl, and lost.
From that day on, the two men became political foes. It was Vassilis
Skoufas, however, who soon gained the upper hand: as a successful
animal thief he came to know every nook and cranny of the foothills,
and rose to great prominence in World War II as a Resistance leader,
acting in close cooperation with the village priest. After the war, he
became the favored local channel for Anglo-American aid, married his
daughter into the highly influential priest's family, and, as the most
prestigious member of the largest patrigroup, held office as village president intermittently over a twenty-eight-year period. His old rival, by
contrast, although by no means poor, never enjoyed comparable success.
It was the latter who finally tried to take over the "small Balkans" revolt
in 1975, wrecking it in the process. While Vassilis held firmly to the
post-Venizelist tradition of voting for moderate political parties, Mikhalis
was the first to endorse the extreme right, taking an increasing number
of the Diakakides with him as time went on.

In 1976, disaster struck. Thanassis Diakakis, agnatic first cousin to
Mikhalis, returned home one night, allegedly from a successful animal
theft, and spent the remaining hours of darkness in jubilant and bibulous

celebration with another agnatic first cousin. Before dawn, when Thanassis was ready to fall happily asleep, Vassilis Skoufas appeared with
an urgent request: would his nephew (Thanassis was the son of Vassilis'
sister) use his newly acquired tractor to tow Vassilis' damaged truck
down to Iraklio for repair? Thanassis apparently protested that he was
too tired, and that in any case he had not yet acquired a driver's license.
Such niceties carried little weight with most Glendiots, and Vassilis—
who was in any case credited with a remarkable ability to "fix" the
authorities—paid no attention. Eventually, of course, Thanassis gave
in, and they set off. Mounted in his tractor seat, exhausted from his
night's revels, Thanassis fell asleep. The tractor suddenly swung off the
road and down a steep bank, and Thanassis was killed immediately.
Vassilis, seated at the wheel of his truck, had better luck. Just as the
truck was poised to tumble after the tractor, the towrope snapped, and
Vassilis was saved.

Vassilis, although no coward, deemed it politic to stay away from the
village until the general response became clear. He suspected, rightly
as it turned out, that some would be delighted to place the blame squarely
on his shoulders. His two sons, however, went to the dead man's funeral,
to test the Diakakides' temper. Since Thanassis had been a skilled animal
thief, he had acquired many "friends," who consequently attended in
force; the funeral was thus a good occasion to test the brothers' public
mien. When Thanassis' brothers accepted Vassilis Skoufas' sons' prof-
fered handshakes of condolence, the latter advised their father that he
could safely return. Quietly, he did so.

Thanassis' brothers were not initially interested in fighting their uncle,
who was so much more powerful than they were and with whom, what
was perhaps more important, they had been on excellent terms. Vassilis
had extended substantial credit to them to cover the costs of their winter
pasturage, and only a few days earlier had arranged Thanassis' release
from jail, where the irrepressible nephew had been serving a brief sentence for threatening another man with a pistol. Thanassis' brothers thus
initially declined to make a public issue of the bitterness they perhaps
already felt against their maternal uncle. While they were certainly not
anxious to speak with him, moreover, it is certainly significant that they
had already done so at the Iraklio hospital where Thanassis was pronounced dead; once again, removal from the village context allowed a
gentler interaction than was shortly going to be possible.

Their agnatic first cousin, Mikhalis, was determined to make sure of
that. For him, sad though the loss of his cousin may have been, the
accident came as a golden opportunity to unseat his old enemy. His
immediate goal was to detach Thanassis' brothers from Vassilis Skoufas'

economic and political patronage and bring them under his own wing. Further, he clearly hoped to use the whole business to his own political advantage, as a means of discrediting Vassilis Skoufas.

His greatest advantage lay in his agnatic relationship to the dead man. In the weeks that followed the accident, two contrasted uses of kinship were heard. The supporters of Vassilis Skoufas kept stressing that he more than anyone had reason to be upset, that he "felt guilty" for what had happened, and that he could not possibly have desired Thanassis' death since, after all, he was the latter's "uncle" (*barbas*). The use of this term is highly significant: a man who speaks of his *barbadhes* in a generic sense, especially when stressing their role as his mentors in any matter affecting vengeance or animal theft, usually means agnatic kin (mostly FB). But the bilateral kinship terminology allows *barbas* to be used quite freely of a uterine uncle also, and Vassilis Skoufas' relationship to the dead man could be stressed in this way as a means of insisting that he had already suffered enough.

Mikhalis Diakakis' advantage, by contrast, lay in stressing his agnatic solidarity with Thanassis' brothers. The more he did so, the harder it became for them to adopt a conciliatory stance toward Vassilis. Once again, the assumption of a critical village audience, coupled in this case with an already ferocious name for demonstrative *eghoismos* and with a skilled manipulation of agnatic loyalties by their far-from-disinterested cousin, made it virtually impossible for them to let the matter drop. On one occasion, indeed, they armed themselves with knives and pistols and rushed to attack Vassilis in his coffeehouse. Vassilis himself was luckily absent that day, and his wife rushed out through the back door, leaving only her two small grandchildren in the coffeehouse: grown men would never attack children. That no blood was shed may in fact have been to the assailants' advantage. In acting as they did, they demonstrated a proper respect for agnatic and sibling solidarity, but they also avoided killing a kinsman whom all the village recognized as their frequent benefactor.

Responsibility for Thanassis' death was clearly no straightforward issue. In variously assigning blame, villagers renegotiated the whole system of ideas about blood debts according to their respective relationships with the principals. Intent to kill, for example, is not *necessarily* a factor in attributing the moral responsibility for accidental death, nor is grief for the deceased *necessarily* a basis of extenuation. Those who sided with Vassilis insisted that as the dead man's *barbas* he must be feeling deep remorse and could not possibly have wished for his nephew's death. Mikhalis Diakakis, on the other hand, explicitly cast all responsibility (*efthini*) on Vassilis and even went so far as to claim that Vassilis had braked suddenly and thereby actually caused the accident. He had to drop this more specific accusation rather hastily when the police officially exonerated Vassilis of all legal responsibility; unlike most villagers, he was in no position to mock at the police, since—doubtless in accord with his own "law and order" brand of politics—he had encouraged one of his own sons to enter the force. His argument thus blunted, Mikhalis was thereafter unable to influence the course of events very effectively, and after a few minor eruptions of anger from Thanassis' siblings the matter was allowed to fade beneath the surface—if not, certainly, from memory.

This gradual readjustment is reflected in the widow's obviously conflicting loyalties. Before her husband's death, she had certainly had every reason for gratitude to Vassilis, who had protected Thanassis on so many occasions from the consequences of his swashbuckling actions. Immediately after the accident, her initial reaction to Vassilis was one of bitter, undiluted fury, and she adopted her late husband's patrigroup's public view, according to which Vassilis should not have insisted on making a tired man undertake such a risky task. She also treated the matter as a patrigroup fight, submitting wholly to the authority of her husband's brothers. On several occasions, she threw herself murderously at Vassilis in public. One such confrontation took place in the district capital; talking about it afterwards, she described the man who prevented her from completing her attack as "Skoufas," thereby showing that she still saw the quarrel as primarily a feud between patrigroups.

Meanwhile, however, the pro-Vassilis faction was explaining events in its own way. The writ of fate can only be read retrospectively (see Herzfeld 1982b:649), but it is precisely this quality of the cosmological framework that makes it so amenable to negotiation and variable reading. Those who believed that Vassilis should not be made to pay for the death of Thanassis contrasted Vassilis' own survival with Thanassis' death, by saying that the uncle "had years" (i.e., still to live), whereas the nephew did not. The widow rejected this argument outright. "I'll tell you what luck is," she railed. "It's when someone comes in the night to get you out on a job and you say, 'Later—if I finish my own work first!' " Her passionately improvised lamentations (*miroloya*) filled the village whenever she walked to or from the graveyard, and villagers worried that her grief and anger would plant in her impressionably young children the seed of future revenge.

Little by little, however, the general concern softened the young widow's stance. Half a year later she was speaking of Vassilis as "my uncle" (*o thios mou*)—a more formal term than *barbas*, perhaps because she was still uncomfortable about acknowledging the relationship—and exonerating him from personal blame. Although she admitted that the sight of Vassilis still fed an irrepressible hatred within her, she no longer seemed homicidal; and her children giggled openly when she mentioned the very thought that she might have killed Vassilis—an improbable act for a woman in any event. Her fury had been redirected. Now she claimed that she no longer believed in God, especially as the shrine that had been erected to commemorate someone else's narrow escape at the same spot had failed to save her husband. Still lamenting—

> My admired one!
> My [piece of] amber!—

she now blamed only God, who, she stormed, "commits all the sins [*amarties*]!" She claimed to be quite ready to go and smash up the church.

The shift in her allocation of blame utilizes a familiar rhetorical device—that of accusing some distant, supernatural force in order to avoid accusing those whom she might legitimately claim as "her own people." As she began to accept Vassilis as her uncle once more, it was to be expected that she would cast around for some more abstract object of her ire. In this, she was yielding also to the weight of public opinion, encapsulated in the critical observation that Vassilis was, after all, the uncle of the deceased. Other factors urged her along the same path. When one of her brothers-in-law prevented her from accepting money from an important local politician who also happened to be a patron of Vassilis Skoufas, she could only wonder at the seeming indifference, in contrast, of the Diakakides' own current patron, who had not so much as spoken a few words of comfort to her.[15] Other pressures came from closer to home. In particular, her brother had married the daughter of Vassilis Skoufas' brother. As the initial furor died down, these competing ties, though not agnatic, vied for attention and respect.

Vassilis' own demeanor, moreover, helped to defuse the crisis. He allowed his beard to grow, and adopted a slow, stiff walk on the rare occasions when he appeared in public—both signs of deep mourning. There were still some dangerous moments. When Vassilis set up a shrine at the scene of the accident in thanks for his own salvation, the Diakakides took this as a serious insult. During the fortieth-day memorial service, Vassilis' wife sparked off a further outburst by failing to close their coffeehouse door as an indication of respect when the mourners' procession filed past. But the Diakakides' anger was quelled by the general disapproval, and after a few weeks Vassilis cautiously tried turning his television set on—at normal pitch for the news, but lower when the signature tune came on, since music is a symbol of joy. Gradually, the fear of further violence receded.

The principal point to note here is that agnatic solidarity is associated with crisis. As crisis fades, other ties become more important again, and force the actors to adopt a stance more in keeping with the official desire for law and order. Agnatic solidarity is *performed*—as, notably, when Thanassis' brothers turned up fully armed at Vassilis Skoufas' coffeehouse, or at the "double wedding" where the Skoufades' awesome firepower—symbolized by the five hundred cartridges that were allegedly used up—was interpreted by all as a collective threat against any possible resumption of hostilities by the Diakakides. At another wedding, the relative absence of gunfire was put down to the fact that few Skoufades had shown up. These displays of firepower are hard to argue with. They do not threaten the foe directly. Instead, they symbolize a claim to collective masculinity: *pistola* is a common metaphor for the penis, and *balothies* (gunshots) are the hallmark of a good Cretan *ghlendi*. Gunfire is unambiguously aggressive and technically illegal, but in contrast to actual bloodshed it is by far the lesser evil, and the sheer numbers of arms-bearing Skoufas males put the Diakakides at a disadvantage. By being peacefully aggressive, as it were, the Skoufades were able to maintain their own supremacy in the dispute, while the Diakakides found that their threats met with less and less sympathy or respect.

In the competitive performance of masculinity, however, the Diakakides had one powerful rhetorical weapon: the widow herself. Immediately after the accident, she appeared swathed in voluminous black, with the merest slit for her eyes to peer through. In this way, the brothers' control of her sexuality was emphasized. Since she was pregnant at the time, they were careful to let this be known: had it been revealed very much later, unsympathetic covillagers might have cast aspersions on the child's paternity, I was told. After birth, the child was given his paternal grandfather's *paratsoukli* as his own *baptismal* name, since there was already an older boy with the grandfather's baptismal name. This unusual procedure confirmed the agnatic group's control over the widow, and the patrigroup's "ownership" of the offspring.

As the crisis receded, the widow's public demeanor became less dramatically restrained, though she continued to wear black. In a sense, she reasserted control of her public self: from the definitely female *miroloya*, or lamentations, which are regarded as an inspired but irrational and incontinent form of utterance, she moved to discussion of her future and the problems her children would face. Since her earlier "irrationality" was associated with her histrionic injunctions to her children to kill their father's "murderer," the gradual shift to a more composed and self-controlled mode of speech allowed those demands to appear increasingly ridiculous, until even her children found them amusing. In this way, the male ideology of vengeance became reduced to a "female irrationality" that the widow herself defused by progressively rejecting it.

This progression throws interesting light on the attributes of male and female in Glendi. In general terms, these follow the pattern already so well documented for other parts of Greece: men portray themselves as rational, self-controlled, and strong, in contrast to the affectionate but also gullible, incontinent, and often weak-willed women.[16] But the formal opposition thus suggested is actively negotiated in social interaction. We have already encountered a woman whose *unsuccessful* adaptation of male behavior brought upon her the ridicule of the coffeehouse clientele. Conversely, men who fail to demonstrate their strength of mind and body are derided as effeminate; farmers, in contrast to shepherds, are "people of the house" (*spitaridhes*), while old men, as they lose their physical and mental strength, come to resemble women more and more, especially in the "unmanly" regularity with which they begin to attend religious services. While meat is a definitively male food, in contrast to green vegetables and beans, people of both sexes do in fact eat both kinds of food; it is only during highly ritualized events, or at the dramatic point of a narrative, that food consumption reproduces ideology with any clarity.[17] But this is the crux of the matter: it is at moments of crisis that the rigid demarcation between male and female attributes becomes salient and well defined. As crisis recedes, the collective masculinity of the agnatic group succumbs to the domestic logic of women. Women who help to hide stolen meat when conflict and discovery threaten may lash their menfolk with contempt for the whole activity when the moment of danger has passed. By the same token, the male-controlled incontinence of the recent widow gives way to a more pragmatic self-control that preys far less on the tension between agnatic groups, and rejects the act of vengeance instead of urging it upon the next generation of males.

This negotiation of the symbolic balance between male and female attributes is also reproduced in the process of transition between two modes of kinship. At first, it will seem strange that the Glendiots, for whom agnatic kinship is evidently important, should use a bilateral kinship terminology, while at the same time they have no term for the kindred as a collectivity. The apparent contradiction is resolved, however, if we treat the Glendiot kinship system not as a terminological abstraction, but as a set of structures that are revealed in social process. At moments of crisis, men act in groups—agnatic groups. For these groups, they have single terms (*soi, fara*, etc.), which play an important part in the imprecations and obscenities that often replace or herald physical violence. An infuriated Glendiot curses his enemy's *soi* rather than the man himself. With the restoration of calm, however, people begin to think again of "my uncle" or "your father-in-law," and to deploy their personal loyalties in the interests of peace. For Glendiots, then, agnatic kinship is a system of *group* categories, while the kindred, which has no autonomous political or social existence as far as they are concerned, is a system of *person* categories. Conversely, their agnatic idiom lacks distinctive categories of person. To single out *specific* agnatic kin categories would violate the encompassing cognatic ideology of church and state without enhancing the collective nature of agnatic unity. At the level of family and kinship values, Glendiot agnation has no place in official ideology, and is "muted."[18] At the level of local conflict, it is expressed overtly: such conflict itself openly clashes with official ideology, and represents the distinctiveness of the Cretan ethos at the same time—and by the same means—as it expresses the *eghoismos* of particular agnatic groups.

The tensions between the two systems, and their conflation in everyday experience, are most fully expressed through elections. These are state-operated events that the Glendiots have converted into arenas for the conduct of crisis in their own idiom. Elsewhere in Greek communities, it is true, kinship plays a part in determining voting patterns (for a detailed study, see Loizos 1975). But in Glendi the agnatic bias is so strong that villagers still cite a violent quarrel between a political candidate and his son-in-law who refused to vote for him because they were of different patrigroups. Here, the bureaucratic format of elections has been converted into a mask for the expression of tensions that directly contradict the official ideology. It is a symbiotic arrangement that gives a peculiarly dramatic form to the Glendiots' love of contradiction and tension.

CHAPTER THREE

THE USES OF IDEOLOGY

Debating Identity:
Politicians and Parties

Although municipal elections are ostensibly about village concerns, and parliamentary elections about national ones, both are radically affected by two further levels of identity. Of these, patrigroup membership dictates voting patterns to a more obvious extent in municipal elections, where party platforms are in fact clearly identified as agnatically based coalitions. The other level of identity that plays a decisive role in elections is that of being Cretan. This factor is hardly felt in municipal contests, except in the sense that some candidates may be derided for supposedly failing to match up to stereotypically Cretan ideals of decency and masculinity. In the conduct of national elections, by contrast, the nature of Cretan identity is as hotly negotiated as are the conflicting claims of the various hopefuls to represent it.

For this reason, elections in Glendi provide an important context in which to observe the complex interrelationships between the various levels of collective identity that concern the villagers. Villagers, whether candidates or merely voters, take stands that foreground their individual interpretations of what distinguishes a Glendiot from other Cretans, or the Cretans from Greeks in general. Candidates and voters alike negotiate the subtle boundaries between idealized images of a land free of animal theft and blood feuds, on the one hand, and a pragmatic vision in which various forms of political protection can be arranged, on the other.

Local politics also reflect some of the dominant concerns of national political evolution. Villagers feel that Cretans in general have been systematically excluded in the past from their just share of political power. They look to the career of Eleftherios Venizelos, the Cretan politician who first became Prime Minister of Greece in 1910, as the one moment when the island came into its own; and they view as the result of Great Power machinations the ignominious failure of what were essentially his irredentist plans only two years after his own defeat at the polls; in the 1922 disaster, the Turkish armies swept the encircling Greeks back from Constantinople and out of Asia Minor altogether. The discredit that this calamity brought upon the Venizelists did not seriously erode his personal reputation on Crete, where, if anything, it became a means to identify the Cretans' subordination to continental Greek interests with the larger humiliation of the whole nation by the evilly conniving Great Powers. Crete remained a staunch fortress of antimonarchist sentiment. It provided solid support for Venizelos' return to power (1928-32), and the same local sentiment backed George Papandreou, the leader of the liberal Center Union party, who defeated the conservative Karamanlis in 1963. By that time, however, conservative politicians of local origin were already making successful inroads into the electorate by manipulating their own kinship ties at home and political alliances in Athens. As the Athens government collapsed in the aftermath of a spectacular quarrel between King Constantine II and George Papandreou over the latter's desire to appoint his own son Andreas as Minister of Defense, conservative and liberal politicians alike took full advantage of the resulting confusion to compete over the voters' increasingly perplexed loyalties. In 1967, the military staged its now notorious *coup*, and, with some personnel changes and with the abolition of the monarchy, remained in power until 1974. In that year, increasing unrest at home was followed by the Turkish invasion of Cyprus, an event for which the junta was badly unprepared despite its role in provoking it. The junta collapsed, and Constantine Karamanlis returned from his self-imposed exile in Paris to manage the country's return to democracy. After winning two rounds of national elections in 1974 and 1977, following a plebiscite in which the abolition of the monarchy was formally confirmed, he later accepted elevation to the presidency of the Hellenic Republic and in this role, in 1981, saw his own party go down to defeat at the hands of his erstwhile rival's son, Andreas Papandreou, now leader of the rapidly growing Panhellenic Socialist Movement (PA.SO.K.). The younger Papandreou had successfully consolidated his position at the expense of more centrist contenders for the mantle of his father and of Venizelos, displacing several splinter groups of broadly liberal persuasion as the prime alternative to conservatism.

The Cretan contribution to this rapid electoral reversal of the established political order was significant. In the plebiscite on the monarchy, Cretans voted overwhelmingly against it, many of them apparently recalling the long battle that Venizelos had waged against an earlier king

(Constantine I). Moreover, many of them had by now experienced life as *Gastarbeiter* in the West Germany of Willy Brandt and Helmut Schmidt, and were convinced of the virtues of socialism and embarrassed by the image that they thought the established Greek pattern of endemic patronage was giving the country in the West. Above all, however, they perceived the rise of the socialist movement in Greece as a real opportunity to recapture for Crete a dominant political role consonant with the island's turbulent and rebellious history. For such people, to be a *pasokatzis* (the local form of *pasoktzis*, or supporter of the Panhellenic Socialist Movement) was to realize the cultural identity of the Cretan in political terms.

Political arguments thus provide an excellent opportunity for examining the poetics of social interaction at work. They are not just arguments about what is right or wrong. They concern what is right or wrong *for* the village, or *for* the island or the nation. The rhetoric in which they are couched, moreover, is not so much a matter of words as one of choices. Political decisions also "speak" in the idiom of village values. Thus, for example, in the 1977 parliamentary elections, it was far more in character for the New Liberals, with their extremely localist appeal and base, to make use of a candidate with strong agnatic backing in Glendi than it would have been for the Socialists to do the same. The New Liberals based their campaign on a barely implicit suggestion that Cretans did not need to discuss actual issues, since their traditions and ideology would lead them to follow the right path. The Socialists, on the other hand, so effectively worked up the appeal of political ideology that any reliance on their part on the traditional allegiances of agnation and patronage could only have backfired.

National elections represent an important conjunction of Glendiot interests and national personalities. Many of the politicians who have represented the Rethimni *nomos* in the Greek Parliament are from Psila, which immediately creates conflicts of loyalty for the Glendiots: should one oppose these individuals as Psiliots, or support them as representatives of the *riza* (lit., "root," i.e., the foothill ridge that includes Glendi, Psila, and three or four other villages)?

Nor is this the sole dilemma faced by Glendiot voters. A further difficulty is created by obligations incurred to powerful political patrons; sometimes, a single individual may be indebted to more than one patron. Then again, such moral restrictions (*ipokhreosis*) increasingly conflict with new commitments to political ideologies. Indeed, the greatest tension of this kind affects Glendiots who are beholden to conservative politicians for favors rendered in the past, but who now want to transfer their electoral allegiance to PA.SO.K. The PA.SO.K platform includes a flat rejection of all political patronage, but the moral force of existing patron-client ties within the village community pits concepts of obligation against the appeal of the new ideology. All these conflicts are fought out in terms of Cretan identity. Supporters of each position imply that their stand represents the only true embodiment of Cretan values, and local history and folklore become resources to be disputed and redefined through intense argument.

To illustrate how the seeming constant of Cretan identity is in practice negotiated through discourse, let us begin with a nonelectoral example. In 1976, Cretan farmers blocked the main road into Iraklio with a lively demonstration against the government-regulated price of raisins. Since by this time many Glendiots had begun to produce raisins commercially, the pricing regulations affected their own economic future, and their coffeehouse discussions centered on the extent to which they should get involved. The brothers Eftikhis and Dimitris Koumbis, both shepherds but both beginning to look forward to owning vineyards of their own, argued in support of the demonstration. Eftikhis specifically observed that the Cretans are "famous [as] men" (*ksakousti andres*), and should therefore show their pride by demonstrating. His brother speculated that the blockade would leave the "town" (*politia*) without food so that people would die of starvation; for "dying" he used a verb (*psofao*) normally applied to the death of animals, emphasizing in this way the mountain villagers' ancient contempt for the urbanites.

Their attitude translated Cretan identity into the terms of modern politics through the medium of a performance whose main effect was to foreground the speakers' own claims to Cretan manhood. Ideologically far different, but performatively lodged in the same idiom, was the reaction of another, older shepherd, who prided himself on the purity of his adherence to the pastoral life. For him, demonstrations were a corruption of politics, since they entailed methods that had nothing to do with the fierce loyalty to a patron that was the basis of the shepherd's survival. But then he, unlike the Koumbis brothers, also openly boasted of his animal stealing exploits; for him, the only arenas for the perform-ance of manhood were the traditional ones of the mountains and foot-hills—places where both men and the very air itself were pure and uncontaminated by practices that he could not recognize as Cretan. Note, however, that *both* sets of attitudes entail resistance to authority as the hallmark of Cretan manhood. The divergence does not concern the prin-ciple of Cretan distinctiveness and independence; it concerns the forms that these should take.

If the content of Cretan identity is negotiable, so too is that of specific ideologies. An irate villager remarked that the doctor who allegedly refused to treat him was from near the Turkish border, and a secret communist to boot. Remarked the villager, "He was either a communist or a dictator!" For this particular Glendiot, a Socialist supporter from one of the smallest patrigroups, both these terms meant "antidemocratic." The doctor, an educated man, represented the evils of the city *as well as* a suspiciously marginal Greekness—the latter a feature which the association with communism, often labeled a "foreign dogma" in official rhetoric, could only reinforce. Add to these circumstances the villager's high profile in local politics (he had successfully secured election to a village council seat) and his notorious hypochondria, and his description of the doctor's behavior becomes several statements at once. It expresses his political convictions; it stresses his identification of himself with the oppressed villager who cannot get decent service from a city-bred doctor;[1] and it presents his politically weak position within the village as a homologue of the Cretan's experience at the hands of other Greeks. It thus implicitly tars all his enemies with a non-Cretan brush, and identifies their behavior with political attitudes that no true Cretan should espouse. An ingenious rhetorical performance, it apparently satisfied the poetics of Glendiot self-presentation. Again, it contrasts with the "traditionalists' " use of the same devices; they, in part perhaps angered by the hostility of socialists and communists alike toward animal theft, treat *all* parties of the political left with dislike.

For many purposes, the touchstone of Cretan identity is provided by the historic figure of Eleftherios Venizelos. His peculiar blend of liberalism and antimonarchism at home with active irredentism abroad would have appealed to the Cretans' self-image on its own; but Venizelos' Cretan birth and his early political career on the island virtually guaranteed him the support of whole villages and even districts in any electoral confrontation. Until Venizelos' death, all Glendiots eligible to vote cast their ballots for the Liberals. Shortly after that charismatic leader's demise, however, a Khloros opted to support the conservative Popular Party. When this was discovered—secret ballots being a transparent fiction at that time—the wretched man was beaten up by a group of his covillagers, who saw his defection as a betrayal of both the village and of Crete. Some years later, however, largely as a result of his ongoing feud with Vassilis Skoufas, Mikhalis Diakakis threw in his lot with a conservative party then led by Constantine Karamanlis. This time, there were no reprisals. The Diakakides voted virtually as a bloc, and gradually attracted the votes of client agnates, affines, and some uterine kin. Even with these expansions, however, the conservative vote was long regarded as a Diakakis vote. The Center Union Party (E.K.), led by George Papandreou, was regarded as the continuation of the old Liberal Party, and Papandreou himself came to be viewed as an honorary son to the now deceased Venizelos.

The period of "apostasy" in Greek parliamentary history had a profound effect on local politics in Glendi. This was the four-year phase between the Center Union's election victory of 1963 and the colonels' 1967 putsch. It was marked by royal and foreign intervention in national politics, with consequent switching from party to party by opportunistic parliamentary deputies. Glendiot's political loyalties were severely tested. Voting obligations conflicted with a growing unease about their political patrons' apparent cynicism, and the collapse of parliamentary democracy was initially viewed by some villagers as a welcome relief from the antics of Athens. There was a price, of course, and Glendiots gradually came to resent it. Precisely because the new regime wanted to eradicate all support for the moderate-conservative factions and at the same time impose its own authority as the sole source of law and order, it imposed especially severe sanctions against animal theft—as, in fact, the comparably authoritarian regime of Metaxas had already done in the pre-World War II period.

With the Cyprus debacle and the restoration of democracy in 1974, many of the old politicians were seriously discredited. All those whose opportunism had allowed the military junta an easy access to power were considered especially culpable. Many of the Glendiots who had been favorably impressed by the West German Social Democrats had by now returned to live in the village. The way for a local Socialist victory seemed open, especially as the PA.SO.K. leader, Andreas Papandreou, could be represented in strictly agnatic—if not always in ideological—terms as the successor of his more centrist father. Here, effective political performance rested on being able to *background* the use of the agnatic theme—since, as we have seen, it was technically ill suited to the ideological goals of PA.SO.K.—while still *making use* of it. To do this properly, another theme had to be foregrounded in place of the older devices; and the choice, not surprisingly, fell upon "ideology." This is in no way to denigrate the motives for their choice, but simply to illustrate the way in which it could be made socially acceptable among Glendiots in general.

Glendi did not return a Socialist majority when the second round of post-junta national elections took place in 1977. To understand why, we must look at the progression of events from the municipal elections of 1975 through the Skoufas-Diakakis feud already discussed, and beyond to the conduct of the 1977 parliamentary election campaign in Glendi. The Socialists were fighting against a firmly entrenched set of loyalties. Gradually, it is true, their own successful manipulation of the local rhetoric began to tell, and they more than established themselves as a force to be reckoned with in 1977.

The rhetorical battle shows that electoral success depended in some degree on the ability to represent a new ideology in terms of received categories. Thus, Papandreou's evocation of his father's memory, and hence of the Venizelist mantle, was reiterated again and again by PA.SO.K. supporters in the village; agnatic loyalty provided a perhaps unexpectedly pliable symbol. Then again, where the conservative politicians had created ties of spiritual kinship with—it was alleged—as many as a thousand baptisms in a single election campaign, the PA.SO.K. enthusiasts responded to the seductive appeals of traditionalists that they had "been baptized in an ideology" and so could not now change—an ironic recapturing of the older sense of *ipokhreosi*. To desert the new faith now would have been an affront to their Cretan pride, and especially to the binding "word" (*loghos*) of the stereotypical Cretan.

"Obligation" implies a lasting moral bond. Clearly, the way an individual Glendiot decided to vote was contingent on personal and historical circumstances, and the apparently immovable moral commitment of *ipokhreosi* would then be deployed in support of that choice. Even though PA.SO.K. officially forbade its candidates to utilize or expand spiritual kinship ties as the basis for vote catching, the party could not prevent its local adherents from profiting from these connections. I heard two ardent PA.SO.K supporters designing a letter to friends now living in Athens, urging them to return to Glendi to exercise their votes there; in such a small community, these votes might make a difference. The letters were to begin, "*Sindekne* [spiritual kinsman]!" The villagers' electoral behavior can only be understood through the prism of "obligation," that seemingly immutable moral concern to which every ideology and every faction constantly appealed for legitimacy. Whatever form it took, each villager's electoral choice had to be presented as a blow for the preservation of both individual and collective *eghoismos*, and hardly a vote was cast—at least by male villagers—without some prior advertisement of intent in precisely these terms.

For those who chose to continue with the old paths of patronage, the advantages were clearly defined and practically useful. A politician who had stood as godfather (*sandolos*[2]) to one's child might later be persuaded to help that child get a first job in a government office or get relocated nearer home while in military service. Moreover, a powerful political patron could—or at least, so it was said—get a convicted animal thief out of jail and back to his village faster than the policeman who arrested him could return to his post. This, always a raw point with the less fortunate shepherds, became a major political issue in 1981. The tie of sponsorship through baptism was also associated with animal theft in that *sindekni*, those so related, could always call on each other for help in locating stolen livestock in each other's villages. This kind of spiritual tie, however, was more obviously mutual, and additionally entailed reciprocal hospitality and the exchange of locally useful information, such as where the cheapest place was to buy grazing rights. The *sindeknia* offered by politicians, by contrast, too often turned out to be a false gift, at least in the villagers' estimation: the expected favors did not always materialize. A not inconsiderable groundswell of discontent on this score added to the appeal of the Socialists' polemical rejection of political patronage in the old mode.

In all of these rhetorical struggles, the ultimate symbol of legitimacy remained the highly idealized figure of Eleftherios Venizelos. His portrait hangs in almost every coffeehouse, regardless of the proprietor's political affiliation. Liberals claim him as the founder of their party; socialists appeal to the Venizelos-Papandreou link; moderate conservatives and extreme rightists, appealing to an essentially populist rhetoric, also claim him as their own, at least to the extent that they, too, are sons of Crete. In the municipal as much as in the national elections, the ubiquity of Venizelos' bearded, bespectacled face reminded candidates and voters alike that no platform that failed the twin ideals of democracy and Cretan freedom could expect to survive. The spirit of Venizelos inhabited the entire community, but was segmented through the social divisions of patrigroup and political party according to the exigencies of each successive event. It is hardly too fanciful to see in his image the secular counterpart to the icon of the Holy Virgin, an emblem of both domestic independence and yet also of communal and regional solidarity.

Segmentary Politics:
A Municipal Election (1975)

The conduct of elections in Glendi gives us a very clear view of the relationship between the village and the bureaucratic state. It illustrates some of the ways in which Glendiots bend official structures, notably those of the electoral process itself, to the specific internal needs of their society. It amplifies the social conditions that generate so much of the rhetoric that concerns us here. Above all, it helps to explain how every localized action or utterance can encapsulate allusions to many levels of social identity at one and the same time. Any account of the poetics of Glendiot manhood must address the ways in which villagers move between the several hierarchical levels of social and cultural differen-

tiation, the varieties of distinction between *edhiči* and *kseni*. The rhetoric
of Glendiot identity is not vented in a social vacuum. It derives from a
richly textured collective experience, of which many diacritical elements
are brought into prominence by both municipal and parliamentary elections.

The collapse of the junta in July 1974 was widely hailed as the
restoration of democratic life in Greece. National elections were soon
held, giving the moderate conservative New Democracy party of Constantine Karamanlis a comfortable lead. The majority of Glendiots had
voted for the opposition Center Union of George Mavros, continuing a
long tradition of commitment to liberal leaders and as yet unsure of the
electoral viability of Andreas Papandreou's emergent Pan-Hellenic Socialist Movement. While the municipal elections were conducted along
party lines in many areas, the Glendiots remained faithful, for the time
being, to their time-honored system of voting in municipal elections
according to the dictates of agnatic solidarity. Superficially, this system
meant that Glendiots were cut off from the mainstream of ideological
ferment that the collapse of the junta had engendered. In practice, it
provided a means of recasting the national experience in local terms,
without necessarily stifling serious consideration of what the relationship
between Glendi and the larger national entity should be. If the major
electoral focus as such was on the personalities and kinship allegiances
of the candidates, this in itself proved to be a reaffirmation of the villagers'
view of politics as a male-dominated, male-oriented activity, and a
preliminary exploration of how far they might eventually expect to penetrate the larger political system on their own terms.

At the beginning of the pre-election period, there seemed to be little
doubt about the local outcome. Vassilis Skoufas, as leader of the Skoufades, and a man of incontestable influence (*kozi*, "knuckle") with the
power brokers in Iraklio and Athens, commanded a large following among
the smaller patrigroups. This was important because of the electoral
system itself. Each local "party" had to put up a presidential candidate
and at least six candidates for seats on the village council. In the case
of Glendi, the presidential slot would usually be occupied by the leader
of one of the larger patrigroups (a Skoufas or a Potamitis); smaller
patrigroups would then be represented by one council candidate apiece,
in order to capture the votes of as many patrigroups as possible; each
eligible villager had only a single vote. The victorious *sindhiasmos* ("coalition") was the one that gained the larger total of votes, and its presidential candidate, who could receive no direct votes, was automatically
installed in office. The council members were the six leading contenders

from the victorious coalition, plus, as a makeweight, the winner of the greatest number of votes from the opposition coalition.

This system was easily adapted to the requirements of agnatic organization. In practice, it was rare for anyone who was not a member of the two largest patrigroups to become village president. Since Vassilis Skoufas was affinally connected to the highly influential Khloros patrigroup, the third largest in the village, his electoral position had seemed virtually impregnable; moreover, his affinal connection to the Potamitis patrigroup had even allowed him to run unopposed in at least one pre-junta election.

In practice, however, matters worked out very differently. In a stormy patrigroup meeting, formally described to me as a "council" (*simvoulio*) and held in one of the coffeehouses, other Skoufades criticized Vassilis for his dictatorial practices and suggested that another Skoufas candidate ought to be allowed to stand. With a carefully sustained nonchalance, Vassilis responded that nothing would please him more, that he was tired from so many years in office, and that he would welcome the chance to step down. Despite his show of unconcern, he was in fact much embittered by what he saw as his patrigroup's collective ingratitude, and for a while would not speak with the close agnates of the man who was suggested as his successor. This individual, known as "Big Yoryis," was not at the meeting that placed him at the head of the patrigroup, but does seem to have been aware of the machinations that were going on in his favor.

Vassilis Skoufas' fall brought other plans tumbling down with it. He had originally wanted to include the leader of the Potamitides, Thomas, in his coalition, and apparently had even proposed a deal that would allow Thomas to assume the presidency after two years (i.e., for half of the full term of office). But this plan might never have worked anyway. One of the politically most energetic Potamitides, Mitsos, had already challenged the suitability of such an alliance, on the grounds that Potamitides should never allow the Skoufades to ride to power on their backs! Indeed, he threatened, he would rather vote for another candidate *against* his patrigroup leader, if the latter persisted in such a disgraceful arrangement.

This was a radical threat indeed. Only about twenty years earlier, Glendiots assured me, a man would not have voted for his own father-in-law if the two were not agnates; the first time this extreme restriction was violated, a huge fight had erupted. Mitsos was thus challenging the very foundation of Glendiot political morality. In implicit self-justification, he asserted that voting against the Potamitis candidate would have been a better option in any case, since he would then have been free to choose the best among the whole range of remaining candidates, leaving aside all considerations of kin. The habit of dismissing village ideology as inimical to "progress" is widespread, especially among the younger PA.SO.K. activists, of whom Mitsos is perhaps the most prominent. For this reason, too, Mitsos reacted angrily when another villager attributed his hostility toward the Skoufades to agnatic *eghoismos.* "*Kakos* [(You have judged me) badly]!" he protested, using a linguistic purism for moral emphasis.[3] Even though he himself had benefited personally from Vassilis Skoufas' tenure of office, he went on, "change" (*allayi*)— especially after twenty-eight years of the same village president—always brings good." Since *allayi* is the rallying cry of his party, PA.SO.K., his stance effectively converted an old-style agnatic hositility into modern ideological rhetoric, reinforced by his insistence that candidates really ought to be elected on the basis of ability rather than kinship obligations. Nevertheless, to at least one disgruntled Skoufas, his patrigroup had "played the priest"—a common metaphor for deceit—by deserting the original agreement to put up a single coalition slate for the election.

Big Yoryis' camp took an analogous view. They refused to cooperate with the Potamitides, regarding any such move as demeaning since they had more votes to command than any other single patrigroup. Big Yoryis' brother Manos pointed out that the village was in danger of becoming dependent upon a single man; when Vassilis died, he demanded, would the Glendiots have to send abroad for a president? Besides, he pointed out, Big Yoryis also deserved a turn. To soften the implied rejection of Vassilis, however, and in order to emphasize the agnatic solidarity that encompassed even these weighty disputes, Manos turned to a truly evocative analogy: the great Venizelos himself had been exiled because of his opponents' jealousy. Since competitive jealousy (*zilia*) of this sort is viewed as a kind of *eghoismos*, and therefore as generally productive rather than destructive, this appeal to national history actually placed the politically divided patrigroup in a morally positive light.

As the election approached, the Skoufades became increasingly despondent. Disaster had loomed from the very beginning. As soon as the news of Vassilis' fall from power became generally known, the Skoufades' client patrigroups began to desert, largely because Big Yoryis was not felt to have the "clout" (*kozi*) of Vassilis. As a result, his slate consisted entirely of Skoufades. The Khlorides split in two, with Vassilis Skoufas' powerful affines leading the pro-Skoufas faction, and the coffee shop proprietor Panos heading the internal opposition. In fact, Panos became a candidate for one of the council seats himself.

The Skoufades sat tight. Although it became increasingly clear that they were going to lose the election by a substantial margin, their attitude was that of men caught in violence: despite the inevitable outcome, the only respectable response was to fight back the whole way. Even when rumors began to circulate to the effect that Vassilis Skoufas was going to vote for the opposition and was persuading his friends to do the same, the Skoufades remained outwardly firm. That they viewed even the unlikely prospect of victory with misgiving emerged only later, when they had already been thoroughly trounced. They did not expect to win. Even had they done so, the resulting village council would have looked suspiciously like a put-up job, with one of the principal candidates the nephew (FBS) of the prospective president. Even while they were bracing themselves for defeat, the Skoufades thus also had to confront an only slightly less embarrassing outcome, in which they would rule the village almost alone, their council an all too obvious travesty of democratic principles.

The reason for this lies in a revealing adaptation of patrigroup segmentation to the official electoral process. When it was clear that the Skoufades could expect only the scantest help from members of other patrigroups, and this only on the basis of scattered votes rather than of a wholesale agnatic commitment, the Skoufas patrigroup divided into segments in order to capture the largest possible number of votes through affinal, uterine, and spiritual kinship connections. The Skoufades were caught in a painful dilemma: whether to expose themselves to charges of group hegemony, on the one hand, or to invite mockery by failing to put up a good fight, on the other. That they chose to stand together argues a continuing commitment to the patrigroup, and also, in all probability, a sound assessment of what would eventually do the least damage. They lost the election, it is true; but it did not take them many years to recapture control of the council, and meanwhile they had kept the mockery of outsiders within reasonable limits.

It is not exactly clear how the council candidates were chosen, except that the four major branches of the patrigroup were all represented, as was the single group of *kollisaridhes*—a group descended from someone who had "stuck" (*kollise*) himself to the Skoufas patrigroup, no doubt because of the tactical advantages this would bestow on someone of hitherto minor standing. Given the relatively high endogamy of the Skoufades, this tactic reduced the number of voters who could defect to the opposition: anyone who seriously thought of not voting for his agnates still had to contend with the expectations of his affines. The *kollisaridhes'* representative, who could not hope for many votes, explicitly stood in order to bring the slate up to full strength, as the electoral law required; any other Skoufas candidate would simply have split the vote with the other representative of his segment, and this might have led to harmful tension within the already battered patrigroup. So urgent was the need to complete the all-Skoufas slate once the client patrigroups had deserted that the *kollisaridhes* did not even hold a segment gathering of their own to choose a representative, as they would ordinarily have done. Instead, the candidate's name was put forward at an emergency meeting of the Skoufas patrigroup, and this action was gladly accepted as the solution least likely to cause internal dissension.

In the days immediately before the election, the Skoufades fought hard to avert further erosion of their position. Not all villagers were equally committed to the principle of agnatic allegiance; indeed, members of smaller patrigroups sometimes found it expedient to stress other kinds of obligation. One voter decided to vote for his sister's husband rather than for an agnate, on the grounds that if everyone was going to vote according to kinship he preferred to vote for someone who was more closely related to him than the candidate of his patrigroup. In this case, moreover, we see very clearly how the moral weight of the brother-in-law relationship, which serves to reinforce solidarity in patrigroups large enough to practice endogamy, works in the opposite way for the small patrigroups. For them, the tyranny of large-patrigroup hegemony was something to be resisted—a theme on which the PA.SO.K. supporters were to play most effectively in the subsequent national elections. Thus, for members of small patrigroups, voting for a *kouniadhos* proved a means of resisting the oppressive implications of agnatic ideology even while appealing to seemingly "traditional" principles of kin solidarity. Since the Potamitides had captured the support of several smaller patrilines, and had even managed to add an extra Koumbis candidate to their list, strategies of this kind heavily favored their cause.

Affinal links had to be weighed carefully. Household heads controlled their families' votes almost without exception, and would therefore not only have to decide how to cast their own votes but also whether a mixed distribution of their dependents' votes might not be politic. One of the Skoufas candidates expressed anger at his "uncle" (*barbas*), a Diakakis, for giving all four of his votes to the Peristeris candidate on the opposition slate, instead of reserving one for him. He certainly did not expect to get all four for himself—the other candidate was the voter's wife's brother's son, whereas the disappointed Skoufas was only his wife's brother's daughter's husband, and so had not actually grown up calling him "uncle." He even claimed to have told the voter to give the Peristeris the other three votes, on the grounds that the two of them enjoyed stronger ties of reciprocity than he did with either. But he thought that some residual sense of obligation might have garnered him the one vote.

Other maneuvers appealed to agnatic values, but in a rather roundabout way. A Peristeris had decided to vote for the Skoufas slate because his brother's son-in-law was collecting votes for the Skoufas candidate with whose brothers he played music for weddings and similar occasions. The Kozalis candidate took him aside and expressed shocked disbelief: he did not want this Peristeris to vote for *him*, of course, but the man should most certainly vote for his fellow-Peristeris! The voter, suitably chastened, agreed. The Kozalis and Peristeris candidates were, it should be remembered, colleagues on the Potamitis slate.

If the ballot is secret, how are people's votes so well known? To some extent, the answer is that they are not as well known as local pundits would like to suppose. Secrecy, although not always maintained purely for reasons of political morality, serves both social harmony and individual self-interest. One village entrepreneur told me that he would split "his" votes between the two slates, but that he was not prepared to reveal more, as doing so could provoke irate covillagers into turning to his business rivals from other communities. Even those who openly declare their preferences may in fact be practicing *tapa* ("bluff, deception"; literally, "plug"). By and large, however, the villagers are able to make shrewd assessments of each other's intentions, largely because each voter is liable to "perform" his electoral preference as an expression of local sentiment. Competition is indeed at the level of public performance, however much the final resolution may depend upon the secret ballot. The reasons for voting for one candidate or another, while by no means as clear-cut as the agnatic ideology might suggest, are negotiated in the open, and concern matters of "obligation." Making sure that a successful candidate knows that one has voted for him may be a profitable ploy. And however wily the voters may be in their attempts to maintain some degree of secrecy, the very fact that individuals can control as many as seven or eight votes means that the risk of *collective* exposure is correspondingly high: one of the group, at the very least, is bound to talk.

At most, the Skoufades could expect to muster 150 votes. The Potamitides had fewer than eighty of their own, but could add some two hundred from other sources. The final figures came very close to this reckoning, so that even the agonized choices that voters had to make between different categories of kin and affines actually made little difference to the result. The Skoufades returned to their work, glad that the embarrassment of the election had come to an end. Some activists on both sides began to plot ahead for the national elections, where the outcome of the municipal contest could affect the deployment of "loose" votes. A few mourned the fact that there had not been time to constitute a PA.SO.K. slate that might have cut across agnatic lines and saved the village from a struggle that left the Skoufas camp divided and the village itself under inexperienced managers. The conservative impli-

cations of the Skoufas slate's name, "Prosperity," can hardly have comforted the more left-leaning voters among the Skoufades, especially as
the victorious party was called "Progress-Labor." Even if the bonds of
agnatic ideology could not be shaken off entirely, they were certainly
going to have to adapt to the newly insistent demands of "ideology." But
before the national elections took place, other events in the village—
especially Vassilis Skoufas' conflict with the Diakakides over the towing-
accident death—reaffirmed the ties of agnatic solidarity and delayed the
shift to a politics more in harmony with the concerns of the national
leadership.

Patrons under Fire

Long before campaigning began for the 1977 national elections, the
institution of political patronage had attracted severe criticism throughout
rural Greece. The indifference of politicians who had assiduously courted
votes with baptisms and promises, the impossibility of getting a hospital
bed without some form of patronage, the use of influence in high places
to leapfrog over others in virtually any bureaucratic procedure—these
conditions had become irksome to a significant proportion of the rural
population. In the mountain areas of western Crete, where some large-
patrigroup shepherds had strong interests vested in maintaining the
system, political patronage became a local election issue and strengthened the hand of the PA.SO.K. candidates and their supporters.

Before the junta, few Glendiots challenged the propriety of patronage.
Each villager, it was thought, should make the best of any opportunities
available to him—once again, *rousfet[h]ia* (political favors), as essentially political, externally directed activities, were handled exclusively
by male villagers. In 1964, a group of Glendiots had appealed to a
parliamentary deputy, with whom two Khlorides had an active patron-
client relationship, to have their papers for emigration to Germany handled as expeditiously as possible. The papers, including passports, came
through "on the same day." When the emigrating Glendiots went to the
Ministry of Labor to process the papers, the official who dealt with them
stared in astonishment; others had awaited the same documents for two
years! Many years later, after returning from Germany and living out the
junta years in Glendi, one of the Khlorides had become deeply disgusted
with the whole process. It was he whom we encountered earlier, calling
on his *sindekni* in Athens to cast his vote in Glendi on behalf of the
strongly antipatronage PA.SO.K. slate.

Even those who still expect to benefit from political patronage may be frankly amused by what they regard as their benefactors' venality. The advantages of such a relationship are, of course, well understood:

> Do you know the saying, "Fear restrains wild actions"? Well, if I were afraid and said that if I went rustling at this moment and they caught me I would rot in jail and never get out, I wouldn't have gone [raiding]! But since I know well that I will have support from one or two personages, or whatever, I do go, because . . . the thief . . . when he has, let's say, a Cretan parliamentary deputy [in his pocket], he goes with more bravado.

While they may benefit from patronage, moreover, active animal thieves do not necessarily admire the venality that makes some politicians serve their interests. The following is a comment on the less visible side of a much-publicized case. A shepherd from a village near Glendi was convicted of raiding and appealed to a senior government official, whom he happened to know:

> He says to him, "Mr. Minister," he says to him, "such and such, and so forth [a common expression indicating that the hearer will understand the content from the context]."
> And he says to him presumably . . . "All right," he says, "tomorrow we'll arrange things and I'll help you," he tells him. . . .
> I heard it with my own ears! He told him that he'd help him. And not even ten days earlier—not even ten days!—that . . . he'd gone to [a public meeting about animal theft in the district capital of] Perama and was shouting all about how he was against animal theft and the rest of it. Whereas, at . . . the baptism, he says to him, "All right. . . . We'll help you."

And the speaker, himself a frequent beneficiary of protection, if his own accounts are to be believed, commented ironically:

> What a joke it was! . . . a government minister, now, with the shepherds. With the thieves!

These stereotypical comments on political venality parallel similar remarks about priests, who, villagers say, should keep to their religious tasks and avoid politics or commerce. Senior government officials implicitly demean themselves by behaving like shepherds, and especially through their imputed association with those who systematically break the law. In actual practice, these alleged patrons may not have done much more than pressure witnesses or plaintiffs to withdraw their evidence while stipulating that, in return for this intervention, the thieves promise never to raid again. Although they may genuinely have hoped thereby to reduce the scale of animal theft, their motives are not often *perceived* in such altruistic terms—and voters' perceptions, cast in a well-tried rhetoric of skepticism, can easily threaten even an apparently forthright declaration such as this: "I do not want a single animal thief as a voter [i.e., in my camp]!"

Of course, striking the right balance is far from easy. One rightist politician found it expedient, during the 1977 campaign, to stress that he had grown up as a "shepherd lad" (*voskaki*) in these same parts. Even this observation, pregnant though perhaps it was with promises of sympathetic action that could not be spoken out loud, could also be construed as merely tactless. The politician was one of several whose origins were actually Psiliot, a source of irritation to Glendiot pride. And, to make matters worse, relations with Psila were not at their friendliest in 1977. On the other hand, his claim to sympathetic understanding was nicely ambiguous: he could claim to know all about the practical difficulties that beset the villagers' lives, but also about the need of many for politically effective support.

The shepherds are almost all committed to this system of patronage, which supposedly protects them from the law while allowing them to represent their patrons as beholden to *them* for votes. The shift to farming has weakened the appeal of *rousfethia*, and younger and better-educated villagers are anxious to escape its clutches altogether. Among this group, the antipatronage policies of PA.SO.K. have the greatest appeal, tempered in some cases by the fact that recent converts to farming still feel obliged to vote for their established patrons in order to secure jobs and other advantages for their children.

One exshepherd tried to use his political connections to advance his two sons, one of whom had trained as a teacher while the other secured a university degree. Both told him that they would abandon "letters" if he went ahead; they wanted to achieve their professional goals without any kind of patronage. Another young and well-educated man, who had trained in agricultural science, was less sanguine. Finding that he could not obtain a government post suited to his talents and training, he despairingly—and accurately—predicted the eventual outcome: that he would be forced to accept the patronage of a powerful local politician in order to get his foot on even the bottom rung of the professional ladder.

Some *rousfethia* gave individual Glendiots exceptional opportunities to control events in the village. For example, limited funds for road construction result in small stretches of paved road away from the main street, and these are a fair index of where the local power lies. Such advantages, however, can often be the long-term downfall of a too conspicuously successful local official. For many years, the leading Diakakis family controlled the single village telephone. Again, political patronage protected them against such charges as refusing to call opponents to the phone for an incoming call—which might otherwise have cost them their privileged control over the main channel of communications with the outside world. When Mikhalis Diakakis attacked Vassilis Skoufas over the towing-accident death, Vassilis' son had to go to a neighboring village whenever he wanted to make a call. Ironically, he used a phone belonging to a Diakakis of recent Glendiot origin; the latter was from a patrigroup segment that regarded all other Diakakides as *kollisaridhes* ("attached agnates"), however, and stood to gain much more by being helpful to the powerful family of Vassilis Skoufas than by siding with the Diakakis belligerents.

Many patron-client links are founded upon the kinds of protection needed by a shepherd in the earlier stages of his career: access to grazing land, help with the red tape of banks and government offices, and protection from the law. But the link need not lapse when the client gives up herding for agriculture, as many Glendiots have done. Some villagers hope to reactivate an old connection on behalf of their children, or to create new ties for the same reason. One man asked me if I "had" any kind of military officer, as he wanted to get his nephew, then doing his compulsory military service, relocated from the northern border zone to Iraklio.

Hospital care was, at least until recently, also still heavily dependent on having the right connections. An angry Skoufas, asked outright by a surgeon whether he "had" a parliamentary deputy to intercede on his behalf, finally got his treatment by threatening total mayhem. When I inquired why he had not instead threatened legal action, he told me that the surgeon would then probably have given him a fatal injection and claimed afterwards that the Glendiot had suffered a heart attack. Such deep pessimism about the morality of those whose superior education gives them power, coupled with the villagers' no less profound distrust of the legal process, faces local voters with two alternatives. Either they side with the more conservative powers and accept the status quo, or they must vote for a left-wing party in the hope that a socialist victory might eradicate patronage altogether. Since the conservative politicians' local support comes largely from those who see recourse to the law as an act of "betrayal," moreover, there is little impetus for change *within* the conservative ranks.

In pre-junta days, the patronage system was also supported by a close identification between the corporate interests of a patrigroup and the political allegiances of its leaders. Heads of larger patrigroups naturally had more to offer the vote seekers. Men belonging to the minor patrigroups were often the most vociferous in their condemnation of the patronage system, largely because they had least to lose. One such voter, having hedged his bets early on by getting the principal politicians of both the conservative and liberal parties as his spiritual kinsmen, announced in 1977 that he might even desert to the communists. If anyone took this threat seriously, it is certain that not many cared. "His" votes were few, and his consistent rejection of the very idea of patronage had kept him very far down on the village power ladder. He even refused on one occasion to go to the village Secretary to request a perfectly legal document that would have entitled him to free medicine, on the grounds that he preferred to avoid getting involved with all kinds of people and regarded the transaction as a kind of *rousfeti*. A Skoufas told him not to be a fool; but still he would not budge. His stand on principle did him little good: avoiding involvement with others is the mark of a politically inept man, and in this case clearly emphasized the villager's small-patrigroup status. Those who reject *rousfeti* must also have some practical benefit to show for doing so: then, and only then, their stance might become poetically as well as politically effective.

By 1977, it is true, the close association between whole patrigroups and political parties had already begun to crumble. Even so, there were many constraints against desertion. One Psiliot patrigroup, for example, had enjoyed a long and close alliance with the Skoufades of Glendi because both patrigroups were committed Venizelists. Feuds between the two villages, as well as a personal quarrel between members of the respective patrigroups, had begun to weaken the link, and political disenchantment threatened to complete the process. The moral imperatives of spiritual kinship ceased to bind the two patrigroups in the political unity that had once transcended the intercommunal boundary between them. A certain Yoryis Skoufas, a loyal member of his patrigroup who had stood for election on the patrigroup slate in 1975, was one of those who enjoyed a relationship of spiritual kinship to the Psiliot patrigroup, having invited one of its members to baptize his own child. Yet he now seriously contemplated deserting to the ranks of the conservative New Democracy. He had decided that Papandreou would sell out to the United States, while he thought that the New Liberals' leadership represented the kind of corruption that he, as a poor shepherd reduced to near-penury by animal raids and unable to gain much protection from his more powerful agnates, had come to detest. But then the entire situation changed for him. His agnate Kostas had decided to stand as a New Liberals candidate, and the good name of the patrigroup and of the village itself was at stake. One should always support a covillager because, explained Yoryis, the village is like a "little state" (*mikro kratidhio*)—a nice illustration, this, of the way Glendiots assimilate the concept of the state to their own ideology of segmentary solidarity. Explaining further why he finally voted for Kostas, he replied, "I have my conscience (*sinithisi*) at rest."

In Glendiot speech, "conscience" and "custom" are virtually indistinguishable from each other.[4] And custom demanded that a man respect his moral obligations to patrigroup and patron. Yoryis was prominent among those villagers who complained bitterly about the indifference of the patron-politicians to village concerns at all times except during elections. This might be an argument of some force when political allegiances were being discussed in a purely theoretical vein. Everyone knows, after all, that "some eat while others vote [*alli trone, alli psifane*]." Yoryis may even have broken ranks later on, after the 1977 election and once he had finally disposed of his flock and turned to farming; at that point, he would have fewer consequences to face as a result of being politically separated from the mainstream of his own agnates. But for now, conscience was as custom did. A closer look at the 1977 election will show how and why custom was able to retain its hold longer than many villagers themselves had been able to predict.

Segmentary Politics Extended: A National Election (1977)

While Glendiots say that municipal elections *ought* to be fought over the candidates' abilities rather than on the basis of kinship, they insist that this *is* the guiding principle in the conduct of national elections in the village. These claims are undoubtedly made in good faith. It was not until 1977 that the Glendiots had to contend with the challenge of choosing between local (i.e., Glendiot) and other candidates, and the ties binding particular patrigroups to particular political parties were neither absolute nor entirely stable.

Thus, while agnatic bloc voting was certainly not unknown or unrecognized, it was also far less obtrusive than in municipal contests. While each patrigroup took pride in its voting record, the fact that virtually all Glendiots sought to represent their electoral choices in terms of keeping faith with the memory of Venizelos meant that questions of ideological purity were foregrounded. The role of agnatic allegiances in determining *which* alleged embodiment of true Venizelism one adopted was correspondingly downplayed. Nonetheless, the segmentary implications of their choices were never entirely lost on Glendiot voters. And when, in 1977, they had to choose between two local candidates whose fathers had been engaged in a bitter feud only the year before, the nature of the villagers' political choices became clearer than at any other time in living memory.

These candidates were none other than the sons of Vassilis Skoufas and Mikhalis Diakakis. Stelios Diakakis was the first to declare his candidacy, prompted—it was widely believed—by a huge financial inducement from the ultraconservative National Flank. The Diakakides already had a record of strong support for the political Right. They were the only patrigroup in Glendi to have produced a policeman, the ultimate symbol of state authority, and they had also been the first to shift their votes away from the official heirs of Venizelos, the Center Union. Some embarrassment was experienced by Diakakis stalwarts during the campaign, since the National Flank—largely promonarchist, and widely suspected of harboring warm sympathies for the recently (1974) ousted military junta—seemed to stand for the very things that Glendiots regarded as antithetical to their own values; only their strident anti-communism allowed their local candidate to claim a share of the Venizelist heritage. One Diakakis, salvaging his own personal standing with the cleverly ambiguous humor that Glendiots admire, went around shouting his enthusiasm for the architect of the original military *coup* of 1967: "Long Live Papadopoulos!"[5] Making a joke about his patrigroup's somewhat disreputable politics allowed him to escape guilt by association, but permitted him to vote with his agnates when polling day arrived.

If their commitment to the extreme Right embarrassed some of the Diakakides, it infuriated almost all other Glendiots. It was seen as a public abandonment of the historic commitment that the Glendiots, as self-conscious localists, had made to the ideals of Venizelism. It also put the majority of Glendiot voters in a painful dilemma. If they failed to vote for Stelios Diakakis, the people of other villages would deride them for failing to close ranks as a community. If, on the other hand, they did vote for him, they would be collectively tarred with the rightist brush.

Into the breach stepped the Skoufas candidate. He, too, had faced a difficult choice. Filled with hatred for everything that the junta had stood for, and distrustful of the conservative and liberal elements that had paved the way for the junta's original assumption of power, he was widely believed to sympathize with the Socialists. Whether or not he actually made overtures to them (as many thought he had), his most effective connections were still with the liberals; his father had been a staunch supporter of the old Center Union, and retained close ties with those of its members who had split off to form the New Liberals. Enormous pressure was put on him to declare his candidacy. For a while, he hedged. But then, dismayed by the prospect of seeing Glendi vote en masse for an ultraconservative candidate because communal loyalty so compelled them, he made up his mind. Beating the declaration deadline by a few hours, he announced that he would serve as running mate to Pavlos Vardinoyannis, a prominent local politician who had served as a government minister in the pre-junta era and who was now the Deputy Leader of the New Liberals. In this case, too, not all of the candidate's agnates were entirely happy with his decision. Paralleling the embarrassed Diakakis' mock enthusiasm for the rightist plank, one Skoufas sneered that some members of *their* patrigroup were turning from Socialists into Liberals! Again like the Diakakis, however, he was effectively protecting his right to vote with his agnates while dissociating himself from the—to him—distasteful ideological implications of their collective commitment.

One of the most remarkable features of the ensuing campaign was the mutual courtesy shown by both local candidates. Each expressed polite disagreement with the other's politics, but each also showed respect for the other's person. Every effort was made to avoid reviving the inter-patrigroup hostility of only a year earlier. Instead, the tension that could so easily have erupted between the mutually suspicious groups represented by the two candidates was ostensibly transformed, thanks to their decorous sense of occasion, into a choice between blocs. The ideological debate was scarcely more explicit than the personal one, although both candidates made a few halfhearted remarks about the reasons for voting for their respective parties. But it was realized by all concerned that any actual confrontation on matters of ideological substance could very easily translate into a renewed feud between households or agnatic groups, with results that could only be disastrous for the village as a whole. The nice sense of restraint exhibited by both candidates allowed, instead, a delicate play of nuance and suggestion. Which level of opposition was paramount? It was certainly not clear; and it was not allowed to become clear. The more aggressive tone of other performances was replaced by a subtly different poeticity, as was indeed thought appropriate to a contest in which one of the protagonists had a univeristy degree and the other an official bureaucratic job. That it was indeed an example of poetic self-presentation on both sides is shown by the interplay it captured between the different levels of opposition, never allowing one to predominate over the other, but always making the polite mode of avoidance and respect speak entirely for itself. Had either candidate opted for a more aggressive stance, he would almost certainly have made a fool of himself, since the other's restraint would have made him look like an inconsiderate troublemaker.

Whether Stelios Diakakis would have collected many votes had he stood unopposed is a moot question. One Skoufas loyalist even asserted that he had actually *gained* as a result of Kostas Skoufas' declaration of candidacy, since it would now be all but impossible for any Diakakis not to vote for him. The rest of the village represented a different proposition altogether. We have already seen that segmentary solidarity does not necessarily lead to mass support, and it is entirely possible that most Glendiots would have felt their communal image better served by voting for other candidates. Certainly, there was a generous choice of alternative justifications, all of which could be used to present the Glendiots as a morally superior community: the recognition of existing obligations, a modernizing trend that put ideology and candidate quality above all other considerations, and disgust with any form of right-wing extremism. Kostas Skoufas' decision to stand, however, disposed of the problem at a stroke. While some villagers were unhappy at his "choice" of party, and others thought that he was being sacrificed to party interests, none could deny the respectability of his affiliation, especially in comparison to that of Stelios Diakakis. From this point on, any Glendiot who decided to vote for Kostas Skoufas needed no other justification than that he would vote for "our covillager [*o khoriano' mas*]." It was never necessary to ask *which* of the two covillagers was intended.

Not only were both local candidates extremely circumspect in their public utterances about each other, but they made few public appearances in the village at all. The battle was being fought; but it was fought almost silently. Stelios Diakakis made no effort to collect any votes within the village; he argued that to do so would have gone against his "pride" (*perifania*). In fact, he must have realized immediately that he could count on almost all the Diakakis votes, with the exception of one household with a binding commitment to the principal New Democracy candidate, and that he could expect virtually no other votes at all. Outside Glendi, Stelios and his father did campaign actively, calling on their various *sindekni* to support their cause. The Skoufades could deploy much more effective forces than the Diakakides: every evening, convoys of Skoufas trucks would depart with much honking of horns to barnstorm the neighboring villages and extract as much electoral capital as possible from the Skoufades' impressive network of *sindekni*. As soon as Kostas Skoufas declared his candidacy, the Diakakides knew that they would have to content themselves with a much smaller vote within the village, and a reduced one elsewhere. But still they did not resort to violence. On the contrary, both sides avoided any action that might reflect adversely on the reputation of their home village.

Within Glendi, it was hardly necessary for the candidates to campaign.

Kostas Skoufas made only one speech, on the final day of the campaign, when he accompanied his senior running mates to the village. He confined his remarks to bare generalities, principally invoking the loyalty and affection of his covillagers, and leaving political issues to the others.

His local opponent, Stelios, had one trump card. He was the only major candidate (in village terms) whose party did not have a single Psiliot on its slate. Tension between the two villages had been running high in the period immediately before the election, vastly exacerbated by the discovery of the body of a Glendiot shepherd boy—later shown to have committed suicide—close to Psiliot territory. Some even thought that opponents of the Psiliot candidates might have deliberately arranged for the boy's murder, in order to harness Glendiot anger to their own purposes. While that rumor hardly gained any currency, I mention it as an indication of the deep suspicion that divided the villages, and undoubtedly influenced the course of the campaign.

Stelios Diakakis certainly stood to benefit from it. While he did not make any public appearances of his own, his better-educated younger brother gave the only speech of the Diakakis campaign in Glendi. It was suggestively staged: instead of standing in a public place and declaiming to an assembled crowd, as Kostas Skoufas had to do on the occasion of his single campaign speech, Stelios Diakakis' brother read it over the loudspeaker system. The text sounds a consistent theme:

> My dear covillagers! Our village has opened up a road in parallel with Psila. It is our obligation and our honor to follow it as do the Psiliots. It is our honor that in the district and in the region of Rethimni and even further afield, the name of GLENDI should be heard. The road is open, with two candidates that we have. One in the National Flank and the other with the New Liberals. They are struggling to raise our village up high. It is our duty that all of us should follow this upward road. All in general! And know then that the vote is [each one for] one person, who alone represents himself, his own personage. The vote is therefore holy and each person commands his own. So, for that reason, vote alone, beloved [friends], without let or hindrance, and with the hope that tomorrow we will see our village raised still further.

This extract, which constitutes the major portion of the speech, demonstrates the Glendiots' earnest desire to avoid an unseemly confrontation at all costs. Villagers thought that it could only work to Stelios Diakakis' advantage, if it had any effect at all, since it portrayed him as placing the community's good above his own. Reinforcing this message, and at the same time implicitly damning the other camp, is the insistent theme that Glendiots should see in this election a chance to show themselves to be as capable as the Psiliots. They should elect one of their own; and what better than to elect a Glendiot who had no Psiliot running mates, and who in fact did not have to play second fiddle to any running mates at all? The rhetoric of the speech appeals to values both local and official—to ideas about honor and obligation, in particular—and utilizes linguistic formalisms (e.g., *oli en yeni* for *oli yenika*, "all in general") that contrast significantly with both the stern demoticism of the Socialists and the affectation of local speech favored by the older Liberal and New Democracy candidates. In these ways, Stelios' brother manages to suggest that the Diakakides' cause is a national one, as their party's name indicates, and that they have succeeded in transcending the more ephemeral concerns of village and regional politics. This was a particularly telling ploy since the New Liberals were known to be almost exclusively Cretan-based and worded their own campaign literature accordingly.

In the political discussions that occupied men's leisure hours during the campaign period, national as well as local issues were heatedly discussed. In discussing a segmentary view of the world, it is perhaps misleading to separate the two levels at all. A Zonaras remarked on the distressingly high proportion of Psiliots among the candidates, and, alluding to the several feuds that have taken place between the two villages, compared the resulting hostility to that between Turkey and Greece.

At the intermediate levels, too, the enemy was always a symbolic Turk. Leftist and liberal voters saw in the name of then Prime Minister Karamanlis the evidence they sought of his un-Greek origins,[6] while "the Americans are first cousins to the Turks!" In the same way, one's vote could be represented as both a defense of local interests and a rejection of "enemy" ones. Since the United States government was seen as implacably pro-Turkish, moreover, every vote cast could be represented as a vote against American interests. For those who voted PA.SO.K. or for the communists, this was straightforward enough: many conservative-liberal politicians had become suspect during the 1963-67 epidemic of party switching, widely seen as a deliberate destabilization promoted by infusions of American money. For those who now—in many cases because of agnatic loyalty—intended to vote for the New Liberals, alternative arguments could be advanced. One man, who had voted PA.SO.K. in 1974, now asserted that Papandreou's aim was to collect the entire left-wing vote so as to hand the country over to the Americans; this voter was therefore going to express his severe disaffection by voting New Democracy! Another Skoufas, also a passionate critic of American foreign policy, now insisted that PA.SO.K. was actually supported by the Americans because it opposed Greek membership in the European Economic Community. Yet another patrigroup member, uncomfortable at his desertion of PA.SO.K., comforted himself by saying that under Andreas Papandreou's leadership the party had, in any case, become less of a socialist party and more of a personality cult.

Other Skoufades who had earlier expressed a commitment to PA.SO.K. were less willing to be seduced by the call of agnatic allegiance. At least one opted for a tactic not unlike vote splitting. Distressed to find himself morally compelled to vote for the New Liberals merely because the local candidate was his agnate, he told another *pasokadzis* from the Zonaras patrigroup to remain faithful to the Socialist cause: his own patrigroup (*soi*) would have to vote as a bloc, but that did not necessarily implicate the rest of the village as well.

Faithful Skoufades acted very differently. Panos Skoufas told the very same Zonaras Socialist, who also happened to be a close affine of his, that he should most certainly vote for Kostas Skoufas no matter what his party affiliation. After all, the Zonaras had a son in Athens; if Kostas were elected, imagine what he could do for him! And he went on to predict darkly that those who failed to vote for their covillager would be sorely embarrassed afterwards.

Kostas was at a considerable disadvantage by having declared his candidacy at the last moment. The strongly partisan Panos Skoufas went with a group of agnates to another village where he had spiritual kin (*sindekni*) known to belong politically to the New Liberals' camp. There, he was told that his friends would vote for the senior New Liberal candidate; they promised to vote for Kostas Skoufas in the next round of elections, but felt that they had not been given sufficient opportunity to get to know him this first time. Such disappointments were common. They did not prevent Panos, and many other enthusiasts, from exerting intense pressure on possible waverers. Panos' own brother-in-law (WZH), Sifis Zonaras, was a much favored target: since Panos and Sifis had together been active *pasokatzidhes*, Panos clearly felt that if one of them could switch allegiance so could the other. In addition, Sifis was actually related, though not closely, to Kostas Skoufas. Kostas' own brother joined Panos one evening in a concerted attempt to talk Sifis and another PA.SO.K. loyalist, a Khloros, into casting their votes for Kostas. Sifis expressed some unhappiness over this pressure. While acknowledging the importance of even a nonagnatic tie of kinship, he felt that Kostas had declared too late—and had previously given too many signs of supporting PA.SO.K—for others to be able to adjust their loyalties in time. Once one has been "baptized" in a given ideology, he added, it is difficult to change again.

The Khloros presented an even more intractable problem. He worked closely with his Skoufas brother-in-law (WB), with whom he shared a small business, and Panos Skoufas thought that this circumstance would prove persuasive. Since the brother-in-law himself did not want to get involved in anything that might create strains between the two of them, Panos assumed that another brother of the Khloros might be persuaded to make a special trip from Athens to exert pressure in his place. I do not know whether in fact the attempt was ever made; but it is almost beyond question that the Khloros stood firm on polling day. He was further alienated from Kostas Skoufas' cause by the conviction that the New Liberals were a losing proposition, since virtually their entire power base was localized in western Crete; and he regarded its two leaders as architects of the political apostasy that had brought the military regime to power. What good had a vote in that direction ever done Glendi, he demanded, except to get a few animal thieves released from jail? He would have voted for Kostas Skoufas had he stood for one of the three major parties (New Democracy, Center Union, or PA.SO.K.), he claimed; but under the present circumstances he saw no reason to throw his vote away.

This last objection seriously hampered Kostas' campaign. Perhaps it provided embarrassed covillagers with a reasonable-sounding excuse not to vote for him; but it also reflected a serious concern with the localized character of the New Liberals' party structure. The New Liberals tried to turn this feature to their advantage, and their campaign literature spoke of going forward with "the God of Crete with us!" This was not the Zeus whose local birth was such a matter of pride in Glendi, but a "segmented" deity opposed to the mainland oppressors' God—a surprising usage in Orthodox Greece, perhaps, but one that would strike a responsive chord among resentful islanders. [7] And Panos Skoufas, passionately endorsing his kinsman's appearance on the New Liberal slate, praised the party leader as someone who could finally relieve Crete of her "orphan" status as a land without a leader of her own. None of these localist arguments did much good. Those who voted for the New Liberals mostly cast their votes for their patrigroup-mate or fellow-villager Kostas Skoufas, or, in a few instances, recognized long-standing obligations to Pavlos Vardinoyannis. Outside the Skoufas patrigroup, hardly any of the declared *pasokatzidhes* seem to have endorsed the Skoufas candidacy.

Within the patrigroup, however, the line held fairly well. That active pundit, Panos, was probably close to the mark in predicting that a large number of disgruntled affines would finally cast their ballots in Kostas' favor simply because they were Skoufades. Even the one Skoufas who had openly sided with the conservatives (and even expressed royalist sentiments), perhaps because of his close affinal ties with the Diakakides, threw his considerable influence on Kostas' side, and went off to the other villages of the district to campaign as energetically as any. Another Skoufas, a prominent member of the Lefteriani segment (see fig. 6), glared half-jestingly around his father's coffeeshop—a Lefteriani stronghold—and announced that no Lefterianos would dare vote for anyone except the Skoufas candidate!

Several non-Glendiot candidates visited the village to campaign. The PA.SO.K. group staged the first rally, with each of their three candidates given charge of a set of topical political themes. The New Democracy was principally represented by the highly visible presence of Yannis Kefaloyannis, then a vice minister in the national government. He held a rally in the coffeehouse of a somewhat discomfited PA.SO.K. activist (who nevertheless could hardly refuse use of his establishment without giving the village a bad name for rudeness), then moved on to several other coffeehouses. Most of the questions addressed to him concerned local issues: why was Glendi, the first village in the area to suffer an outbreak of hepatitis in over ten years, still without a sewage system? What were the chances of seeing a kindergarten built in the village? Had any progress been made in the government's plans to develop some of the village's natural resources for tourism? To all of these, he answered with a suave assurance that contrasted deliberately with the much more aggressive style of the PA.SO.K. candidates, though it left the villagers as full of skepticism about men in office as they had ever been.

The use of "enemy" coffeehouses for political rallies illustrates an important feature of Glendiot political activity. There is a strong feeling that the *kafenia* are public places, arenas for the emblematic performance of male roles. The norms of hospitality also make it virtually impossible for a proprietor to refuse a visiting politician the right to use his space for a public meeting. But even without this consideration, the nonpartisan character of the coffeehouses contrasts both with the owner's political preferences and indeed with what has been reported from other rural Greek communities. It seems to be strongly felt that political exclusiveness contradicts the role of the coffeehouses as places for skilled agonistic displays of wit and repartee. Performance is more important, in this context, than one's specific political allegiance. A Skoufas loyalist openly proclaimed his pleasure at the active involvement of PA.SO.K. supporters, for example, on the grounds that only through "give-and-take" (*andidhrasis*, lit., "reaction") would the correct path be found. Kostas Skoufas' cousin (MFBS), possibly the most active *pasokadzis* of them all, emerged from Kostas' father's coffeehouse carrying posters for Kostas' campaign. What could he do? Kostas' mother was overjoyed when the candidates gave their speeches from a balcony belonging to yet another member of her natal patrigroup, much to the latter's chagrin.

And a Skoufas who put New Liberals *and* Center Union (EDIK) posters up in *his* coffeehouse justified this by saying that the coffeehouse was, after all, a public place. "And a *democratic* one," affirmed his nephew (BS), emphasizing the desire of all Glendiots to adopt a morally respectable collective image. Just as the two local candidates avoided conflict in the interests of a performance of harmony that nevertheless subtly suggested the existence of conflict, so the coffeehouse proprietors view their establishments as public places in which the text of discord can be all the more deviously elaborated.

The greatest drama of all surrounded the last-day rally held by the New Liberals, when the village's very own candidate was seen standing together with the senior candidate—a man toward whom Glendiots, whatever their misgivings, expressed the polite respect appropriate for a former government minister with many years of active political life behind him. Before the four New Liberals candidates arrived, excitement mounted and a huge crowd gathered in the street in front of Kostas' father's coffeehouse. The evening darkness was cut by strips of lights hung across the street by the candidate's maternal uncle, who conveniently happened to be the village electrician. Meanwhile, in another remarkable gesture of unity and mutual respect, the candidates were making their first stop at the coffeehouse of Mikhalis Diakakis. When the candidate's car finally drove up to Kostas' father's own coffeehouse, the church bell rang out noisily—presumably at the behest of Kostas' close affine, the priest. Then the crowd pressed forward, bouquets of flowers were presented, and after much handshaking the principals went inside to be welcomed officially. They soon reappeared, went up to the balcony of the facing coffeehouse, and made decorous speeches to a crowd consisting—we may safely assume—of the already converted and the sardonically curious. The outcome of the campaign was already virtually decided. Only a failure to treat the village to this sign of respect might have had some effect on the voters' temper. But the speeches themselves were not viewed as anything more than a formal, if necessary, gesture. When the candidates were ready to leave again, they were given a nostalgic send-off by one of the oldest Skoufades, a man who had himself held municipal office:

> Go, my friends, to the good and to a good time,
> and may your road fill with roses of all kinds!

The formulaic verse, so familiar to all Cretans as the expression of friendship and hospitality, reciprocated the politicians' claim that their party represented the interests of the island.[8]

The next day, Glendi filled with people I had never seen before. Most were villagers domiciled elsewhere but still registered on the Glendi electoral roll. While national law forbade the sale of alcohol on election day, for fear of violence, conviviality ran high. There was nothing to worry about, and no surprises were expected. When the results were announced, they conformed to the general expectation:

Kostas Skoufas	225
Senior N.L. candidate	21
N.L. total	246
PA.SO.K.	93
New Democracy (most to senior candidate)	65
Stelios Diakakis (sole National Flank candidate)	51
EDIK (Center Union)	22
Communist Party	4

Although these results appear to give Kostas Skoufas an impressive lead, they represent only the pattern in Glendi itself. They also show the swelling appeal of PA.SO.K., which grew to irresistible force by the 1981 elections, and which was able to withstand all the blandishments about village solidarity. The insignificant communist vote includes at least one nonresident. The poor showing of EDIK, the revamped Center Union, is evidence of how far it had already been displaced as the bearer of the Venizelist standard by the New Liberals and—in the end much more effectively—by PA.SO.K.

The elections gave free play to Glendiots' concerns about their place in the nation's political future. They were locally conducted with a restraint that came, at least in part, from the knowledge that the results had more to do with voters' moral commitments than with the negotiation of specific local issues. It is true that the senior politicians' appearance in the village allowed Glendiots to vent their unhappiness with the lack of material help from official sources, especially over the sewage problem. Even here, however, the importance of demonstrating respect for the educated, wealthy, and powerful—whatever one may say about them in private—circumscribed the possibilities for substantive debate. Robert Pashley, who explored Crete extensively in 1834, recorded the striking politeness of the islanders at that time (1837: 82-83). It is clear that the ability to adopt an "official face" is not new to this part of Greece.

But the fact remains that even the national election of 1977 was locally conducted along lines that conflicted ideologically with the national model. However anxious Glendiots may have been to avoid the implication that their electoral behavior was largely determined by considerations of agnatic loyalty, this is quite clearly what did happen. It was successfully introduced by the locally experienced leaders of the two parties that fielded Glendiot candidates; they realized that this action would effectively muzzle the emergent appeal of Papandreist socialism in the village, and in fact they managed to contain the PA.SO.K. challenge in 1977. In 1981, however, the combined strength of the small patrigroups, whose members had grown thoroughly disgusted with the alliance of large patrigroups and conservative-liberal politicians, was sufficient to make for a convincing PA.SO.K. victory in Glendi and in the whole Rethimni electoral district.[9]

This point partially addresses the issue of how representative of Greece a community such as Glendi can be considered, and in what sense. To the extent that the Glendiot vote could be taken so seriously by nationally important and successful political figures, Glendiot social institutions leave their mark—however muted—on the political life of the country as a whole. As the ethnographic description now moves to the forms of agonistic discourse, we enter a world that seems to have less and less to do with the officially acceptable face of the national culture—and nowhere more so than when we look at animal theft. But the nexus of agonistic discourse is precisely what gives elections in Glendi their peculiar form. The men who participate in these elections—candidates as well as voters—perform their roles according to poetic canons of a distinctive kind. In Glendi, elections enact the Glendiot political vision, and it is a vision in which Glendiot distinctiveness projects itself as the ultimate good in its own right.

CHAPTER FOUR

IDIOMS OF CONTEST

Domains of Male Discourse

The distinctiveness of Glendi as a community, as well as that of Crete as an island, is reproduced in the *eghoismos* of the individual performer. While elections provide a forum for the expression and negotiation of collective idiosyncrasy on a wider, national stage, everyday life furnishes countless opportunities for the celebration of male selfhood on a more intimate scale. That elections are indeed male activities is shown by several features: the male control of household vote blocs and the electoral passivity of wives, mothers, and daughters; the focus on agnatic allegiance in the actual voting; and the public debate over parties and issues.

In this debate, moreover, men vaunt a distinctiveness that goes with being Cretan, or being Glendiot, as they understand these identities. To take but one example, the dissident Skoufas who has cast his lot with the conservatives does so, according to the general understanding, out of a form of *eghoismos*. His own argument, that he likes to side with the underdog, allows him to present the hitherto dominant right wing as a legitimately *Glendiot* cause—a cause to which few Glendiots had flocked until now in part, at least, because it was very far from being that of an underdog. The Skoufas in question is able to ward off some of the inevitable hostility to his conservative choice by performatively identifying the royalist party with the oppressed condition of Glendi and of Crete! That the nature of the identification is diffuse and inexplicit makes it relatively immune to destructive criticism; it is, in short, an effective deployment of poetic principles for political ends.

But electoral involvement is only one dimension of these principles of male self-presentation in Glendi. In this chapter, I examine some more everyday aspects of the mode, in order to anchor the description of political attitudes and actions in a more general understanding of Glendiot concepts of the male self. These concepts are given expression in many domains of day-to-day experience. One who is, in the Glendiot phrase, "good at being a man [*kala 'ndras*]" must know how to wield a knife; dance the acrobatic steps of the leader (*brostaris*) of the line (see illus. 5); respond in elegant, assonant verse to a singer's mockery; eat meat conspicuously whenever he gets the chance; keep his word but get some profit from it at the same time; and stand up to anyone who dares to insult him. He must protect his family from sexual and verbal threats, and keep his household at the level that befits a "master of the house [*nikokiris*]." He must dispense hospitality at every possible opportunity, deprecating the poverty of his table whilst plying his guests with meat and wine. He must be ready with clever humor. And in all these agonistic domains, his every action must proclaim itself a further proof of his manhood. An action that fails to point up its own excellence is like the proverbial tree falling in an empty forest.

Take drinking, for instance. At every wedding, young men circulate with jugs (illus. 7), offering a pair of drinking glasses to every two men in turn so that they may drink together. Some of the toasts are standard ones that do nothing more threatening than wish good health. Others are more obviously competitive:

> *Skoutelovarikhno sou! / Č' egho andistenome sou!*
> I strike your mug! / And I give you as good as I get![1]

Even less obviously aggressive toasts entail a formulaic matching that suggests the importance of balanced power:

Stin afedhia sou! / Kalo' na orisis t' onoma sou!
To your lordship! / May you own your name well [i.e., may you enjoy a fine reputation]!

And these more flamboyantly and self-consciously *Cretan* toasts are usually thundered in a deep-throated roar and with a closed /a/, which everyone recognizes as the sign of a true Cretan man.

These vocal tricks are also used in ordinary conversation, as when a bass "*ne!* [yes]" puts some impertinent questioner in his place. They are viewed, along with the distinctive retroflex [l] stressed in such phrases as *kala 'ndras*, as typically Psiliot devices. Much as the Glendiots profess to dislike the Psiliots, they concede at least symbolic superiority to them in all performative modes in which manhood is emphasized: readiness with words, singing, dancing and instrumental music, sheep rustling, and even ability with "letters"—a convenient explanation, this last, for

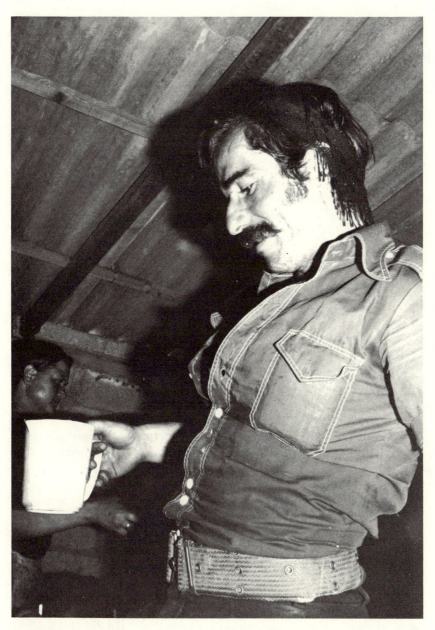

7. Wedding conviviality.

the undeniable prominence of the Psiliots in local politics. But we should also note that Psila is physically higher than Glendi, and that this, in the local symbolism, gives it an implicit moral superiority as well.

Drinking involves the substances of masculinity, sexuality, and death. Another toasting exchange makes this explicit:

> *Stsi khare' mas! / O Theos na kami to zare mas!*
> To our joys! / May God take care of us!

This seemingly innocent exchange, usually uttered between married men, actually reproduces at the level of social tension the balanced opposition we hear in its sound shape. "Joys" is a term commonly used for "marriage"; when flung mischievously by one married man at another, however, it is understood by both to play on the conventional analogies between marriages and funerals—two rites of passage whose structural similarity is a constant theme in Greek rural imagery.[2] If that were not clear enough, the response clinches it.

In this exchange, several messages reinforce each other. First, men confront death by confronting each other. It is not necessary to fight with lethal weapons in order to affect contempt for death; joking will do as well, and with less social destruction. As black-clad, mourning women went from coffeehouse to coffeehouse with trays of *kolliva*, the ritual food of the dead that is made for memorial services, one man boomed at a friend, "To yours too [*če sta dhika sou*]!"—an ironic use of the traditional formula addressed to unmarried youths at weddings. Not only is this a clever improvisation on the common analogy between death and marriage, but it flings a truly agonistic challenge at the addressee either to find a clever riposte or to face its implications with aggressively good humor. The speaker poetically draws attention to his own devil-may-care stance as one that befits a true man whether he faces death or his fellows, or indeed both at once.

The act of drinking is in itself both a link between death and marriage, and an affirmation of manliness. We have already seen that red wine is likened to the blood that defines agnatic descent. It also symbolizes youth and marriage; at the funeral of a young man, taken by death before he could reach the married state, red wine is conventionally substituted for the colorless *tsikoudhia* as the substance used for drinking to his memory and wishing God's forgiveness for him. Wine, too, is the substance of commensality, along with meat, at the reconciliation ceremony (*sasmos*) that resolves a dispute between men, and potentially converts their mutual hostility into alliance. The pugnacious toasts are also accompanied by a physical display of male strength. Glasses are banged on the table and then raised in salutation, toasts are roared out, and then the glasses are clinked and banged down on the table a second time—this last part being a departure from standard Greek practice—before the contents are quaffed at a single draught. Men do not usually sip their drinks, but drain them each time a toast is called.

Wine is no longer drunk in the coffeehouses. There, the commonest alcoholic drink is *tsikoudhia*—a grappa whose ferocity matches the all-male context. It is tested by throwing a small quantity on the fire beneath the still (see illus. 8). If it explodes it is kept; if not, it is poured over anise to make ouzo, a far weaker drink. Men who visit from other villages are treated to a glass of this strong liquor; having toasted their bene-factors, they are then expected to stand a round to everyone present. A man must show himself to be *kouvardas*—generous with his money and open to all. In the hot, dusty summer months, the drinks are accompanied by slices of watermelon or cucumber; in the spring, a farmer may happen by with a batch of wild artichokes, which he is forced to surrender to the convivial crowd; they are eaten raw, with a little salt and lemon juice, and leave a dry blackness in the mouth that invites further drink-ing. When neighbors cooperate on house construction, every household contributes male labor, while the women circulate with *tsikoudhia* and food (illus. 9). At times, coffeehouse patrons may decide to play a game of cards for a kilo of meat, in which case the smell of frying soon fills the air while the players contest who will pay the butcher. At other times, cheese, peanuts, raisins, or dried chickpeas accompany the liq-uor. The food, though necessary, is secondary to the drinks, through which men announce their genial disregard for the toughness of life in general:

> *O Theos na mas ta vghali!*
> May God take them away from us!

At this point, someone always asks, "*Ti omos* [But what]?" And the reply, no less invariably, comes back:

> *Ta strava mas ta eksodha!*
> Our crazy expenses!

It is not that God is really *expected* to help, or there would be no real humor in the jest. Rather, it is by making light of their burden—of time that has to be "passed" if life is to be at all bearable—that men express their commonality as well as, with varying degrees of explicitness, their ability to stand up to life's travails as well as to each other.

In each social encounter between Glendiot men, the structure of their relationships emerges again and again as a format of mutual, if often amiable, opposition.[3] The pairs of wine glasses at weddings eloquently

8. Making *tsikoudhia*: women's labor, men's drink.

9. Cooperative building: neighborliness.

express this format, their mutton-greased rims a forcible reminder that by the very act of eating and drinking together men give expression to the identification between rivalry and friendship, between opposition and alliance. Meat and wine are the appropriate agents of conversion from the hostile to the affectionate forms of rivalry because they are quintessentially male substances. When a man admits to you—*andristika* ("in a manly way")—that he has stolen from you, or done you some other injury, you know that he is worthy of your respect and friendship— worthy, in short, to take food and drink with you.

Similar competitiveness marks the consumption of food. A host who serves only a small amount of meat feels embarrassed since a meal without meat is not considered a meal at all. At wedding and baptismal feasts, huge amounts of boiled and roast lamb and mutton, roast pork, and sometimes also chicken and organ meat are consumed. Women who have come as guests from other villages eat with studied decorum; local women are usually fully occupied with the preparation of the food. The men, in contrast, make a huge display of tearing strips of meat off the bones with their knives and making critical remarks about the quality of the meat as they chew. They also boast of famed eating occasions, such as the time two shepherds, trapped up on the mountainside by vicious weather, ate seven sheep in seven days! The ambiguity created by the metaphorical use of "eating" to signify "stealing" emphasizes the association of meat consumption with masculinity.

Meat (*kreas, kriyas, mavrilidhi*) as a category includes only the flesh of flock animals. Chicken, although eaten, does not count: it is a domestic product, appreciated for its taste, but not regarded as especially prestigious. One returned migrant from Germany recalled how he had learned to enjoy it while he was abroad, but that its taste had rapidly palled once he returned to Glendi. He was a member of a small patrigroup, had never owned a flock, and had now become a small entrepreneur in a construction business he ran with his two brothers; but the Glendiots' food aesthetic, with its emphasis on the values of the pastoral life, was evidently still strong enough to affect his taste.

The consumption of meat serves to index both the ecological and the symbolic idiosyncrasies of Glendi. People from the towns and lowland villages attribute to Glendi the poverty, illiteracy, and social backwardness that they stereotypically associate with pastoralism; they conventionally see the transhumant way of life as a form of nomadism that conflicts with the desired ideal of being in control of one's own land. The Glendiots' own view is characteristically ambivalent. On the one hand, they accept that sedentarization brings many conveniences, not the least of which is that they can avoid the two- or three-day trek—or even the less onerous but financially burdensome truck transport—to winter pastures on the coastal plains in central and eastern Crete. On the other hand, they see the transhumant shepherd as "king" (*vasilias*) of the land. Increasing numbers of shepherds are now solving the problem by buying out the landlowners whose winter pastures (*khimadhia*) they formerly rented, thereby enjoying the prestige of both the substantial landowner and the owner of a large flock.

The constant factor in these recent changes has been the significance of meat. Most Greeks, even pastoralists (see especially Campbell 1964:140) regard meat as a luxury. Even on Crete itself, the one dietary deficiency of the rural population has generally been in animal foods (Allbaugh 1953:18). Yet this was clearly never the case in Glendi, where men recall how even the most terrible famine never meant a lack of flock meat. Stories of the German Occupation, and even of the closing years of Turkish rule, show that among the various foods consumed by villagers, meat alone never became completely unavailable. The harsh terrain around Glendi did not favor the growing of grains or olives, so that bread and oil might occasionally disappear altogether; but there always seem to have been animals available for slaughter—if not from one's own flocks, then through raiding the lowlanders or sneaking a few animals away from the flocks sequestered by the invaders.

For these reasons, Glendiots do not regard meat as the rare treat it seems to be elsewhere in Greece. This is not to say that they despise it. On the contrary, they take pride in the austerity and hard pastoral life that its consumption, especially when unaccompanied by other foods, symbolizes for them. It is this ennobling association with hardship, so unlike the more common Greek view of meat as simply a luxury item, that makes it manly. The wilder young shepherds, being closer to nature because they are "outside" (i.e., *up* in the hills), also eat it in its most "natural" and therefore "harshest" state (raw), while boiling—pragmatically regarded as a safer way of treating stolen meat, since it makes less smoke than roasting—represents an intermediate stage. Meat thus becomes a medium for encoding the relative values of Glendiot manhood, and its variable treatment symbolizes degrees of distance from untamed nature. Glendiot symbolism allies this common theme of culinary symbolism (e.g., Lévi-Strauss 1968:395-411) to the special needs of an outlaw perspective by exalting the moral excellence associated with the more *natural* rather than the more cultural forms. For Glendiot shepherds in their capacity as animal thieves, it is the demanding purity of nature that corresponds to true male excellence.

The association of an exclusively meat-based diet with the rigors of pastoral life, however creditable to the masculine self-image, brings in

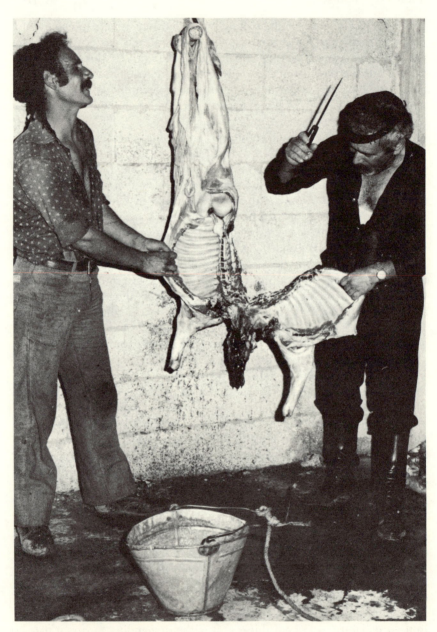

10. Meat, the symbol of manhood.

11. Hospitality for the ethnographer.

its train a deep appreciation of the comforts of home. A middle-aged
man recalled boyhood times spent as a *mandradzis* (messenger boy who
took food from the village up to the shepherds working in the hills):

> Between eleven o'clock and twelve I would arrive at the place where
> the sheep were quartered, where we kept them. As soon as I got
> there, all the *stironomi* (shepherds in charge of the male animals)
> gathered together. . . . So they were all sitting there, greedily eating
> this food which I took them, food cooked in oil (*ladhomeno fai*).
> They had become sick of eating stolen meat all the time!

The oil-cooked food was always cooked by the shepherds' wives and
mothers. It came under the category of *mayirepsimia* ("kitchen-cooked
food"), conceptually opposed to *ofta* ("roast foods," definitively handled
by men). Beans were at a premium to the meat-sated shepherds:

> . . . lima beans, greens, dried beans, whatever kind of beans,
> whatever there was. But above all they had a special preference
> . . . for green lima beans. . . . In season! When it was the season
> for them, green lima beans were the most wonderful food for them.

Oil-cooked vegetables represent the luxury products of the plains. Even
though Cretan olive trees had the highest yield of the whole Aegean and
Adriatic zone even before the last war and furnished the basis of the
agricultural economy (Allbaugh 1953:17), their oil was a scarce item in
pre-war Glendi. Eating oil and vegetables expresses control over the
sources of comfort, which "belong" to the relatively "female" men—the
farmers (*spitaridhes*, "men of the house") of the rich lowland farming
land. By an extension both analogical and metonymical, Glendiot men
also thereby express their domination over the characteristic work of the
women of Glendi itself.

Meat, then, was the main source of physical nourishment for the men
who worked with their flocks. As it was also usually stolen meat, the
shepherds were understandably nervous about letting the boy be caught
with it:

> So one of them would get out a piece [of meat] to give me. Then
> another would get one out, and then the next one, so they would
> fill up another bag for me, so to speak, up there, and I could sit
> right through from the evening without sleeping, without anything,
> eating meat all night! Whatever was left over the next day in the
> morning, you'd keep on eating all day, and in the evening, about
> this time, they'd tell you, "Go on, leave now!" Now they did this
> since I was a child, in case someone got hold of me and made me
> betray the fact that they had stolen meat and that they'd given me

some to eat. Do you get the point? They kept it secret. This was a secret of the shepherds, in other words. They'll have said to themselves, "He's a child, he might give us away. And just for that reason, they don't let me leave until I've finished up the meat."

The young adolescent go-between, mediator between the women's world of oil-cooked food and the men's world of stolen meat, was still not old enough to steal and cook his own meat. But his initiation into manhood might not be long delayed, and stuffing him with stolen meat was a suitable mark of his transitional state of passage between the two worlds. The position of the *mandradzis* (lit., "sheepfold person") is that of a less than totally manly being. Significantly, Psiliots say that they regard all Glendiots as *mandradzidhes*—that is, as inferior shepherds whose role is to serve those of greater manliness than themselves. The act of dispensing hospitality in the form of meat is thus, at a more general level, a claim of true *eghoismos* in this sense also: the guest is placed in a symbolic dependence upon the host, just as the *mandradzis* takes his meat—and his communion with manhood—from the true shepherds up in the hills.

In the village houses, meat is often served out of a large cauldron (*tsikali*) in which it has been cooked by women. Its preparation, however, is again often begun by men, who do the initial cutting of the meat with their personal knives. A meat stew offers an important convenience to large families, or to households that are particularly likely to have to entertain unexpected guests.

A possible crisis arises whenever unexpected visitors show up at a house where there is no meat at hand. Nowadays, with seven part-time butchers plying their trade in the village, this is hardly a serious problem; on the mountainside, shepherds are usually quite willing to slaughter an animal to entertain an honored guest. But even when large amounts of meat cannot be found quickly enough, the host may be able to emphasize his generosity, and above all his manhood, in another way. He may apologize for the poverty of his table, pointing out that the guests would have to be content with "whatever can be found" (*to vriskoumeno*). This phrase invokes a crucial principle. Ability to improvise, to make the most of whatever chance offers, is the mark of the true man. It is unthinkable for a Glendiot to refuse to entertain extra guests; on the contrary, he is expected to make the most of what he has, announcing that "food for nine [people] also *defeats* ten!" Note the agonistic quality, the claim to moral victory, that this attributes to his hospitality. It is a quality that combines well with the ability to improvise a meal out of nothing, and that attests to his control over the female household members who actually do the work of preparing and serving the repast.

Improvisation, dominance, and competition are all aspects of a single poetics of male selfhood, a poetics that is perhaps best summed up in the term *khoui*—the perspective that allows the male Glendiot to insist on his eccentricities as evidence of a fundamental conformity to the canons of Glendiot identity.

Improvisation and Opportunity

The good host who serves up "whatever can be found" is the epitome of a larger principle. The significance of flexibility and an ability to make the best of any situation are key components in the definition of the true man. Each successful demonstration of *eghoismos*, especially when manifested in the bending of fickle chance to the actor's own ends and the comfort of his guests, suggests an infinite swathe of possibilities—none of them explicit, to be sure, but then it is in this very indeterminacy of suggestion that the poetic qualities of Glendiot male self-presentation lie.

Women, too, are honored for their ability to cope with the unexpected, though their ability to do so on occasion is taken by the men as a limiting case. The ultimate example of social excellence (*filotimo*[4]) is given as the poor widow's reaction to unexpected guests; her offering of a glass of water and a handful of olives, the best she can do, is valued as an act of total generosity. It is often a wife, too, who shoos her husband off to the butcher if she has no meat at home, while she prepares the rest of the meal; and her own hard work at providing the creature comforts of home life is often highly visible from the street or even, if one of "her" men is the proprietor, in the coffeehouse (illus. 12-14). But her actions in this regard are viewed as a metonymical extension of her husband's *eghoismos* as a host, as are her verbal duels in defense of her home and her marital patrigroup.

Even in such definitely male domains as sheep rustling, women have some opportunities to display this kind of personal flair, but this again occurs specifically as a means of defending the home. A woman who stole animals would presumably be regarded as having overstepped the boundaries of legitimacy, and to have attempted to assume an impossibly literal masculinity for herself—just as did in fact happen, for example, in the case of the "man-woman" who broke the rules of coffeehouse decorum. While women express principled disapproval of the act of theft, and thereby emphasize the fact that they are *not* men, on the other hand, their very innocence makes them ideal agents of concealment. At the approach of the police, one woman cut up some stolen meat and hid

12. A rare moment in a male domain: preparing a spindle in her husband's coffeehouse.

13. Making *ploumista*.

14. *Ploumista* on display.

it in a water pitcher, which she then calmly carried down to the well;
another pushed a haunch of meat down the effluent pipe of the family
toilet so that it vanished for good.

But women's dexterity at concealment is largely derived from their
characteristic privacy; recall, for example, the young woman whose
defense of her chastity allowed the stolen meat to remain undisturbed
amongst her underclothes. Men, by contrast, are constantly called upon
to articulate their performative skill in public. They have many arenas
for this: the dance, the song contest, drinking, eating, and card playing.
Bride theft and animal rustling, while more covert, involve skills that
also get talked about once the immediate risk of exposure has faded. In
recounting stories about animal rustling, moreover, men can display
their skill at two levels simultaneously: the narrative level reproduces
that of the event. And just as stolen meat is tastier, so, too, animal
thieves are said to put plenty of "pepper" into their stories.

Glendiots admire what Bourdieu (1977:8) has called the *"necessary improvisation* that defines excellence." They have scant respect for the hack, whether in the dance or in concocting verse. The ability to fit an utterance or an action to a context is best shown in the degree to which a man can present his own deviations from the stock manner as an improvement, while at the same time managing to suggest that his opponent lacks the strength of character needed to challenge the conventions. In Glendi, a society where self-regard is socially positive, the hack's failure to stand out from the crowd hurts his status. The social character of *eghoismos*—and more especially that demonstrative eccentricity called *khoui*—is thus matched by a socially acceptable range of idiosyncratic performance.

In the Glendiot social aesthetic, certain key constructs are enunciated repeatedly. Central to it is the concept of *simasia*, loosely glossed as "meaning." Meaning is impossible without some degree of obvious connectedness (*sinekhia*) between events—as, most explicitly, between the verses that make up the give-and-take of a competitive sequence. But connectedness is not enough; the events themselves must "fit" (*teriazoun*) both the context and each other. And the actor must not seem to have pondered his moves. On the contrary, he should seem to have "chanced" (*etikhene*) upon the flock he raids, the verse he suddenly thought up, the food he is able to serve his unexpected guests. A teasing song, made up on the spur of the moment, "came out by chance (*tikheos evyičene*)." Had it seemed otherwise, the opposing singer might have held the verse up to ridicule by the simple expedient of parodying it.

Such principled serendipity makes an adventure out of every encounter. Life is uncertain, fleeting: *kosmos pseftis* ("the world [is] a liar"). Death is a talented thief in Greek symbolism[5]—something Glendiots are more able than many to appreciate. They certainly have an appropriate response: "We'll steal one of Death's bad hours [i.e., one of the hours that Death had instead hoped to steal from *us*] from him [*tha klepsoume mia ora tou Kharou kači*]!" The Glendiots' mockery of death is no index of fundamental disrespect. On the contrary, Death thus anthropomorphized is a truly worthy opponent.

Glendiot concern with *simasia* indicates an awareness of the poetic qualities potentially inherent in all speech, and indeed in all action of any kind. If speech is a kind of action, so action can be said to speak. Glendiot usage is particularly explicit about this when *denying* the value or significance of some deed: *dhe lei prama* ("it doesn't 'say' anything"). This is the essential component of meaning, without which life itself is worthless. A well-lived life is a life of well-stolen moments, each one unique.

This does not mean that repetition is absent from Glendiot discourse. In fact, we were repeatedly struck by the villagers' ability to derive huge amusement from the endless repetition—at their request—of anecdotes about Churchill's skill at political repartee. But this is precisely the point: the stories recounted a model of quick thinking with which the Glendiots could identify, just as they seemed to enjoy well-tried tales about clever sheep raids. In these cases, the narratives did what otherwise the actions would have to do for themselves: they presented the protagonists' improvisational skills in a favorable light.

In the case of a witty remark or a successful raid, it could also be said that a verbal account was necessary to preserve a unique and possibly very private event. With highly public acts such as dancing, on the other hand, these stories would soon pall; a good *fighoura* (acrobatic ornamental step) can soon be replaced in people's memories by many more of the same. A young man, stooping as he leaped to pick up a fallen cigarette, may be demonstrating serendipitous excellence of a high order, but his action could easily be duplicated many times over. By contrast, the witty remark, feeding police officers stolen meat, or a rude comment elegantly fitted to verse and made to sting a specific person—these events are unique to particular casts of characters, and repetition of such stories always entails generous circumstantial detail. The stories themselves enter the repertoire of received wisdom.

In such cases, the unexpected is drafted into the service of convention. At a memorial service held for some Glendiots who had been executed by the Germans, held a few days after that tragic event and on the very spot where it had taken place, a Glendiot became extremely drunk on the *tsikoudhia* with which the mourners were asking God's forgiveness for the victims. Suddenly he shouted, *"Panda se tetia* [such things forever]!"—up to that point, apparently, a festive toast without any special implications. While some of the villagers were scandalized at the time, the drunkard's embarrassment made a superb joke. As a result, whenever Glendiots today start drinking heavily, they are liable to yell, *"Panda se tetia!"*—and then to check around to be sure that all present have appreciated the allusion. A remark that may once have caused considerable hurt has, in a relatively short time span, been assimilated into the Glendiots' humorous confrontation with death.

The constant recourse to an oral archive is a fair index of what events, verbal or otherwise, are considered to have *simasia*. Particularly in the case of *mandinadhes*, the rhyming or assonant couplets that are the Glendiots' favored song and verse mode, the best evidence of which texts are thought to have the greatest significance may be the extent to which they are remembered.

Authorship of these verses is not attributed on the basis of text alone. The apt use of a familiar verse in a novel context also qualifies as original, and will be remembered as such. Except for a few proverbial distichs, moreover, Glendiots do not see much sense in reciting texts without some description of the circumstances of performance, the point being to celebrate an individual singer's *etimoloyia*, or "readiness with words."[6] Note that the main emphasis lies on the verbal dimension. While musical form can invest a performance with some excitement, the minimal variation in tunes seems designed more to highlight the singers' verbal ingenuity by emphasizing the tightly disciplined sound structure within which they have to operate. Other devices that support the same strong contrast between disciplined form and adventurous content include phrase repetition, the imitation of syntactic formulae, and the use of both phonological and syntactic parallelisms to emphasize semantic incongruities. Each well-regarded verse is "diagrammed" in ways that focus attention on its form as itself a significant element of the performance (see Jakobson 1960), and which may also take account of the performative context as well as of the purely textual content; the local concept of *simasia* demands this. Verses that fit well with each other or with the situation at hand are said to "match" (*teriazoun*)—a term with sexual and romantic connotations, and sometimes glossed as "having kinship" (*singenevi*). Finally, the musical structure and a set of highly conventionalized decorative phrases may be used to emphasize these textual and contextual features. They are not subsequently remembered, however, and do not in fact seem to be entirely necessary to a good performance; in fact, a well-remembered *mandinadha* may have been performed in an ordinary speaking voice.

Here is an example that illustrates most of the principles of good *mandinadha* performance. A young Glendiot man had gone to the lowland village of Voriza, a place despised by Glendiots as merely agricultural and a good place to raid without fear of retaliation. The locals started to goad the Glendiot youth with suggestions that he should marry into their village. Irritated, he announced:

Kallia 'kho   na me thapsoune stsi   asfendias   ti riza
Better-I-would-be to-be-buried   at the asphodel's   root

para na paro kopelia na' ne 'pou ti Voriza!
than to take a girl   who is from Voriza!

An old Voriza woman, standing nearby, heard the verse and replied:

Kallia 'kho   na me thapsoune se mia khiroskatoula
Better-I-would-be to be buried   in a   puddle-of-pig-shit

para na paris   kopelia na 'ne Vorizopoula!
than that-you-should-take a-girl   who is a Voriza-girl!

The appreciative glee with which this was recalled many years later *in Glendi* shows that a good performance may be acknowledged and remembered even if it entails the temporary humiliation of a covillager. What made it clever?

First of all, the old woman introduces an irony about the Glendiot youth's actual performance. She takes his romantic formula of "the asphodel's root," a common motif in love verses, and converts it into something all the funnier because it can be accommodated to the same verse structure. Devices that accuse an opponent of conventionality are effective weapons; Glendiots say that one should get new verses "from one's [belly-]bag." The replacement of one way of saying "a girl from Voriza" by another further foregrounds the old woman's verbal dexterity, although singers are allowed to use the same rhyme for more than one pair of verses in sequence. The virtual reproduction of the rest of the Glendiot's verse for a very different meaning is a hallmark of poetic skill.

The social relationship between the two performers—a young man and an old woman—is sufficiently antithetical in its own structure to lend further force to the play on verse form: each antinomy reproduces the other. Precisely because such daring versification is usually (though by no means exclusively) attributed to men, the woman's success was all the greater. Her performance provides an extreme of sorts, rather like that of the widow whose meager fare is cited as the ultimate in hospitality: for a man to be openly put in his place by a woman is thought to be especially humiliating, and the Voriza woman's age allowed her to speak up where perhaps a younger woman might have transgressed the limits of acceptable daring. Knowing how far to go is the key to a successful negotiation of the balance between personal idiosyncrasy and social acceptability.

Often, a clever verse riposte serves to restrain physical violence. To respond with knife or fist would demean the assailant by suggesting that he was incapable of responding with some witty line of his own. In the following example, an enamored young man exclaims:

Akhi ke na iksera   ekini pou mou meli,
Ah! if-only-I-knew her   who is-in-my-future,

na tin daizo zakhari, karidhia   me   to meli.
I'd feed her sugar,   [and] walnuts with honey.

This youthful outburst provoked a sardonic retort:

Ma to Theo katekho tine, ekini   pou sou meli:
By God,   I know her   —the one who's-in-your-future:

stou Skoufadhonikou tin avli tin ekhoune   dhemeni!
in Skoufadonikos'   yard   they have her tied up!

To any Glendiot, the meaning is obvious: the imagined bride is a donkey!
Had this been said in so many words, a violent response might have
been inevitable: calling someone a donkey is one of the gravest insults,
since the donkey is taken as the epitome of a being totally lacking in
social worth. As it was, however, the cleverness of the response restricted
the young man's options to responding in kind or keeping silent. Allusion
both furnishes a more potent insult, and yet also protects the speaker
more effectively, than any direct attack could do. It not only attacks the
speaker at a personal level, moreover, but through its mocking focus on
the young man's formulaic diction—"to feed her sugar, [and] walnuts
with honey"—it casts doubt on the latter's manliness itself. In a community where manhood requires a constant exhibition of performative
skill, the clever *mandinadha* can reduce an opponent symbolically without giving him the chance to respond in any other domain.

Some *mandinadhes* make their insults explicit; several that I recorded,
for example, do explicitly call the opponent a donkey. The idiom is one
that takes great daring to carry across gender boundaries. Occasionally,
however, a woman dares to engage a man in verbal combat in this way,
and may even gain a certain admiration from other men if she manages
to hold her own. In 1960, Sifis Skoufas met a girl who, he claimed,
"had an *eghoismos*" to compete with a man at singing *mandinadhes*. He
told her that he was from the Mylopotamos region; she replied, equally
haughtily, that she was from Iraklio. Then she launched into verse:

Ame more   sto dhiaolo, sardhella   vromesmeni,
Go,   you wretch, to the devil, [you] anchovy that stinks,

ki   apopata tou vareliou, pios dhiaolos   se theli?
and dregs   of the barrel, what devil   [would] want you?

He replied:

Etoutana t' apopata ta kanoun stin Evropi,
These   dregs   are made in Europe [i.e., are of high quality],

ma si 'se apo čiena pou kanoun   i anthropi!
but you are of   those that are made by people [i.e., excreta]!

The clever play on *apopata*—"dregs" as well as "excrement"—is reinforced by the patterned repetition of the verb *kanoun* ("they make"). At
the same time, the reference to "Europe" implies failure to meet a

standard of "civilization": the male singer equated cultural superiority with his own values.

The woman hesitated, afraid—according to the man, at least—that he might continue. He did, too:

> *Apo inda pervoli ta 'vghales,   skila, ita kremmidhia?*
> From what garden did-you-take-them, bitch, those onions?
>
> *T' aghrofilakou   tha to po pos ise 'si 'pitidhia!*
> To the field warden I'll tell   that you're skilled [as a thief]!

A woman would steal *vegetables,* and onions are offensive because they *stink,* a condition that Glendiot men associate with both female sexuality and inadequate masculinity. Such behavior warrants the otherwise un-thinkable appeal to authority. Irony is heavily applied: "skill" of this sort is hardly admirable in a woman, the man implies, and fits, as the rhyme does, with the stink of "onions." But just to make sure the message is well understood, he reinforces it with a contemptuous dismissal of her "masculine" skill at versifying:

> *Gabadhokaftis   tha yeno   na keo   tsi gabadhes.*
> [A] cloak-burner I'll become and burn the cloaks.

> *Maimouni, pios s' armenikse na vghanis   mandinadhes?*
> Monkey,   who taught-you   to make up [lit., "get out"] *mandinadhes?*

If this last distich seems somewhat inconsequential, that is apparently the point of it. The first line imitates a well-used formula largely asso-ciated with love verses (e.g., "A little swallow I'll become and come to your pillow . . ."). For him to be a "cloak-burner" is as silly as, the man suggests, it would be for a mere woman to try to sing good *man-dinadhes.* The use of a parody phrase is doubly mocking, since it also suggests that the woman's singing is mere hackwork, and that the man can run rings around it. But she was not yet out of the contest:

> *Sapia sanidhia   dhe pato,   yati   'kho   meghalia,*
> [On] rotten boards   I don't tread, because I have pride,
>
> *se tethia ipokimena dhe   dhidho simasia.*
> to such objects   I don't pay   attention [lit., "meaning"].

But the refusal to attribute "significance" was too much for a man to accept from a woman, and he turned on her the ultimate insult—the suggestion that all she was interested in was marrying into his patrigroup:

> *Me   tsi tomatas   to zoumi kam' alousa ke   lousou.*
> With the tomato's juice   make a bath and cleanse-yourself.

Dhe benis   *is to soi mas,*   *vghale t' apo*   *to nou sou.*
You aren't entering   our patrigroup,   get it   out of   your mind.

The force of this lay in the implication that the woman would herself
have no "meaning" unless she married, and that her own menfolk's
collective name was no match for that of the male singer's patrigroup.

This sequence illustrates some of the key features of competitive
mandinadha-singing. The constant play on over-familiar formulae, the
agile re-use of phrase structures, and the significant emphases given to
rhyming pairs are all devices that allow the performer to highlight the
quality of his performance. When the performer is a woman, the same
qualities seem to be appreciated; the man of this particular contest
seemed to harbor no resentment, and indeed expressed a barely qualified
admiration for his opponent, although he had certainly not hesitated to
take advantage of her female status for the purpose of scoring points off
her in the actual song duel. His admiration, however, entailed attributing
a quality of masculinity to her. A woman may engage in the performance
of manhood, but her doing so is conventionally treated by the men as
anomalous even if also impressive.

Much of the *mandinadha* humor is sexual, and this makes overt
confrontations between women and men difficult to sustain without giving
offense. This boisterous humor also goes with the more or less exclusively
masculine atmosphere of the *kantadha*—the rollicking progress of a
group of young men from house to house as they improvise bawdy couplets
on their way. One winter, while the snow still lay on the ground, we
wended our chilly way with one such group as its members put their
arms on one another's shoulders and sang uproariously, both *mandinadhes* and a couple of the more famous west Cretan *rizitika*. At each
house, they formed a dance circle while the woman of the house hastily
prepared food and drink. One inebriated member of the group paused
in the doorway of one house, and, catching sight of a tempting length
of sausage, cried out:

Tetia   andera   omorfi   dhen idha   sti zoi mou,
Such   a gut,   [so] fine,   I've not seen   in my-[entire]-life,

na 'ne   etsaparomia   osan tin edhiči mou!
that was   so   similar   (like) my-own!

If references to donkeys are insulting, they also form the basis of a
special category of *mandinadhes*. These are sets of couplets recounting
the reactions of various villagers to the death of an animal—not, in most
cases, one that people would ordinarily eat, but a beast of burden such
as a donkey or a mule. The verses satirize the personalities of the

neighbors. One bibulous elder is portrayed as counseling, "Sit down and let's think;/ we'll need wine, and we'll have to find some!" Another man who had many offspring "went and took its skin,/ to turn it into a blanket for his children to sleep on." A near-dwarf is ridiculed as "he was there but couldn't lift it [i.e., the meat],/ he could only lift everyone's [herding] sticks." When he threatened to leave the sticks behind if people didn't take him seriously, the song goes on, someone else told him that in that case he would tear up the notebook in which everyone's share was recorded. The point of these various satires is to underscore men's love of meat, which is so great that they may even eat it in the proscribed form of carrion, and are prepared to quarrel violently in order to increase their shares. Men actually did eat donkey meat in the harsher moments of the last war, but carrion is normally regarded as an abomination. The songs are therefore described as a "jest" (*kalambouri*)—but note that this term is also used in some embarrassment of the consumption of raw belly-fat. Men do vent their *eghoismos* in the eating of meat, and even these amiable caricatures are invested with a strong sense of what meat means to them.

The songs' foundation of seriousness is also revealed by their strongly contrasted treatment of women. Women are represented as peacemakers who try to calm the inflamed greed of their husbands. When one angry participant tells another that he won't get a single morsel, a woman cries out, "In this division [of goods], let only God judge!" It is a woman, again, who enjoins them "to share [it] out justly, because it is a sin [*amartia*]"—that is, to quarrel over the spoils. This concern with religious precepts is regarded as characteristically female behavior, and, despite the fact that the poets are themselves men, is juxtaposed in telling contrast with the excesses of men being men.

The versifiers themselves are somewhat nervous about the possible effects of their wit. One of them hesitated to tell me some of his verses because he felt that those who had been their butt might legitimately complain. He also sought permission before reciting the verses he invented, just to make sure that he could not be blamed for offending anyone's dignity. This concern is also shown in at least one of the texts:

Kondofthikhis' red mule died,
and nobody could be found to make up a song about it.
Eftikhis [the poet] goes down, makes his way to the coffeehouse
   (*doučani*),
and they all pressed him to make up a song about it.
"I want to make it up about it, but I want you to think [of this]:
if anyone objects, you're to attack him!"

It is enough for the hapless poet to show his manhood in making fun of everyone else. He does not want to get hurt, especially as his task is to satirize male violence itself. That satire encompasses the sympathetic treatment of women's attitudes, as well as barbs directed at individual foibles, and the very idea of eating donkey meat, especially carrion, is itself absurd enough to make fun of male values. The two active "donkey poets" now living in Glendi are both gentle and elderly men, exshepherds whose age and infirmity grant them the sort of licence that perhaps they need.

Glendiots regard jokes about their own system of values as a true index of manhood. Not only do they joke about the posturing of manhood itself, but they happily abuse the solemnities of more official forms and conventions. Two men, one of whom had invited the other to be his wedding sponsor (*koumbaros*), were joking. One was helping his mother and grandmothers make decorative pieces (*ploumista*; see illus. 13 and 14) for the wedding breads for which the region is famous, and his hand suddenly slipped. Said the other, "Gently, *re koumbare*, gently *re paliokoumbare* ['foul old wedding sponsor']!"—an unthinkably rude phrase in more sedate circles. "A 'heavy' phrase!" he then smirked at me. The other man remarked that their relationship was not to be taken too seriously, since the marriage had not yet taken place. But this jesting disrespect is certainly not the Greek norm.

Glendiots evidently enjoy playing with language. Their puns are constructed to poke fun at any kind of solemnity. Thus, while men's jokes do indeed seem to effect a symbolic reversal of local powerlessness (cf. Brandes 1980:133), they also make sly comments on the men's own desire for alliances and for other trappings of male power at the local level. One of the prospective *koumbari* just mentioned commented on what would happen once they were *real* spiritual kin. But instead of saying that they would "become serious [*tha sovaropiithoumene*]," he laughed, "We'll turn into underpants [*tha sovrakopiithoumene*]!" The competitive element in such verbal play is never long absent; but it also has the reflexive capacity to make fun of its own potential seriousness.

Word games also share another feature with the insulting verses, the animal raids, and the many practical jokes of male sociability (such as getting friends to push a truck on the grounds that it had broken down and then driving off at high speed). This is the effective use of opportunity. While these events may vary in the extent to which Glendiots are prepared to invest time and effort in them, they all provide a means of displaying the talents that define a man *as* a man. A pun or a practical joke, no less than a rhyming verse, may "fit" a situation, and this is what gives it "meaning." All these domains, moreover, allow men to "seize a bad hour from death"—that is, to turn the world's lies against the world itself, and to show that true men wrest humor from the very grip of fear. When they talk about raids, Glendiots do not deny the fear inside them; on the contrary, they regard it as enhancing their bravery and sense of adventure. But a man who can turn another's mockery into his own weapon is at least on the way to mastering that ultimate enemy within his own person.

In, Out, and Upside-down

If the foothills of Mount Ida are the setting for dangerous raiding contests, the many coffeehouses already given are no less unequivocally a male domain. Women do sometimes enter, especially the owners' wives and daughters who help with the work of preparing and serving drinks. But men still regard the coffeehouses as their own special arena within the village (see illus. 15). These establishments are where newspapers are passed around and avidly read, political issues are debated, lewd jokes are passed freely to and fro, and where round after round of drinks unite the company in a roaring fellowship.

Glendiot coffeehouses vary considerably in size, degree of modernity, and clientele. The largest and newest ones have vast glass panes for frontage, while older establishments may be little more than an enlarged cubbyhole in the side of a building. Several double as grocery stores, and almost all dispense a few perishables such as commercially produced confectionery.

Inside the coffeehouses, the all but inevitable portrait of Venizelos announces the masculine, because political and above all *Cretan*, character of the arena, a transcendant symbol that unites several levels of identity—Greek, Cretan, and local—through obvious divisions of present-day political interest and allegiance. Beside it, just as they might accompany the domestic icon of the Virgin at home, the proprietor's parents stare glumly out of framed photographs in stiff paired poses, dark shadows of the past in their Cretan waistcoats and kerchiefs. The proprietor serves from a counter where he can make coffee at a bottle-fed gas ring—the minimal equipment, along with the cold water tap, of all these establishments. All now also have a television set, often covered with a hand-embroidered cloth of the type self-consciously described as "Cretan embroidery" (see illus. 16 for several domestic examples of this style), and, while the programs of music and films are often ignored or

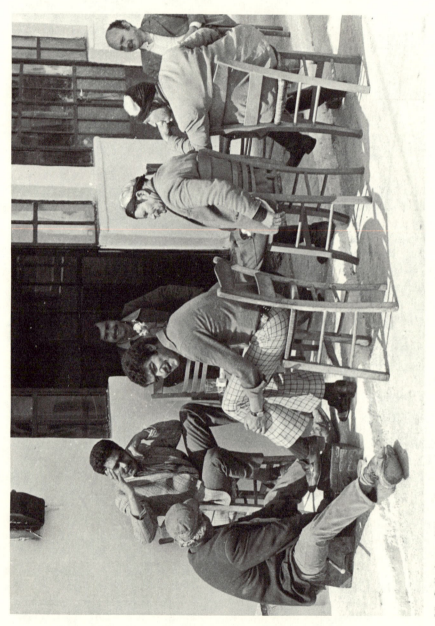

15. Coffeehouse life: outdoor scene in warm weather.

16. Identity on display: Cretan embroidery in the formal living room. (Note the *vouria*, or shepherd's bag, hanging on the wall.)

ridiculed, the news broadcasts usually excite avid attention and debate. Some coffeehouses boast a map of Cyprus as a declaration of national solidarity, and some also have maps of Crete or of the world.

The coffeehouse is a political arena, at once actual and expressive, in which the affairs of Glendi are analogized to those of the nation. The portraits and maps spell out the main rhetorical features of the analogy: solidarity, based on a familial trope, with the oppressed victims of external aggression against the Greek entity. Every so often, a man gets up to examine one of the maps in order to prove a point, or turn the television set up loud so that everyone can hear news affecting the national interest—and roundly curses anyone foolish enough to demand quiet for his own conversation or game of cards. Whatever one's personal reasons for being there, the coffeehouse is a model of the dangerous public world in which individuals, the village of Glendi, and the people of Greece at large are all exposed to the treachery of their foes.

Here, too, men vaunt their male identity in games of cards (illus. 17) and dice. Throwing dice for money, technically an illegal activity, is regarded as particularly something that shepherds do, and these men may gamble enormous sums—sometimes several thousand drachmas in an evening—on the whim of chance. Some card games are also played for high stakes, although the simpler games may involve only the price of a round of drinks or sweetmeats, or perhaps a kilo or two of meat. But even the less daring games are the medium of a rich, metaphorical discourse that plays out some of the essential themes of Glendiot manhood.

Card-game behavior reproduces features of two particularly prominent male domains: animal theft and bride abduction. Whereas these two domains require swift and often silent action, however, the card game provides a forum for skill in that other area of demonstrative masculinity, clever talk. The rules of the games themselves are fixed, and therefore of relatively little interest in the serendipitous idiom of Glendiot life. But the conversational gambits, well-timed gestures, and of course the flamboyant triumph of the winners are all legitimate themes in male interaction. Their insistent suggestion of the other two domains of masculine competitiveness lends spice to what would otherwise be a dully repetitive activity.

The Greek coffeehouse is not merely a markedly male location. It is also a place with "clear boundaries demarcating internal from external space, with a strong disposition to visual communication from outside looking in and vice versa" (Spyridonidis 1980:142). These physical dimensions are given symbolic expression in rules of etiquette that may

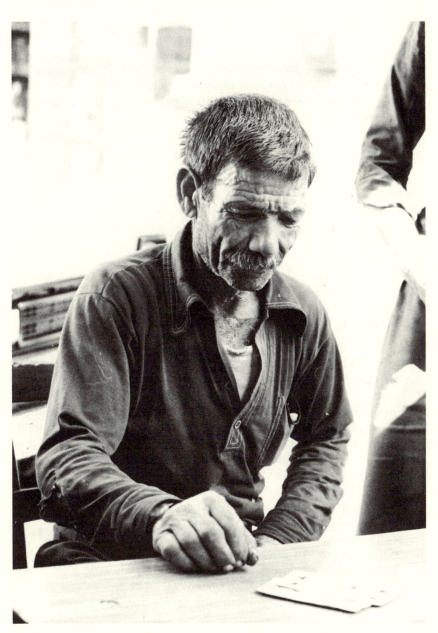

17. Card game.

be found, with slight variations, all over Greece. The Glendiot canon may be summarized as follows:

1. When he enters a coffeehouse, a man should greet all present, taking care that the sweep of his eyes take in the entire company.
2. Once he has done this, and only then, the others return his salutation, and he can sit down.
3. One of those already seated tells the proprietor, "Treat him (*čeras' tone*)!" The proprietor then asks the newcomer what he will have, and goes off to fetch it.
4. When the proprietor brings the drink, the one who is treating pays the proprietor, or puts the money on the tray or saucer. (One variation here is that a close kinsman may pre-empt the right to treat the newcomer at this juncture: treating is an honor, not a burden, and symbolizes reciprocal affection in the form of generosity.)
5. The newcomer raises his glass and toasts his benefactor, who replies with a suitable formula. From this point on, or sometimes even from the moment he sits down, the erstwhile newcomer has the right to treat those who enter after him.

These rules constitute a formal expression of manhood. Glendiots make this very clear when they contrast their own behavior with that of the east Cretans (people from the province of Sitia), whom they regard, furthermore, as *kaka andres*—"bad at being men"—because they are supposedly both "bean eaters" (i.e., not meat eaters and therefore of dubious manliness) and complaisant cuckolds. The most convincing demonstration of Sitian effeteness is, for the Glendiots, the allegation that among them it is often the man who *enters* who treats those already *seated*—a reversal, in short, of dignified male custom, and of the quintessentially male principles of hospitality.

Why should the seated men be obliged to offer hospitality to those who enter, rather than the other way around? First of all, to "sit" in Greek idiom connotes the ease of higher status; it implies that one does not, at that moment, perform manual labor, and that one is in possession of a specific physical space. In general, it is thought that a passer-by should always greet those who are seated, and that it is tactless for the latter to force the issue by initiating the exchange.

But the sharp sense of demarcated space is also a potent factor. One who enters is, in a stricly contextual sense, the inferior of those already inside. For this reason, anyone entering the village on foot is expected to greet those already there; the coffeehouse rule applies essentially the same basic principle. A less frequently articulated rule also has it that those who are walking *downhill* should greet others walking in an uphill direction. This is readily linked to the inside/outside opposition through the use of "going out" (*vyeno*) for "going up" (e.g., *vyeno st' aori*, "I'm going up the mountainside"). Since the higher ground is also the wild place—whether the mountain pastures are meant in relation to the village, or Glendi in relation to the city—it is those who come from the higher ground whose political inferiority is symbolized by their formal obligation to greet first. The animal thieves of Glendi are closer to nature, and this gives them a kind of *moral* superiority in Glendiot thinking: a man who thrives in such a harsh setting is a true "wild animal" (*therio*, an approving term) and must be "full of spirit" (*psikhomenos*). He has, as it were, made a virtue of his exclusion from the effeteness of "culture."

The rhetoric of spatial movement allows Glendiots to frame their political marginality in the wider Greek context. Thus, again, Iraklio—and the wealthier coastal plains generally—are known as *mesa*, "inside"[7] (fig. 7). To be "inside" is to have power; to be "outside" is to lack it. The symbolism of hospitality is similarly predicated on this rhetoric. While Glendiots would certainly deny any attribution of *permanent* inferiority to the guest, a *contextual* inferiority is entailed by the act of hospitality itself. Glendiot hosts not only vie with each other to treat strangers; they are also engaged in a continual competition with one another. Thus, the treat (*kerasma* or *trattarisma*) establishes a fleeting advantage for the giver, an advantage which the latter is expected to redress in the ordinary course of village interaction. Yet the same act of establishing a temporary obligation (*ipokhreosi*) between host and guest also *equalizes* the relationship between the newcomer and the rest of the company. Once he has sat down and accepted his treat, he is on an equal footing with the others and so can be admitted to their more immediate contests over dice or cards.

Contests they most certainly are. One of my own most frequent card-playing companions would announce, "Let's clash lances [*na konda-rokhtipisomene*]!" Card games are often described as "struggling," and valiant opponents as *pallikaria* ("fine young men"). Some basis of opposition beyond that of a friendly game is usually sought; when two kinsmen of different generations were matched against each other, even though they were fairly close in age, an onlooker jocularly justified the whole situation by announcing that it was a contest between the old and the young. Almost every move is made with aggressive gestures, especially by the striking of the knuckles against the table as each card is flung down; note that "knuckle" (*kozi*) is the standard term for political influence of the kind that a man of long local experience and a tough reputation might be expected to possess. And a card player's revenge

Fig. 7. The symbolic organization of inclusion and exclusion: island, village, and coffeehouse.

for earlier humiliation is "returning the blood," just as in the vocabulary of vengeance killing. Clearly, card games provide a symbolic enactment of concerns that elsewhere might cost men their reputations and even their lives. I once heard a Glendiot admonishing players in a vein that sharply reminded me of the origins of some of our own technical discourse: "Now you'll play agonistically [*edha tha pekste aghonistika*]!"

Card games are thus a medium for the expression of contest in emblematic form. They particularly convey the paradoxical sense of potential loss inherent in winning any kind of contest. The winner is said to have "come out"; he is now exposed, as it were, to the others' desire to wreak vengeance upon him in turn. The loser, as the one who is now left symbolically "inside," treats the winner, and thus redresses the imbalance created by his defeat. Card games express the disturbing ease with which positive contests of generosity merge conceptually with negative contests of violence, since the loser suffers material humiliation; but they also, conversely, mediate the transformation of downright hostility into alliances based on mutual respect. The violence is there, in the metaphorical "clash of lances" and in the rich sexual insults the players trade. But the obligation that the loser treat the victor reproduces the transformational relationship between contest and alliance. Just as every cycle of theft may end in spiritual kinship, and perhaps too as killings may in rare cases result in marriage, card players actually roar *sindekne* at each other as they slam their cards on the table. A contest ideally ends in commensality: "[We steal] to make friends."

Card games are accompanied by some distinctive speech idioms that strongly reinforce the metaphorical relationship between the several domains of agonistic discourse in Glendi. A highly specific phrase that is used of a youth's initiation into animal theft, for example, is sometimes also applied to teaching a novice card player: "I brought you out on the branch [*s' evghala sto kladhi*]." More generally, men assess their own performances in card games in terms of manliness. But perhaps the most noticeable feature is the frequent feminization of the names of the cards themselves.

Men talk about the cards as though they were immoral women. Some villagers have developed distinctive phrases of their own, and, as one might expect, improvisation is common. When the game seems to be going against a man, he may exclaim, "She/it [the card, or perhaps the luck of the game] doesn't want me!"—the formulaic plaint of the rejected suitor. Many of the other expressions are less decorous:

1. The king (*righas*) may be called by feminized forms of *Kostas* (the informal form of *Konstandinos*, name of the locally despised

last king of Greece). The suffix -*ara* (in *Kostara*) implies a large, sexually well-endowed woman. One player also called the king both *Kostarina* (another mockingly feminized form) and *koumbara* ("ritual kinswoman [through a marriage sponsorship]"); the latter seems to have been intended as a slur on the "woman's" sexual charms, since sexual relations with ritual kin are strictly pro- scribed—an old man lamented the passing of his virility by saying, "My wife and I have become *sindekni* [i.e., 'spiritual kin through baptism,' and hence debarred by incest prohibitions from having sexual relations]."

2. The queen (*dama*) is often called *poutana* ("whore") or *roufiana* ("female pimp"). Another term is *vroma* ("stink," used with the specific implication of sexual corruption). A game that has gone badly may be said to have "stunk" or have "been corrupted"; again there is a strong if implicit suggestion of the sexual pollution that brings failure to any male enterprise—a theme taken up also in the way men attribute losing a game to sexual contact the night before.

3. The jack (*vales*) is known as *poustis*, "passive homosexual"; the same term is sometimes also used of the king. Both the jack and the king may also be called *pappas* ("priest"), a sobriquet with strong suggestions of sexual immorality and betrayal. A player objected to a kibbitzer who kept giving his hand away, "Are you a devil or a priest?"

4. Number cards are ordinarily known by a compound of the number plus neuter suffix (e.g., *dhio* ["two"], + -*ari*, > *dhiari*). Players frequently feminize these forms (*dhiara*; cf. *Kostara*, above [#1]).

5. One player usually calls any four "the devil's house." It is a house because it is square, he explains; and cards are generally associated with the devil, as are loose women.

6. The ace is sometimes glossed with one of the several terms for "penis" because, as a player explained, it is single.

That the instruments of aggression should also be the objects of pos- session fits with the larger idiom (cf. also Meeker 1979:18). The male organ is feminized (e.g., as a *pistola*) when the emphasis is on its large size, as is the male himself (*andrella*, < *andras*, "man"; compare also the ironical *papadhella*, "great BIG priest"). Another powerful instru- ment, the "pencil" which "writes" down the alleged political misde- meanors of Greek citizens—this comes from the symbolism of police bureaucracy—is a *moliva* (for *molivi*). In attacking their opponents' possessions, Glendiot men are deploying their own, equally vulnerable instruments. "I screw his female kin group!" exclaimed one man of a hated conservative politician. "I screw the cards you're playing!" yelled another, during a game. Villagers commit their own resources, feminized to symbolize the basic opposition between possessor and possessed, to the capture of those of their rivals. The ultimate insult is therefore to represent those men as themselves reduced to the objects of the competition. Such is the implication of the contemptuous dismissal of sheep thieves, especially by those who have decided that animal theft is not a manly pursuit, as "sheep men" or "sheep *sindekni*" (*provatandres* or *provatosindekni*). It is no longer clear whether the sheep or the thieves are primary: the aggressors have merged with the passive objects of their contest.

Good players are like animals in heat. They remember their opponents' cards, giving force to the pun *"thimizi"* ("he's in heat," for *thimate* ["he remembers"]). Their violent knuckle rapping on the table is suggestive, too; *khtipao*, "strike," the verb for this action, is a common metaphor for the man's role in the sexual act, as indeed is *pezo* ("play"). A winner is told, "You're ploughing straight" (*dreta sernis to zigho*)—an explicitly acknowledged metaphor for copulation. But success is denied to the man who has already been polluted by sexual contact. When a player begins to lose consistently, bystanders taunt him, "You were baptizing all night!"—another common metaphor for sexual activity, and one that perhaps gives an ironic twist to the constant cries of *sindekne!*

The explanation here is that a man who has "gone with his woman" is *ghoursouzis*, "unclean." This term is also applied to men who steal animals from their covillagers, to those who are thought to have the evil eye (a sign of envy), and to those who cheat at cards. In each case, the implication is of illicit competition. Thus, the man who has recently had sexual relations is symbolically equivalent to the one who plays foul. All female sexuality is regarded by men as potentially polluting; it is of no significance in this context whether it was with one's own wife or not. One player, finding that he was losing, grabbed the genitals of his prepubescent son on the grounds that the latter's sexual innocence might help his own game; on another occasion, doing the same thing to an older but handicapped man, he simply explained, "Virginal!"

Freedom from sexual contact is clearly associated with success in the battle against other men. In earlier days, or so at least it is said, men would abstain from sex before going off to do battle with the Turks; raping Turkish women, on the other hand, was less serious, because it was essentially an attack on their husbands. One villager described animal theft as *magharisma*, "pollution," thereby emphasizing once again the sense of homology that connects these various domains.

Taking an opponent's cards is thus a sexual attack on his person. A losing player may therefore "castrate" his opponent in order to gain advantage. He does this by dealing the starting cards from the bottom of the pack instead of leaving the dealer to deal them himself from the top, often prefacing this action with the gleeful announcement, "I'll castrate you [*tha se mounoušiso*]!" What he does here is, first of all, to invert a conventional action. More than that, he takes the action entirely away from the dealer, thereby suggesting a kind of impotence: he has been asked to "cut" the deck of cards, and he "cuts" further than he has been asked. The action recalls animal theft here, since the removal of sheep from the flock is also called "cutting," and one of the worst insults that a thief can pay his victim is to cut off the bells of the male animals. Depriving one's opponent of his manhood in this way is supposed to lead to a change of fortune: "the card changes." But it also leads to jesting cries of "Shame!" and to ribald suggestions that the victim's wife will be furious with him: wives are jokingly supposed to keep a sexual tally and to demand that their husbands make up for any missed nights.

There is another act of symbolic reversal that expresses contempt for an opponent: leaving the cards one has captured from him upside-down (i.e., face upwards). To do this stresses the fact that, once captured, these cards are no longer of interest; the analogy with dishonored womanhood is obvious, the more so as the expression used of cards so displayed—*anaskela* (lit., "with their legs in the air")—is formulaically associated with the loss of female chastity. One player actually objected to having a card turned up like this, saying that it was "like the *anaskela* woman" and indicating with a very explicit gesture that he meant one who was easy prey; the physical reversal of a woman's body provides such an apt expression for the loss of chastity that Campbell reports for the Sarakatsani that women actually avoid running for fear that they might trip up (1964:287). The same player, commenting on another's victory, remarked, "He's gotten her out [*evghalen ti*]!"—an expression that suggests sexual exposure at the same time as simply "winning" (see Herzfeld 1979). A card that cannot be put down without being captured may be described as a woman's barren sexual organ. The inference seems clear enough: the pivotal idiom of "possession" articulated in these games is sexual. In accounts of animal theft, this is still more significant, as the act of theft is metaphorically transformed into one of sexual conquest: hence, once again, the "harem" metaphor for flocks owned by Turks. In card games, too, this further analogy is implicitly recognized by at least some players, including the one who repeatedly puns that "nines" (*ennia*) are "lambs" (*arnia*).

The analogies between animal theft and sexual seduction are also recognized at yet another level. Young Glendiot men may claim to have easy sexual access to lowland women, for example, whereas highland women are normally only accessible through marriage—a contrast that parallels the opposition between one-way raids against lowland village flocks and reciprocal raiding among highland communities. This reinforces the Glendiots' contemptuous association of lowlanders with bean eating, cuckoldry, and promiscuity—in other words, with a universe in which the differences between women and men are as unclear as the distinction between possessed and possessor.

The analogy between card games and the conventions of sexual access is also realized in an inverse way: close kin, spiritual kin, and affines rarely play against each other. Where the stakes are high, they avoid doing so altogether; but even when the stakes are comparatively trivial, the avoidance principle provides a good excuse if a man happens not to feel like playing. Those who avoid playing each other at cards are also those who cannot enter into further affinal relations with each other: they may not "take" (a common convention for "marry") women from each other's immediate families. Marriage is a transformation of hostility into friendship and alliance; at the moment it happens, the groom's party may still taunt the bride's people in a *mandinadha* that "we have taken your best bride!" Once the affinal link has been established, however, any further demonstration of tension is considered unseemly and potentially disruptive.

In accordance with the analogy between card games and the competitive search for affinal alliances, then, those who are already linked avoid the risk of anger. When large sums are involved, card games can lead to real violence. Symbolically, too, card games between closely related men are as "incestuous" as internecine quarrels. If women are regarded by men as the source of discord, and above all of "deviltries" (*dhiaolies*), so are cards. Once a hostile relationship has been converted into a productive one, morality dictates that the partners avoid anything that might reverse that process. But competition between closely related men is best avoided from the start: the fickleness of cards, like the unreliability of women, could easily prompt violence between those who are supposed to hold a special affection for each other.

From the foregoing discussion, we can see very clearly the parallels between the three domains of male interaction that give metaphorical force to the card game in particular. The players do not themselves comment on those parallels, and seem reluctant to consider even the possibility of their existence very seriously. This does not mean that they are ethnographically irrelevant. It may indicate a measure of embarrassment about the sexual implications of the idiom, reinforced by an equal measure of discomfort at discussing abduction and animal theft out of their appropriate contexts. But it also, significantly, recalls the well-known reluctance of performers and artists in more familiar settings to examine the multiplicity of meanings their work can evoke (cf. Jakobson 1980:88-89). Inasmuch as card games allude to other kinds of social conflict, they do so in a highly generalized, noncontextual way; and this is the source of their poetic impact. When a player uses a novel term for one of the cards, feminizing it in accordance with the poetic principles involved but in such a way as to highlight his own ingenuity, he does not necessarily want to think about the wider ramifications of his performance; indeed, to do so might very possibly spoil the effect. But the effect is there.

I have suggested that Glendiot men rejoice in the very uncertainty of their lives, since it this that gives them the chance to demonstrate their improvisational skills. In playing cards, that improvisation is most obviously realized in the inventiveness of their conversational idiom—always, however, within the limits set by the guiding analogies between the game itself and other domains of male interaction. The structural principles remain constant. For example, the analogy between incest prohibitions and the conventions of card playing also applies to animal theft: once a potentially antagonistic relationship between a Psiliot and a Glendiot shepherd has been converted into *sindeknia*, for example, these two men are as unlikely to square off over cards—at least in public—as two affines or two brothers.

Card games thus epitomize, in a clearly framed setting, the uses of personal style for converting uncertainty into truce. Although they may occasionally lead to violence, the very fact that they take place in the coffeehouses means that the sources of restraint are at hand. They thus express a potentiality that, in the domains of bride abduction and animal theft, is more often realized when confrontation ends in violent death. But they also express the guiding principle that tension, opposition, and well-matched guile are ultimately the best foundations for alliance.

CHAPTER FIVE

STEALING TO BEFRIEND

"Coming out on the branch"

"Coming out on the branch" is the phrase used of the young Glendiot male's first theft. It is strongly reminiscent of the expression by which, in pre-independent Greece, men used to signify their joining forces with the outlaw groups that plagued both the Turks and the wealthier Greeks.[1] Whether its recurrence in Glendi represents a conscious allusion to national history it is no longer possible to tell; but it certainly implies a degree of conventionality in the initiation of young animal thieves.

Glendiots attribute the continuation of animal theft to several features. Prominent among these are political patronage and the social environment of the village. In the latter category is included the group of friends and peers to whose pressure every Glendiot adolescent is subject. The usual pattern whereby a shepherd boy is initiated into raiding is for an older boy to make the suggestion; the younger lad hopes—often in vain on the first occasion—to make a symbolic claim to manhood:

> I remember the first time that I went on such a "tale," stealing.
> I was with a young lad, the first year that I left school. Thirteen years old! And we set off in the morning, of course we didn't go very far, [in fact we went] very nearby, we went and took five sheep.
> Well, we brought them to their destination, to our own place, but my mother . . . and my friend's father didn't know where we had gone. They were so anxious that they left here during the night and came looking for us up there with the sheep. They found us.
> "Where have you been?"
> Said I, "Nowhere!"
> Afterwards, in the morning, the man who owned the sheep came, and he turned out to be someone we knew. And he took them again and left. Untouched!

>   And we, now, my friend and I, said, "Look what idiots we are
> . . . to go and walk all night and not even get any meat to eat!

This account immediately foregrounds the essential features: the initial responsibility of someone else for the "education" of the young thief, the mother's opposition, the defiant attempt at claiming autonomy ("Said I, 'Nowhere!' "), and the failure of that first expedition judged in terms of meat eating. Particularly noticeable is the specific reason for that failure. The victim was a "friend"—in other words, someone with whom the boys' families had social links. One lesson that still needed to be learned was how to attack people who were socially far enough removed; note how, in this account, the lack of social distance appears to be symbolized by *geographical* proximity. It takes bravery and experience to travel far on the mountainside by night. Equally, however, it was important for these boys to learn an object lesson: if you steal from an ally, you are obliged to return the stolen animals without demur. This, too, is a principle of manhood.

Another young thief was more fortunate. His daring provided a means for creating an alliance of his own, symbolized in this case by his eventual acquisition of an appropriate token:

>   I was then eleven years old. Well, and it was Christmas Eve.
> Christmas Eve! Well, we then had about thirty sheep, my father
> was poor in those days, very poor.

Note the framing of the discourse in terms of poverty. After some more circumstantial detail to back up this claim, the speaker began to describe the theft and its consequences:

>   One evening, there was another person from this part of our village
> here, he was older, he was three years ahead of me in age. Now,
> as we were chatting, he says to me, "Why don't we go find some
> animal or other? To eat?" (I was then a young lad, I tell you, it was
> the first time I went [rustling]). "Hey, you, why don't we go?"
>   "Let's go!"
>   "Shall we go?"
>   "Let's go!"
>   So we got away from there and went to the territory of Tholos.
> Eh! Both of us, young lads together, we gathered the sheep to-
> gether—as they were in the flock, so we gathered them.
>   Well, to take an animal, you have to gather it in. And [so] we
> were collecting them in and I took one, a sheep, and he took two
> lambs. This was suckling time.
>   And I took a sheep with its lamb, and [then also] another sheep.

Well, we brought them away from there, and took them to a cottage. And we slaughtered the lamb on the spot, the one that didn't have its mother, we slaughtered the lambs [*sic*], and we skinned it and hung it and finally roasted it on the spit, each one of us taking half.

Meanwhile, they were looking for us in the village. Of course I used to go down [there] every evening with the sheep, and that evening I hadn't gone down at all. Like, [they must have thought], something's up!

Well then, Damianos [the speaker's brother], who was also a young lad at the time, came. We of course had eaten the lamb and stayed out there, and we'd slept in the cottage. In the morning we got up. I see my own sheep right there! They hadn't moved from there at all. And we went down bit by bit, and saw our sheep, so to speak, each his own—both mine and my friend's. And suddenly we see Damianos down below, our own [family member]. He shouts from where he's standing, but of course we got afraid. He said that he'd beat us to smithereens. And we didn't get close.

Meanwhile, the other boy's father comes up. Well then, I then took the sheep and came down here to the village.

The next day, the man who owned them came here to the village and was asking about them. Well, that was my first theft, and they even got them [i.e., the sheep] back from us, eh? They got them back from us!

In other words, the man who owned the sheep was friendly with my father, very friendly. And he asked my father. Said he, "This and that['s happened], I've had a sheep stolen from me, one that was suckling its lamb. Just ask your boy whether maybe he saw anything, whether he knows anything, whatever."

My old man comes to me and asks, he says, "You are [responsible for this], maybe you know something?"

I was then just a lad and I wouldn't deceive my father, so I told him all about it. I told him, "So on and so forth, we took them!" I told him.

Well, we did manage to eat the lamb [before we were found out], and the fellow afterwards took the other sheep with its lamb and left. He'd learned about the sheep, he learned about it [i.e., where it was], so to speak. He didn't make any [official] accusation or anything.

But when he took the sheep away, he just told my father that I should go the next year to get one [from him], he'd give me a lamb. And I did go and he did make a gift of it to me! He really made a gift of it to me! . . . Perhaps, let's say, because he wanted things fixed up good and proper, so I wouldn't go stealing from him again.

As he'll have said, "The boy's 'coming out on the branch' now. . . . Now he's growing up, and he's 'coming out,' and I'd better give him a lamb so he won't come this way again. . . ."

It was just as he foresaw, so to speak: on account of the lamb he gave me, we later became friends.

This was an embryonic success: the young thief, though found out through the normal channels of mediation, had made an immediate impression on his victim, and was consequently able to acquire a meat animal as a contribution to his own flock. Gift giving is a constant theme in the raiding narratives, since it symbolizes the transformation of hostile reciprocity into reciprocity of more positive kinds. The possession of animals and meat, too, serves as an index of a boy's accession to manhood. One exshepherd recalled how, caught almost red-handed on his first theft, he was forced to return the meat of the animal he and his companion had stolen and slaughtered; the fat (*ksinji*), specially set aside as a valued delicacy, had fallen to the ground while they were handing the meat over, so he picked it up and hastily stuffed it inside his shirt.

The first theft seems to be a memorable event for many shepherds. It is an initiation, however informal, into manhood, and the narratives systematically formalize the experience to fit the rhetoric of male identity. Almost every such narrative I heard concluded with a reference to the acquisition of animals (dead or alive) or to the creation of an alliance, or (as happened with the lad who so impressed his victim as a potential threat) to both at once. The event is well understood to mark an *experience of passage*:

> I was then, I think, thirteen years old. And I went with another person, and the two of us went [raiding].
>
> But it seemed very strange to me, like, how can I put it to you now? I took on a certain "air," so to speak, I took on manliness (*andria*) inside myself, even though I was still a child.
>
> Eh, and after that, I went on [raiding], but, to tell you the truth, I don't steal very much now.

The "air" he acquired is what the thief who has acquired a political patron also feels: the term connotes the swagger that the tough, well-protected, and self-sufficient youth must adopt in order to hold his own.

Stealing poses an excruciating moral problem for the young thief's parents. On the one hand, they are afraid that he may get hurt if he

ventures out prematurely, and they know that once a young man is
committed to raiding he enters a pattern of dangerous activity which, at
least in earlier days, was all but irrevocable. They also worry that the
joy that successful animal thieves claim to feel when they are out raiding
will deter him from aiming for a more ambitious profession; where once
shepherding was regarded as the height of a male Glendiot's ambition,
it is now seen by many as a demeaning life of toil. On the other hand,
however, they are forced to recognize that as a shepherd he will need
to know how to steal, since otherwise he will not be able to acquire a
sufficiently fierce reputation to protect his own flocks from the depredations of others.

The best situation from a parent's point of view is when the lad uses
his own initiative and is not caught. Then he can safely and legitimately
take some pride in his son's prowess, and even perhaps offer a little
advice:

My first *klepsa* ("theft") happened when my father was on his own.

He also didn't have many sheep because people were striking at
[i.e., stealing from] him. He didn't have brothers to graze [the
animals, and so help protect the flocks against raids].

So he was on his own, that is; he had about a hundred sheep,
so to speak, so he was afraid, so to speak, was my father, because,
like I told you, he didn't have brothers, so to speak, so there was
no one to work with him. With the kind of people we've got around
here, if you're going to keep sheep, other people have got to be
afraid that you'll take [animals from them]. Covillagers as well as
outsiders, let's say!

At that time, as a lad, I used to go up [into the foothills], and
he told me, says he, "Stamatis," says he, "So-and-so has stolen a
sheep from us"—a ram, rather. . . . I was furious, even though I
was just a child.

Of course I said nothing to my father—but, say I, "How can I
take revenge on him without my father knowing, so to speak?" I
get up and go. . . . But I was afraid of just about everything, let's
say. . . .

I say to myself, "I can't just take a sheep. . . ." So . . . I cut
many branches, and throw them down into a *sfendona* ["sling," i.e.,
a kind of concealed lair], as we call it, and I hide under there
among the branches.

Paff! and I grab one! A billy-goat, so to speak!

And I cut off its bell—I couldn't take *it* to our own sheepfold, so to speak, and I took off its one bell. So I removed the bell and took it to our sheepfold, so to speak.

Says my father to me, "Where did you find the bell?" so to speak. "How did you find it?" so to speak. "How did you get the billy-goat? Where did you find it?"

Say I, "Father, do you remember that night, the other day when you told me that So-and-so from Stalia had 'eaten' a billy-goat, and so forth?"

Says he, "Yes, my boy."

"Eh, I went and did thus and so, and took off its bell and brought it [here]."

So he says to me, "Now look here, you, why didn't you bring," says he, "the billy-goat?"

Say I, "Father, I couldn't, because it was a big one and I couldn't drag it along."

He says to me, "What'll become of you," he says to me, "my little brave, when you grow up and bring me the billy-goat as well!"

The striking act of defiance—removing a male goat's bell is a far more serious insult than simply stealing an animal—seems to have won paternal approval.

But a father never actively encourages his sons to go out on a raid, however much his stories may initially awaken their desire for adventure. The initial impetus usually comes from a slightly older boy. One father, claiming to know that his son did go animal rustling, threatened that *if he caught him at it* there would be trouble, and this seems to be the point: a father may be impressed by a son's daring in retrospect, but it would be poor training for the kind of self-sufficiency that a thief needs for the father to be actively involved in the boy's initial attempts. That a child seems healthily cunning enough is one matter—the day one male baby was brought back to Glendi from the town hospital where most children are now born, his delighted great-uncle exclaimed, "Tonight he'll go on a raid!"—but no parent wants the direct responsibility for actually training a new thief. Indeed, with today's increasing concern that the shepherd's life is not a boy's best future, fathers who were once notoriously successful animal thieves themselves are anxious to conceal the bad example from their own children. For once a boy has experienced the joy of *klepsa*, Glendiots have come to suspect that he may never want to change profession.

Like women who criticize their husbands and sons for raiding but help them conceal the spoils when danger lurks, so, too, the fathers of young animal thieves may display a marked ambivalence:

> We went to a *mitato* [stone-built shepherds' hut], put the animals in there, and there, of course, we slaughtered them, roasted them, and ate them, too!
>
> And in the morning, just as day was dawning, here comes my father!
>
> He had learned that I'd gone off raiding. Some other people told him, people from here that I used to hang around with. They told him, "Tonight Stelios isn't here."
>
> "Where's he off to?"
>
> "He's off on a raid!" (. . .)
>
> And my father comes. . . . He says to me, "Look how you won't behave yourself, but just go off all night, now what've you done? And what's happened to you?" Well, so he says to me, "What did you do to him?"
>
> "What should I have done? We went after his animals, only what are we to do with them," I say to him, "with these animals?"
>
> So he tells me, "In such-and-such a place there's a hole in the ground, go and put them there until we see what's up."

Paternal disapproval is gradually transformed into involvement as it is overcome by the prospect of serious trouble.

A mother's disapproval is often far more severe. The boy who managed to salvage the fat from his first stolen animal thereupon took to the hills for two days and nights for fear that his mother would give him a memorable hiding. Hunger finally drove him home, and the expected punishment did not materialize. Nevertheless, he recalled, he was afraid of her reaction; mothers did not want their sons to become "thieves" (*kleftes*), no matter how skilled. Another irate mother made it quite clear that her domain and that of raiding should remain entirely apart:

> My mother didn't want such things [as stolen meat], so to speak, in the house. She didn't like thefts, so to speak. Nor did she eat [stolen] meat, she still doesn't eat any now. If you tell her it's stolen [*klepsimeiko*], she doesn't eat any at all! She tells you, "Get it out of the house!"
>
> And they [the owners of some animals he had stolen] were hunting me. She said to me, "Don't [bring it in here]!"
>
> I'm telling you, that was the first time I went home (with such a thing, I mean).

On the mountainside I used to steal, so to speak, I used to "eat,"
but [only] on the mountainside [*aori*]. At home, however—no!

The demarcation between home and *aori* sharply reproduces that between
the domains of women and men, respectively. Note that the speaker
almost sounds as though he were saying that his mother *did not eat*:
from a male point of view, a meal without meat is no meal. At the same
time, for the young male roving the mountainside in search of his prey,
eating and stealing were virtually synonymous. Only a weakling would
eat his own animals when there were others to be had. But what had
clearly irritated the narrator in this tale was the fact that his mother had
flatly refused to *admire* the evidence of his manliness: "She didn't want
to give it any importance (*simasia*) at all!" The Glendiot concept of
"meaning," *simasia*, includes the specifically social aspects of significance; and these—especially between men and women—are open to
disagreement.

An adolescent thief does not usually learn all at once. Early errors
are recalled with raucous amusement:

It was Easter. And we . . . found a lamb. We poor souls didn't
know how to skin it, so we got it surrounded and one of us took
hold of it and pulled by the feet and the other by the skin. And we
took its skin off, we managed it, and we stripped it and roasted it
and ate it!

Despite such embarrassing first attempts, a boy's experiences may
nevertheless prepare him well for the tougher and usually more dangerous
exploits that we will have to perform by the time he has a large flock of
his own. In the following account, a boy learns not only the risk of
treachery from those weaker than himself, but also the folly of attempting
to involve the Divine Will in one's deviltries:

I was a young lad out with the sheep. And two other young
covillagers of mine were grazing other sheep nearby, and I had
mine. And they went and stole a sheep. . . .

But they weren't capable of slaughtering and skinning it. I was
older. They tell me, "We got a sheep that we've got over there,
ready for slaughtering."

So I slaughtered it and skinned it, and we roasted it.

The lads [i.e., the victims] found the ones who had the sheep
out, and got hold of them. They [the boy thieves] told them, "We've
slaughtered it."

"With whom, hey?" They say, "Vassiloftikhis slaughtered it."

I was older than they were!

So they came and took us to put us on oath. . . . Three big brave lads, with me just a young boy! And I was afraid, and they didn't [actually] tell me that I'd stolen it.

"I didn't take it myself, the boys took it, they got it out of the *koumos* [hole in the ground], and then I went there."

"But *you* slaughtered it!"

I denied it. I had my hand on the icon of the Virgin Mary, listen to a miracle! Say I, "No, I didn't slaughter it."

The icon falls away to the ground!

Skilled thieves are reluctant to take others less experienced than themselves on a raid; the risk of exposure is simply too great. As for taking a false oath, that is a truly heinous offense, and the narrator here was lucky that it happened in a relatively trivial context. He had already learned some of the tricks, of course. In particular, he was familiar with the *koumos*, described in more detail by another expert thief:

A *koumos* is, in a hole where there are many stones, you find some sort of hollow and so you shape it out more or less regularly. . . . In the ground, so to speak, like a hole; and you put a rock on top, maybe two rocks, and the animal is inside, and if you pass by there you can't see it at all.

Initiation into manhood is marked by the acquisition of wisdom such as this. But it is not enough to know how to steal; that knowledge must be convincingly exhibited for a youth to win the respect he craves from older men. A boy of about fifteen was taken by his uncle to visit an older and more experienced shepherd, who was engaged in the annual shearing (*koures*, illus. 18) of his flock:

"Let's go . . . and have him treat us to two or three cigarettes."

Eh, in those days, where would you even *see* cigarettes? I'd be up on the mountainside for a whole month, so to speak, and I might have smoked five cigarettes, maybe ten, the whole month!

Their host treated everyone else, but assumed that my informant was too young to smoke:

Say I, "Thanks," I tell him, "eh, I don't smoke," I tell him.

I *did* smoke, of course. But since he points me out and calls me a young lad, I was immediately angry, Mikhalis [i.e., MH], and I say to myself right there, "Look at that now!" Say I, "I'll tell you soon enough whether I'm young!"

Such self-control marked this youth as already a skilled player. His

18. *Koures*: shearing the flock.

diplomatic response enabled him to steal a sheep from the offender without being suspected. He told his companion from the original visit what he had done:

> "But if he gets to hear of it, he'll kill you, you wretch!" (. . .)
>
> In other words, he was again struggling to "break" it [i.e., the enmity], telling me that I shouldn't hang onto my hatred, so to speak. "You shouldn't've!" he says to me. "It's unseemly." "I was dead right to do it, just eat if you want to. If you want to, eat. If not, don't! Just don't say a word." Yes. "You don't want to eat? [Then] get out of here! If you do want to, sit down and eat, and not a whisper!"
>
> "Eh, what the devil am I to do? What?" says he. "I'll eat," he tells me, "so there!"
>
> So we roasted and ate it; and afterwards he told the old man, my grandfather.
>
> Now, my grandfather was someone who had very good relations with the other fellow. So the next day my grandfather was furious [with me]: "Monkey! Cuckold! Scum! From now on you're not to do such things to me, so to speak and so forth!"

At this juncture, the youth's companion (his uncle) explains the circumstances to the irate grandfather:

> So then my grandfather gets up and goes on his own to their *mitato*. He tells him, "The lad did thus and such, *sindekne*, just don't go looking for your sheep. . . ."
>
> "Yes, but are you really serious?" he asks him. . . . "*Poooo!* Look at that," says he, "and I didn't take him seriously," says he, "not a bit. . . ."

A clear message was received. It was further reinforced by the youth's skill at timing, an aspect of personal style that foregrounds the basic theme of reciprocated slight (see also Bourdieu 1977:6). A boy who quickly learns the art of self-control, so necessary for effective social interaction, can expect to be accounted a man within only a few years.

Not all young Glendiot men learn equally fast, or show an aptitude for these high-risk skills. Some may seek their fortune in other ways; one Skoufas who hated the pastoral life with a passion emigrated briefly to the United States, and has since returned to set up a small but profitable business. Neither intelligence nor large-patrigroup membership guarantees aptitude for *klepsa*, though these attributes certainly help. Among those who do remain, "with the sheep," moreover, there is a considerable range of variation in their respective abilities both as herders and as thieves. The rhetoric of "hunger" and meat eating is learned early, and virtually all the accounts of raiding channel experience through these conventions; but even here, personal narrative style is subject to wide fluctuations of vocabulary, brevity, and self-awareness. The *kala kleftis*, the man who is "good at being a thief," however, has to be his own advocate. Men learn young how to spice their raiding stories with "pepper"—not necessarily in the form of lies, but certainly as a narrative skill that reproduces the inventive agility needed for the raids themselves. If the narratives reproduce the quality of raiding, moreover, it is also true that the raids in turn possess some of the expressive properties of narrative. Glendiot idiom recognizes this in the use of *istoria*, "tale," for any exciting event, be it interpersonal violence or adventure in the foothills. "We'll have 'tales'" means that serious quarrels are anticipated. But the term is particularly apposite for animal raids, in which Glendiots are usually eager to acknowledge expressive skills. As the shepherd with whom I began this chapter recalled: "I remember the first time I went on *such a tale*."

"We steal to make friends"

Once a young shepherd has "come out on the branch," he is usually anxious to establish his autonomy as a man to be reckoned with. The first attempts, often ending in varying degrees of ignominy, give way to a more concerted campaign of aggression, directed against those whose reputation recommends them as useful allies. In these more serious raids, the younger man tries to provoke his victim into retaliation, which—in theory, at least—calls for the theft of twice as many animals as were taken in the first raid.

Raid and counterraid eventually lead third parties to intervene. Although this was his objective, the young aggressor initially resists all attempts to mediate, as does the older shepherd. Both are obliged to make a brave show of contempt for each other, and both eventually submit on the ostensible grounds that they are doing a "favor" (*khatiri*) to the mediators, who are usually their kinsmen or spiritual kin. As a solution to the dispute, the mediators usually propose that one of the principals baptize a child from among the close agnates of the other. This, in fact, was the aggressor's original goal—"friends" is often a synonym for *sindekni*—and it may also suit the older man, if he is anxious to store up some useful sources of protection against the all too rapid advance of old age. From the moment of agreement, the principals address each other as *sindekne*, and are morally bound never to raid each other again. More than that, they are supposed to help each other when yet others raid their flocks, and especially to serve as *arotikhtadhes*. These are men who visit their own *sindekni* and kin in other villages and "ask" about the missing animals on behalf of the victims.

So urgent is the need for a cessation of hostilities that often, when no child old enough for full baptism can be found, the principals make a temporary bond by having one of them cut the first nails of a child from the other's patrigroup, preferably from among his closest agnates. This provisional nail-cutting ceremony (*koutsanikhisma*), which has no ecclesiastical status whatsoever, allows the participants to address one another as *sindekne* and commits them to obligations analogous to those involved in baptism.

A young shepherd is concerned to establish as many such links as possible, and as soon as possible. One who is known as an effective thief must have many powerful friends, *sindekni* all, and can protect his flocks all the more effectively. Those who do not have enough "knuckle" to call on shepherds in other villages for the kind of assistance just described will rapidly succumb to attrition at the hands of more effective thieves. It helps to be of a large patrigroup, since *sindeknia* extends to all agnates on both sides of the pact and therefore increases a man's effective reach; villagers say, with some irony, "My *sindeknos'* dog is my *sindeknos* too." (Local custom also permits a man to have many subsidiary *sindekni* at a single ceremony, and this enables him to extend his influence still further and faster.) But if one happens to belong to a smaller patrigroup, a ferocious personal reputation can compensate to a substantial degree. Those who are known as effective thieves may have considerable resources at their disposal; when one young shepherd died in an accident, for example, the huge gathering of shepherds from other villages attested to his prowess at stealing "to make friends."

A theft must always be avenged if the victim expects to be taken seriously. So must an insult, which may indeed be a probe to test a prospective victim's willpower. Young shepherds, in turn, may seek advantage from insults to their infirm agnates, or even to women. For women may not raid on their own behalf; a shepherd who does not go stealing animals is consequently regarded as effeminate, and is dismissed with a phrase otherwise conventionally used of women—*to adhinato meros*, "the weak part" (also reported in the latter sense by du Boulay [1974:123] from Evvia). Thus, avenging an insult to the women of one's family achieves three aims simultaneously. It foregrounds the young man's new status as family protector; it thereby contrastively expresses his manhood; and it may also help to establish a new alliance with the aggressor, or reaffirm a tie that had already been established in an earlier generation, but that the other side was prepared to abandon if it no longer offered any advantage.

In the rather lengthy example that follows, we encounter all these aspects. Note, too, how the formulaic sequence "hunger-revenge-consumption" assimilates this personal experience to a consistent theme:

I had this habit [of raiding]—because I don't go doing it any more—years ago, let's say, I must've been twelve or thirteen years old. In those years, so to speak.

During the winter, when the wind had frozen the snow, and afterwards when the snow was melting down here in the lower-lying area.

And we had sows here in the village—many sows! In those days, people used to go looking for acorns [to feed the sows].

Eh, there was hunger here in those days, now that we're talking about it, and everyone worked with whatever he could find, so to speak. A sow, a chicken, whatever he had.

And my mother, too, as I was saying, goes up to look for the acorns; we had a sow, [so] she went to find and gather acorns up there on the mountain. But acorns were not to be had on the Greek—er, I mean, in our village's—mountain territory. So they were obliged to go to the Psiliot zone, there on the boundaries between our villages, I'm telling you. To be precise, that is, there where we used to graze our sheep. Along the border there [that we share] with the Psiliots. Of course we didn't have any sheep there [then], we'd taken them off [to winter pastures] at that time.

And some Psiliots are around. Now they got peeved that [our women] were gathering the acorns, which they themselves used to take for their pigs. Now by a coincidence, as I'm telling you, my mother happens to be out gathering for herself, and of course she knew those people. They were friends from there.

Now I don't know—did they recognize her? Didn't they recognize her? They *can't* have recognized her, because, had they recognized her, of course they wouldn't have acted as they did, so to speak.

So two or three shepherds rushed down from there, Psiliots again, and just as the women were gathering [the acorns] from the holm oaks there, they went and take the baskets and throw out their acorns.

As though they were saying, "Get out of here, don't gather a thing!"

My mother's alone by a tree, right beside the others, of course, and was gathering.

And one of them approaches. "You too, *koumbarissa*," he tells her, "why are you gathering our acorns?"

Says she, "Well," she tells him, "are these holm oaks yours? Whose are they? Up here in Osia," she says to him, "I know where I am, we bring our animals here"—so as to make him understand whose [widow] she was! and who *she* was! hoping that he'd show respect and not throw her acorns away.

Eventually she was forced to reveal her identity, as the widow of a locally well-known war victim:

"So is your husband going to come and steal our animals?"
Now they *know* that the Germans had killed my father.
"Maybe your husband will come," he tells her, "to steal our animals?"
Says she, "My husband, *bre* [a term of aggressive address]," she tells him, "won't steal your animals because he cannot steal them. But people will be there to steal them from you!"

When her son, the narrator, came home, he was furious:

Eh, the poor old woman had this anger inside her.
As soon as I got away and came here from the winter pastures . . . my mother hadn't told anyone about it. Not even my uncles [i.e., her late husband's brothers] or anyone at all!
She tells me, "My child, So-and-so did thus and such to me." My mother told me details. "You should be aware of it, my child, just don't greet him, don't speak to him. Because he behaved like this to me!"

As a mother, she did not want the boy to be involved in violence. By withholding the ordinary intercourse of speech, she thought that her son could nevertheless deny the aggressor's essential humanity and manhood, without himself becoming involved in actual violence. The boy, given this opportunity to achieve a stronger persona for himself by identifying with his father as both victim of the insult and aggressive protector of the home, had other ideas:

"All right," I tell her. "Mama," I tell her, "I won't speak to him, but beyond that I won't bother him, but just don't tell anyone what happened," I tell her, "not even my uncle Yoryós or any other uncle of mine, and [don't let] any other person besides me get to hear of it," I tell her. "I'll destroy him! Just don't tell anyone!"
I was being cunning, now!

Say I, "She'll be afraid now in case some 'incident' comes out of it, and she'll say to herself, 'I mustn't talk about it.' "

Well, but I was going about it in quite a different way!

Say I, "I'll take my revenge on him on my own!"

During the next several months, whenever he encountered the aggressor, the boy hailed him respectfully, taking good care to address him as *sandole* ("godfather") since he had in fact baptized one of the boy's cousins. Meanwhile, however, the boy was already on the attack:

Two, three, two, three, four. Five! More than that I didn't take off him.

When I didn't have the opportunity, if I didn't have the opportunity to consume them, so to speak, on my own, I'd take five and slaughter [just one] and eat it, and into the ravine with the other four! (. . .)

I don't remember how many of his [animals] I "ate," I don't remember how many of his animals I destroyed, because if I "ate" four or five animals, *literally* ate them in other words, I'd destroy the rest [by throwing them] into a ravine.

Whenever he stopped making inquiries, in other words, whenever he decided to put it out of his mind to find out [about a missing sheep], I'd take another one off him.

"Hey," he'll have said, "where are they coming from to steal my animals? Where?"

In short, he'd completely forgotten my mother's secret. The idea may have occurred to him, [but if so] he forgot it, he didn't remember it. The man had come to the point of madness. He was saying, "Where? How? Who is 'eating' them off me? They're doing this to me as a vicious nuisance. But who? I've no problems with anyone. Why is this thing happening? Where?" he kept saying.

He set mediators to work here in the village, uncles of mine. He was saying, "The sheep are *not* in Glendi!" In Stalia! All around! He'll have said, "Next thing I'll know, someone'll come from really far away just to take two or three animals from me—no!" [This was an unlikely prospect, in other words.]

I destroyed thirty or forty for him, I don't remember [exactly how many].

Finally, Mikhalis, he remembered. Who knows how it came back to him? And you [*sic*] remembered the whole business with my mother, so to speak, up there on the mountainside.

And he sets out that very same hour! And he comes and finds

my uncle Yoryós. "*Sindekne*," he tells him, "I want to tell you something."

"What's up?" he says to him.

"I did thus and such to your sister-in-law last year, and I threw her acorns away, and I made this remark to her."

Right away, my uncle Yoryós understood the whole business. He hadn't understood it [up to that point].

Questioned directly by his uncle, the boy initially denied all. But then his mother admitted to having told him about the insult she had been made to suffer, and he saw that he could no longer conceal what he had been doing:

> But Mikhalis, I had every intention of not leaving him a single one if he didn't remember it! In a word, I could've taken them all at a stroke and thrown away the lot, and after that I'd have had him in fits of agony. Agony!
>
> Five, five, four, five, four, five—just to make him make inquiries, so to speak, do you understand? to make inquiries, to "ask" [i.e., about the location of the missing animals]. Right up to the point where I hadn't left him a single one! That's how determined I was.

And with great satisfaction he concluded:

> I did it, and I think, Mikhalis, that I've never experienced greater pleasure in my life than in this case. I've never done any other deed, in other words, that gave me as much pleasure as this!

Personal satisfaction must surely have been compounded, however, by the certain knowledge that his actions showed him to be a man who should not be trifled with. The destruction of sheep that he could not manage to eat was an insult of a high order, since convention demands that unconsumed animals be returned to the victims of a theft through the good offices of the mediators. In this case, however, a spiritual kinship tie already existed, and the narrator could cheerfully imply that the *aggressor* had only himself to blame if he failed to respect the obligations of *sindeknia*. The insult to the narrator's dead father gave him a particularly effective justification: it was the aggressor, not the offended family and patrigroup, whose conduct put the ordinary rules of raiding in abeyance.

In this case, raiding was used to restore a relationship that had already existed in the previous generation. The boy's revenge was also an attempt to recapture for himself his father's reputation as a man to be reckoned with, and specifically as a man who could effectively protect his household. The challenge, intentionally or not, had the effect of restoring a potentially valuable alliance, since the boy had the skills needed to establish his prowess.

He did not merely show himself to be a skilled thief; he also demonstrated mastery over the communicative implications of raiding. Throwing another's animals into a ravine (*dafkos*) is a particularly contemptuous insult, implying that they were not even worth taking as food. The normative theft, by contrast, is one in which the "choice" (*dhialekhta*) animals are removed; a formulaic way of reporting a theft is to say, "They've *chosen* them and put them in their sheepfold!" To throw another's animals away is analogous to insulting his female kin as morally worthless, and this made the boy's defense of his mother very apt indeed.

Even when raids are conducted in a strictly normative manner, they always suggest a strong analogy with the abduction of women. Both activities are known as *klepsa* (which is also, perhaps significantly, the term for cheating at cards), and it is said that most local quarrels originate over animals and women. Socially, the parallels between raiding and abduction are strong: both entail a contest over claims to manhood by both sides, both involve a high degree of risk to the physical person, and both—if successful—may lead to the creation of an alliance based on mutual respect.

A young man who decides to make a name for himself by raiding a stronger, more experienced shepherd usually anticipates the possibility of such an alliance. Until third parties intervene, however, he and his foe are obliged to continue their struggle, and considerable personal hurt may be inflicted before resolution can be achieved. The term *sasmos*, "reconciliation," has a peculiar aptness here. It is derived from *sazo*, "fix" or, more significantly, "pull taut" (as with a string). As long as a dispute continues, the relationship is complicated by fear and ignorance of each other's intentions. Once reconciliation has been effected, by contrast, these complexities are ideally replaced by a clean, sharply defined tension; instead of contempt for alleged fakery, each party now expresses respect for the other's genuine *eghoismos*. The tension is there—no serious alliance could exist without it—but it is defined by a new directness.

The challenge to raid a powerful shepherd usually comes early in a shepherd's career. In the account we have just been examining, for example, the Psiliot's challenge essentially taunted the widow that she had no capable men left in her family, ability being defined here quite explicitly in terms of raiding. The gauntlet may be flung down even more directly:

Well, I, young lad that I was, used to guard and take care of some goats, of course, around two hundred goats. . . .

Well, one day a man came, and he was a *captain*—that means somebody whose name was noised about in the whole *riza* [foothill zone]—he was a captain and he was from Tholos.

And he says to my boss, says he, "Did you bring him [i.e., the Glendiot who is now telling the story] here, huh!" he says, "so that he can learn [all about the locality] and the next day go off to wherever he's from and come back to steal our sheep? Since you've brought him here, he'll get to know all the terrain, so to speak, and he'll bring others from their neck of the woods so as to come here and rob us of our sheep, so to speak! Why did you bring him?"

Meanwhile—my boss is fooling around, of course—I got furious. And [I was all set] to take revenge on him, since he made this remark—that is, even though I was only thirteen years old, [just] a lad.

The Glendiot was still too young, however, to take effective revenge himself. Instead, he wrote to his brother-in-law (ZH) and another Glendiot, telling them where his tormentor had some thirty sheep just waiting to be stolen. The others acted promptly on this attractive proposal. The Tholiot was beside himself with anger, but when he discovered that one of the thieves had been the speaker's brother-in-law—an exceptionally skilled animal thief—he decided to "fix" the situation in the usual way. The speaker's attribution of motive is revealing:

Meanwhile, this guy [the Tholiot] will have told himself that he [i.e., the speaker] got angry in this way *so that he could turn them into friends*, and he invited my brother-in-law Stelios to go and baptize a child of his, so to speak, and he did actually baptize a child of his.

Since the brothers-in-law were also agnates, this arrangement was certainly far from unhelpful to the Tholiot. Even if the boy did not turn into a skilled thief as he had taunted him, the brother-in-law was already well known throughout the area for his cunning and courage in *klepsa*. Meanwhile, the boy had also demonstrated a certain degree of manhood himself: he had refused to take an insult meekly, and he had designed an appropriate response.

In most instances, a shepherd must himself be a "worthy" (*aksios*) foe, thief, and ally. The challenge is always there; men must show themselves capable of possession, whether the object be animals, women, or even weapons—the very instrument of possession. Two Glendiots had foiled thieves who had attacked their flock. Not content with the mere recovery of their own goods, they disarmed the attackers:

> "You don't have the heart, *bre*, to carry weapons! *Men* carry weapons! You just aren't men!"
> I threatened them, and even if they'd talked back just a bit, I'd've beaten them to shreds, I wouldn't've killed them of course, but I *was* bold with them.
> "But weapons," I tell them, "are not for all to own, and those who are going to own them, *vre* [a possibly slightly politer rendering of *bre*], should be worthy of them, let us say."

The claim to manhood must be established in action. One who has so far lost his manhood as to have been disarmed may not "speak," since this, too, is a male activity. Of the chicken-hearted, a *mandinadha* has it:

> *Min done paris, kopelia, ton asvestokoliari;*
> Don't marry,   girl,   the one-whose-bottom-is-whitewashed;
>
> *pou dhe ghateši na mila   moudhe na rozonari.*
> he doesn't know how to *speak*,   nor   to reason.

The one-whose-bottom-is-whitewashed is, of course, a chicken—a bird whose flesh is often contemptuously dismissed as not being real meat at all. The privilege of "speech" has to be earned, and those who have rejected one another's significance "do not speak to each other" (*dhe miliounde*). And those who have thrown their weapons away have abandoned the manhood that would give them a voice in the councils of true men.

Not all shepherds of a given age are equally powerful. Some allow the pressures of *klepsa* to drive them into farming or small industry. Others develop a reputation as "law-court people." This option is effectively closed to Glendiots, or to the inhabitants of any of the villages in the *riza*, since recourse to legal action is regarded as a form of betrayal and leads to violent reprisals—usually in the form of the systematic dissolution of the culprit's entire flock. Glendiots may take thieves from the immediate area to a court of law in rare cases when the latter have demonstrably resisted all attempts to achieve a reconciliation, since in that case the onus of culpability is on the others. But such cases are few and far between, probably because it is a rare situation in which an absolute impasse can be said to have been reached.

When the "law-court people" are from further away, however, they are relatively immune to systematic destruction, and a compromise may be necessary. Legal action could lead to the economic ruin of the thieves.

In such cases, Glendiots may accept the mediation of people from still other communities, and will feel safer if a *sindeknia* can be arranged. "Now," commented a Glendiot who was involved in one such case, "we've become *sindekni*, and even from afar each hails the other, "Your health, *sindekne!*" There is perhaps a touch of irony here, but the advantages of a peaceful resolution could not be gainsaid.

For the most part, however, Glendiots regard the formal truce of *sindeknia* as appropriate only to those cases where the two sides have demonstrated roughly equivalent strength. In the case just cited, in fact, the Glendiot admitted that neither side was powerful (*dhinamiči*), and gave this as a reason for the relative ease with which mediation was accepted. Among the "men of knuckle" (*kozalidhes*), however, there is only one acceptable pattern. This is the pattern of raid and counterraid, in which the very idea of going to law is anathema to both sides. Here, too, third parties are involved; but whereas the threat of legal action may lead them to intervene in the disputes of minor shepherds out of a desire to avoid the betrayal of local values, their involvement in the fights of "big" shepherds may bring them personal prestige and will also reduce the risk of eventual homicide.

Those who are "good at being men" act within the morality of reciprocal theft. Raiding entails bravery and skill, but it also calls for mutual respect and a sense of style. Any shepherd who violates the canons of *klepsa* is considered to have compromised his manhood. Most of the narrative material that I recorded addresses violations of the code, probably because these cases seemed especially interesting, and also because a man who is able to punish his rival for such infractions demonstrates his own superiority in the process.

"I never deceived a friend"

The cardinal rule of *klepsa* is that one does not steal from the flocks of one's own people. This includes covillagers, especially agnates, and spiritual kin everywhere. In practice, however, even this fundamental principle is not observed. A humorous *mandinadha* expresses the standard justification for stealing in error (see also Mavrakakis 1983: 113-114, no. 45):

Sindekne, skotina 'tone, če ti samia dhen idha,
Sindekne, dark it was, and the ear mark I couldn't see,

č apis tin idha ti samia, mono trianda pira!
and once I'd seen the ear mark, only thirty did-I-take!

This *mandinadha*, which is especially funny in that it replaces a phrase meaning "a small one" with the extravagant "thirty" (*trianda*), parodies a conventional rhetoric. Glendiots do not necessarily assume that a theft from the flock of a kinsman or *sindeknos* was genuinely unintentional, nor is this a question of great concern. What is far more important is that the thief, if caught, should demonstrate respect by *claiming* that he had not realized to whom the animals belonged:

> This is a [statement of] cause, a phrase, so to speak, a justification which justifies everything. And it does make you wonder. . . . He gives you the impression that . . . perhaps he really didn't know.
>
> In other words, this is a rule, a justification.
>
> He can't very well tell you, "I didn't do it, and *that* fellow stole them from you!" There should be "reasons." He comes and tells you, "Yes, I did take them." If there are "reasons."
>
> When there are none, however, what can he say to you? [Would you want him to say,] "I want to begin a family quarrel with you, because I just *want* to"?
>
> That's out of the question!

The great advantage of formulaic self-exoneration here is that the victim is left in doubt about what the thief's real intentions might have been. Raiding is an uncertain activity; even the demarcation between stealing animals to include them in one's own flock and stealing them for food is blurred by the use of "eating" to signify both. Such open-ended uncertainty allows the creative manipulation of events to create more and more extensive alliances. The link between this and the idiom of self-exoneration is explicitly recognized:

> He may do it deliberately. There is a possibility, however, that he may wish [for an alliance], when you are strong [*dhinamikos*]. He may want to be friends with you, so he comes and steals your animals intentionally, so to speak, so as to establish ties with you.

Clearly, the way to achieve this goal is by demonstrating a mastery over the diplomatic niceties that true manhood demands. Once again, we see here the importance of speech in the profile of the skilled thief.

When a Glendiot steals from a covillager, he is approaching the equivalent of incest. Such an act, especially if the victim is a kinsman, is regarded as *ghoursouza*, "pollution." In one case where the conflict was resolved, I was told that the story—and, by extension, the actions that it described—had great "meaning" (*simasia*). But this was said ironically, and with regard to a dispute that had ended amicably enough.

There is little point in stealing from a covillager, since most are already kin or affines; the object of theft is to establish *sindeknies* in as far-flung a range of villages as possible. Significantly, the only Glendiots with numerous ties of spiritual kinship within the village are farmers.

Besides this consideration, it would be very hard for a covillager to claim that he had not recognized the ear mark of his victim's flock. Within each community, there is virtually no duplication. The limited possibilities for creating recognizable and distinctive cuts on the animals' ears (illus. 19 and 20) does mean, however, that as *between* villages there is often a good deal of confusion. With this in mind, some shepherds aim their raids at flocks that bear an ear mark similar to their own, or one that can easily be disguised. One active animal thief even claimed that at the age of twelve he carefully selected an ear mark that "ruins" whatever other ear mark it replaces. The object of this was to preserve as many stolen animals as possible for his own flock; if there is any danger of recognition, a thief always hastily slaughters and eats the animals instead.

There would in any case be little point in raiding a *sindeknos* deliberately. The alliance already exists, and may actually suffer if the victim feels that the thief was simply taking advantage of his immunity from suspicion. Allies in more distant villages are too valuable to be wasted, even if a mistake does happen every so often:

> I had there [in a village to the south] a certain friend, a good shepherd . . . and he had told me, "Here in the lower part [of his village's territory] is [a certain shepherd] . . . come and take his animals."
>
> So I got up and went there to steal his animals, and I took those of my friend [instead]! They were nearby.
>
> He understood the error and came and said to me, "Eh!"
>
> Eeeee, I didn't recognize them as my *sindeknos'* animals there.
>
> "Eh, they just wandered off and left [and that's why I made the mistake," said I.] Well, that business was fixed up too. We didn't get to eat a single one, he got them all back.

After all, to eat the meat of wrongly stolen animals would have been a negation of manhood. Note again the recurrent device of meat eating to symbolize the social message contained in the narrative.

Carefully handled, in fact, the return of wrongfully stolen animals— as, for example, in cases of misdirected revenge—can be as effective as actually "raiding to make friends." One former shepherd recounted

19. Cutting a *samia* (property mark) on a sheep's ear. Had it sported a different mark before? Or no mark at all?

20. *Samies* (property marks) are clearly visible on both ears.

how he had miscalculated but then turned the mistake to very good
advantage:

> They of course got their animals back from me, they took their
> animals away, and we became even more closely connected; but
> we had thought that they were the ones [who had raided us]. And
> they considered us justified, in other words, because they had some-
> how gotten us mixed up in their own affairs. (. . .)
>
> When they came here, they came and we became *sindekni*, that's
> what we became, and I told them right away, "We took your animals
> for such and such reasons." I tell him, "We're not to blame."
>
> "Eh, how come you're not to blame?"
>
> "We are not to blame, we just got mixed up. But *that* man stole
> the animals!"

Asked then whether he had gone back to raid the real culprits, the
speaker explained:

> Those people happened to be cousins of theirs [i.e., of the shep-
> herds who had been raided in error], and for the sake [*khatiri*] of
> our [new] *sindekni*, so to speak, since we'd become *sindekni*, I didn't
> go, Mikhalis.
>
> The first group had come here, however, and had truly shown
> that we had done badly indeed to take their animals, and thus we
> established such close ties that by now you couldn't begin to imagine
> them! Both with the one lot *and* with the other.

By creating ties of *sindeknia* with both the real and the imagined culprits,
the speaker used his original error creatively both as a basis for new
ties and, by extension, as a means of showing himself to be well versed
in the arts of manhood.

The decision to return animals stolen in error, though theoretically a
moral imperative, is not always easily taken. The company of a fellow-
thief can lead a shepherd to an act of probity that he may later regret:

> I untie the animal's feet and take it so that we can leave. I look
> at its ear mark and—it belonged to my marriage sponsor, the man
> who had "crowned" me.[2] He had "crowned" me!
>
> Say I, "Tough on you, but *I'm* not taking this sheep, not even if
> the very earth should be destroyed!"
>
> "Why?" he says to me.
>
> "Because it belongs to So-and-so, who 'crowned' me."
>
> "*Bre aman* [a cry of remonstrance here]!" he says to me.
>
> Nothing doing, in other words. Eh, just as it was I let it go.

Really. . . . And I shouldn't have released it, I should have eaten it. Ah, well!

And his companion of that night's work remarked wistfully that *he* had wanted to taste it.

Animals stolen in error may be eaten—literally—before the mistake can be rectified. In that case, the victim "will make a gift to you of the ones that have been slaughtered," and will expect only those still alive to be returned to him. This is in fact the general pattern, since even a new victim is always a potential *sindeknos* and should not be denied the privilege of commensality.

For this reason, compensation is very rarely requested when some of the animals have already been consumed. If compensation is requested, the mediator provides the substitute animals at his own expense. Almost invariably, however, he refuses to aid the victim ever again. Not only has the victim put his *arotikhtis* to considerable expense and effort, but he has also perverted the course of reciprocity by demanding reparation in this way. More than that, his attitude suggests that perhaps he is not enough of a man to seek recompense by conducting a retaliatory raid of his own, and, should this be true, he is hardly worthy to be one's spiritual kinsman and ally.

Occasionally, the request for compensation is simply a bargaining device. In a characteristic dispute, two Glendiot brothers-in-law had stolen some twenty-five goats. The victim eventually caught up with one of the culprits, who refused to betray his companion but claimed to be solely responsible. There then began a mutual testing:

So we left the others, the rest of the company inside the house. We go outside, and he says to me, says he, "Did you slaughter all twenty-five goats?"

Say I, "I did slaughter them!"

Says he, "Have you no fear of God?"

Say I, "Why should I be afraid of God? So I did *not* slaughter them then [i.e., if you're going to make a fuss about it]! Why are you going on about it, making such a to-do?"

He says, "You should pay me for ten [of the] animals, because I've incurred a lot of expense and you should pay me for the ten animals so that I don't lose out altogether."

Well then, I tell him, "I told you that as a joke, that I'd stolen your goats, I was testing you to see if you were a strong person. And [as things have turned out] it's lucky I did *not* steal them, else you'd even have me put in jail.

He found himself in a state of real crisis. He . . . got upset, he'll have said, "He's telling me neither the truth nor lies. How can I tell?"

At this juncture a shepherd from yet a third village, *sindeknos* to the complaining victim and a friend of the Glendiots, hears of the victim's demands. In response, he plays an effective hand, telling the victim:

"You will never [again] make me go to the Mylopotamos region to 'ask' about [stolen] animals, unless you make a present of them all [i.e., to the thieves]."

And he says to us, "Don't be afraid for yourself, he wasn't about to do a thing. Just tell the truth!"

As a result, the thieves confessed, the victim retreated from his demands, and—at the victim's request—the former foes became *sindekni*:

We went to the house and he cut-the-first-nail—of (*koutsanikhise*) my first daughter.

Evidently the victim was well satisfied with the outcome. His demand for recompense may in fact have been no more than a ruse, designed to secure maximum leverage and especially to put the mediator on his mettle. Without this ploy, he may have reasoned, the thieves might not be willing to accept him on equal terms. He took a calculated risk: the mediator would have been justified, according to the norm, in deciding there and then to have nothing further to do with such a rapacious and unmanly individual. But he did not overplay his hand. On the contrary, he did what was most admirable in Glendiot terms: he staked his very reputation on a hazardous diplomatic maneuver, so eventually gaining the respect of a man who might otherwise have continued to despise him.

His action could easily have gone against him: this was its ultimate éclat. Seeking reparation denies the most commonly cited purpose of raiding, that of creating a network of alliances. Similarly, too, refusing to admit responsibility when one has been confronted with the evidence is a cowardly and unmanly way to behave; and it, too, rejects the possibility of a useful alliance with one's erstwhile victim. It is a matter of pride to be able to say, "I never deceived a friend."

Deceit of this kind, moreover, usually provokes an unmistakable denial of the offender's manhood from the intended dupe:

As we were saying, some animals of ours had been stolen.
Afterwards, we were "asking" about them, and they didn't tell us. That is, we got some people to ["ask"] about them.

But the culprit refused to own up. The Glendiot victims were certain about the thief's identity, and decided to vent their rage on him:

> And we collected up his animals and took off all their bells (*sklaveria*). We wrecked any that weren't any good and hung them, all bashed in as they were, on the sheep.
> And we took three [animals] and castrated them.

The Glendiots were highly satisfied with their symbolic revenge. They did not actually tell their victim that they had removed the bells or castrated the animals: it was not necessary. After a short time had elapsed, the thief himself came to them and owned up, admitting—as his self-exoneration—that he had been afraid to take responsibility for the original theft. The Glendiots, anxious to prove their superior manhood, admitted their part in the matter, and the quarrel was satisfactorily brought to a conclusion with the baptism of the daughter of one of the Glendiots by the other shepherd.

When a shepherd admits to having performed a raid, but untruthfully denies that any of the animals are left alive, he is rejecting normative obligations. If he is found out, his offense causes great anger:

> Well, one time someone had stolen animals from me. For revenge, I take a friend of mine along and off we go. This fellow had of course put his own animals in the lower part of his house. I go with my friend, we open the door in order to take them.
> But he heard us. So he gets up and chases us from behind, so to speak, While this was going on I tell my companion, "Stop," I tell him, "right now, and I'll chuck a hand grenade at him to kill all of them during the night."
> My friend, of course, didn't let me. "No," he tells me, "you shouldn't," and so on.
> Well, then we took ourselves off.
> I was of course very angry with him, because this fellow had made fun of me. He'd told me that he'd slaughtered all the animals that were mine—meanwhile, he didn't slaughter them, but kept half of them alive and slaughtered them later, let's say, for the wedding. I heard of it afterwards, that's why I was rarin'—so to speak—to go take such a heavy revenge on him.

Explicit in this account is anger prompted not by the theft as such, but because the thief had tried to make a fool of his victim. Since an important component of manhood is the ability to "ask" effectively, deceit on these occasions calls for a massive retaliation that leaves the question beyond any shadow of doubt.

That the concern in these retaliatory raids is with the claim to threatened male identity is also very clear in the usual reaction to the theft
of a male animal. The castration of rams and billy-goats is, as we have
seen, a profoundly insulting act. But even merely to steal a male animal
challenges the owner's masculinity. Thus, if thieves "see that it is a
varvato [i.e., 'well endowed with testicles'], they unleash it. They don't
steal it." Although the ostensible reason given for this is that the male
animals are essential to the constant regeneration of the flock, the shepherd's manhood and person is also deeply implicated. The youth who
brought back a bell to his father made an effective claim to manhood
even though he was not able to manage the billy-goat as well. In fact,
although his reason for leaving the animal itself was a merely practical
one, shepherds do occasionally remove the bells but leave the actual
animals on purpose: the message of contempt is all the clearer for it.

The removal of an animal's bells is a symbolic realization of this
principle. It can be done on a scale calculated to provoke an immediate
response:

> One time, my son-in-law's animals were stolen. And he was
> "asking" this way and that, and he learned about the animals [i.e.,
> where they were].
> They didn't square with him.
> He'll have said to himself, "So-and-so are the thieves, but they
> didn't own up," because they were afraid of him.
> They'll have said to themselves, "If we confess to [having stolen]
> them now, we're lost!"
> Says he, "Fine!"
> So then he goes once more with this fellow [a fellow-Glendiot]
> . . . and they collect together a flock of animals at Nidha. And they
> take eighty bells off them. So they take them and straight away hung
> stones on the animals, on their throats, and left them there. (. . .)
> And they got the idea right away: "Who did this to us? So-and-
> so did it! No one else could have done it."

An important principle is illustrated here. Shepherds want their raids
to be read, and read correctly. There is usually some residual ambiguity
concerning the identity of a thief; but when a raid is conducted for
strictly retaliatory ends, the victim is usually thought to have no difficulty
in identifying the source and reasons for his present discomfiture. The
principled indirection of such a communicative mode, however, allows
for the ever-present possibility that the original victim may have retaliated against the wrong person. In that case, as we have seen, the
innocent victim has the option of accepting the explanation that the raid

was conducted in error, whether or not he finds this genuinely convincing. If he chooses to do so, both he and the raiders stand to gain a new social tie, or at the very least—through the demonstration of their forthrightness—to increase their social standing.

Clearly, then, this is a system in which a good improviser stands to gain from the pervasive ambiguity of raiding. The sources of possible error are legion, and include: the limited range of identifying ear marks and the crudeness with which many of them are cut (see illus. 19 and 20); misinformation spread by a thief anxious to conceal his own actions; even false claims to being the culprit oneself, advanced in order to secure an alliance without all the effort of actually raiding:

> The Vrondades [a segment of the Skoufades] had once lost some sheep and were "asking" for them. They "ask" this way, they "ask" that way.
>
> And a certain individual presents himself at Spithiana. Says he, "Hey, *I* stole your animals!"
>
> Whereas he hadn't stolen them at all!
>
> Says he, "So *I* slaughtered them."
>
> Eh. "So you slaughtered them? All right!"
>
> These folks, the Vrondades, relaxed, like one might say, "So he took them and slaughtered them [i.e., and there is nothing more to be done about it]."
>
> But Stavros [one of the Vrondades] . . . said to himself, "But screw it all, that guy stole my animals from me, and I've given them up," and so on. "This business doesn't look right to me. . . ."
>
> [He searched] this way, that way. Stavros discovered where the animals were.
>
> So thereupon the Vrondades started shouting at him [the man who had "confessed"], "Here's this one! Here's this one!"—until finally they prove to him that he had *not* slaughtered them, that he hadn't played straight.
>
> So he owns up and says that he'd acted this way, says he, deliberately, in order to make friendships and all that. "So that I could 'ask,' so to speak, for my animals, so that people could 'ask' for my animals in Glendi, and all that, and so that we could initiate friendships."

This confession of falsehood was extremely offensive to the Glendiots, who treated it as *atimia*—a term that may perhaps best be translated as "failure to conform to the expectations *socially* appropriate to one's *personal* standing" (see also Herzfeld 1980a). The offender claimed a manhood that was not his to claim. He did redeem himself somewhat by confessing to the falsehood, and the Vrondades signaled their acceptance of this by agreeing to baptize his child.

Nevertheless, my informant—himself a Skoufas—continued to express a considerable amount of indignation over the man's misbehavior. While Glendiots associate raiding with specified forms of cunning and deceit, these are still *normative* deceits. To confess to a raid that one has not performed violates the norm because it constitutes an attempt to gain an alliance on false grounds.

Perhaps nowhere more than in this aberrant case do we see that raiding is considered a test of manhood and, as such, a necessary preliminary to friendship. But beyond that, the case also shows that the secrecy that allows shepherds to perform as men requires that they be constantly on the alert for just these violations of principle. Vigilance, no less than daring, is an essential component of manhood. Its importance is derived from the secrecy which enfolds all raiding activities, but which then itself has to be "performed" in public. The secrecy of a *kala kleftis* is thus appropriately paradoxical: it must be performed in public. It is not enough to know how to conceal one's moves; one must also convey to other villagers, and to shepherds from outside Glendi as well, a clear impression of one's ability to act silently and effectively in the defense of home and flock.

"Don't investigate what you eat"

Much of the secrecy displayed by animal thieves does serve practical ends. Some parents are anxious not to let their children hear raiding stories, for fear that these would exercise a corrupting influence; but others are more concerned that their children might unwittingly betray recent thefts. A similar concern led some villagers to doubt whether I would ever be allowed to hear of very recent exploits, as these, if bruited about, were more likely to provoke retaliation.

"If you've eaten meat [in the village]," the conventional wisdom has it, "you've eaten stolen meat." Especially at weddings and baptisms, where the massive consumption of meat calls for emergency measures, it seems to be generally assumed that some part of the meat provided must have been stolen. So certain is this assumption that, on one occasion when the police were unable to identify the exact culprits behind a raid that seemed to have been prompted by a wedding celebration, they arrested the groom as a symbolic collective punishment.

While Glendiots happily assume that some of what one has eaten at a celebration must have been stolen, they avoid any direct allusion to its origins. Etiquette demands that one never inquire about the source of what one eats:

> Once, up on the mountain, I had my bag full of meat. Full! Stolen meat!
>
> So someone sees me and calls to me then, and I go over to him.
>
> And he says to me, "Are you carrying," he says to me, "bread to eat? Because, [if you are,] I am," says he, "crazy with hunger."
>
> Bread, yet. I was hearing [him talk about] *bread*!
>
> Say I, "I am carrying some," I say to him, "as much as you can."
>
> And he takes a piece of meat and he was eating it, and as he ate this here first piece of meat, now, he says to me, "But where did you find it," he says to me, "this meat?"
>
> "Eat, you!" I tell him, "and don't talk."
>
> When he'd eaten another mouthful, he says to me, "But," he says to me, "is it stolen?"
>
> "Eat, you," I tell him, "and don't talk!"
>
> I was eating a little bit, too, and the man happened to ask me again, "But hey, where did you find the meat?" he says to me. "What meat is this?"
>
> So I got furious, and I took my bag and tied it on my back and made off and away.
>
> He says to me, "Hey, stop!"
>
> "Get out of this place," I tell him, "you stinking scum!"

And the speaker turned to me in order to emphasize the moral: "Now you, too—wherever you may chance to be, don't investigate what you eat—what it is, whether it's stolen, whether it's bought."[3] Stolen meat symbolizes the Glendiot respect for improvisation. Because it must be concealed and disposed of rapidly, it is by definition "unweighed" (*azi-yasto*): it does not pass through the legitimate channels of market control. Stolen animals also become fair game for further depredations because, of course, the secrecy that surrounds their original disappearance makes them hard to trace. A Glendiot found a stray black lamb, and mentioned it to a passing shepherd from another village. The latter, scared that his theft of the lamb might be unveiled, denied any knowledge of it. Some while later, the thief came looking for the lamb, but this time the Glendiot simply said that *he* knew nothing—although in fact he already had the missing animal "in my belly". Two weeks later, the thief reappears:

> Says he, "Hey you, that lamb must have been lost somewhere around here, but where? How?"
>
> "Well, if I tell you that I've eaten it, what will you do?"

Says he, "Nothing."

"Do you remember how many times you asked me? And told me that it wasn't yours?"

Says he, "Yes!"

"That very evening I slaughtered it. What the hell, with stolen meat it's easy come, easy go!"

"It's all yours," he tells me.

Tales of thieves stealing animals from other thieves, knowingly or otherwise, are not uncommon, and emphasize the importance of the snatched advantage, the moment of sheer insolence, in the way Glendiots view male interpersonal relations.

Improvisation is also a necessary component of concealment. Women cramming stolen meat into a waste pipe or water pitcher, a boy who stuffs a piece of fat into his shirt, shepherds who hurl stolen animals into a ravine—all exhibit a keen ability to avoid being caught. It is not only shepherds and their families who need to practice such vigilance; a butcher who receives stolen goods is also liable to sanctions both official and local. One butcher in a nearby village who often received stolen animals from Glendiot and other shepherds had a narrow escape:

> On one occasion I happened to have gotten hold of twenty animals. The fellow who owned them came looking for them. To me! I had bought them [though they were stolen].
>
> Meanwhile, I'd taken one of the animals from that lot to the village of Portokali and sold it there, and I said to myself that since he was here trying to seek the sheep from me, he'll also go to Portokali. And he'll find the sheepskin.
>
> So as not to be caught, I went and slaughtered one of my own animals from here and sent the sheepskin to him [i.e., his contact in Portokali].
>
> And I said to him, "If they show up looking for the animals, show them this sheepskin."
>
> That's just how matters turned out.
>
> The fellow left here and went to Portokali, and said, "This and that and so forth. I want you to show me the skin of the sheep that you slaughtered today. The animal you slaughtered today!"
>
> So I said to him, "Here you are, sir!"
>
> And he was persuaded that the animals were not his, and got up and left.

Given their extensive experience of methods of concealment, detection is a real test of wits among the shepherds. "The folds of his belly" (*i dhiples tsi čilias dou*) seems an apposite metaphor for a shepherd's devious cunning: as the belly conceals stolen meat, so the face of the shepherd secretes the wiliness needed to avert detection of his own thefts or to hide his success in detecting the thefts committed by others at his expense.

The paradox of this kind of secrecy is that it has to be performed. A man must be *known* as one who can keep a secret, and also as one who already has enough secret knowledge of his own to make him a formidable enemy or ally. When *arotikhtadhes*—"those who ask [i.e., about stolen sheep]"—come striding into the village, villagers may affect to be uninterested or ignorant of their reasons for being there; but this mask disguises avid curiosity. The *arotikhtadhes* are taken to their friends' homes, and then to the coffeehouses. From the latter, they may come out for a while to stand huddled in the evening shadows with their Glendiot friends, conducting their business of inquiry. Everyone knows why they are there; few know exactly how the inquiry is proceeding, or who is most directly involved. The affectation of generic secrecy—which also had some informants coming surreptitiously to our house to talk about their own exploits, even though virtually everyone in the village knew that *in general* this was going on—discourages more specific inquisitiveness. It also gives a shepherd the reputation of being skilled at investigation and well connected throughout the shepherding villages of the area.

Villagers, using the rhetoric of modernity, say that the successful detection of stolen livestock requires both psychology and diplomacy. "Psychology" here means the ability to deduce who is likely to have stolen the missing animals in the light of known quarrels or previous incidents, as well as of reputation as a successful thief. "Diplomacy" means the successful manipulation of existing ties, and especially the ability to coax a confession out of a recalcitrant *sindeknos* or other associate. One of the Glendiots' favorite instances of the latter talent concerns not animal theft, but murder, although the incident is taken to illustrate the cunning that supposedly characterizes shepherds above all others. A Glendiot had been thrown into jail along with several others on suspicion of their being collectively involved in a murder. The Glendiot, who knew perfectly well who the killer was but did not want to take the responsibility of reporting him, kept fuming, "I screw the mother of the man who committed this murder!" Eventually the murderer could stand it no longer, and screamed at the Glendiot to cease his insults— and the guard overheard the whole exchange. All but the true murderer were then released, and the tale is still told in Glendi as an illustration of the cunning diplomacy in which the shepherds are so expert.

The most effective "diplomacy" is the skilled acting out of a role that
is totally discrepant with people's expectations (cf. Goffman 1959:141-
166). A young man with revenge or profit in mind may actually wait
until he has given up shepherding before starting a series of devastating
raids. He knows that people are less likely to suspect him then: raiding
is regarded as morally acceptable only among active shepherds, since
only they possess the means to make it a truly reciprocal activity. Farmers, for example, are viciously attacked if they steal animals, on the
grounds that they do not own flock animals that their victims can steal
in return. And a man who has become respectable with a small business
can say, "I've given up raiding" (*eksevosčepsa*)—a statement that seems
to preclude the very possibility that he might still be an adept thief.

By the same token, a youth who has not yet established a fearsome
reputation can often escape detection on exactly that basis. Herein lies
the crucial paradox. On the one hand, he wants immunity from discovery
for long enough to do some telling damage. On the other, however, he
badly wants to be identified once the damage has been done. But the
longer he can escape detection, the greater the credit that accrues to
him once the truth does emerge. Style calls for good timing, and in
reciprocal raiding the stretching of tension over a long period can reinforce a man's claim to excellence to great effect.

Much, too, can be achieved through the careful assumption of an air
of unconcern, the modest refusal to show anger in public, and the
cultivation of a good and recurrent alibi. It is considered smart to steal
from more distant villages, because suspicion is less easily excited: the
hardship of traveling fast over a long and difficult trail deflects suspicion
while also emphasizing the manhood of those hardy enough to do it,
with the result that *cunning* and *toughness*—those two fundamental components of Glendiot manhood—combine to serve the same ends.

Again, the boy whose mother was insulted in the incident over the
spilled acorns tried for a long time to escape detection, since the longer
he could maintain his incognito the more damage he could inflict. To
his mother he was especially careful to give nothing away, both because
he knew that she would be displeased at his exposing himself to such
danger and because, apparently, he wanted the satisfaction and benefits
of inflicting revenge for himself alone:

> I used to avoid [doing anything obvious], that is, but I'd be looking
> for a chance. I'd be sitting here in the coffeehouse up to ten or
> eleven o'clock, making like I was going home to sleep, and I['d] go
> by the house to tell my mother, "Mother, I'm going up to the

mountainside tonight, and not staying here. I'm going over there to
see how the sheep are doing."

I'd go on up, I'd go and take his animals and slaughter one, and
fix up the meat and hide it, and chuck the rest into the ravine, and
in the morning I'd show up, so to speak, with the sheep, herding
them in that direction.

From the [early] evening I'd be here, the same in the morning,
and every evening again I'd come back down here.

They couldn't find me out, I tell you.

I didn't do anything else.

People would say, "If Eftikhis [the speaker] were going to take
the sheep off him, he'd take, for example, Manolis or Mikhalis—
someone else. On his own, what could he do?" (Did you understand?)
"No meat's been found on him, what would he do with them [i.e.,
the animals]?"

Once he was forced by his uncle to confess, his success in keeping the
secret for so long redounded to his credit, and contributed to his rapidly
established reputation as a skilled and cunning opponent.

Once he ceased herding, however, that reputation eroded: the connections he still enjoyed from his shepherding days were no longer
reliable. As he commented with some bitterness, in another context:

Eh, today, where am I? On the side of what's good for people,
so to speak. A social person. A gentleman! I know how to talk to
you. . . . I respect the next man, I respect everything, let's say,
I'm politely attentive.

All those who used to greet me from afar, eh? and used to say
to me, "Eftikhis, how are you? Your health!"—while I now sit in
the coffeehouse in my chair, these people pass by and don't greet
me, Mikhalis. Since I don't steal and since they're not afraid of me!

He is tempted to restore the balance of fear:

And sometimes, so to speak, I get angry, and say to my uncle,
"A devil upon their cross," I tell him, "if I don't sometimes think
of taking from this cuckold, of, of, of splitting fifty [animals from
his flock] and chucking them into the ravine. For his disrespect,
so to speak! Whereas *he* knows . . . how much friendship and so
on we used to have; and the moment I sold my sheep and I stopped,
stopped, stopped stealing, he doesn't show up to greet us!"

Angry stutters notwithstanding, however, Eftikhis knows full well that
he has gone too far along the road of respectability by now.

"Diplomacy" and "psychology," and the use of spiritual kin as on-the-spot agents, are by no means the only devices open to a shepherd investigating his losses. Some methods that more obviously resemble police detection bring a successful investigator credit for his native wit. In the days long past when Glendi and most of the other villages had no vineyards, the discovery of grape seeds in a trail of excreta led one shepherd straight back to his stolen animals in the only local village where there were some vines. In a much more recent case, a Potamitis was convinced that some sheep he had lost had been stolen by fellow-Glendiots, because three grains of corn, evidently the remains of a lure to get the sheep out of their pen, seemed to be of a size consistent with that of a government issue that had been distributed to the Glendiot shepherds only a few days previously.

While Glendiot detection is directed to discovering the identities of the actual raiders in each case, the process of detection and "diplomacy" fulfills another purpose as well. It establishes the range of *probable* raiders, and in this way helps a shepherd to select promising future alliances. If he wrongly accuses a powerful man, and raids him, he may return all the stolen livestock if the truth emerges. Even if he has slaughtered and eaten some of the animals, however, there is a reasonable probability that the wronged victim will make him a gift of them—that is, by not retaliating or demanding compensation. But even if he does retaliate, there is still a good chance that the new exchange of hostilities will end in a further alliance. Thus, retrospectively, it may matter a great deal less that a mistake was made than that it was productively exploited as a good opportunity to create new social ties.

Mistakes are perceived as inevitable, and the claim to have stolen in error is an acceptable excuse. Nevertheless, some shepherds prefer not to confess even though to do so might be to their long-term advantage. When they are caught in such a lie, their victims usually express great anger. In no case is this truer than when the thief falsely denies his misdeeds on oath, for then he has risked even the wrath of God in order to show contempt for the social values of men.

"Finally we ended up in church, on oath"

To put a shepherd on oath is a sign of deep mistrust, for it shows that one has no faith in his protestations of innocence up to that point. Glendiots are reluctant to go this far: it entails a blank refusal to believe anything the suspect says, and it challenges his manhood by suggesting that perhaps he had not been brave enough to own up. Above all, it places a heavy burden of responsibility on the suspect's shoulders, without necessarily dissolving the suspicion itself: if the suspect swears falsely that he is innocent, the weight of sin that falls upon him is thought to be shared by the man who forced him to go to such an extreme. *Na paris orko* can mean simply "to take an oath," but it can also mean, specifically, "to take an oath falsely"; the conflation of these two meanings suggests a lack of confidence in the oath as a test of innocence. Thus, when a shepherd puts a suspect on oath, he knowingly takes a risk that he has connived at perjury in the eyes of God. Finally, asking another shepherd to swear to his innocence on oath presupposes that the one who asks can also exact violent punishment for a refusal. At least in theory, a determined opponent can call this bluff, knowing that the weaker shepherd's inability to take effective revenge for the insult will invite protracted and persistent derision.

For all these reasons, shepherds use the oath only as a last resort. They prefer to rely on *filotimo*—in this case, the moral obligation to admit to theft when correctly challenged:

> I would get hold of you on the basis of *filotimo*, and you would tell me that you'd "eaten" my animals.
> "Tell me about it, friend, and I'll make you a gift of them. I'm not putting you on oath."
> Because, listen to me: "For [both] just and unjust matters," they say, "keep away from the oath."
> In a word, the oath is a weight. Oath? A sin, a weight!

The moral responsibility is clearly not borne by the perjurer alone: his interrogator has to accept some moral reponsibility for having put him in a position where lying might have been difficult to avoid. But there is also a social reason for the shepherds' reluctance to resort to the oath. Once a shepherd has sworn on a holy icon or on the Gospel, it is impossible to express open doubt about his word unless irrefutable proof can be found; and it is precisely the lack of proof that necessitates using the oath as a test in the first place. Doubting a man's oath means impugning his good faith. Even for Glendiots who profess disbelief in the teachings of the church, this is a serious affront: it challenges their *social* worth. In this context, it is worth recalling that *Khristhianos* means a *socially* good person, rather than a believer.

Even religious skeptics take the oath seriously in principle:

> I say that I don't believe. But when I go and take the oath there, no! I don't know, now, as it were, it's impossible for me to take an oath [falsely]. No! However much I say I don't believe, so to speak,

in religion, and I don't believe in the things that it [i.e., religion] writes, it still seems to me, how should I put this to you? as to what is written in the Gospel, I'm of the opinion that these things are very correct, and I shouldn't trample on them.

Perhaps so; but it should be noted that there is an expectation that oaths will be broken, whether made in church or taken on the Gospel in court; and, in fact, on another occasion the same speaker had not been averse to letting his own godfather's perjury protect him from a jail sentence for animal rustling.

When a shepherd does insist on demanding that his suspect submit to the oath test, he hopes that the latter will confess at the last moment. Often, this happens quite literally at the church door. In one such case (and the pattern is probably not uncommon), just as they were about to go inside the church, still shouting angrily, one of the pair of shepherds suddenly explained that he was indeed the culprit, acting in retaliation for an earlier theft. "In any case," he pointed out, "we're all square." The two shepherds shook hands and never entered at all; there was no point facing the ambiguous virtues of the sacred icon once the truth had been established and the shepherds had been able to recognize each other's manliness.

When "finally we ended up in church, on oath," a double bluff may be attempted:

> Because, since they insist on taking us to the oath for us to deny that we'd "eaten" a bunch of animals of theirs, we later suspect that . . . it must mean that they had "eaten" some of ours and that they think we know, and for that reason they insist that we were "eating," that we "ate," sheep of theirs. . . .
>
> In other words, you tell me, "Eftikhis, I don't believe you, I'm going to put you on oath."
>
> "But why, my dear Mikhalis, should I eat your sheep, so to speak? and not say 'Excuse me' to you, after all, for example, that kind of thing?"
>
> Sometimes you've "eaten" sheep of mine and you're of the opinion, you think I know it. And afterwards, when you tell me that we should go to church to take an oath . . . you'll tell me, "Eh, I have changed my mind anyway, and I'm convinced that you don't know anything."
>
> Then *I* get wise to things, and if I've lost sheep and haven't found out where they are, I say, "Hey! the cuckold! the way he's insisting that we go and take an oath and that he doesn't believe me must

mean that the sheep I lost at such-and-such a time were 'eaten' by *him*—and he thinks I know about it, and that's why he's doing this!"

To make his point more forcefully, the speaker gave as an example an occasion when, the original accusers having backed off in just this way from their demand that he take an oath, he then demanded that *they* do so. In the particular case in point, in fact, both sides were innocent, and the oath taking served the useful purpose of reassuring them of their mutual friendship—an especially important development since all concerned were fellow-Glendiots.

There is some fear of supernatural consequences for those who perjure themselves. The most common portent is the movement of the icon away from the perjurer's hand. A local monastery has an icon of St. George that is credited with terrifying efficacy: "The Saint used to give out miracles. If you knew that you were taking [an oath falsely], he'd hand you a miracle and you'd be shaking, shaking, shaking! And you'd own up."

The monastery's icon of St. George is credited with truly miraculous powers. Local ecclesiastical authority attributes this to the monastery's possession of a relic of the saint. The icon is specifically said to have turned away from a perjurer who denied having stolen a head of cheese; when the two principals left the church with the abbot of the time, the victim prayed to St. George for a miracle, whereupon a whirlwind arose out of nowhere, blew a pebble into the thief's face, and gouged out his eyeball.

The key terms associated with oath taking are the verbs *mologho* ("confess") and *metaniono* ("repent"). Both are terms with strongly religious associations, and have precise meanings in ecclesiastical dogma. Despite the ecclesiastical setting of oath taking, the use of these terms in that context is strictly secular, in the sense that "confession" is simply an admission of culpability and "repentance" a decision to own up despite initial displays of obduracy. No divine grace is expected in either case. Rather, both acts aim at the creation or restoration of *social* relationships, and the bitterness felt toward the perjurer seems similarly to be motivated by dislike for the social consequences of his dishonesty. "Confession" is actually a concept for which Glendiots evince some distrust, since it is possible to "confess" the thefts of others—an act of betrayal. Thus, the sacred context of oath taking, though accorded the awe due to any supernatural power, bypasses the offices of the church altogether. Those who go to the monastery to take their oaths carefully avoid contact with the abbot or his monks, and generally prefer the dead of night so that they can avoid meeting lay servants too.

Here we return to the theme of secrecy. Although the special efficacy of the monastery's icon of St. George is thought by local clergy to derive from the presence of the relic, the location of the monastery itself seems to be a powerful factor. It is set in the wooded countryside, accessible to all the surrounding villages but removed from all. It is thus neutral territory, and has the further advantage of permitting a much greater degree of secrecy than would be possible in a village church. Both factors may play a part in the selection of other settings for taking the oath. For example, if Glendiots and Tholiots want to avoid being seen, they may settle on a small and almost deserted church in the tiny village that lies between their respective communities. Such secrecy prevents others from learning about the rift between two men who now expect to present themselves to the world at large as good friends. The danger that unfriendly gossips might try to disrupt the new alliance is thus minimized as far as possible.

It is not even necessary to go to a church at all. Two cothieves put each other on oath because, when their booty suddenly disappeared, they became extremely suspicious. (In fact, someone else had seized a chance to steal it.) They selected a stone: "On the rock, we made the sign of the Cross, and he put his hand there on it and took an oath. Then I too put my own [hand] on it and also took the oath." The words were no less terrible for being out in the open air: "May God have nothing to do with the [i.e., my] soul if I took the meat!" Apparently it persuaded the conspirators; and their faith was shortly thereafter borne out by the discovery of the real culprits' identities. The speaker became *sindekni* with the real thieves, who turned out to be covillagers of the original pair—a potentially explosive situation that needed immediate repair.

The material presented in this chapter shows how Glendiots adhere to a fairly explicit set of rules of conduct in their raiding activities. When they break these norms, they hope to succeed in impressing others with their flair. More often, they incur reprisals in which it is the avenging victim who performs the more striking role, through a poetic justice that has to be matched by a well-flavored account.

The pattern of raid and counterraid reproduces in certain structural features the agonistic matching that characterizes such verbal activities as verse insults. The counterraid is not merely an economic retaliation; indeed, shepherds are adamant that the destruction of livestock entailed in raiding is far more likely to create an economic *loss* to both parties, although they recognize the more indirect but substantive benefits that a widespread net of *sindeknia* relationships can bring. Also, of course, *failure* to retaliate would invite economic destruction, since a weak shepherd is regarded as fair game.

But what seems particularly important to the Glendiots is the *style* of retaliation. Here the notion of "matching," so explicit in local commentary on the verse insults, is helpful. The examples given above show that a successful act of revenge is one that so appropriately caps the original injury that it draws attention to its own significance. Here is a true poetics of action. A ram is stolen from an apparently defenseless, lone shepherd; his young son steals a bell and lets the animal go. Thieves refuse to own up to their deed; their own goats are given stones instead of bells—surely an apt comment on their failure to behave according to the canons of manly forthrightness. A Psiliot insults a Glendiot widow; her son mocks his manhood by using the very fact of his own youth as concealment.

These actions succeed as *mandinadhes* succeed, by playing with poetic form. The narratives about them perpetuate and reproduce analogous principles of structure and variation, foregrounding at yet another level what it is that makes Glendiot men distinctive in their own eyes. In the structures and style of the raiding narratives, we find still further elaborations on the theme of Glendiot manhood. These elaborations are not only conducted at the level of explicit narration; they also entail the expressive negotiation of the narrative form itself.

CHAPTER SIX

RECIPROCITY AND CLOSURE

Context and Structure:
Preliminary Observations

An ethnographer receives information in a form already shaped by the ethical and aesthetic values of the community being studied. Just as the moral content of the discourse undergoes constant revision and reinterpretation, moreover, so too the form and structure of that discourse reflect a continual negotiation of the narrative aesthetic. The very distinction between moral and aesthetic values blurs: both are negotiated through social performance; both project "eternal verities" in which consistent form masks uncertainty and contest over interpretive content; and both achieve an appearance of self-evidence through what Douglas has called "backgrounding" (1975:7).

For the purposes of this analysis, however, it may be useful to retain the distinction a while longer. In the previous chapters, we have seen how the poetics of everyday performance entails strategies of male contest, specifically male contest over feminized "objects." The discourse, though abetted by verbal symbols, is semiotically much broader than a purely verbal concept of poetics would imply; the verbal symbols themselves do not so much dominate the discourse as serve to foreground some of its structural features. The entire gamut of symbols deployed in this discourse signifies a disciplined tension, which includes the tension of contest over how well individuals perform the discourse. Such a degree of systematic reflexivity suggests that the verbal part of the discourse might predictably yield further, illuminating evidence of the poetic principles at work.

It is something of a truism that texts cannot be read well except in relation to context. But the contexts themselves are constructed by the authors of the texts. Indeed, the Glendiot concept of *simasia* recognizes this: meaning resides less in a particular text than in the *relationship* between text and a provisionally defined context. All previous textual material—as in a string of *mandinadhes*—is part of the context to which the emergent new text must respond.

From this point of view, any distinction between "how the Glendiots tell stories" and "what actually happened" is entirely artificial. Both the event and the narration of event are social constructions, each reinforcing the other: the context of event is thus also a text in its own right. Again, Glendiot theory recognizes this in the conflation—as it must seem from a literalist perspective—of the concepts of *exciting event* and *story* in a single term, *istoria*, which also significantly happens to be the official term for "history."

This is not to say that Glendiots never tell lies. From their point of view, however, lies, like thefts, are strategies to be employed creatively in the performance of the self. The rueful comment that many animal thieves laced their narratives with "pepper" was not uniformly censorious. True, it probably represented a certain reluctance to admit me, an outsider, to the whole range of the "folds of the Glendiots' bellies." But love of strong-tasting food bears approving witness to a shepherd's manliness.[1]

Although most of the material I collected was given to me in the comparative privacy of my house, a few narratives were performed in what, for the villagers, seems to be the most usual context: in a coffeehouse. Not every such establishment is equally appropriate; some are too large, or have too diverse a clientele, for the appurtenances of intimacy to be maintained—for intimacy, like secrecy, must be performed. The ideal setting is a small coffeehouse, frequented by closely related agnates and their more trustworthy associates. Thefts are also discussed in the privacy of the home, and this seems to be the primary means by which boys begin to learn the principles by which they will be expected to emulate their fathers.

The foregrounding of secrecy is consistent with a number of features already discussed. Perhaps most important of all is the fact that it shows the narrator to be capable of comporting himself well before others. Then again, it suggests an ability to steal effectively: keeping secrets is essential to successful raiding. Verbal continence, moreover, is metonymically indicative of the self-restraint that marks a powerful man, one who does not need to boast: for boasting invites retaliation, as happened when a Glendiot shepherd disproved a colleague's assertion that none could rob him, by setting fires all around his sheepfold and driving the animals out into his own waiting arms. Thus, to be secretive while, at the same time, letting others know of one's skill is a delicate balancing act, which itself is a sign of manhood that others may try to dispute; it calls for a finely tuned sensitivity to what constitutes an appropriate time and place for the recounting of raids. Like a singer who emphasizes his excellence by demurring when invited to perform, the animal thief must demonstrate a commendable reticence when urged to speak of his deeds.

My own involvement as audience to the narratives reproduced in this book has undoubtedly also had some effect on their style and content. Some aspects of this influence are revealing, both with regard to the more general problem of the ethnographer's effect on the generation of data, and more specifically for the analysis of the raiding texts themselves. Constant checks to see "whether I had understood" provide a valuable reminder of the somewhat atypical circumstances under which, simply by being an ethnographer, I was hearing the accounts of raiding. Initially, I encountered an entirely understandable reticence about the whole phenomenon of raiding. Villagers clearly thought that I might embarrass them before their fellow-Greeks, whose contemptuous view of all Cretans as "goat thieves and knife pullers" causes them so much distress. They were also concerned, at a broader level, to deny the Greekness of raiding.

These circumstances now give me the opportunity to illustrate how narrative form can reproduce social relations. Many of the raiding narratives I heard began with some kind of disclaimer about the role of raiding in Greek or Cretan society. Again, it is important not to take these remarks in conjunction with, for example, the story about the Greek who offered to get Christ out of jail, as proof that one party or the other must have lied. Rather, the tension between introspective self-recognition and extroverted self-presentation, the ideologically motivated struggle between two mutually opposed semiotic systems,[2] is a pervasive feature of all Greek social discourse; nowhere is it more so than in Glendi, where peculiar circumstances allow villagers to challenge the official discourse and decompose its encompassing claims.

The tendency to begin a narrative with such a disclaimer before plunging into a description of some highly illegal activity indicates and reproduces this tension. We might be tempted to complain about an apparent internal contradiction. For the Glendiot shepherd, however, such contradictions between the outer and inner realities of his collective identity—at the national, local, village, and patrigroup levels alike—are the very substance of social experience. They are also a requisite part of effective performance. That they are limned in the sequential structure of a raiding narrative, especially one that has been addressed to an inquisitive foreigner, shows how narrative form does indeed reproduce social experience, and how the expression of that experience can never be independent of the audience for which it is being recounted. Narrative sequence is not necessarily a reproduction of temporality, though this may be an expectation in some cultural settings. It is more likely to express what the narrators themselves regard as a significant relationship between experiences (cf. Herrnstein Smith 1981:223; Ricoeur 1981:175). Thus, when raiding narratives open with statements about the nonexistence of raiding in Greek culture, and especially the role of Turkish misrule in engendering it, we should read that progression as an expression of the ideological tension that itself gives meaning to every act of raiding. It is only to experiences that *lack* tension, whether personal or ideological, that Glendiots are unwilling to attribute "meaning."

Consider the situation. A shepherd has come to see me after dusk, when his visit, if noticed, will be treated as appropriately secretive. His unobtrusive style of arrival shows respect for the village canon, according to which he should not display the less respectable aspects of village life to an outsider. On the other hand, everyone knows by now that I am aware of the high incidence of animal theft, and my visitor is not averse to impressing a new audience with his courage and skill. Thus, in beginning his tale in rather formal language and with a disclaimer, he is first building a wall of words around the central theme. As he warms to his task, his language changes. More obviously dialect forms creep in; the excitement of remembrance glows in his twinkling eyes; and the voice may drop to a deeper growl, itself a symbol of pastoral manhood. At the end, he may use some formulaic phrase to indicate closure: "And [so the story] ended." We have returned to the more public world.

The self is heavily invested in the performance of these narratives. The narrator is usually either the thief or, in a few cases, the mediator. When his raid is unsuccessful, the narrator cannot present himself in a conventionally heroic cast. No matter: such instances provide free rein for an ironic self-mockery, and perhaps also offer an attractive opening for other audience members as well. The following example illustrates one way in which failure—especially failure in a good cause—can be converted through personal restraint into a symbolic compensation. It continues an incident we have already encountered.

After stealing a sheep, the speaker discovered that it was the property of his marriage sponsor (*koumbaros*). Over the objections of his hungry companion, he let it go:

Ah, well; I let it go. Yes, and then I chance upon (*mou tikheni*) a feather in the moonlight, as we were wending our way back. We hadn't achieved a thing, we were returning home along this way, and on the road I came across this hawk feather.

Say I, "A pox upon you! Just let me take you, as it were, for a remembrance."

So, well, I take it and put it in my waist like a knife; look, I was holding that there hawk feather like a knife. Do you see it [*pointing to the actual feather*]?

Here his wife broke in, with apparent irony: "He brought it as meat." And her husband took up the cue immediately, and without any evident awareness of irony on her part: "Yes—instead of meat. And we came back without having achieved anything. We didn't do a thing!" By combining the modest concluding disclaimer with the wistful symbolism of the souvenir hawk feather, the speaker suggests that he had not genuinely failed. He had indeed grasped the offering of opportunity, the feather that he "chanced upon" on the moonlit road. This is the verb that a raider uses of the sheep he "happens to come across" in the high foothills, and which he then steals more or less as a matter of course; it is the term applied to the way in which a *mandinadha* "comes to" an inspired singer.

But it is his wife who offers him the opportunity to convert the feather into symbolic meat. Her intervention completes the pattern his narrative has begun. He has given up the stolen animal, judging—probably correctly—that his manhood would be better demonstrated by this action than by eating an animal so easily obtained. He stood up to his friend (who is a key member of the audience to which he is presently telling of the exploit), insisting on a scrupulous observance of the conventions. His loss of the meat is balanced by a gain. In this case, the gain is a feather which he holds "like a knife" before placing it close to his body. His wife then completes the conversion process, allowing him to claim, only half-jestingly, that the feather was a prize analogous to the meat he might have expected to gain from the raid:

1.	2.	3.	4.
ITEM LOST	1ST GAIN	2ND GAIN	3RD GAIN
actual meat $\rightarrow$	hawk feather $\rightarrow$	knife $\rightarrow$	as-if meat

The *agent* of the final conversion is the speaker's wife. The whimsical initial conversion of a feather into a knife is iconically reinforced by the gesture of tucking it in the belt; as an instrument-possession in the mode already described, it is marked by a curious dialectological feature that allows Glendiot speakers to "feminize" certain words" here *mašera* for standard *makheri*). Its further conversion into meat, however, has no iconic conventions to reinforce it, and relies principally on the wife's understanding of her husband's motives. At this point, the woman herself becomes the female instrument—the husband's possession, as it were— for converting the object at hand into meat. From her own point of view, as opposed to the androcentric perspective expressed by the husband, the situation perhaps called for irony. But the husband's unhesitatingly matter-of-fact incorporation of the image into his narrative flow—"Yes, instead of meat"—shows that for him, at least, the symbolic conversion had proved quite acceptable.

This example is especially valuable in that its performative context is probably much closer to everyday narrative behavior than most of what I was able to collect. Above all, the audience included both pro- tagonists—with their internal differences over whether the sheep should have been killed and eaten or not—as well as the speaker's wife. Our own presence was thus somewhat diluted; the other actors were talking to each other as well as to us. The narrative reflects these circumstances, and bears comparatively few traces of the editing that some informants seemed to feel was necessary.

The sequence of this narrative follows the temporal sequence of events fairly consistently. It also exhibits structural features that seem to emerge at least as strongly in other narratives in which literal temporality appears far less significant. In particular, the resolution in terms of symbolic consumption, especially of meat, expresses the affirmation or denial of manhood.

The feminization of the possessed object is also strongly marked, not only in the gender of the "knife" image, but also in the gender changes of the stolen sheep earlier in the story. "The animal" begins as gram- matically neuter (*to zo*). Once it has been captured, it is no longer an "animal" or a "sheep," but simply a *feminine* "it" (*tine*). Then, when the thieves make ready to leave, the "animal" reverts to its noun des- ignation, but as the disagreement between the two thieves erupts its gender becomes ambiguous. The righteous speaker tells his companion that he "won't take *this sheep* (*toutine to provato*) even if the very earth should be destroyed!" *This sheep* is feminine in ostension ("this" [*toutine*[F]]— i.e., the one we are stealing) but neuter again inasmuch as it is a sheep (*to*[N] [art.] + *provato*[N]). This is not a question of simply matching gram- matical categories to genders (i.e., noun:neuter::pronoun:feminine [or demonstrative:feminine]), since there is *also* a feminized form of the noun (*provata*), which shows up at suggestive points in these narratives. Rather, such gender changes seem to mark shifts in the animal's status from mere beast to disputed possession and back.

These grammatical peculiarities, which "violate" the norms of standard demotic Greek, are viewed by Glendiots as evidence of their cultural exclusion from the Greek mainstream. As such, of course, they are apt markers for the narration of events that pit the villagers against the law. Villagers often express much the same kind of embarrassment about their language habits as they do about endemic animal theft. In the actual narratives, then, the use of grammatically distinctive forms in conjunction with the imagery of male contest contrasts tellingly with the use of rather formal opening phrases for the expression of embarrassment that Crete should ever be host to anything so reprehensible. A more detailed exploration of these textual features is in order.

Context and Structure: Signifying through Sequence

Many accounts of raiding exhibit three distinct moments: the self-justifying preamble, the climax of the raid itself, and the formal closure. Not all are represented equally often, or with uniform emphasis; nor should they be taken as clearly defined *parts* of the narratives. But all three are common enough, and conventionalized to a sufficient degree when they do occur, to permit identification.

THE PREAMBLE

This introductory moment, which may not reappear in stories subsequent to the first one of a session, usually carries a strong statement of collective self-exoneration. The entire phenomenon of animal theft is conventionally attributed to Turkish oppression; within this framework of extenuation, there is often a more general allusion to "hunger," a device that allows the narrator to identify the thief's momentary condition with the hapless state of the Cretan people. A young thief may simply attribute his action to hunger, or he may make a more explicitly ideological statement.

The following account illustrates the relationship between a very brief preamble about deprivation and the consumption of very large amounts of food at the end:

> *Klepsa* is a [result of] deprivation. Just now, on Monday evening, my sister [had a child of hers] baptized. Well, in order to have enough money to pay for the meat which they'd be getting for the occasion, she'd've had to shell out at least thirty thousand [drachmas]. Forty!
>
> Well, I happened to be around at the time, this was about five or six days ago, and I was passing through, having taken some

animals to a certain place, some sheep, and the place where I took them was my sister's village.

So I chanced (*'tikhe*) to drop in on her. To see how she was getting along. And when I came by and then learned about all this, when she told me later, she said, "On Monday," she said, "I'll be baptizing my child."

So I said, "What's this I hear about having a baptism?"

Said she, "Yes," she said, "we're going to baptize him, and we were going to telephone you to tell you to come to the baptism."

My brother-in-law was there, and as we chatted he told me, "I'm in difficulties," he said, "and I don't have a penny. Where will we find the five or six animals I'd need," he said, "so that I can do the baptism? For six animals at the 5,000 that you need for each one I'll have to pay 30,000."

So I said to him, "Don't go," I told him, "even to get a single kilo of meat! I'm going to bring it to you," I said, "right here."

I had some animals, sheep, in a fenced enclosure [i.e., where they were kept after being stolen from their original owners], and I told myself that I'd bring him five or six animals from there. So I set off with my truck, and put eight animals in it. And I took them there, and we slaughtered them right there, after putting them in an animal shelter of theirs. And he [i.e., the brother-in-law] slaughtered them and hung them up right there.

There aren't many thieves there at all. Thieves, in that village, simply don't exist. It's a *small* village.

So, he slaughtered them, and there wasn't any business with certificates or official seals or anything.[3] He slaughtered them, skinned them, and put them in the ovens. And so he met their obligation.

Now if I hadn't been around, if I hadn't been on my way through there so that he could tell me about the forthcoming baptism and that he didn't have a penny and all that, he'd have been in debt to the tune of thirty thousand, perhaps forty thousand drachmas; if he had to sit tight and look around for the money, his children would have gone short. All because of the forty thousand for the food so that he could pay off the sheep that he wanted to slaughter for his child's baptism. Whereas I got them free of charge! Unweighed [*aziyasta*]! Now I, I took care of things for them, and looked pretty generous, eh? saying, "Eat, eat!" He told me he needed six animals, but I took him *eight* animals!

For this speaker, the depredations of the Turks had merely been replaced by other, governmental rapacities. Animal theft, in his judgment, was a response to need, and hunger justified all. The preamble cues the listener to expect a victory over the hunger to which it alludes.

Other narratives are even more explicit, especially when they locate the event in a period of unusual distress such as the German Occupation. In those texts, the *pina* ("hunger") of that terrible time almost invariably sets the scene for a massive capture of livestock:

> I once went raiding, during the Occupation, in '43. . . . Twenty-five goats! And we brought them here and sold them. It was the Occupation, we were in dire straits. We slaughtered them, we ate; we were hungry.

Such an introduction again cues the listener to expect success at the end of the story: the victim demanded compensation, but was persuaded out of his unmanly insistence and the principals became *sindekni*.

The German Occupation was a harsh time for the Cretans. The practices that had seemed so localized hitherto could now be presented in terms of a curse that had afflicted the entire nation:

> Once, during the Occupation, I thought I'd go and steal some sheep. Then, of course, people were hungry. There were Germans in Crete, and in all of Greece. And we hunted for sheep and goats, whatever we chanced to find.

He and his companion stole a hundred sheep, one-fifth of the victim's entire flock. Although "hunger" was the expressed motive for this raid, it was certainly of a very long-term variety: "Later, we shared out the sheep and "made them sheep"—that means, we made them our own animals—and we also slaughtered some and ate them." The actual eating seems to have come as something of an afterthought. But since "eating" includes theft, "hunger" is also a synonym for the deprivation that justifies such actions.

The preamble is usually brief, when it appears at all. Among Glendiots, it is hardly enunciated, but it does serve as a useful boundary to mark the incorporation of an inquisitive stranger into a more intimate sharing of Glendiot experience. In this regard, it parallels the official, national ideology in its reluctance to accept raiding as a genuinely endemic phenomenon: the causes are always sought in foreign influence or domination. But, concurrently, it expresses the Glendiot perspective on *all* forms of imposed authority. As long as there are governments of any sort to oppress the villagers, there will be hunger; and as long as Glendiots are hungry, they will eat. The play of these concepts is elaborated in the main body of the narratives.

THE CLIMAX OF THE RAID

Perhaps the most striking stylistic feature of these narratives, but also of Glendiot speech in general, is the play of grammatical gender to which I have already alluded. In particular, the usual neuter term for sheep (*provato*) is replaced by feminine pronouns (or occasionally by the feminized forms *provata* and *provatina*).

This is not just a linguistic nicety, to be treated as irrelevant to the more usual concerns of social analysis. The regularity with which these gender alterations occur also suggests that they are not usefully treated as simple errors. Glendiots, when asked about such usages, may dismiss them as poor grammar, but this is evidently one side of the disemic phenomenon: the very fact that I, an outsider, could ask about something so far removed from Athenian speech invited an "official" rather than a "local" level of response. The gender alterations occur with a high degree of consistency, and must clearly be treated as indices of symbolic value. Systematic violations of an officially endorsed grammatical code reproduce the local response to the official regulation of social life (see also Kevelson 1977).

In Glendi, at least among men, possessions as well as the (possessed) instruments of possession are often represented as feminine in gender. The conversational conventions associated with card playing provide an especially elaborate illustration of how this conceptual principle organizes male relations in Glendi. The male subject is represented as active, in contrast to the passive female subject. This, as has been noted with regard to modern literary form, is characteristic of a male-authored discourse (Berks 1982:50) and is brought into sharp relief in Glendi by two circumstances: the political dominance of the men, and their own claim to controlled speech as a symbol of that dominance. From their androcentric perspective, their very words have the status of instruments under their guidance: speech is a political tool. That the women express similar sentiments in public does not necessarily indicate that they share the same perspective at all times, of course, and their own more "muted" discourse usually only surfaces in more intimate settings as a gentle irony.[4] But in the political arena, in which I include animal rustling as a major basis of political alliance, male discourse has the floor. In this setting, gender-related peculiarities of male discourse are unlikely to be insignificant.

Often, the narrator does not specify whether the animals are sheep or goats. This is significant, since, while *provato* ("sheep") is grammatically neuter, goats are usually called by sex-specific terms (*traghos*, male; *egha, arogha, katsika*, female; the generic neuter *katsiki* is comparatively unusual). All the terms used of "animals" are neuter, without exception. *Ozo* is recognizable as the standard *zoo; zoumbero* and *ekhnos* are local forms and recognized as such; and *miaro* is an east Cretan term affected by some of the longer-ranging transhumant shepherds, apparently to indicate their expertise in matters far from home. Thus, when animals are described with the object pronoun *tsi*, which can be either masculine or feminine (i.e., as the Cretan equivalent of the standard Greek accusative plural pronouns *tous* [m.] and *tis* [f.]), the listener is alerted to a shift of emphasis. (The neuter accusative plural pronoun, *ta*, is the same as in standard Greek.) It seems that the pronoun here is unambiguously feminine: adjectives in the same position are given unambiguously feminine suffixes.

Here are some examples:

1. In describing a retaliatory raid, a shepherd said, "We took four [*tessera*^{N}] choice [*dhialekhtes*^{F}] slaughter-animals [*sfakhta*^{N}] and took them [*tsi*$^{F/M}$] and left" (actual order: *tessera sfakhta dhialekhtes*). The animals are described as being for meat: this will happen at the *end* of the theft, when the beasts cease to be an object of ongoing contest. At the moment of "choosing" the animals, however, the thieves are in the process of contesting possession, and this is conveyed by the feminine gender of the adjective, with its active-verb connotation.

2. A young thief "had gathered together some thirty sheep in various places in the area, so to speak, and had them [*ts'*$^{F/M}$] together with my other [*alla*^{N}] sheep [*provata*^{N}], marked [*samomenes*^{F}] with the same ear mark." The "other" sheep were no longer in dispute; the successful disguising of the thirty that had been stolen recently, however, was still a matter of concern. This speaker did go on to talk of "my own" sheep using the feminine form for the possessive adjective, but here there was some implied doubt as to whether he would be able to claim permanent custody of *any* of the sheep in his possession; the young man in question had relatively few animals that he had not acquired through theft.

3. From the foregoing, it may look as though there is a simple correlation between grammatical unit and gender, and this might cast doubt on the specifically social implications of the gender transformations. Here, then, is a counterexample. In the story about the replacement of bells by stones, which are grammatically feminine in Greek, the owners "went in the morning and they see the [*tsi*$^{F/M}$] stones [*petres*^{F}] hung [*kremasmena*^{N}] on the animals. . . ." Here the metaphorized genitals are transformed into

grammatically neuter replacements; remember that the penis itself is often feminized as an instrument of aggression and possession.

The third example shows how feminization can also be reversed. Taken together, all these instances demonstrate the ideological implications of grammatical form at two levels. At the more inclusive level, they defy prescriptive official norms; their very changeability stems from the refusal to adhere to absolute canons that characterizes Glendiot responses to the official world generally. At the level of local interaction, the grammatical play on gender reinforces the ideology of male possession and domination, and the deployment of that ideology as an expressive weapon in male contests.

The climactic moment of a theft is the "eating" of the stolen livestock. This is usually bracketed with the feminine/masculine pronoun (e.g., $ts'^{F/M}$ *ifagha*, "I ate them"). But the act of "eating" is, as we have already seen, extremely ambiguous. Given that some shepherds prefer not to admit to their thefts immediately, the claim that they have "eaten" the animals may imply a continuation of the contest. When, on the other hand, they manage to preserve the animals alive and to incorporate them into their own flocks without being detected, the usual pattern is for the animals to be described using neuter grammatical forms. At this point, they have ceased to be objects of contest: they are no longer interesting to the appropriately agonistic male.

CLOSURE / RESOLUTION

Preservation of the live animals represents one definitive narrative closure that also constitutes a resolution of tension in the social relationship. Since successful *arotima* ("asking") normatively entails the return of all animals that are still alive to their owner, the absorption of the animals into the thief's flock means that no immediate social benefit accrues to either party; the tension of the successful raid is not replaced by that of a satisfying alliance, and the animals rapidly cease to be counters in a social game.

This rapid diminution of social interest is indicated by the concluding phrase of most narratives about such cases: "I turned them into sheep" (*ta 'kama provata*). The implication is that the animals have ceased to be something other than themselves. For "sheep," a narrator may use the term "live ones" (*zondares*[F], *zondaria*[N], *zondarika*[N], *azondana*[N]). The feminine term is comparatively rare; it seems to be used mostly in generalized descriptions of how raids are conducted. In narratives of specific raids, the neuter forms supply emphasis to the closure: since the animals have been fully absorbed into the flock, they have ceased to be the objects of male contest.

A good illustration of this is provided by a narrative in which there was no expectation of continuity. A man in his mid-sixties was taken on a raid by his son, who told him that he ought to be able to boast of having been able to steal animals even at his advanced age! The fact that father and son went together announces the idiosyncratic nature of the raid. Father and son, or two brothers, normally avoid raiding together, as the danger that both might be killed in a fight is considered too much of a risk for their families, even though fatalities are actually quite rare. Especially in the case of brothers, a survivor is always expected to take responsibility for the household of the deceased. Father-and-son raiding also means a generational category confusion, since raiding is to some extent the activity by which the son lets his father know that the time for a change of family leadership draws near. But in the present case, pride in the father's vigor sufficed to overcome these normative expectations. The frame of the raid was not the usual one of creating new social relationships, since the father had long since established a more than adequately fearsome reputation for the purpose, and had widespread contacts as a result. This was a raid conducted for pure bravado, which I was told about as I had inquired whether he would tell me about his very last one:

> We left from Ksilia when I was sixty-five years old. And we went because he was taking me, he said, for the last time to go for a theft.
>
> We went, we saw the shepherd, and he took fright and left, and we then herded the sheep together and took three or four, I don't remember how many, and we went and released them [into our own flock] and I turned them into *zondaria* and they made many animals for me [i.e., through births]!
>
> This was my last theft!

The shepherd was clearly not a desirable ally, since he ran away from an elderly man and his son. But why be concerned? This was one raid in which the creation of new social ties had not furnished the pretext or the context; and so the raiding text itself closes a lifetime of pastoral success with socially neutral, and grammatically neuter, mother sheep.

A second, and contrasted, form of closure is provided by the narratives that end with the creation of a social bond. The young shepherd who sent his brother-in-law to raid an enemy concluded:

Meanwhile, this guy will have said to himself that "he [i.e., the speaker] got angry in this way so that he could turn them [i.e., the raiders] into friends"; he invited my brother-in-law Stelios to go and baptize a child of his.

At this juncture, questions invite a reaffirmation of the same closure. I asked whether it was Stelios who had baptized a child from the other side:

Yes, he baptized a child of his, of this guy's. Even though he was then saying, like, he'd show them what he was made of [*tha kani tha dhiksi*, lit., "he'll do, he'll show"], once he finds out where his sheep are, so to speak. Afterwards, however, he invited my brother-in-law and he baptized a child of his just so that this thing could come to an end.

Here the story ends with the explicit conversion of enmity into alliance. The raid generated the social tie; the young shepherd had demonstrated his knowledge of the norms; and his brother-in-law had gained a new ally.

The baptism is not always so obviously related to the events that preceded it. In one narrative I recorded, it simply supplies the formal closure in what, outside of simple considerations of narrative structure, seems an inconsequential progression. The protagonist stole thirty sheep and took them to another village, not Glendi, where he and his companion slaughtered them all:

. . . and made merry because we had been slaughtering and we were eating and we got drunk and we made merry there for two days! And we made merry, and I also did a baptism! I also baptized a child.

When I questioned him, this speaker insisted that the baptism had no connection with the theft: "There happened to be [*etikhen*] a child there, and I baptized it!" In short, he took advantage of an opportunity that turned an otherwise rather insignificant theft—one that might have yielded merely financial profit—into the basis for a social tie. Here, narrative sequence *transforms* an undistinguished exploit into one in which conspicuous consumption joins hands with the exhibition of improvisatory skill: "There happened to be a child there, and I baptized it!" By closing his narrative with this event, the speaker manages to convey the idea that he has successfully extemporized his personal flair.

Another set of transformations is generated by failed raids. The progressive conversion of the hawk's feather into a knife and then into meat illustrates one tactic, whereby the speaker replaces the key possession by a metaphorical substitute. Telling of an early failure, a mature narrator may dwell on how he successfully eluded capture, or on some incident (such as those in which a boot sole comes unstuck) where disaster and fear were overcome by flamboyance, if not by actual success on the raid. There is little reason for a narrator to tell of his own failures, unless it be to dramatize the hazards of the raid. Fear is not something to be suppressed; rather, its cold presence endows the account of even an unsuccessful raid with respect for the raider's courage.

Thus, in general, the forms of closure mostly serve to highlight the prowess of the raider, who in the majority of instances is also the narrator. In the progression of events from tension to equilibrium, the objects of contention are quite specifically *neutralized*. When, as in most raiding events, the progression is instead from negative tension (hostility) to positive tension (alliance), closure is marked contrastively by a social act such as baptism. Baptisms entail the massive consumption of meat, the object of contention now becoming that of commensality. Indeed, in a few tales, a peculiarly daring form of improvisation entails inviting the victim to eat the meat of his own animals. This is not an insult so much as a challenge, and it is appropriately answered by the contract of *sindeknia*. "Turning them into sheep" marks an *absence* of new social ties. In contrast to this, eating the meat marks the *creation* of such ties. Not all social ties follow the norms, however, and here the idiom of meat eating provides an expressive medium for negotiating the significance of some of the variations.

Transformations of Reciprocity

Both in physical action and in narrative form, Glendiot shepherds express a high regard for poetic justice. Insults are repaid with raids, or in extreme cases by puncturing the offender's cheese-making cauldrons; economic waste reinforces expressive contempt. In particular, the use of meat eating as a closure device provides a malleable idiom for representing some of the variations on normative reciprocity.

In the act of eating meat, shepherds convert hostility into a more affable relationship. One form of poetic justice that plays on this theme is to treat one's own victim to the stolen meat. If the victims should be police, of course, the act represents a victory for Glendiot values, and one that the police themselves are hard pressed to punish if they ever find out:

> In 1949 or '50, I was in grade school at the time, I remember that two people—thieves, let's say!—had brought a flock of stolen animals to my father, and he bought them.
>
> Well, these were from outside the area, from the other side of Mount Ida.
>
> Well, they say to him, "How much will you give us to leave them [here]?"
>
> "This much!"—for example—he told them a price.
>
> Says he [i.e., the thieves' spokesman], "Take them!"
>
> Of course, with the money that he gave them then, that money would have bought two sheep whereas there were [actually] thirteen.
>
> Well, when he'd given them their money and they had left, my father says, "I'll go down and slaughter one, for sale [i.e., as meat]." He went down and slaughtered a sheep, and then he comes up [again].
>
> At that time, there were detachments of police patrolling around all the time. As soon as he had brought the meat up for my mother to put it in the cooking pot, he shouts—still from outside—saying, "The police are making a search! the police! the police!"
>
> Now he had the twelve remaining sheep inside the house.
>
> Says he, "Phew! what am I going to do?" He goes down again and slaughters the twelve sheep. And we had a hay store. Hay. He goes and digs into the hay and throws them in there, and the police came and made an inspection.
>
> Actually, the thieves themselves had "nailed" [i.e., betrayed] him to the police, [saying] that he had stolen sheep inside.
>
> So the head of the police [detachment] says to him, says he, "They nailed you good and proper," he tells him, "but you understand how to do your work even better [i.e., how to conceal the stolen meat so that we cannot find it]! Keep your wits about you," he tells him, "wherever you take on stolen goods! Because they're out to ruin you."
>
> Anyway, he says, "As you can see," he says, "I, now, I don't have anything [like that]. I'm just cooking [*psino*]," says he, "two or three lima beans [*kouča*], and if you'd like to, sit down, and we'll eat them."
>
> They sit down, and my mother puts the meat out on the table.

Says he, "But—are *these* the sort of lima beans you have, Mr. Manousos?" he asks him.

Says he, "Indeed! These are *my* kind of lima beans!"

Manousos actually gave himself away slightly, since his word for "cooking" (*psino*) more properly signifies "roasting," and is most commonly applied to the preparation of meat. Also, even though his wife was doing the actual kitchen work, he claimed to be the one who was cooking. Unless meat were involved, this would sound improbable even as a fixed phrase; men more often say that their *wives* are cooking, as a pretext for inviting a friend in to eat.

The invitation is couched in a slightly exaggerated form of the mock-modest style that Glendiots commonly affect. A true meal must have meat, especially when guests are involved; thus, the "two or three lima beans" are a variation of the formula by which the host excuses the poverty of his table and the need to "make do" with "what one has" (*to vriskoumeno*). Again, the phrase cues the listener to expect a magnificent display of food: understatement of this order is ironical.

The story ends with the verbal conversion of lima beans into meat, and Manousos' triumph over both his betrayers and the by now thoroughly baffled police—who clearly realized that they have been brilliantly mocked, and yet could not avoid accepting the ostensibly polite hospitality they were offered without causing grave offense:

Eh! After they'd eaten, now, and drunk, and had really got their appetites going, he tells the head of the detachment, "What's left of the sheep that they 'nailed' on me I've got downstairs, but there isn't more than one. The others," he tells him, "have left."

Says he, "How come? Since we surrounded the village and have been watching it all night, how *could* they have left?"

Says he, "They've left! A helicopter came and took them!" [*Laughing.*]

There, it's finished.

[*After further thought*]: Whereas the sheep were inside the house, so to speak!

His triumph was total: with truly poetic irony, the police had eaten part of the evidence and totally failed to find the rest!

While the consumption of stolen meat by the victim or by the police can furnish a telling closure, there must be a precedent to justify the caustic implication. Otherwise, this act may warrant a more violent response. The young lad who brought a bell home in retaliation for the theft of his rams was especially incensed because the thieves, not content with stealing and slaughtering male animals, had encouraged a mutual friend to feed the boy on the meat and then swore this third person to absolute secrecy. In this case, they had not even carried out the ironic jest for themselves, and their manhood was consequently at risk.

The "conversion" of beans into meat is a symbolic claim to manhood. Like all such rhetorical strategies, it is reversible: some narratives/events entail depriving an unmanly male of his meat and replacing it by vegetable foods suitable for "female cooking" (i.e., foods in the category of *mayirepsimia*). In the following illustration, this symbolic opposition is further reinforced by two circumstances: the response is to the humiliation of a female dependent who could not legitimately respond with violence of her own; and the event occurred in a village that Glendiots profess to despise as singularly lacking in the hospitality that marks true manhood:[5]

> During the [German] Occupation, my wife went to Agora and she wanted to get carobs. And they told her the price of the carobs.
>
> So she took two sacks and filled them. Meanwhile, she went down below and they told her that the carobs were [too] cheap[ly sold at that price], and the person says not to give them to my wife. So my wife was obliged to pour out the carobs again onto the heap where they had been.
>
> She comes home in the evening and tells me, "I went to Agora to such-and-such a house, and I filled sacks with carobs and for a single *lepto*, for a ten-cent piece more, they wouldn't give me the carobs."
>
> Say I, "Let him be, it doesn't matter!"
>
> The next day I get up and go down there. Nighttime! And I go and open the gate to his courtyard. He had two goats inside, and a pig. So I get the goats out and take them, and the pig remains behind. As I was getting out into the alley, one of them got away from me, and only the other goat remained—so *I* took care of it in my belly, and *he* ate the carobs!

A true man does not steal pigs; the only *klepsa* I heard involving a woman was about the theft of a pig. More to the point here, the thief has challenged the Agoritis' manhood by *taking* meat while *leaving* the carobs for him—an inventively poetic extension of the Agoritis' rapacity. His action says, in effect: you are right to hang on to your carobs, since you are not man enough to look after your meat.

The gift of meat or of a live animal to a young thief who has just "come out on the branch" represents his accession to manhood. Conversely, the *refusal* of meat to a man who conducts an agricultural business in a socially unacceptable way, in an already despised village that is physically located *below* Glendi, connects a personal rivalry to symbolic cartography. By insisting on purely financial gain, the Agoritis associated himself still more firmly, in the Glendiot's eyes, with the supposedly effete values of those who live "down below."

To some extent, this contempt extends also to Glendiot farmers. The term for a farmer, *spitaris* (lit., "house person"), suggests "female" domesticity. If farmers ever steal, as some did during World War II, they take only fruit and vegetables. A farmer may not steal livestock, and the reason for this is quite explicitly stated: he has no animals for his victim to raid in retaliation. Glendiots are careful to stress the reciprocity of normative animal theft, since this is the basis of its deployment in the forging of new social links.

Two narratives about what can happen to farmers who have the temerity to raid reinforce their moral with dexterous sequencing. In the first example, at least, the story was well remembered, as the narrator had served as mediator and knew the other actors intimately. Apparent temporal distortions may thus not be the product of imperfect recall. In any narrative sequence, temporal ordering may always be overcome by other forms of classification (Goodman 1981:115), and the problem is then how best to identify and read the sequence in terms of salient categories. In Glendi, food symbolism is explicitly associated with the poetics of social identity, and seems to provide a common marker for stages of narrative progression. In examining these two incidents in which farmers in effect claimed manhood by stealing animals, the order of food-related events seems to overcome linear temporality to the point where the message of those events stands out more clearly.

The conceptual structure of the first of these two raiding stories is that of the *adynaton*. This is an extremely common figure of speech in Greek, and has associations with both the return of the dead ("when the crow turns white . . .") and the successful pursuit of a hopeless romance ("when people sow barley at the bottom of the sea . . .").[6] In the present narrative, the specific message of the implied figure of speech is that farmers eat meat when they can prove their manhood—a cruel taunt when flung down by shepherds, and all the more so when it is limned in actual events that are still well remembered:

He was a *spitaris*. And he used to "eat" many sheep.
Well, I'd be the one to go and ask him about it. He owned up to [having stolen them] all. He trusted me, let's say. He never concealed his doings from me. He'd tell me, "I stole them, but don't

tell," and I never did. Secret, always! And if he had cause to tell, at any time, I fixed up the business for him myself.

So he never went to jail, never paid a price for it. That's why he would tell me about them [i.e., the stolen animals].

Well, if he didn't go one day and bring back a sheep from Vrissi. Daytime, too! And he set it to boiling in their house.

But the owner from Vrissi left his village that night and came looking for it, and came to my house.

It was raining. And he says to me, "My sheep was stolen today. You find it for me, here in the village!"

Say I, "Sit down here, and I'll go out and take a stroll." And he was sitting in the house, and I go to [the farmer] Lamboyoryis, I'd felt right away that Lamboyoryis had stolen it.

Pressed to be more specific about how he had guessed, he said that he had "psychologized" the farmer:

Because he was a regular.

And really, I go to his house and say to him, "Like, the sheep of So-and-so from Vrissi, did you take it?"

He just stopped there a moment, and his wife rushes forward and tells me, "He did take it." And his wife told it just the way it was. "He took it, and you should take it away from him. Don't tell the other man about it, because he [i.e., Lamboyoryis] is a poor man."

Eh, he admitted doing it after that, and he says to me, he says, "I took it, and I still have it alive." "Eh, come on, hand it over to me!"

So I get out a rope, and tie it up [i.e., using the rope as a lead] and take it to the house of the man from Vrissi.

The man from Vrissi got all enthusiastic, he was so pleased: "Send him along to me tomorrow, and I'll give him ten *okadhes* . . . of cooked food, so that his children may eat."

And he sent it to him and went along himself, he gave him ten . . . *okadhes*, as they were in those days—we should tell the truth, eh?[7]—food for his children to eat.

And the food that he sent was a mixture of beans and green vegetables, highly prized but hardly a man's diet.

In addition to the conversion of male/shepherd/meat into female/farmer/vegetables, there is a concurrent theme that derives from the same ideological matrix. This is the view that theft is the result of deprivation; thus, the vegetables were sent so that the farmer's "children could eat"— a formula through which the man from Vrissi acts both hospitably and in a manner expressive of his status. Recall that a diet of meat alone is seen as exemplifying the hardship of the pastoral life; shepherds are far from averse to eating "cooked foods" themselves. But a theft of meat implies nominal "equality in contest" (*isopalia*) between thief and victim, and this the Vrissiot was not prepared to concede. By first recovering his animal through effective use of his connections in Glendi, then by showing his generosity in a way that explicitly *substituted* vegetables for meat, he managed instead to state his own moral superiority in un-equivocal terms. To have let the thief go undetected would not merely have cast doubts on his personal influence in the area; it would also have implied the possibility of a reciprocal relationship, and hence one of equality—clearly an unthinkable resolution under these circum-stances. His solution was triply effective: it marshalled the fundamental assumption that the giver is superior to the taker (cf. Mauss 1968 [1923-24]), blocked any possibility of a reciprocity that would have restored the balance, and made effective use of the symbolism of food without directly insulting the offending Glendiot. From rhetorical skills of such a kind is highland Cretan reputation made.

The narrative sequence reinforces this message. The tale begins with a statement of the relationship between the narrator-mediator and the thief, a statement that shows the former to be a man of trustworthiness, compassion, and good judgment. Then the tale moves to the theft itself. We are immediately alerted to the possibility of symbolic inversion: the theft was carried out during the daylight hours, a dangerous and perhaps even inappropriate undertaking. The victim, by contrast, anxious to reestablish his superiority over this upstart farmer, comes at night.

The sheep has been "set to boiling" in the would-be thief's house. Near the end of the story, however, it is led off alive! This apparent contradiction can be resolved if we interpret the first action as a statement of *intention*, in which the claim to manly status is made through the symbol of preparing meat. Boiling, too, is a thief's best strategy to elude detection when he cooks on the mountainside; here, however, we are already in his house, the domestic sphere, and this fact alone compro-mises his claims.

Lamboyoryis first denies everything. If he were a shepherd seeking an alliance with the injured party, this would be the correct stand for him to take; but we already know that he has no flock of his own. It is his wife who acts as the agent of conversion here, adopting the stereo-typically male role of protector and shamelessly alluding to her husband's poverty in order to save him from jail. At this point, it is revealed that the sheep is alive still: there was no flock here to absorb it, and the claim to meat-eating status has been found hollow. Now the boiled meat is transformed into "cooked food," as the narrator called it in discussing the story afterwards. Since the shepherd has succeeded in redressing the balance, he can afford to be magnanimous to a man who must rely on his wife for safety. The Vrissiot's success is further emphasized by another feature of the narrative sequencing: having been left in the mediator's house, he now suddenly reappears in his home village when the sheep is actually restored to him. Again, this does not seem to be a case of distortion or false recall, so much as one of the poetically effective uses of narrative structure and sequence. Back in his home village, the erstwhile victim is once again in control of his situation; for that is what "sitting in one's house" means in Glendiot speech. His restored control is sharply drawn in another contrast: whereas Lambo-yoryis had tried to take the meat to Glendi, the Vrissiotis turns the tables by having Lamboyoryis come to Vrissi for the vegetables.

By inversion, the significance of "sitting in one's house" is corroborated in the second story:

Vrondis had sheep, and some fellow from Osidi gets up and goes and steals his sheep. Later, he [the Glendiot] learned about them.

Well, and you see, the fellow from Osidi didn't have any sheep. He didn't have any sheep for Vrondis to steal from *him*, but he found out that he had two goats and so Vrondis ups and goes, because he was a really tough guy, there wasn't anyone stronger in our village, and he ups and goes to Osidi to the other fellow's house.

The house had two levels, and the man lived upstairs and had the goats down below.

So Vrondis goes and takes the door off. He takes it right off the hinges! And he takes it and, if you'll excuse me, pisses right on the door.

And then he takes the goats and leaves.

It's as though he said, "I've taken your goats, now you just eat what I left for you on top of the door!" (. . .)

It's like saying, "Sir, I didn't bother you, why are you bothering me? Did I bother you? Why did you steal my sheep? Since you knew they were mine!" (. . .) "And don't you steal from me again! . . . If you do, I'll come and sit in your house."

Here the response is more violent. The removal of the door not only violates the secrecy of the private home, but it also suggests a proverbial retribution:

Min gamis	*mi sou kanoune,*
Don't do [things to people]	*so they won't to you,*

min   bis   na mi sou poune,
don't   talk   so people won't gossip to you,

stin kseni   porta mi   khtipas če   ti dhiči sou spoune.
On another's door don't beat   lest your own   they break down.

Antisocial behavior is behavior that violates the principles of genuine reciprocity. Gossip is evil because it is hard to repay effectively; theft is polluting when it cannot be reciprocated; and the violation of a house demands equal punishment in return. All these social offenses are more or less equivalent to each other. Thus, a man who raids shepherds without having a flock of his own is, as the story very explicitly points out, inviting a poetic retribution of this kind.

Here, moreover, the meat is converted into a symbol far more contemptuous in its implications. The original offender is specifically told to "eat" what has been left on his door: he has forfeited the right to eat solid meat, or indeed anything fit for ordinary human consumption, and has instead been given liquid excreta to eat. The reversal of consumption reinforces the other violation of his manhood, the invasion of his house. For a man to "sit in his house" is a sign of respectability, of being worthy to be greeted by those who pass by outside; for someone else to sit in it, then, symbolizes his utter humiliation. The audacity of removing the animals from the man's own house, just as happened in the case of the carob merchant in Agora, serves exemplary notice on all farmers: those whose very name (*spitaris*) betrays the crucial role of the house (*spiti*) in their self-definition are the last ones who should so brazenly risk all they own.

Shepherds traditionally treated farmers with enormous contempt. Since shepherds generally have lower status than farmers in rural Greek mixed-economy communities, the Glendiots' elevation of the pastoralist emblematically expresses the paradox of Cretan identity: that the economic and social margin can be recast as the moral center. It is said that a prospective bride would formerly not so much as consider marrying a farmer if she herself came from a good patrigroup and shepherd's household. Not everyone is equally happy to accept this version of the past, understandably enough, and there are hints that the supposed dominance of the shepherds in generations gone by may even then have been tempered by a realization that other ways of life gave better access to the comforts and luxuries associated with economic and political power. One illustrative tale—which, significantly enough, I heard from a member of one of the smallest patrigroups, and which may well not be recent in origin—reverses the conventional wisdom entirely. What is more, it does so through the same symbolism of "eating" that we have seen play so prominent a part in the shepherd's narratives:

> Once upon a time, they say, a covillager of ours here found an in-marrying male [*ghambros*—one who marries a woman of Ego's patrigroup], and in this way he'd be getting married to a kinswoman.
>
> Well, but *she* said she wanted a shepherd, like, someone who was a thief [*kleftis*] or something like that. . . .
>
> But the first man wanted to arrange for a kinsman to marry her, who understood how to give her a good life, who was richer.
>
> She didn't want any of it! She said, "He's a farmer [*spitaris*]," and all that.
>
> She won, and instead of marrying the man whom the first man (who was some kind of uncle of hers) wanted her to, she goes and gets herself a shepherd. The thief, so to speak!
>
> Later on, after some time had elapsed, she got married to this fellow that she had been looking for, and all that, and then her uncle passes by the house and asks her how she is getting along.
>
> Says she, "Don't even ask," she says. "Poverty! evil! and I don't know what besides!"
>
> Yes, she'd kept on about how he was from a big patrigroup, this groom she'd married. She'd *wanted* to marry the guy! And now [her uncle] passes by and asks her, "How are you getting along now?"
>
> Says she, "Hunger [*pina*], I don't know what else! Poverty!"
>
> Then [the uncle] in turn says to her, says he, "Eat," he says, "a patrigroup now [*fae, lei, edha soi*]!"
>
> In other words, earlier on she'd wanted him since he was of good patrigroup [*ikhene soi*, lit., "he had patrigroup"], he was from a big patrigroup, he was from a big *ratsa* of the kind whose surnames last. And he says to her, he says, "Eat," says he, "a patrigroup now!"

Here is a reversal indeed. Now it is the desirability of the thief that is held up to ridicule, and "hunger," instead of justifying his way of life, has become a source of reproach to *him*.

While the story undoubtedly epitomizes the attitude of many small-patrigroup Glendiots in the past, it also represents a view of the pastoral life that is steadily gaining currency in the village as a whole. The new farmers, with their holdings in the lusher lands of villages at lower altitudes, their mechanized transport, and their substantial bank balances, have prospered to the point where it is no longer true to say that they are generally despised. Their profession, moreover, is less subject to the kinds of pressure that make a shepherd depend so much on having many close agnates: the work can be interrupted, the property is harder to loot than a flock of sheep, the life itself is fully sedentary.

Money has become an acceptable medium of power, of "eating." Now, suddenly, the valiant hunger of the shepherds looks much less attractive: the alternatives are gaining ground. To self-consciously traditionalist shepherds, their farming covillagers have begun to look suspiciously like lowlanders; but it is hard not to envy their sudden wealth. The farmers, for their part, have negotiated their way into their new status with the rhetoric of the traditionalists. In this tale, for example, "eating" has become an irony: big-patrigroup manliness has had to feed, as it were, on itself. Today, it is those who have money who "eat." A story like this, then, allows the hitherto lowlier members of the community to shake off their older status. A youth who was listening to the tale, and whose own patrigroup had dwindled to a shadow of its size two generations before, scoffed sourly, "And she didn't want [the man he had chosen for her], she wanted the one who was from a [large patrigroup] and was poor, and didn't want the one who was from a small patrigroup and had money!" Money has certainly not replaced animals as the single greatest source of prestige, although it is certainly the major medium of defining wealth. The transformation is in progress, however, to variable degrees depending on the status, occupation, and age of the speaker. Money is still viewed with a measure of suspicion: bank balances resemble flocks in their distressing vulnerability. But bank balances, as villagers have long since learned, are more stable than cash in hand. One villager, explaining how he had built himself up economically, recalled that he had worked for payment in English gold sovereigns, which used to be a common medium of exchange in Greece. As soon as he was able, he converted these extremely vulnerable *lires* into cash over which he had greater control. In describing this conversion, he remarked, "I turned them into money [*ta' kana lefta*]"—structurally, the same phrase with which a shepherd expresses the incorporation of stolen sheep into his flock. Given that gold sovereigns were long a popular medium of exchange, "turning them into money" is as impenetrable to a literalistic reading as the turning of sheep into sheep, and calls for greater attention to the specifically *social* implications of the phrase.

It is not merely that linguistic style has survived social and economic change. The closure phrase "I turned them into sheep" marks not only a narrative termination, but the absence of new social relations. Glendiots complain that the new commercialism they have experienced in the post-World War II period has undermined all the old reciprocities. Some regard this as an evil thing, and the end of hospitality; others see it as a product of "evolution" (or "progress"), and the basis of a less intensely pugnacious way of life. Whichever view a villager chooses to adopt, however, the central theme echoes a truly Maussian plaint: monetary exchange undermines the totalizing reciprocity of yesterday and obscures the bonds between people that gifts—and, we should add, thefts—create (cf. Mauss 1968 [1923-24]:258-260; Blok 1983:46). The closure of narrative form is a closing of social form, a conclusion to the active experience of mutuality; and the use of such a bleakly terminal phrase as "I turned them into money" also suggests the closure of an older idiom of social life.

Glendiot rhetoric is well illustrated by the narrative materials just explored. Their internal sequencing helps us to understand the significance of particular formulae when they appear in everyday speech. For the Glendiots themselves, the distinction between everyday speech and narrative is blurred by a poetics that informs both the entire range of verbal discourse and the range of social action: an *istoria* is *any* interesting event, be it narrative or experiential. It is only when we try to argue that the shepherds "never" or "always" eat only meat that we also impose too rigid a distinction between narrative and event, image and actuality, fiction and fact. When a Glendiot picks up his knife and starts tearing strips of meat off a bone, or jestingly refuses to sit down to a meatless meal, he is not excluding the possibility of *ever* eating vegetables; rather, by his carefully nuanced behavior, he emphasizes those elements of his interaction that make a contextually appropriate claim to manhood. Tales of raiding are, in this sense, just another form of poetic action, like the deeds that they describe. If they are more accessible than the raids themselves, they are also more fragile precisely because they appear not to be "the thing itself." They can be derided as improbable, as seasoned with too much "pepper." But when they succeed, they establish the speaker's identity as a man whose words are of a quality to match his physical actions. In both, he is a poet of his own manhood.

SIN AND THE SELF

Negotiating the Self

The negotiation of personal identity always also entails the testing of social values. Even the most inventive displays of male self-regard must prove acceptable if they are not to backfire, but the truly skilled performer tests and stretches the tolerance of his peers to the limit. Given the exaltation of tension in Glendiot social life, moreover, the ability to carry off a needling verse insult or an outrageously daring raid is highly prized. In this regard, Glendi differs markedly from many other Greek communities, where the self-regard known as *eghoismos* evokes ambivalent assessments at best (see Herzfeld 1980a).

Even among the Sarakatsani, for whom *eghoismos* is a social virtue in a man, its positive aspect is taken as a sad comment on the fallen condition of humankind: by appealing to the doctrine of Original Sin, Sarakatsani are in effect enabled to justify attitudes that conflict with the humility enjoined upon all Christians by their religion (Campbell 1964). In Glendi, however, such considerations are taken less theologically. At most, villagers assume that the human condition as such precludes social harmony. More specifically, they attribute their own institution of animal theft to a *political* version of original sin, the "fall" of Christian lands to the oppressive Turks and their successors—including, of course, the present-day bureaucracy.[1] All aspects of their life that do not harmonize with official values are so excused: endemic theft, quarrelsome social relations, violence, uncouth speech with strong evidence of Turkish influence. Politically imposed hunger breeds ethical sin. Gendiots resent a world in which their own definition of wrongdoing stands so far removed from that of the encompassing nation-state.

The social ideology of most Glendiots is exemplified by one woman's blunt assertion that "bad *eghoismos* doesn't exist." In Glendi, men (and to some extent women also) constantly challenge social tolerance because challenge itself is a social norm. For those who fail, usually because they lack the ability to maintain an aggressive stance once they have initiated it, the label of *pseftoeghoistis* ("pseudo-*eghoistis*, faker of *eghoismos*") may lie in wait.

Not everyone agrees, of course, whose *eghoismos* is genuine and whose is not. Farmers, too, are much less anxious to claim *eghoismos* for themselves, attributing it instead—and somewhat disdainfully at that— to the shepherds. The conventional view of Mediterranean value systems as based on a complementary opposition between honor and shame is particularly inapplicable here, as a key component of *eghoismos* and of *filotimo* (the term most commonly translated as "honor") is the notion of *dropi* (usually rendered as "shame"). Viewed through the prism of the usual honor-and-shame gloss, it would be hard to make sense of a Glendiot's remark that he had left Germany and returned to his native village "out of *eghoismos*, [out of] *dropi*": he meant by this that loyalty to his home community would have made him deeply embarrassed had he not left behind all the pleasures of life abroad.

Dropi, as the sense of embarrassment which a man affects to have felt when confronted with an angry opponent, is a doubly essential component of manhood: one must have it, but there are also occasions on which one should ideally also overcome its constraining effects on the self. It is thus somewhat like the fear that must be felt and then overcome if a man is to make a convincing claim to courage. For example, if the victim of an animal raid rightly accuses another of being the culprit, the latter may subsequently attribute his failure to confess to a sense of *dropi*. This is an acceptable rhetorical strategy, and seems in most instances to permit a peaceful resolution:

> "You said," I tell him, "that you slaughtered such-and-such an animal, and meanwhile this same animal came [wandering this way]." I tell him, "This therefore proves that you held back the animal."
>
> Says he, "Since I did this to you, Eftikhis, please forgive me, as I was embarrassed (*endrepomouna*) and didn't tell you, as it were, I was embarrassed before you (*se drapika*), and all that, and that's why I wanted you to leave the village [i.e., without learning the truth]." He justified himself to me right there.

Dropi (with which the verb forms *endrepomouna* and *drapika* are cognate) is thus the counterweight to the arrogance that makes a man a true *eghoistis*. Soon after the confrontation he describes, the speaker in this passage came to accept his enemy's friendship; it was the successful appeal to *dropi* that rendered the latter's previously hostile behavior acceptable. A false *eghoistis* would have tried to swagger his way out of the situation altogether.

Eghoismos, like "individualism," is a *social* rather than a psychological phenomenon. In Glendi, it is characteristically displayed through actions that focus on the self as a potential or actual patrigroup head or as a possible founder of a future agnatic segment. Since Glendiot men are known by a combination of the name (or nickname) of an apical ancestor and the baptismal name of the individual bearer (e.g., Sifis + Nikos > Sifonikos), the common Greek view that one is "resurrected" in the baptismal names of one's descendents becomes doubly true. When a man has a particularly distinctive nickname, this greatly enhances the prospect of immortalization through naming. This form of commemoration has little to do with the remembrance of an actual personality, since the repetition of baptismal names in alternate generations actually deindividuates them over time. As a *social* marker, on the other hand, these double names effectively link the living individual to an agnatically defined social grouping at the subpatrigroup level.

Take the example of Sifis Skoufas. His nickname was unusual, and he apparently disliked it so intensely as a youth that he would pick a fight with anyone who dared use it. By the time I arrived in Glendi, however, he had reached middle age; he had sired nine children; he had prospered economically; and he had succeeded—as he proudly boasted to me—in splitting his patrigroup's political allegiances, taking a small splinter group with him into the royalist-conservative camp. This last action may be quite significant in terms of patrigroup fission, since, if his name does become that of a patrigroup segment, that group will already have traces of a distinctive political character to mark it off from the other Skoufades.

He owns a large truck, which roars in and out of the village almost every day, bearing his nickname on its side in large printed letters. When asked why he did this, when everyone else used a formal or legal name, another Glendiot remarked that this man was an *eghoistis*—meaning, apparently, that he wanted to maintain a distinct identity. He was in fact quite daring: as he was a principal in one of the current feuds, his name could have been read as an open challenge.

Others apparently thought that his self-aggrandizement was merely a pose, and charged him with untrustworthiness and fakery. In such disagreements, it is not only the reputation of individuals that is negotiated; the values themselves undergo constant redefinition, even though they appear as fixed moral certainties. At times when his political dissidence was to the fore, his agnates distrusted him; when he joined the Skoufas campaign effort in 1975, he apparently overcame some of that distrust; and when he found himself caught up by his complex kinship ties in the struggle between Mikhalis Diakakis and Vassilis Skoufas, some sympathy was expressed for his situation. Although the changing circumstances undoubtedly ranged him with different strategic interests at different points, the evaluation of his public mien—which did not itself change appreciably—reflected some uncertainty about the correct moral approach to crisis. Every time such a man's *eghoismos* was discussed, the notion itself was open to reconsideration.

His progression from hatred for the nickname to boasting about it represents a common pattern. The acquisition of *eghoismos* entails pride in the self that others have tried to denigrate. Most nicknames are none too complimentary: they make fun of people's physical defects, temper tantrums, or even discreditable experiences. The ability to wear these defiantly, and to make the world accept one as a man of value, is central to the definition of manhood: it represents that ultimate skill of being able to snatch success and pride out of the threat of humiliation, and it allows the wearer to remind others of his possession of that skill until the end of his days.

Significantly, whereas a man's official name (baptismal, patronymic, and surname) is how "he is written" (*ghrafete*), his *paratsoukli*, or nickname, is "how he is heard" (*ghrikate*). The official name is regarded as primarily a documentary tag, useful in dealing with the bureaucratic world, but—because of the commemorative use of baptismal names—too common within the village to be distinctive. Indeed, some bureaucratic offices now use the nickname as an additional identification. Within the village, the nickname is "heard" in the sense that it immediately sets its bearer off from the crowd, and so supports his *eghoismos*. So distinctive are some *paratsouklia* that one old man, whose name was a compound of his father's *paratsoukli* and his own baptismal name, wanted to drop the baptismal part altogether. He seemed to be trying to displace his own father as apical ancestor even while saying that he wanted to be known by the same name as his father: his own sons accepted the conventional format (nickname + baptismal name) readily enough. In fact, there are many middle-aged and older men whose nicknames turn out to have been their fathers'. Apparently, the ability to express filial pride, while effectively inducing a variety of "structural amnesia,"[2] serves the aims of *eghoismos* at two seemingly contradictory levels at one and the same time: the patriline is glorified, but vested in the living person. In one case, a Skoufas leader was so powerful that his brothers also acquired the composite *paratsoukli*—an unusual concession within the same generation, and clear evidence of a remarkedly successful projection of *eghoismos*.

Nowhere do we see the intimate connection between *eghoismos* and *dropi* than in the attitude Glendiots adopt toward their own nicknames. Many of these nicknames are none too complimentary, and each may initially provoke vast amusement at the bearer's expense. Some (e.g., "Penis") are implicitly sexual, in a manner which might satisfy the male boasting that goes on within the village but which would certainly occasion embarrassment when heard outside it for the first time. Some allude to amusing personal characteristics; there are at least two "cats" in the village, one so named for his straggly whiskers and the other for his imputed tendency to claw and hiss at everyone in sight, and they are distinguished from each other by suffixes. Yet others allude to irascible tempers (e.g., "Roarer," "Brawler"), short stature (suggested in one case by a simple application of the diminutive suffix), large or exceptionally muscular build (again often conveyed by suffixes), or peculiar hair resembling the horns of an animal (e.g., "Goat"). Finally, there is a group of nicknames conferred as the result of some social connection; it is not uncommon for villagers to acquire the nicknames of their godfathers, for example. Married women are known, almost invariably, by a composite form of their husbands' nicknames, and may initially react as negatively to their negative implications as do the men.

But the male bearer, at least, must overcome his initial embarrassment, although what is acceptable within an intimate circle may remain too undignified to bear repetition among strangers. I sometimes experienced difficulty in learning people's nicknames, still more in finding out how they were acquired; once equipped with this knowledge, however, I was encouraged to use it, and occasionally would be asked like a performing animal to show off my linguistic tricks. Glendiots were slightly embarrassed but also amused at my interest in nicknames and village dialect, both of which they regarded as uncouth but intimate aspects of their daily lives; without that information, I might have found it much harder to gain any insight into still more concealed facets such as animal theft. They begin the process of name acquisition early; when a villager called a young boy by what would probably become his standard village name in due course (i.e., his father's *paratsoukli* plus his own baptismal name), I picked it up, too, and the child petulantly struck me in reply.

Since members of the largest patrigroups recognize several levels of segmentation, each marked by the name of the apical ancestor, they may sport several *paratsouklia*. This allows them to use the most inclusive when they travel outside the village; they are often hailed by some fairly anodyne combination such as the "Sifonikos" form mentioned above. The more intimate the social context, however, the more specific the *paratsouklia* that are used, and the more likely it is that the other members of the conversation group will be aware of the disreputable or humorous events to which the nicknames allude. To the extent that a man is prepared to vaunt a name that originated in some humiliating past history, he shows that he has conquered the *dropi* that limited the exercise of his *eghoismos*.

By contrast, the Classical Greek names that some village men have are usually inappropriate for compounding with agnatic *paratsouklia* and still more so for becoming patrigroup names themselves. Names such as Themistokleoyannis or Yannothemistoklis do not occur: they are aesthetically unacceptable. Perhaps, too, their intimations of official nationalism make the comparatively long Classical names too grand for such characteristically local combinations. *Paratsouklia* belong to the introspective, intimate side of village life, not to its official face. A name of obviously Classical form and origin "does not fit" (*dhen deriazi*) with ordinary baptismal names to make a *paratsoukli*. A man who has such a first name would need to acquire a distinctive and obviously local nickname in order to provide a new patrigroup segment with its requisite ancestor.

This is not to say that patrigroup fission is based entirely on aesthetic principles. Rather, to revert to the point I made earlier about the artificiality of distinguishing between moral and aesthetic values, a man's excellence—his *eghoismos*—is known only through the performance he provides his selfhood. His acquisition of a nickname is a test of his ability to overcome the constraints imposed by his inner sense of *dropi*, and thereby to demonstrate that excellence; as it becomes more widely known and used, it also becomes a mark of his success in that regard. Only a man who has developed a strong reputation, one aspect of which is to have sired many sons, can expect to found a new segment. Thus, the progression from anonymity to distinctive identity, and from *dropi* over a caustic nickname to proud display, is the definitive career of the "man of knuckle" and potential segment founder.

The conquest of *dropi* entails actions that frequently conflict with both bureaucratic and ecclesiastical laws. Humility has little place in Glendiot men's lives: however much they may profess to regret the fact, the humble man—more than anyone, the shepherd who does not steal for himself— cannot expect to be socially effective. Sin, in the ecclesiastical sense, is thus a necessary condition of social existence. This is less true for women and old men than for those who must engage in the daily struggle. For all Glendiots, however, it calls for some form of expiation, whether through the office of the confessional or through some more secular means.

A Weight upon the Soul

Sin, *amartia*, is the general category under which the church classifies many of the activities that constitute Glendiot everyday experience. Clearly, theft is a major element of this complex, which also includes taking lives, quarreling, exhibiting pride, blaspheming, and cheating. The components of both *eghoismos* and *poniria* are thus all included: what is moral behavior in Glendi may look very different from an official or ecclesiastical perspective.

Although Glendiots do speak about sin themselves, moreover, they have arrogated the term to their own purposes. We have already seen their attitude in the sweeping comment that priests "are the [real] sinners"; in the characterization of a bridegroom's arrest on his wedding day for receiving stolen meat as a "sin" against ordinary decency; and in the young widow's cry that "*God* makes all the sins!" Clearly we are dealing with a concept of sin far removed from that of the religious or secular authorities.

A more precise gloss on the Glendiot use of *amartia* might be "responsibility for what happened." This is well illustrated by an incident that took place when Crete was still under Turkish rule. Some Glendiots stole a Turkish cannon, and hid it in the village for fear that the Turks might find out and conduct reprisals against the whole community. Then three other Glendiots stole it, and sold it. The other inhabitants were dismayed, and, under protest, the village priest finally agreed to pronounce a curse on those unknown individuals who were responsible for the disappearance of the cannon. Before the entire congregation, he first advised the culprits to step forward before he pronounced the anathema, so that they would not also be guilty of perjury: each villager had to swear to his own innocence. Nobody came forward until afterwards, when it was too late. Then one of the culprits admitted to his offense, and the priest told him that he "had the *amartia*" through not owning up before the priest had pronounced the solemn words on the Gospel.

Amartia is considered something to be avoided whenever possible. It is of no consequence that the sin has been committed against an evil person, or to destroy wicked spiritual forces. Even destroying the force of the evil eye (*thiarmos*) is a sin in this sense. A curer pronouncing the spell against the evil eye may weep copiously, and this is attributed to the assumption of *amartia* through the destruction of the wicked emanation:

> Eh, now, since I take the *thiarmos* and make it go away, I have, they say, this *amartia* then. That's how it is. (. . .) Just as the wild animals choke the lambs and I "bind" them [with a spell], and when I bind them my eyes weep like a river running to the ground. Well then, they say [that it is] the *amartia* because the wild animals also expect [sustenance] from the animals that *we* eat.

But this is not a theological position:

> Many tell me, "Don't 'bind' the wild ones, because you [will] have *amartia*."
> So I told the priest about it, and the priest tells me, "No, you don't have [*amartia*], since you are curing. . . ." And that's the way it really is!

This declaration of faith apparently did not prevent the old curer, who was also an ex-shepherd of once considerable power, from hesitating every time he was called upon to pronounce the spell. The concern with *amartia* reflects a view that every injury will eventually have to be paid for. This is also the sense in which old men go to church "in order to cure the sins that they have committed": and here, at last, the secular concept of sin begins to give way to the religious.

"Having the sin" is to be liable to blame for whatever happens to someone or something. Thus, sin in the eyes of God takes second place to sin in the eyes of man. This is consistent with other Glendiot attitudes to the supernatural; male confession is more often that between two thieves (as when they take the oath at the dead of night) than between a sinner and his priest; and divination, which in pre-Christian times had become the exclusive prerogative of priest and emperor, is a secular activity among irreverent shepherds (see below). In much the same way, the concept of *amartia*, though based on an implicit appeal to divine writ, serves Glendiot men as the basis of a negotiation of morality among themselves. One who "has *amartia*" has it in relation to a fellow-human, and it is to the latter that he is most immediately accountable.

Penitence, too, is a social concept. When a man "repents" (*metaniono*; cf. Classical and New Testament *metanoia*) of his refusal to admit to a theft, for example, his response is not necessarily an inward enlightenment. Glendiots distrust psychological attributions, as we can see in their conflation of the New Testament concept of *suneidēsis*, "conscience," with the moral social emphasis of "custom" (*sinithio* > *sinithisi*). Insofar as they do consider the problem of the inner state, Glendiots call an awareness of unmet or unrequitable responsibility a "weight on one's soul" (*varos sti psikhi tou*): it was to avoid this, for example, that led the kinsman of a recently deceased Glendiot to return to the village and deliver a memorial tribute, having heard about the death only after the funeral. For Glendiot men, repentance is less a response to the imperatives of conscience than a tactical decision to gain the best advantage from a difficult situation:

> Sometimes, you've "eaten" sheep of mine and you are of the opinion, you think, that I know it. And afterwards, when you tell me that we should go to church to take an oath, you may repent [*na metaniosis*], you'll tell me, "Eh, I've-changed-my-mind [*emetaniosa*] anyway, and I'm convinced that you don't know anything."

Here, the act of repentance is a tactical decision to withdraw from the contest before it shifts to one's disadvantage. Confession, too, is primarily a secular concern for the men. While they do have the option of going to take the rite of confession, and may do so before Easter in order to take Holy Communion, their avoidance of church attendance in general places the weight of confession in another sphere. Instead of confessing to a priest, shepherds "confess" to each other. Just as *metanoia* precedes confession in the ecclesiastical sense, so a change of mind precedes owning up to one's misdeeds in order to obtain forgiveness (*signomi*) and friendship from another shepherd. Confession in both spheres is expressed by terms of the same etymological base (religious *ksemologho*, secular *mologho*).

But "confessing" is a betrayal of secrecy: "If we admit [*moloyisoume*] [to having stolen] them now, we're lost; he'll 'eat' all of ours!" Sometimes, the term is used for deliberate acts of betrayal, as well as for the accidental betrayal of theft by an inexperienced child. In matters of vengeance, including retaliatory raiding, the term has the significance of a "dangerous leak," which might cause a further round in the revenge cycle. Talking about his own preference not to know anything about such matters, one villager remarked, "Yes, I could put him on oath on some occasion and afterwards tell on him [*na tone moloiso*]!"

Significantly, this commentator likened the act of "telling" to the role of priests. Another villager remarked that had he been a priest, he— like the present Glendiot incumbent—would have refused to take confession; it is often best to know little or nothing about the secrets of others. Generally speaking, there is a pervasive fear of confiding in priests through the confessional rite. Experience has taught the villagers that this can prove to be one of the most dangerous sources of leakage.

Thieves confess to priests, and priests "confess" these confidences to the world at large. A *mandinadha* expresses the general sentiment:

| *Kallia 'kho 'na ghaidharo* | | *na me ksemoloyisi* |
| Better | for me to have a donkey | to hear-my-confession |

| *para na pao stom bapa na me kseyevendisi.* | | |
| than to go | to-the priest and have him expose me! | |

Villagers thus blame the ecclesiastical establishment for the breakdown of confessional privacy: in this rhetoric, confession becomes betrayal, and the priests can indeed be viewed as the true sinners in the Glendiots' secular axiology:

A: I believe, let's say, in God, let's say, in Christ, let's say. That is, I believe as a Christian, let's say, and all that, basically I do believe. But I don't want either to go to church or to set eyes on priests!

B: Right, by my Virgin Mary! If I were to go back to church, there are *lots* of priests, so to speak [i.e., so many that one cannot escape them].

A: Yes!

After some more in the same vein, a third speaker takes up the theme:

C: I'm the same, I can't stomach them. Why so? Because they're not human (*dhen ine anthropi*)! Eh, no, when the priest tells you, and says, "If you don't vote for So-and-so," so to speak, and all that nonsense, that's what the priest tells you, *I* say, "You cuckold, since you're a priest, so to speak, what are you doing getting mixed up in party politics?" (. . .) In other states, they liquidate the priest! Eh, they don't want anything like priests! Because *these* are the sinners!

The rejection of the priests' "humanity" reflects a general view of them as antisocial beings, whose abuse of spiritual authority renders them morally inferior to any lay offender. To be an *anthropos* is to participate in the normal reciprocities of social life; and this, according to Glendiot perceptions, priests are either unwilling or unable to do. Part of this passionate anticlericalism springs from the supposed venality of the priests, who are said to exact substantial amounts of money for hearing confession. One villager gleefully recounted how he had tricked the local confessor into hearing his statement out in the fields (instead of in church), merely in order to tease the priest when he demanded payment. On another occasion, two closely related Glendiots, a man and his female cousin, announced in a mock-solemn, ecclesiastical singsong that "the servant of God is fasting because he has no bread!" This parody of the baptismal rite ("the servant of God is baptized Nikolaos") reveals through humor an assumption that even relatively prosperous Glendiots make—that the appurtenances of the church were designed to feed the hierarchy at the expense of the people. That assumption certainly fuels the villagers' deep suspicion of the entire confessional rite.

It is not clear whether the Glendiot priests' refusal to hear confession— they delegate that duty to a priest from Vrissi—springs from a fear of being accused of betraying confessional confidences, or from their re-luctance to assume responsibility for prescribing penances. The older priest (father of the present incumbent) eventually succumbed to pressure from his superiors and agreed to serve as a confessor; but he has confined his services only to those who insist on using them.

Theological and social explanations of his reluctance mesh. The priest can hardly be unaware of his male covillagers' unwillingness to tell him of their more serious offenses:

> . . . since many things happen which should not be spoken about under any circumstances, that's why the priest doesn't hear confes-sion. Because he knows that if he came and heard my confession, for example, I can't tell him [everything].

The problem is that a person who makes only a partial confession is committing a sin if he then goes on to take Holy Communion. A com-passionate priest realizes, too, that the penitent may be suffering con-siderable misery through his inability to confess all. The villager whom I have just quoted attributed the priest's reluctance to hear confession to the fact that "he is a covillager and . . . a person who is very good, very good indeed." Another local clergyman confirmed that "they don't tell the truth during the confessional," and gave this as a reason why he, too, preferred to avoid administering the rite.

Another villager saw in the old Glendi priest's attitude an intelligent management of the problem of personal responsibility. In this view, the priest "didn't want to take the sins [amarties] [upon himself]." Even when the penitent confesses everything, the "weight on the soul" passes from penitent to priest as soon as the priest permits the penitent to participate in the ritually purifying Communion rite. The priest would naturally not be thought willing to accept the entire burden of sin of so pervasively dissident a community as Glendi. But the ambiguity of whether the sin actually passes to the confessor is somewhat like that associated with the oath. Whether or not he is telling the truth, a shepherd, as we have already seen, regards "taking" the oath in *any* sense as an almost intolerable burden, since he is thereby committed to personal and moral responsibility. In much the same way, the priest who hears confession and agrees to let the penitent take Communion must bear the ultimate moral responsibility if, in fact, the penitent has not told the truth at all.

There is the further consideration that anyone who hears all the secrets of the village comes under constant suspicion of indiscretion at best. Here, there is a clear analogy between the local priests' reluctance to hear confession and the location of monasteries suitable for oath taking on neutral territory: to be effective as a mediator of wrongdoing, spiritual authority must be removed from the immediacy of social pressures. Priests who hear confession are the prime suspects when news of some illegal act "leaks" to the authorities. An irate villager, betrayed by a confessor to whom he had admitted participating in a homicide, demanded, "Are you a priest or a devil?"[3] Another confessor in the area explained, "As I said, if we suppose that someone came and confessed and I speak of it aferwards. . . . then I have the *amartia* upon myself." Here, "sin" has come to mean something entirely practical: the responsibility for getting another person into trouble. Recalling the "sin" of sending a man to jail on his wedding day, we can see that the local clergy endorse some, at least, of the secular definitions of the concept.

Even a conscientious priest must face extremely difficult decisions which, apart from the moral dilemmas they pose, place the priest in a delicate situation socially:

> And for that reason [i.e., the difficulty of making the right decisions] exactly, I have of course heard many accusing a confessor.
>
> Yes! The discussions in the coffeehouses! I'd hear them accusing [*sic*] Alpha along with Beta, saying that Alpha along with Beta had caused [*sic*] this sin, and they confessed. Both confessed, and [the priest] instructed Alpha [*sic*; but the speaker presumably means the Beta of what follows] to take Communion, but told the other man, "No, a year or two must pass before you can take Communion."
>
> "Why this difference?" says he. "I reject that!"
>
> And I say to him, "Is Alpha married?"
>
> Says he, "Yes, he is married."
>
> "Does he have a family?"
>
> "Says he, "He does."
>
> "Does Beta have a family? Is he married?"
>
> "No."
>
> "Should Alpha have got up from his bed, left his wife, left his children, and gone to commit this crime along with Beta, who is

free of family obligations? That is why he gave Beta [a slip of the tongue: *read* Alpha] permission to take Communion. . . ."

Here, the ecclesiastical position comes relatively close to the social values of the villagers: the married man is more culpable because, in addition to committing the sin of theft, he has also failed as a family head. Here, in fact, the self-justifying rhetoric of the dispossessed seems to have some theological basis:

> . . . he didn't give it [permission to take Communion] to you because you are married and have your wife. The other man was not married.
>
> And this makes a difference. It is one thing to sit in your house and to have your bread, and to have your meal, to have your olive, this and that, and [then] to get up and go to the mountainside to go and steal a sheep, and something else for the one who is [already there] on the mountainside and doesn't have bread or anything else. It's a big difference! So to the one man [the priest] will mete out a punishment, to the one who goes from his house and has his bread and his cheese and money, and [still] goes and steals. Whereas the other man is on the mountainside and doesn't have anything: he is more justified.
>
> The same [applies] in court, because one of them leaves his house and goes and steals, [whereas] the other finds it [i.e., the stolen animal] around him. "I'm hungry [*pino*]," he says. There's a difference!

The idiom of self-exoneration is familiar: the shepherd's hunger is contrasted to the wealth of one who "sits in his house"; he does not seek his prey so much as "find" it by chance; and his dependence on meat is contrasted with the agricultural abundance available to the householder.

The priest's perspective, however, is more rigidly defined than that of the shepherd. Whereas the shepherd uses this rhetoric in defense of all raiding, and in defense of the proclivity to animal theft in general, the priest sees his role as that of a judge, charged with assessing penalties appropriate to crimes and their circumstances (illus. 21). The priest, too, is supposed to be the sole recipient of information given during confession, and may not speak of it thereafter. When he *does* betray such confidences, he reduces himself to the level of a lay sinner: "he takes the sin when he speaks out [*perni tin amartia otan moloyisi*]," as a local confessor explained. By speaking out, "confessing" the misdeeds of another person, he places himself on the same level as his penitent, and shares in the latter's culpability. From an ecclesiastical perspective

21. The views of the church.

he has violated the rite. From a secular point of view, on the other hand, he has committed the social sin of violating personal trust. Since this is theoretically a rare situation among shepherds, the priests may indeed be seen as "the worst sinners." Although the ecclesiastical and secular reasons for condemning his behavior are not the same, they mesh in a conceptual complex that allows the Glendiots to deny the priests' fundamental humanity while insisting on their own identity as Christians. Every breach of confessional trust both confirms the villagers' hostility and increases the priests' concern that fewer and fewer shepherds will come to take the rite.

Men, unlike women, are more concerned with the political than with the religious notion of original sin. They see their isolation from the worlds of power and wealth as determinative of their present attitudes and actions. They are not thieves by profession or role, in the standard anthropological sense; indeed, they are very insulted by the merest suggestion that they might be. In strictly professional terms, those who own flocks are *vosči*, "shepherds"; a few with comparatively large flocks (over five hundred animals) rejoice in the title of *kouradharidhes* (from *kouradhi*, "flock"). They do apply the term *kleftes*, "thieves," to themselves, but only in a contingent sense—when narrating some exploit, for example, or celebrating their own courage.

Being a thief is, as we have seen, a mode of "occupation" in the Burkean sense of a categorical ascription of social identity in accordance with the circumstances of the moment (Burke 1954:237-238). As Burke points out, people constantly seek to "ethicize" such occupations, and to make a virtue out of what circumstances have already created. At this point, the sinner's act of expiation may be a repetition of the sinner's categorical offense. The Glendiot shepherd ethicizes theft on the grounds of irresistible political circumstances; each raid he commits expiates his fallen condition by confirming his exclusion from the political pale. In this way, "the *categorical* motive may serve as a motive for a corresponding *personal* motive" (Burke 1954:290): each raid reaffirms the conditions of its own justification.

The confessional denies the values that theft exalts. But this does not mean that Glendiots reject it out of hand. First of all, as older men see death approaching, they are expected to be more concerned with retribution in the afterlife, and consequently to attend confession more readily. Women go to confession at an early age as a matter of course. Their commitment to church procedure forms a complementary opposition with the men's secular confession. Both confession and owning up to a theft are regarded as morally good but dangerous activities: a woman may be betrayed by her confessor, a man by those to whom he admits his guilt in a raid. The difference is that a man can reject or punish an unfaithful *sindeknos*; unlike women before their priest, Glendiot men do not attribute to any specific individual the special status of receiver of confidences. In telling each other about their raids, they reject the total concentration of power in a single man's hands. Instead, they collectively arrogate to themselves, and secularize, the idiom of penitence and confession.

Their dislike for the institutions of the church, Glendiot men insist, does not prevent them from accepting the existence of some Higher Power. What they reject is the political domination of the ecclesiastical authorities, whose supposed venality has earned the church the title of "little store" (*maghazači*). In the next section, we turn to another area in which the villagers have apparently taken over and generalized access to the supernatural. Their *eghoismos* allows them no less.

Bones of Contention

Glendiot shepherds perform a kind of scapulomancy, or divination with the shoulder blade of a sheep or goat. Far more than a method of anticipating the future, this practice constitutes a genuine semiotic of social, ethical, and practical concerns. These concerns are all matters about which Glendiots exhibit considerable anxiety: marriage, death, wives' fidelity, childbearing, social worth, the size of flocks, the incidence of raids, and the behavior of the natural elements, as well as the acquisition of material wealth and the general well-being and prosperity of the household.

Perhaps this form of scapulomancy should not be called divination at all. It purports to allow the practitioner to "read" the future, but one's first impression is that its predictive role is not taken very seriously. In this respect, it closely resembles Glendiot attitudes toward fate and chance. Glendiots do not tailor their actions to negative assumptions about the future, but use rhetorical devices such as destiny to explain the past. In their social aesthetic, chance is not something to anticipate: to do so would destroy the very spontaneity on which artistic self-presentation rests, and deprive men of the opportunity to "steal one bad hour from Death." In the same way, the reading of the *koutala* ("shoulder blade"; lit. "large spoon," a feminized form of the commoner neuter *koutali*, "spoon," and hence a grammatically appropriate object of male possession) does not fix future events so that they can be circumvented. On the contrary, it emphasizes the dangers of ever relaxing one's guard:

it provides a performative context in which men explore the deep uncertainties that may one day enable them to show off their true prowess.

Glendiot men often display the same ironical agnosticism with regard
to the *koutala* that they exhibit toward religious matters generally. "Sometimes," remarked an elderly former shepherd, "it happens [*tikheni*] to
show [i.e., the future]." But it is clearly not thought to be infallible,
even by those who insist that they believe in its general efficacy. The
uncertainty of the prediction reproduces the uncertainty of actual social
experience, in which "chance" (*tikhi*, here represented by the cognate
verb *tikheni*) provides both the threat of ruin and the possibility of
overcoming it.

That uncertainty, moreover, provides a general context for the striking
of what initially seem to be quite inconsistent attitudes toward scapulomancy. One speaker flatly denied belief in the *koutala* (or anything
else)—"just like Kazantzakis, who doesn't believe in anything!"[4] Here,
identification with the best known of all Cretan authors led the speaker
to express a skeptical response. But the same man also claimed that the
predictions of another, older man had always come true. This is hardly
the expression of a totalizing disbelief. Instead, it transpires that the
significance of successful divination lies less in the occurrence itself
than in the retrospective telling of it. Even those who dismiss the entire
practice as "lies" are calling it by the same name that they use for life
itself, and for the world in which they live.

While there may well be some villagers who strongly believe or disbe-
lieve, they are united in their willingness to recognize the efficacy of
scapulomancy in the past. Taken together, their various comments suggest that the *koutala* offers far more of a way of prodding and probing
the febrile skin of social experience than of planning for the future.
When a villager justified his failure at predicting accurately by claiming
that the bone had probably come from too young an animal (which should
be at least a yearling), he still attributed *simasia* to scapulomancy *seen
as a general principle*. Another informant justified his own skepticism
on the grounds that he had personally never seen a divination actually
come true, but went on to add that he believed in scapulomancy nonetheless since it was "according to the tradition of our forefathers."

Perhaps the most revealing comment is the jest that the bone lacks
simasia unless it has meat on it. The bantering tone in which this remark
is conventionally offered should not deceive us into treating it as a literal
rejection of scapulomancy. Rather, it alerts his audience to the speaker's
unwillingness to reject the practice out of hand: give him a shoulder
blade with some meat left on it, he says, and he will have appetite
enough to try a reading. Any activity that recognizes his manhood—

here, by means of the meat—has *simasia* for him. In his agnostic mockery
of scapulomancy, he dares the supernatural to do its worst; and in this,
he reproduces the stance of a true man toward his fellows. Meat is
something one acquires, ideally, by chance; so, too, is success in scapulomantic prediction. Even in more law-abiding communities, the agonistic relationship between men is replicated in the collective attitude
toward nature (see Friedl 1962:75). The Glendiots, whose mockery of
death disguises rather than replaces fear, adopt a similarly irreverent
rhetoric toward everything that lies beyond everyday experience. The
contexts in which they practice scapulomancy are, appropriately, highly
informal ones. A shepherd strips the meat off a shoulder blade, and
jestingly begins to "read" it as trusted friends and kinsmen gather around
with a mixture of curiosity and mockery (illus. 22 and 23).

Scapulomancy is usually practiced with bones from animals of known
ownership, since the point is to couch the entire discourse as though it
were person-specific. Since the Glendiots do not literally expect all the
predictions to come true, however, and as a result are ultimately more
interested in the much more general question of whether prediction is
really possible, they were apparently happy to demonstrate it in the
abstract. Hear what one Glendiot was prepared to say about the owner
of the animal whose *koutala* he was "reading" for my instruction, without
knowing at the time who the owner really was. (My teacher on this
occasion was also the author of the more detailed explanatory diagram
[a] of the two that I have reproduced in fig. 8.) He began: "He has much
money . . . he's married . . . he's in very good shape." The speaker
could discern no evidence of offspring. "This fellow can't have any
filotimo at all," he continued, observing that "since" he had no *filotimo*
the shepherd in question must have a lot of money.

The owner of the sheep was then declared to have a wife of dubious
morals: "From the point of view of chastity, she isn't doing too well!"
Then came a quick switch to weather conditions: "It isn't raining these
days." Immediately after this, the speaker returned to the shepherd's
personal problems: his family life was in difficulty, he had no sheep
(perhaps the one from which this *koutala* came was a house animal?),
he had no immediate fear of death or sickness, he was so lacking in
filotimo that he wouldn't even give you water to drink! The wife's fidelity
was not so much disproved as problematical: usually, the wife's infidelity
is marked by a single dark spot in the center of the end joint (see fig.
8a), but this had two or three such spots, none of them well centered.
The ambiguity of this reading was matched by a corresponding ambiguity
as to whether the owner had any children and, if so, how many. The

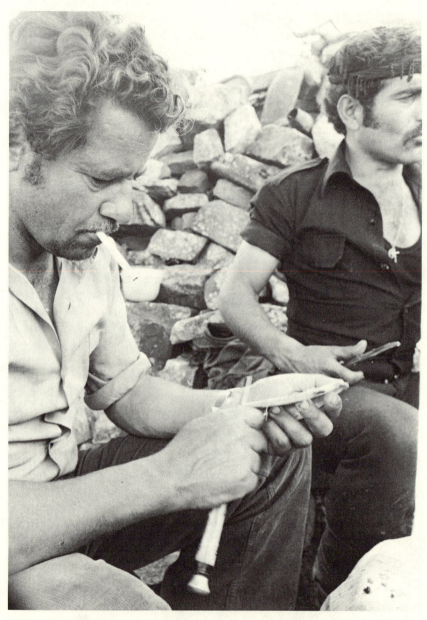

22. Cleaning meat off the *koutala* allows the shepherd to read its message.

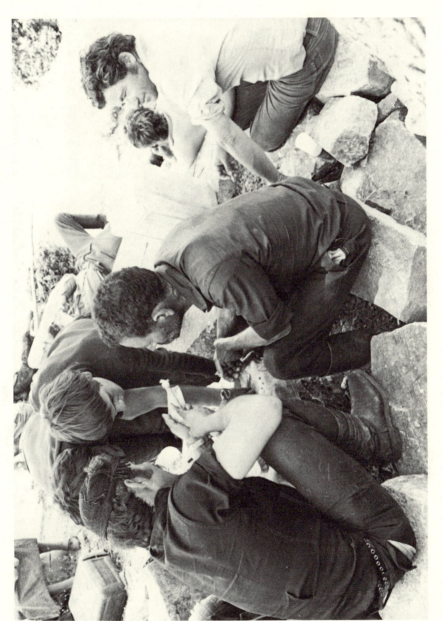

23. Gathering around to learn the message of the *koutala*.

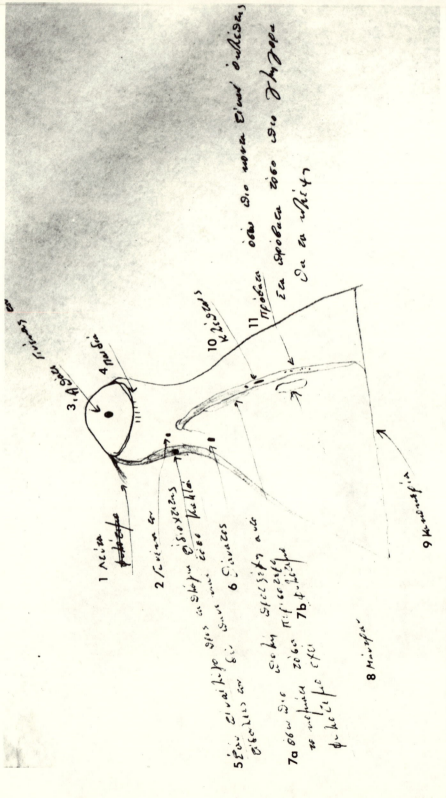

Fig. 8a. A detailed explanation of the *koutala*.

Translation of explanations: 1. Money. 2. His wife. 3. Deceit by his wife. 4. Children. 5. If the owner [i.e., the mark representing him] is a little to the side, his business isn't going too well. 6. Death. 7a. The more this piece sticks out, the more *filotimo* he has. 7b. *Filotimo*. 8. Sheepfold. 9. Bad

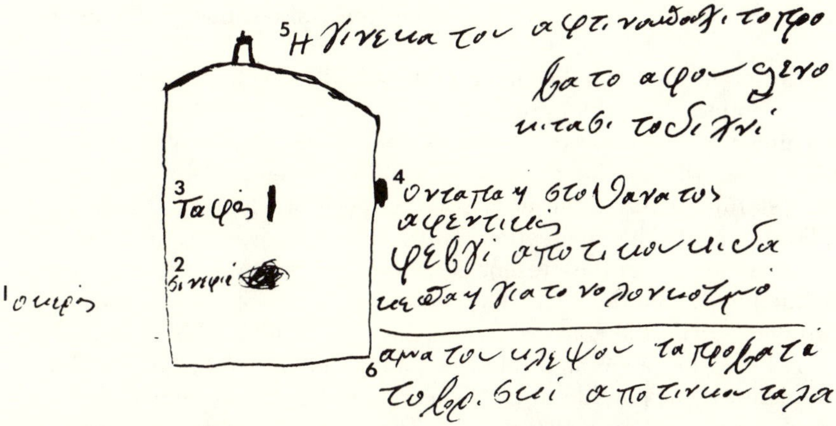

Fig. 8b. A further drawing of the *koutala*. Although less detailed than fig. 8a, it confirms the essential concerns of Glendiot scapulomancy.
Translation of explanations: 1. The weather; 2. Cloud; 3. Tomb; 4. When the owner is going to his death, [this mark] leaves this mark and he goes to the other ? world [i.e., of the dead]; 5. If the wife of the man who owns the sheep is sleeping with someone else, it [the *koutala*] shows it; 6. If his sheep have been stolen, he finds it out from the *koutala*.

bone was too small to be sure on this point, the diviner claimed, and it was confusing to read. There were no signs of [animal] thieves.

The speaker thus covered almost all the possible signs on the *koutala*, some more definitely than others. His diagram (fig. 8a) corresponds in some details to comparable material reported from elsewhere in Greece, as does a second, less detailed one (fig. 8b),[5] although there are also significant differences. Whatever the regional variations, the Glendiot *koutala* correlates clearly with Glendiot ideas about what has *simasia* in social life. There are some variations in local practice, notably a marking that is held to indicate Cyprus gradually drawing near to Greece, but these individual versions fall well within the topical range of what might be expected to interest villagers generally.

The *koutala* is divided into three principal position categories for the purposes of divination. These are the membranous flat area, the ridge, and the several edges. On the flat area, we find all the marks of ordinary, natural events: wife, children, weather, death—the last being marked by a slight depression, which elsewhere in Greece signifies plague. Note that weather conditions are physically closest to the flock, where they will have the greatest impact in actual life: they are not directly responsible for a person's physical or commercial position, but affect both through their effect on the flock animals.

Children, proverbially equated with wealth, are placed on the swelling of the joint, rather than precisely on the flat section. This is apparently significant: a man's prestige is augmented by the size of his progeny, and especially by the number of boys. Children are the product of a successful marriage, the normative purpose of which in Glendi is explicitly stated to be procreation. Thus, just as death succeeds the married state as the end of the present generation, children ensure the survival of the family into the next generation: note the pivotal positioning of the wife/mother on the *koutala*. When the wife is unfaithful, however, she falls below her appointed role: this is a half-concealed, "inner" flaw in the family, comparable to the general sense of failure indicated by the mark on the left side of the bone. The contrast between the good wife who secures her husband's posterity by bearing his children and the bad wife who ruins her husband's present status is clearly reproduced in diagrammatic opposition on the *koutala*.

Note also the position and representation of "money." It is symbolized by a cartilaginous obtrusion, the distinctive softness of which symbolically reproduces the fickleness of cash as well as of those who own it: recall the diviner's ironic assumption that a man with so much money could not possess much *filotimo*. Money *can* be good: the money signifier stands out from the flat area, as do both the swelling on which children are marked and the ridge with its signs for sheep and *filotimo*. The juxtaposition of "money" and "children," as well as the diagrammatic contrast between them, suggests the ambiguity of the proverbial claim that "many children are wealth"—a statement that encapsulates the idea that many children *replace* individual wealth, since they must divide their patrimony into correspondingly smaller parts. This connection between wealth and offspring is schematically reproduced on the *koutala*.

The ridge, on the other hand, displays signs of a socially positive nature. The higher it is, the more *filotimo* the owner is supposed to have. In the ridge is located the sheepfold, the symbolic and physical location of a shepherd's main source of prestige. On the top are both sheep and thieves; the closer together they appear, the nearer to the flock the thieves have come. The juxtaposition is apt: the more sheep a man owns, the greater the likelihood of raids, especially if he is also thought to have the degree of *filotimo* that will ensure a socially appropriate response from him—a response that will lead to mutual respect and alliance. The *koutala* thus expresses a clear correlation between flock ownership, *filotimo*, and liability to raids. Like money, moreover, *filotimo* based on flocks is an index of external rather than endocommunal relations, a structural homology that is drawn by the *koutala* through having both attributes represented by protuberances rather than by parts of the "everyday" flat section.

We have already seen that the higher ground is the morally purer in Glendiot spatial symbolism. It is at least suggestive that the predictions of both good and bad in the *koutala* entail removal from the flat center. Not everything in the center is unambiguously good, certainly, but death and bad weather are inevitable and natural. This is not true of infidelity, wealth, or *filotimo*, all of which entail some degree of public exposure.

This exposure is reflected in verbal idiom. One who is deceived "comes out ridiculed" (*vyeni koroidho*); one who copes well with danger finds his name "coming out" in a positive sense. The lability of this idiom reproduces the ease with which every increase in power and prestige brings a correspondingly greater risk of failure and humiliation. Such is the "chance" which the Glendiot shepherd must seize if he is to earn his manhood, but which may, if he is inadequate to the challenge, bring him down. Furthermore, "going out" means ascent, especially of the mountain tracks. The higher a shepherd goes with his flocks to the summer pasturage, the more closely he approaches the moral purity that *filotimo* entails. And the higher he goes, the greater the chances that he must take, and the larger the risk of attack. It is surely no coincidence that the two shepherds with currently the greatest reputation for *eghoismos*, Skoufades both, have the highest summer pasturage. It was one of them who boasted, "We're the free Greece here!"

The physical deployment of signs on the *koutala* iconically reproduces the spatial symbolism of the Glendiots' social world. That world is brittle with uncertainty and ambiguity. For a villager to read a *koutala* as though it offered absolute certainty would thus run counter to his own experience and knowledge: the impossibility of forecasting events is suggested here by the opacity of each reading. Excuses about small bones or unclear markings are an integral part of this idiom, verbal ploys that the self-appointed diviner produces in the course of his performance. That successful predictions appear as a thing of the past rather than of the present emphasizes the same message of uncertainty: as the uncertainty of Glendiot social life had increased, so contact with the supernatural has deteriorated. It is far from unlikely that the previous generation said much the same thing about *its* precursors (cf. also Herzfeld 1983b).

The *koutala* thus represents the internal tensions of village life. As a semiotic of indigenous social theory, it also stands for the eccentric status of this society within the larger national entity. Its very existence flies in the face of ecclesiastical disapproval. Historically, as Grodzynski has argued (1974:267-276), all popular forms of divination came to be regarded as a usurpation of imperial as well as divine authority. Despite official and ecclesiastical condemnation, however, the particular practice of scapulomancy appeared in Greece early in the Christian era. The Byzantine writer Michael Psellos devoted a long descriptive passage to it, and a lengthy manuscript, probably of early thirteenth-century date, records the method of divination in such detail as to permit comparison with modern ethnographic examples (Megas 1926). Its appearance in Greece has been attributed to barbarian (specifically Gothic) influence, and it seems to have flourished only in politically marginal areas with predominantly pastoral populations and a decided aversion to the rule of law.

Its marginality suited the aims of nationalist writers. In commenting on the thirteenth-century manuscript description, for example, Megas asked, "But how should we explain the mention of the name of *Turks and barbarians* in the title of a book whose intention is to record Greek customs and Greek beliefs? It is a common belief that the magical skill of people of different language and religion is more perfect" (Megas 1926:6). In this way, the folklorist is able to demonstrate a measure of agreement between his own conclusions and popular attitudes, as well as with the very similar insistence of Psellos that scapulomancy came from Persia. In each case, the practice is regarded as un-Greek.

This cultural marginality reproduces the *social* marginality of those who still practice scapulomancy. In the pre-Independence period, scapulomancy was most commonly found among the mountain-dwelling guerrillas (Megas 1926), people whose way of life closely resembled that of the Glendiot shepherds in important respects—notably the institutionalized resistance to authority.

If the internal disposition of the Glendiot *koutala* furnishes a semiotic of prevalent social concerns, as a unit this ritual object can also be read as an index of the Glendiots' political alienation from the center, especially in the light of these scattered but internally consistent historical precedents. This is not to say that Glendiots are aware of the historical background; but the continued disapproval of the church and the specific location of "thieves" in the nexus of scapulomantic signs together make the use of the *koutala* an effective expression of what makes Glendiots distinctive. To that extent, the *koutala* is both a diagram of internal social concerns and a symbol of the community's external relationship with the encompassing forms of officialdom. Scapulomancy can usefully be treated as a device for thinking about subsistence activities, as Tanner (1978:100) has suggested in an entirely different ethnographic context. Glendiots clearly use their version of the practice, however, for much more than thinking about the activity from which it is immediately derived, although the vicissitudes of pastoralism are well represented in it. It is also concerned, at a radically more general and encompassing level, with the necessary indeterminacy of *all* significant experience in Glendiot life.

Sometimes the predictions "chance" to come true. But the very uncertainty of this is significant: the heyday of moral excellence in which men could predict with confidence contrasts tellingly with the present impossibility of certain knowledge about the future. Men are men because they grapple with that uncertainty, of which the political expression is a segmentary view of social relations; they deal with chance and serendipity, not with the security of advance knowledge. When they "read" the *koutala*, they are reading the inscrutable present rather than the determinate future. Perhaps it has happened in the past that a prediction came true; perhaps this will happen again. But who knows? The only meaning, *simasia*, that can be attributed to scapulomancy is that of the ritual performance itself. As an expression of manhood, it plays on the need to take every chance event as it comes, spurning the hack's desire for a safely anticipated outcome. This is the implication of maintaining that only a *koutala* that has meat upon it has "meaning": only one with meat on it can be of interest to a true man. For meat, which at its tastiest and best is stolen, symbolizes the uncertain chance successfully seized.

The *koutala* thus reproduces the structure of ideas about manhood, relating the internal tensions of Glendiot society to the external uncertainty of Glendi's relations with the bureaucratic state. Perhaps this seems a little too portentous a statement to make of something that the Glendiots joke so freely about. But joking is not a sign of triviality. On the contrary, people who joke ironically about death and danger are clearly exploring matters of deep concern to them. *Simasia* is the crucial term of their jokes about scapulomancy, and *simasia* is the Glendiot canon of "meaning," "relevance," "significance"—all those ideas that stand contrasted with triviality. Jokes are fragile and contingent, "a temporary suspension of the social structure . . . a little disturbance in which the particular structuring of society becomes less relevant than another" (Douglas 1975:107). At one time or another, all Glendiot men are placed in this normatively subversive role: they are all jokers.

That is why the recurrent discussion of humor plays so much greater a part in this ethnography than we find in descriptions of more conventionally law-abiding communities; the very condition of outlawry demands a constant exploration of both the internal and the external ambiguities of social experience. For the Glendiots, all life, the whole world, is a lie. To joke with and about it is to venture a little way into the concealed truth behind that lie—the truth that nothing can be known of the future with absolute certainty, and the truth that the prescriptive discourse of statist ideology is not the place to look for an understanding of present insecurity. Truth, like stolen animals, must be seized on the opportunity of the moment. It is evanescent and highly resistant to definition. This, the Glendiot performance of scapulomancy announces, is where the lability of humor provides greater insight into the nature of social experience than any set of official rules and definitions.

CHAPTER EIGHT

TRANSFORMATIONS

Visions of Change

"As long as there is a Mount Ida, there will be animal theft!" This is the pronouncement of a man still heavily implicated in the practice which, depending on one's viewpoint, has made Cretans either notoriously beholden to powerful patrons or a shining example of political independence. Yet there are clear indications that conditions are changing.

It may be too early to judge whether the prevalence of animal theft will really dwindle beyond the point of no return. At least twice, repressive regimes—the Metaxas government (1939-40) and the military junta of Papadopoulos (1967-73) and Ioannidis (1973-74)—have tried to suppress animal theft in a systematic and sometimes brutal way. These regimes of the extreme right were committed to a cultural policy that stressed the ancient virtues, and were determined to reduce the entire country to a state of virtually military discipline; they tried to control everyday life in every detail down to the dress and hair length of the people and the kind of music played. Not surprisingly, they could not countenance any form of banditry: not only did it flout their authority, but it presented an image of Greece that conflicted with their idealizing purism. Since these governments were dictatorships, moreover, they did not need to court voters, and could afford to offend even the most powerful shepherds of the region. On both occasions, however, as soon as these harsh governments were replaced by milder and more democratic administrations, animal theft flared anew. Expressing a firm conviction that certain politicians saw in it the best means of controlling large blocs of votes, especially through the combined obligations of agnation and *sindeknia*, the *aorites* returned to practices that had not so much ceased as gone underground. While many Glendiots felt that they had suffered repeated disillusionment at the hands of their political patrons, they also claimed to have few alternatives. Since their experiences gave them little faith in democratic process in general, moreover, they accepted the patronage for what it was worth and otherwise looked to their own traditions and values.

After the collapse of the colonels' junta, however, the rise of PA.SO.K. did seem to offer a new start. Indeed, the party's battle cry of *allayi* ("change") appealed to many villagers. The old pattern of patronage no longer seemed impregnable, and the Socialists' attacks on it had enormous appeal for families that had been edged out of the pastoral economy by the depredations of well-connected thieves. From the evidence presented in this book, it should be clear that animal theft articulates values and ideals central to the Glendiots' collective and individual self-images; and it is unlikely that anything so deeply entrenched, and so well anchored in both rhetoric and social experience, could be stamped out overnight. Nevertheless, the fact that even before the change of government some of the more sensitive representatives of the law were beginning to adopt tactics of persuasion—rather than of outright repression—means that the groundwork had already been laid.

Police tactics are not confined to merely verbal persuasion. Prominent among the legitimate methods available to the police are regular patrols, much aided by the recent construction of dirt roads in the wilder reaches of the mountain grazing zones. Roadblocks on the main arteries also enable the police to check on the trucking of stolen animals to urban butchers—a convenient and profitable means of disposal, though quite at variance with the norms of the traditionalists. Police informers are thought to be everywhere. But the police have come to realize that it is only by resorting to locally recognized forms of mediation, and to the local idiom of persuasion, that they will ever have a reasonable prospect of eradicating endemic animal theft.

The principal device through which they sought to operate for a few years after the restoration of democracy in 1974 was that of local committees, consisting of powerful representatives of all the significant patrigroups in each village. While this may have served as something of a deterrent, it proved ineffective as a means of bringing thieves to justice. In Glendi, for example, one year's crop consisted of a single thief, a Skoufas who was reported by an agnate who was serving on the committee. What would hitherto have been regarded as a gross betrayal could be justified now on the grounds that animal theft damaged the good name of the village, and was therefore a far greater betrayal in itself. Such arguments did not, however, outweigh the general reluctance to turn one's kinsmen over to the authorities, and the committee project petered out after a year or two of unproductive operation.

The difficulty with judging the success or failure of virtually any attempt to deal with the problem rests on the accessibility, or otherwise, of evidence. It was only at the end of my initial, four-month tour of fieldwork that I began to get systematic information about animal theft or frank admissions that it was still going on. Today, precisely because many villagers support the Socialists' platform, they may be especially reluctant to admit to a way of life so markedly at variance with it. The fact that animal theft reappeared so promptly after the fall of each dictatorial regime, moreover, raises the (under the circumstances) rather ironical likelihood that a return to more conservative politics in Athens might have a similar effect. Glendiots in fact often point out parallels between the Socialist program and that of the colonels—a curious juxtaposition, certainly, until one recalls that the colonel's major power base was the countryside, that their rhetoric was heavily populist, and that they, too, were vehemently opposed to the continuation of endemic animal theft and its political manipulation. In both ideologies, otherwise so radically divergent, the political corruption of the moderate conservative establishment is presented as responsible for the persistence of animal theft. This argument could hardly fail to appeal to the Glendiots: it proposes that animal theft is not autochthonous, and so reproduces at the local level the rhetoric that treats it as imported or as a response to foreign occupation at the national level. It also implicitly echoes the Glendiot's eagerness to view the political world of Athens as a continuation of the *Tourkokratia*.

Some success in reducing the frequency of raids could already be claimed before the change of government. Much to the embarrassment of the local party bosses, the regional PA.SO.K. and K.K.E. (Communist) leaders made common cause with two major groups: the small patrigroups in the mountain villages, and the more docile sheep farmers among the lowlanders and *notičotes* ("southerners" from the opposite flank of Mount Ida). Both these groups had been progressively victimized by the depredations of powerful highland shepherds, and had accumulated a rich reserve of resentment against the conservative politicians whose eager acquiescence, they felt, had maintained and even reinforced this sorry state of affairs. As a pre-election strategy, local representatives of these two political movements began urging to support for a public protest meeting, to discuss the problem of animal theft, and—less explicitly, though quite effectively, as it turned out—to embarrass their conservative foes.

The meeting, at which I was present, was held in the district capital.

It was attended by representatives from a large number of villages; by the local parliamentary deputies representing PA.SO.K., the New Liberals, and the New Democracy party; by the regional police chief; and by perhaps two hundred shepherds from the region. Even before the meeting really got under way, there were doubts about what it could achieve. Many of the most active sheep thieves were sitting at coffee-houses a stone's throw away from the meeting place, hugely amused—or so it was said—at the proceedings.

The meeting addressed a variety of issues. There was some discussion of how sheep could be more effectively marked for ownership, since the system of *samies* clearly played into the hands of skilled thieves; a new method of tagging, already tried on an experimental basis, was much touted by a few proponents, but did not arouse any obvious enthusiasm. The formation of antitheft committees in the villages, already tried with mostly unimpressive results, was briefly mentioned. But the two dominant themes in the discussion were also the most revealing of the present political dimensions of animal theft: the shaming of known thieves, and the role of politicians in maintaining the institutionalized forms of animal theft.

Shaming as a mode of punishment has a long history in rural Greece. Its appearance as a means of dealing with animal theft in western Crete, however, probably derives directly from the acuity of several local officials, who have come to appreciate the importance of ethical rhetoric as a means of negotiating change. Through their insistence that *animal theft is not a manly activity*, they appeal to the eternal verities of Cretan society in order to advance social change. This is a subtler approach than outright repression; but the evidence suggests that it is beginning to produce results, aided by the steady shift away from pastoralism and toward agriculture and small industry.

At the meeting, police officials and left-wing politicians found themselves in remarkable harmony, since they could agree on the necessity of encouraging the public humiliation of villagers caught by their fellows in the act of raiding. They were also able, in this way, to turn responsibility back to the villagers for the eradication of what all present agreed had become a "scourge" in the area. But whereas the official representatives of law and order were anxious to avoid embarrassing the powerful conservative politicians by raising the second issue, that of the abuse of political patronage, and whereas the left-wing politicians were careful not to become directly embroiled in an unseemly wrangle, many of the local supporters of the latter were only too happy to tell stories of sheep thieves who had been saved from jail by high-level intervention.

The organizers of the meeting made somewhat ineffectual attempts to stifle this part of the discussion, hoping instead to focus attention on actual methods of dealing with the problem. Some of the shepherds present were not so willing to let the political bosses off lightly. As a result, the leading New Democracy and New Liberals deputies for the region, both of whom were present, were forced to make explicit statements condemning animal theft, and denying their complicity or desire for it. Some heated exchanges and a good deal of virtuous generalization did little to allay the sharpening political polarization in the room.

To judge from subsequent comments, most of the shepherds present doubted whether anything of great import had been achieved; most seemed to regard the entire event as more of a clever political ploy—as perhaps it was. Nevertheless, the fact that the meeting took place at all is highly significant. It symbolized a new sense of Cretan pride, already expressed in Glendi by disgruntled farmers and smaller shepherds, and it may also represent a strategic exploitation of that pride by those who had the most to gain from the suppression of animal theft. The island's national and even international reputation was being eroded by the constant, unfavorable press treatment of animal theft, and some awareness of this had already begun to fuel a growing desire to remove its cause.

The unfavorable treatment of animal theft in the national press continues the nationalist historiographic tradition of regarding all forms of brigandage as foreign to Greek character and tradition. One report dwelt critically on the emergence of large-scale, motorized raiding as a variety of "Mafia" activity; another described a shoot-out between raiders and prospective victims as "scenes out of the Far West."[1] Such devices are intended to deny the Greekness of the entire phenomenon—a sensitive issue for Cretans, whose (to other Greeks) notorious distinctiveness now becomes a liability, since it removes them from the symbolic cultural center.

The rhetorical shift, moreover, serves the same goal as the emergent view of raiding as "unmanly." If to be a Glendiot and a Cretan is, from the men's point of view, to show oneself a true man, then clearly what is "unmanly" must also be "foreign." To some extent, the preconditions for this reinterpretation are already contained in the conventional village rhetoric, in the device of blaming animal theft on the Turks and other foreign occupiers. Until recently, however, the majority of the men of Glendi were shepherds,[2] there were no viable left-wing political alternatives to the patronage-ridden parties of right and center, and too few Glendiots had enjoyed the education or experience to identify with outsiders' opinion of their society. The village was internally dominated by the more powerful male members of the largest patrigroups, and farming was regarded as an effeminate occupation fit only for those who could not defend their flocks while decimating those of the neighboring communities. Now all that has changed. Even some of the most powerful shepherds, men whose flocks would have qualified them for the title of *kouradharidhes* in the previous generation, are also tilling the soil. With this change comes a drastic reevaluation of the moral universe.

Rhetorical and Pragmatic Realignments

Apart from the terraces above the village, where they grew poor wheat, barley, and animal fodder, and from the tiny garden plots within the inhabited zone of the village, Glendiots initially had few usable fields at their disposal. In the early 1920s, an innovative proprietor and grocer planted the first vines, and this experiment proved so successful that soon many other Glendiots followed suit. Over a decade later, a consortium of Glendiots acquired some fields in the comparatively nearby Portokali territory, and began to produce both table-wine grapes and olives at a level approaching self-sufficiency. But it was not until after the Second World War that Glendiots began to give serious thought to larger-scale agriculture. The acquisition in 1951 of some 169,000 square meters of fertile land in Portokali by a consortium consisting of the village president, the priest, and three other well-respected village leaders opened up novel possibilities. Close social ties between those concerned demonstrated that the acquisition of land was not incompatible with traditional loyalties, or disruptive of them (see fig. 9). In 1963 the construction of a properly paved road linking Glendi with the agricultural communities in the lowlands as well as the towns meant that villagers could now conceive of farming in yet more distant communities while continuing to live in their mountain homes. But still the old view persisted—that only the pastoral life was fit occupation for a serious man.

Effective change began soon after 1960—first with large-scale temporary emigration to West Germany and elsewhere in Europe; then with grain subsidies provided by the government of George Papandreou in 1963-64 and a consequent decrease in the degree of self-sufficiency; and, most dramatic of all, the large-scale purchase of lowland properties, made accessible through the acquisition of motor vehicles, at an ever-increasing pace.

This last development was made possible by two major factors: the existence of reliable information networks through which Glendiots could ascertain the availability of good land at low prices, and the rural exodus from the farming communities. Both of these enabling conditions have

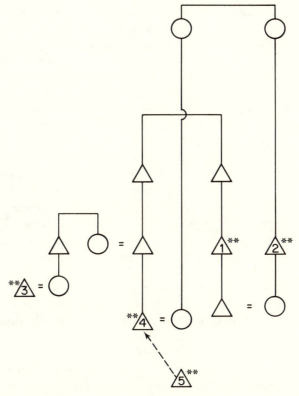

Fig. 9. Relationships among joint purchasers of land. Double asterisk indicates the parties to this arrangement. Partner 5 baptized a child of partner 4.

their special ironies. To take the information networks first, these largely derived from ties of *sindeknia* both with the owners of winter grazing land and, still more ironically, with other thieves. In the latter case, it was not only mutual assistance to confront other raids that *sindeknia* conferred on both parties, but a commitment to provide each other with any information at all that might prove economically useful. While it is clear that the degree to which this commitment was honored in practice varied hugely, there were some instances in which a spiritual kinsman alerted a Glendiot to attractive land prospects.

The second irony concerns the sources of land. The first Cretans to move in large numbers to the major Greek cities and abroad were not all mountain villagers; indeed, a much more devastating demographic decline hit the coastal and plains villages in the postwar period. The process continues at an ever-accelerated pace, so that there are some villages now in which between 30 and 50 percent of the total agricultural land is owned by Glendiots. As the populations of such villages decline rapidly and are swallowed up by Athens and Iraklio, and as its own inhabitants seize opportunity after opportunity to cultivate the rich vineyards and olive groves now available to them, Glendi continues to grow in size. Returning from Germany, many former emigrants are particularly reluctant to return to the hard life of the shepherd, and are correspondingly keen to take advantage of the new possibilities; earning enough money to do so, moreover, was a frequent motivation for the original act of emigration. Farming extracts considerable toil, but only at certain seasons; and it permits freer access to the urban centers, as well as greater flexibility in the diposition of one's working hours. Thus, since about 1975, equipped with much inflated bank balances, some of these returned migrants have acquired properties costing as much as one million drachmas.

Some Glendiots have managed to retain their flocks while diversifying into agriculture. This is usually done by buying previously rented winter grazing land and turning some of it over to agricultural purposes. Lowlanders who only a few years ago regarded the Glendiots with fear and disgust are now only too happy to sell them their properties as they, in turn, move to the towns. Glendiots who take advantage of these situations often acquire or build a home on their new property, so as to have a decent place to live both in their farming properties and back in Glendi. In many cases, they eventually vacate the Glendiot property; and it seems at least probable that the present demographic increase of Glendi will soon be reversed as this pattern becomes more general. Meanwhile, some of the biggest shepherds of all—including the Skoufades whose fathers owned the highest *mitata*—have adopted the dual economic pattern. One of these men has served prominently on the local committee opposing animal theft.

Under these circumstances, it is easy to see why the older association of animal theft with manliness has weakened. Other symbolic assumptions, too, have died with it. Fewer young men sport extravagant mustaches, and some, all farmers, had even given up smoking at the time of my 1981 visit. Wealth is no longer counted in sheep, but in the size of one's bank balance and the opulence of one's habitation (although it is true that some of the grandest houses belong to successful raiders). Even those who have opted to remain shepherds for the time being are gradually becoming less concerned with having large flocks than with the quality of the animals they raise.

But one internal feature above all others has turned local opinion against animal rustling. This is its sudden escalation at the hands of a small number of entrepreneurs, who use motorized transport to "lift" as many as fifty or sixty sheep in a single raid. Those who engage in it are not after personal revenge or the creation of new ties of *sindeknia*, but immediate financial profit. Other villagers condemn this new activity as "commerce" (*emborio*), thereby classifying it, even amongst themselves, as "non-Glendiot" and—perhaps more significantly—"non-shepherd-ing." Instead of treating it as a *response to* hunger, they view it as a way of *inflicting* hunger on others. Instead of viewing it as a game against chance, they describe the things that make it almost foolproof—the involvement of several conspirators in each "gang" (*spira*), the use of radio communication to warn of police blockades, the elaborate involve-ment of wealthy urban patrons who can provide legal and financial protection. The increasing evidence of such extended networks that appeared in the national and local newspapers fed a growing disen-chantment with practices that many Glendiots had once, in a different form, regarded as very much their own. Meanwhile, it had become common knowledge that many of these entrepreneurial animal thieves were able to secure protection and even active help from within the official ranks, and this can hardly have helped them to maintain any kind of standing as representatives of a gloriously insubordinate Cretan identity. Under such circumstances, even—or perhaps especially—the most staunch traditionalists express disgust with this commercialized reincarnation of animal theft.

Some of their complaints were given a thorough airing at the district meeting. Indeed, the heavy focus on the commercial transformation of animal rustling overshadowed the continuation, admittedly on a reduced scale, of more "traditional" modes. The new, commercialized thieves, with their trucks and radios, have furnished the authorities with a far more compelling argument against animal rustling in general than they ever had before. How can a raid in which the odds are so much on the raiders' side be invested with the *simasia* of manliness? Both the ex-clusion of risk and the adoption of a commercial ethic alienate the two groups on whose judgment the continuation of animal rustling would eventually depend: the older shepherds who still openly praise the old rustling mode, and the educated young who feel embarrassed at the damage that *all* raiding does to the image of Crete.

The new raiders themselves fight back in terms of the familiar rhetoric, which provides a rich symbolic capital for the negotiation of social values. They argue that rising inflation and the impossibility of escaping the clutches of rapacious politicians do not leave them much choice, and that the corrupt bureaucracy only makes matters worse. The greater wealth of those who have turned to farming makes for increased social competition: houses must now be grander and better appointed than ever before in the interests of securing a good marriage, and both farming and small-scale industry entail new kinds of expense for equipment and materials. The assumption that one who is no longer a shepherd will "therefore" avoid raiding actually increases the temptation, since such people are rarely among the prime suspects as long as there continue to be active shepherds in the area. It is probably true, as Glendiots maintain, that there are extremely few active thieves of the new kind in their area, let alone in Glendi itself. The vastly increased difficulty of knowing who they are, however, increases the menace they pose to the local economy and to the reputation of the region and of Crete as a whole; and their jealously guarded anonymity completely subverts that fundamental principle of the older mode of raiding, which was "to make friends." Although they argue that they are driven to raiding on such a vast scale by a new version of the Cretan's symbolic hunger, the obvious prosperity of the area as a whole undermines their attempts to present that position as metonymically Cretan, as their fathers were able to do for their own practices, and such deprivation as villagers do mention in this connection is invariably attributed to the *victims* instead.

Thus, by extending the principles of *kleftouria* for their own ends, the new thieves have only succeeded in eroding the social principles on which it was based, and hence also in transforming the poetics of Glendiot male performance. Raids have lost their power of identifying the individual performer's *eghoismos* with that of *soi*, village, region, island, and nation. Instead, they are now seen as explicitly and prosaically directed to a single end, by means that directly harm—and certainly do not augment—the pride and self-respect of all these concentric social entities. They give few or no openings for narration, since the consequences of discovery would be far more serious and ramified than used to be the case. The little that is known about them is predictable and stereotyped: ingenious tricks are kept from public knowledge since the thieves are more interested in preserving their professional skills and advantages than in achieving "knuckle" in the area. They are detested by even the toughest animal thieves of the previous generation, men now in their forties or older, as violators of normative reciprocity. As far as most Glendiots are concerned, in short, they lack the poeticity that gives *simasia* to male action: they have become, not so much "feminine," as simple "unmanly."

The Passing of a Style

The political and economic changes described in the preceding sections have not yet obliterated the practice of raiding other shepherds' flocks, and some of the conventional, small-scale raiding continues. Nevertheless, the embarrassment occasioned by the few commercialized raiders is alone a strong deterrent; villagers openly worry about its effect on the national and international reputation of Crete. The advent of television and the high-school careers of many village children, too, may be distracting young men away from the other performative skills, notably the singing of *mandinadhes*, that contribute to the projection of an idealized male self.

Within this current reformulation of social life, the increasing penetration of village discourse by official values and goals, and the integration of the village into an economic system in which raiding is both impracticable and disruptive, more and more villagers have come to espouse the legal morality of the state. Every attempt to exploit the conventions of raiding brings further discredit on it. Some new kinds of theft, for example, violate the code, and demand a change of response. A once highly active sheep thief, finding himself the victim of a purely agricultural theft, first decided to try traditional methods of learning where his property had been concealed. Finding that this led him nowhere, however, he complained to the police. It is true that his action occasioned some negative comment; some villagers thought that it had completely ruined his chances of ever finding out who the culprits were, "since he *knows* the customs of the place!" But what matters is that it took place at all, and that it did so in response to a deed that was itself—since it involved agricultural produce rather than livestock—a violation of the existing norms. The aggrieved party was a man of considerable local stature and an active political force within his patrigroup, and he had by this time become a successful farmer and landowner. What is more, the whole village soon knew what he had done.

While there was widespread surprise that he would do such a thing, the original act had also been a violation of traditional categories: agricultural materials, however valuable, were not among the things that serious shepherds stole. Only a farmer would admit to stealing watermelons, for example, as something worthy of comment or pride. Now, with the increased value of agricultural produce and the intensified involvement of the Glendiots in farming, an agricultural theft took on much more dangerous implications, and reporting it to the police eventually signified little more than that *all* the old reciprocities were now in decay in the face of an increasingly commercial outlook.

Another element in the increasing identification of the villagers with the bureaucratic *kratos*, rather than with the idealized *ethnos* alone, is their growing dependence upon the former. They receive much-needed loans from the Agricultural Bank, especially through the offices of their own Agricultural and Pastoral Cooperative. Some of them are employed directly by it: one villager has even become a policeman himself. Much though they resent its restrictions, the villagers' increasing lack of economic self-sufficiency and their corresponding reliance on officially sanctioned markets for their produce effectively mean that a life of virtual outlawry puts any individual seriously behind in the competition for all the things that carry prestige: a good home and large property (for which loans are needed); impressive jobs for one's offspring; the right to drive a motor vehicle; and even papers needed to travel abroad. The roads that entangle and surround the would-be thieves on the mountainside symbolize the strangulation to which theft itself is now subjected.

As a result, animal theft is increasingly spoken about as a thing of the past. This is not a strictly accurate assessment of the situation; talking about it as something long gone by is a rhetorical device often used with strangers. But the local conditions are increasingly unfavorable. Since the mid-1970s, animal shelters have obviated the need for transhumance, thereby complementing in winter the effect of the increased control of the mountain pastures by the police in summer. As the number of active shepherds itself declines, it seems that the pattern of reciprocal raiding cannot but follow suit.

It does so, however, on its own terms. As we have seen, the only rhetoric that seems to be effective against it is derived from the same ideology of selfhood, broadly defined, that informs the very practice of raiding. It is an ideology that insists on the primacy of the male and on an identification between the self and all the concentric social realities to which it belongs. But it is also an ideology that conflicts directly with the pyramidal conception of statism, whereby authority is exercised by a bureaucracy on behalf of all citizens. Glendiot selfhood opts instead for relative autonomy: it is conceived in terms of a segmentary relationship with the *ethnos* rather than of a pyramidal one with the *kratos*.

Today, however, this selfhood has other outlets. Even a comparatively poor nonshepherd can lay claim to respect by public evidence of his self-sufficiency (see illus. 24). Men compete in urbanity, and appreciate a protuberant belly more than the lean toughness of the shepherd. A

24. Basketmaking.

young exshepherd who had opened a sweetshop in Iraklio was praised for having put on weight: his newly chubby grin represented an achievement more realistically within the Glendiots' reach than ever before. In former times, a shepherd was criticized for being *adhinatos,* "weak," in the sense that he was not a good enough thief; today, the same term means "thin," and describes the condition of one who has failed to achieve sufficient wealth and leisure.

Today, too, the identification of local with national interests has become harder to escape. Newspapers and other media bring to the village a consciousness of playing a part in international politics: Cretan resistance to the implementation of E.E.C. agricultural policy, for example, while at odds with the stance of the government then in power, removed the level of debate to that of regional and national identities that would be seriously damaged by a continuing reputation for local banditry. Glendiots have become passionately aware that, as one farmer put it, the only way the Rethimni region ever gets into the news is through some sensational new coverage of animal theft. Those Glendiots who support protest demonstrations and blockades do so *as Cretans*, subordinating their local identity to a collective resentment against the domination of western European (and American) capitalism; here there is still a place for *eghoismos*, on a grander scale than ever before, and the rhetoric of oppression and insubordination expresses a bitter collective experience that the Glendiots share with their compatriots in general. In terms of a comparison with their erstwhile life as transhumant shepherds, they have ceased to be "hungry." On the international scene into which their economic activities have now thrust them, however, they face new sources of resentment and rebellion to which the animal-rustling past is only analogically relevant.

The decline of animal theft, even though presented to the villagers in terms of their own rhetoric of manhood, entails something of a victory for the statist ideology. This does not mean that Glendiots will henceforth meekly accept the dictates of elected or appointed authority. It does mean, however, that it becomes more and more difficult for them to insist on the positive evaluation of personal, agnatically based *eghoismos*—that celebration of unruly selfhood that constitutes the core of this book. The hierarchy of social identities is clarified into an administrative schema, so that the paramount loyalty to the state—if not to particular governments—suppresses those sentiments of cultural difference of which every act of lawless pride boasts. The poetics of manhood is replaced by a legalistic and literalistic morality, in which the contextual nature of *simasia* is converted, step by step, into the reified culture of definition.

Every year, the Cretan sheep graze more peacefully, newly confined in their enclosed pastures as the actions of Cretan men are newly defined in a bureaucratic code. Even the countinuing acts of lawlessness are recast in this way: they serve one purpose, an economic one; and if they speak at all of hunger and deprivation, they do so only in the mouths of those whose slow economic growth has put them in the hands of outside entrepreneurs. Besides, ever fewer Glendiots are willing to jeopardize the new prosperity. Betrayed by the extension of its own rhetoric into activities that have little to do with the familiar reciprocities and undermined by an economically attractive recasting of the relationship between the individual and the state, the poetic celebration of Glendiot manhood threatens to yield to a more prosaic vision. Instead of expressing all the many levels of collective identity through individual performance, Glendiots increasingly subordinate their selfhood to the single level at which all the other collective identities are bureaucratically controlled and defined.

Yet the transformation is neither complete nor consistent. There is a danger in writing in the "ethnographic present," as most conscientious anthropologists would agree. By the same token, however, it is all too easy to yield to the opposite fashion and deny the relevance of Glendiot ideals of manhood for understanding the "real" present. Such an approach would only yield an equally absurd caricature. I have taken much of the material on raiding, revenge, and agonistic social interaction from recent events in the village. Had the Glendiots surrendered their poetics of selfhood to the external forces of cultural and social homogenization, I could never have written this book. How far into the future the specific feature of animal theft will survive is unclear; events gave the lie to earlier forecasts of its imminent disappearance. The Glendiots' own attitude to literal prediction, revealed in their scapulomantic practices, should teach us not to be so hasty.

Thus we return full circle to the lessons that the Glendiots themselves can teach us. Their ideas about the meaning *of* and *in* social life make a mockery of the distinction between theory and ethnography. Their social concepts clearly belong to both of these categories of our own discourse: they can be described as a feature of Glendiot culture and society, but they also engage productively with the theoretical capital of our own discipline. The Glendiots are not professional ethnographers; but, like ethnographers, they are committed to unremitting *social diagnosis* of their own community and of those who have the temerity—but also the privilege—to enter it as guests. In this book, I have not merely tried to ask for a sympathetic understanding of their social institutions, though I believe that anthropologists are professionally equipped to take that side of the discussion far beyond the conventional platitudes about custom and criminality. I have also asked that we take the Glendiots seriously as commentators upon their own condition. Given all that I have learned from them, I suggest that this is an entirely reasonable position.

The concept of a poetics of the social self is, of course, an extraneous device. If I have succeeded at all in rendering it unobtrusive, this is because it seems to gloss so much of what the Glendiots themselves have to say about the nature of social interaction in their community. In particular, the definition of poeticity as a set toward the message itself, a focus on form and style, brings into sharp relief the performative dimensions of Glendiot *eghoismos*. Similarly, the detailed textual analyses that I have presented are translational devices: their purpose is to suggest the range of associations that particular linguistic and other semiotic forms take on for Glendiots.

In the end, however, the main focus rests on what the Glendiots have to say about *simasia*, about their own understanding of meaning. Here, indeed, there may be a basis for further comparative research. Much current anthropology is predicated on the view that the search for meaning is a universal feature of the human condition. But is meaning always the same? What does it mean to say that it is? The Glendiots' *simasia*, certainly, is a conceptual framework for their own, idiosyncratic lives, but its example suggests possibilities for comparison with other societies. Meanwhile, it can be approached on its own terms and in its own context, if we are willing to hear what the Glendiots have to say about it. For them, it is the evanescent experience of social life that only true poets of the self can snatch from the remorseless passage of time.

APPENDIX

SPECIMEN GREEK TEXTS

1. See pp. 188-189.

Μιά φορά που λες επήγαμενε μ' ένα στην γλεψά, και πιάνομ' ένα και ξανοίγω το ζο εγώ. Μμμ, του λέω, φέρε μου το σκοινί να την μπουζάσουμεν 'παέ, δηλαδή, 'α ξανοίξουμε να πιάσουμ' άλλο ένα ζο. 'Α πάρει καθαείς μιά. Και μου δίνει αυτός σκοινάκι, τήνε βουζάζω. Ζυγώνουμε δα ύστερα να πιάσουμεν άλλο ζο, ζυγώνουμε, πάε στριμώνω, 'παέ ξέρω εγώ τι, δε πιάνουμε άλλο ζο. Ωστόσο, ξεπατώνεται του ορτάκη μου το οτιβάνι και πηαίνει αξυπόλυτος. Και τον εφάγαν οι αγκάθες, ϗι αναγκάστηκα να τόνε φέρω. [At this point, a listener makes an exclamation of disbelief or irony.] Σοβαρά. Όϊ ψευτιές, και τού 'πα, Ναί. Λοιπόν, τ' αποτέλεσμα είναι, μου λέει, Δε γίνεται, μόν' άδε να φύγομενε να πάρουμε το ζο κειόν', να φύγουμε. Πάμενε. Ξεβουζάζω το ζο ϗαι να το πάρουμε να φύγομενε. Ξανοίγω τη σαμιά ϗαί 'τονε του κουμπάρου μ' που μ' έχει στεφανωμένο. Μ' έχει στεφανωμένο. Λέω, Κακομοίρη, μα τούτηνε το πρόβατο δεν τη παίρνω 'γω για, άνε χαλάσ' η γης. Γιάντα; μου λέει. Γιατί 'ν' του Τάδε που μ' έχει στεφανωμένο. Μπρε αμάν, μου λέει. Τίποτα, δηλαδή. Ε, καθώς είν' και τη μολαίρνω. Πραγματικά δηλαδή, τη μόλαρα. [Then, to a comment from the other speaker:] Απου δεν ήπρεπε να μουλάρω 'γώ, ήπρεπε να τήνε φάω. Τέλος-πάντων.

2. See pp. 171-173.

Μιά φορά πάλι θυμάμαι, κ' ήμουνε, τότ' ήμουνε πολύ μικρός, ήμουνε δεκαπέντε χρονώ'. Εκεί-μέσα. Και πήγαμε σ' ενούς τσι κουρές. Εβλέπαμε τα πρόβατα μου και κούρευε ένας γείτονας, νά 'με, όχι και κο, κοντά γείτονας, να πούμε, αλλά λίγο πιο μακρυά. Λέ', Άδε βρε να πάμενε κει στο, στο Τάδε να πούμε να πα' τόνε βοηθήσομεν, να πάμεν κει στο Οσίδι να μας κεράσ' δυό-τρει' τσιγάρο [sic]. Ε, τοτεσάς εδά, τσιγάρα που να δεις, νά 'με; Εγώ 'κανα στ' αόρι ένα μήνα νά 'με, και αν είχενε καπνίσω το μήνα πέντε τσιγάρα, δέκα. Λοιπόν, πάμε στη μάντρα εκεί και κουρέγανε. [There follows an account of how the host failed to offer him a cigarette. The speaker decides on revenge.] Μόλις εσυχάσαμ' τώρα τα πρόβατα ϗαι κοιμήθηκεν τώρα αυτός, την κοπανίζω εγώ. [Laughs.] Και λέω, Θα σου πάρω δυό, δε σηκώνει άμα του πάρω δυό, γιατ' ίντ' 'α τσι κάμω; Να μ' αποκαλύψουνε τούτοινε. Λέω, Μιά θα πάρω. Δεν ημπορούμουνε ϗαι να πάρω ϗαι παραπάνω. Πάω λοιπόν στα πρόβατα ἤει, κάτεχα βέβαια αφού τσι κουρεύαμε νά 'με το, 'ην ημέρα. [Note that here he does correct the gender of the article, and compare with what follows.] Ἇαι πιάνω μιά, μα διαλεχτή όμως, ε! [Chuckles.] Ἇαι τήνε παίρνω και τή σφάζω επί τόπου. Δεν ξέρει τώρα ο άλλος τίποτα. Αρμέμ' 'μεις το πρωΐ τα πρόβατα. Ἇείνη την ημέρα δεν έψησα ϗείνο το, μέρα νά 'με, καθόλου. Τό 'χα βέβαια φυλαμένο σ' ένα σημείο που σεν μπορούσε να το, ουτε σκύλος ούτε άνθρωπος να το βρει. [Explaining:] Τρύπες νά 'με στο βουνό που χώναμεν ϗρέας, νά 'με. Το πρωΐ βέβαια αρμέει αυτός, μετρά τα πρόβατά του, λείπει μιά. Σου λέει, Πε! ίντα γίνηϗε, μου πήραν το πρόβατο, ξέρω εγώ. Γυρέει, δεν τη βρήνει. Σου λέει, Πήρασί μου την απόψε.

3. See pp. 164-165.

[Asked about his first raid:] Αααα, εϗείνν' έχει ϗαι σημασία, ε; Λοιπόν. Ήμουνε τότε ένδεϗα χρόνων. Ένδεκα χρονών ήμουνα. Λοιπό'. Και ήτανε παραμονή Χριστογέννων. Παραμονή Χριστογέννων. Λοιπόν. Εμείς τότε είχαμενε καμμιά τριανταριά πρόβατα, ο πατέρας μου ήταν τότε φτωχός, πολύ φτωχός, ο πατέρας μου ήτανε πολύ φτωχός. Λοιπόν. Και μ' είχε ϗαι τά 'βλεπα να πούμε 'παέ μέσ' στα φαράγγια, ϗαι τα βάλαμε κάθε βράδυ μέσ' στο σπίτι μας, τα βάλαμενε μέσα. Χειμώνας ϗαιρός, σου λέω, τω' Χριστογέννω'. Λοιπόν. Μία βραδυά, ήτανε άλλο ένα από τη χωριοδάϗι μου ϗειδα, πιο μεγάλος αυτός, ήτανε δυό-τριών χρονών πρώτος. Όπως εκουβεντιάζαμεν τώρα, μου λέει, Δεν πάμενε, λέει, να βρούμε γιανένα ζο; να φάμε; Εγώ τότε πιτσιρίκος, σου λέω, πρώτη φορά που πήγα. Μώρε συ, δεν πάμε; Πάμε! Πάμε; πάμε. Λοιπό', εσηκωθήκαμεν αποϗεί, πάμενε τότε παέ στα Θολιώτικα. Ε. Πιτσιριϗάδες τώρα ϗαι οι δυό, μαζώνουμε τα πρόβατα, τό, το κουράδι όπως ήταν να πούμ' το μαζώξαμ'. Λοιπόν, ϗαι για να πιάσεις ζο πρέπει να το μαζώξεις. Ἇαι μαζώνουμε ϗαι πιάνω εγώ ένα, ένα πρόβατο, ϗαι πιάνει ϗι αυτός δυό αρνιά. Τότε βυζάνανε. Ἇαι πιάνω δ'λ'ή το πρόβατο με τ' αρνί τϗη ϗ' έναν άλλο ένα. Λοιπόν. Τα σέραμεν εμείς αποϗειδα, ϗαι τα πάμε σ' ένα οπιτάϗι. Ἇαι σφάζουμεν επί τόπου τ' αρνί, που δεν είχενε μάνα, σφάζουμεν τ' αρνιά, ϗαι το γδαίρνουμε ϗαι το καστένουμ' να πούμε ϗαι το σουβλίζουμε τελικά ο ϗαθαείς το μισό.

NOTES

PREFACE

1. See especially Fernandez 1976-77, on verse humor and social categories; Galaty 1983, on the poetics of ritual; and Brown 1977, on the aesthetics of sociological texts.

CHAPTER ONE

1. The information is contained in a pamphlet published privately by Steryios M. Manouras some six years ago, giving local statistics and concisely outlining specific problems currently facing the village. A later reference, in Marinos Tzane Bounialis' *The Cretan War* (1685), shows that a community had existed here during the Venetian period, although the Turkish document is the earliest administrative record. No earlier named reference to Glendi exists, even on maps, but this does not preclude the existence at some earlier date of a small settlement or shepherds' encampment where Glendi now stands.

2. The extent of foreign intervention is a matter of considerable bitterness to many Greeks today. A good general historical survey is Couloumbis, Petropulos, and Psomiades 1976, while Freeman 1975 provides a revealing, if somewhat more sectarian, account of the critical period from 1944 to the end of the colonels' rule in 1974. Couloumbis and Iatrides 1980 add a well-documented discussion of the specific role of the United States. On the political role of foreign powers in Crete, the most complete and up-to-date work is Papamanousakis 1979. Some of the articles in local publications, notably *Kritikes Ikones*, provide examples of a more xenophobic idiom. Herzfeld 1982b contains a discussion of the rhetoric of political responses to foreign interference in Greek affairs generally.

3. Villagers admit quite freely that fresh meat was always available, and there is scattered evidence—for example, in song texts from the area—to support this (e.g., Mavrakakis 1983:244, no. 3). Meat was the product of a hard life or of theft, and therefore "wilder" than the kinds of "cultivated" food of which the Glendiots were often more literally deprived. See also chapter 4.

4. The official census data for Glendi are as follows:

1881 390	1951 926
1900 590	1961 958
1928 728	1971 1,056
1940 789	[1981..........1,425
	(unofficial estimate)]

The growth in population has taken place despite an increasing tendency to limit progeny to a maximum of three children per household, especially among those who have given up herding. The need for several brothers to share workshifts with the flocks has been supplanted by a desire not to let landholdings fragment too rapidly in succeeding generations, and to provide more luxuries and better education for the children.

Glendi's demographic robustness stands in marked contrast to what has happened in most of the coastal and eastern areas, even in the fertile Messaria plain. See especially Burgel 1965:95-125.

5. The tension between extroverted collective self-presentation and introspective collective self-knowledge is given ideological significance in Greek culture through the phenomenon that I have elsewhere dubbed "disemia" (Herzfeld 1982c). This is the existence, in a wide range of cultural modes of expression, of a contrast between a formal code designed for external consumption and a relatively informal code that expresses, through both form and content, the unexpurgated stereotype that Greeks hold of themselves. "Disemia" is best known in its linguistic form, diglossia, with its contrast between the neo-Classical *katharevousa* and the everyday *dhimotiki* ("demotic"). But the phenomenon is by no means confined to language. In architecture, for example, neo-Classical façades may mask unpretentious interiors. Disemic tension has ideological implications: the neo-Classical stereotypes, for example, embody an image of Hellas that owes much to Western European influence and political control, and that has been especially favored by the political Right within Greece. Disemic tension does not only occur at the national level; Cretans, for example, may talk about their home island very differently in an all-Cretan setting than they would before mainlanders. At the same time, as this book is partly intended to demonstrate, their attitudes also *identify* Crete with Greece, in both idioms: because Crete has an extremely ancient history, Cretans can claim neo-Classical respectability without necessarily sacrificing their distinctiveness, but they can also take a more familiar but perhaps less respectable trait such as *poniria* and treat it as a sign of their unadulterated Greekness.

6. So deeply rooted is this polar opposition that "Bulgarians" has

often been used as a synonym for "communists," while anticommunist political literature is full of allusions to "foreign dogmas" and "Slavic threats."

7. Some may object that this is a mistranslation, on the grounds that *kleftouria* was a historical phenomenon with a specifically heroic and patriotic cast. The translation does, however, respect the essential significance given to the word by Glendiots, and there is little reason to suppose that it was not also so used by the guerrillas of the period of the War of Independence. That it was cast more as a *heroic* lifestyle in nationalistic historiography is hardly surprising, and does not commit us to the same interpretation.

8. There is an increasingly valuable literature on this subject. See especially: Kondoyoryis 1980; St. Clair 1972:35-40; Vasdravellis 1975. For an illuminating study of the post-Independence development of relations among bandits, Greek officialdom, and foreign observers, see Koliopoulos 1979, 1982. In spite of the deep hostility evinced by successive governments toward the bandits, Koliopoulos shows that even in educated circles there existed a certain amount of "guarded admiration" for them. Commenting on an 1835 article, he observes: "The lifestyle described is unmistakenly drawn from the klephtic tradition— or, rather, what appeared at the time and later to have been this tradition. . . . There must have been . . . a positive attitude towards brigandage perhaps, reflecting no doubt a growing tendency to identify post-independence brigands with preindependence *klephts*. The attribute of a national function to brigandage, though never officially admitted, was not difficult to conceive" (1982:41). Such attitudes doubtless delayed and hampered the effective suppression of brigandage on the mainland. We meet them again in the quandary faced by police and other officials in confronting the very similar problems posed by Glendiot animal raiding. Similarities of this kind, while to be treated with caution, certainly suggest that ethnographic analysis of the west Cretan *kleftouria* of today would help to illuminate the historiography of Greek brigandage by providing comparative materials. The crucial step is to recognize that a genuine basis of comparison does indeed exist, and this insight has been made far more accessible through the researches of the scholars mentioned here.

For a brief ethnographic preview of this material, see my account (Herzfeld 1983d).

It is also worth noting that the terminological tug-of-war over what term is appropriate continues today, and may more generally be a feature of countries in which a central government, succeeding to a colonial heritage, struggles to assert its legitimacy as the true representative of all its subjects. A single example will serve here to illustrate: "Eleven people have been hacked to death at the Namalere agricultural research station in Uganda by men described by the Government as bandits—a term for rebel guerrillas—Radio Uganda reported" (*The Times*, London, #61,593 [July 25, 1983], p. 6 [col. 8]).

9. For example, at the churches of Panaghia Kera at Kritsa (Merambello), and St. John the Baptist at Axos (Mylopotamos) (Gerola 1961:57 [#297], 85 [#568]). Both churches were painted during the main period of Veneto-Byzantine wall painting (13th-15th centuries). The scene reproduces a popular punishment, apparently widespread throughout Greece before the enactment of specific antirustling legislation, for the shaming of thieves (see Anagnostopoulos 1955:63-64).

10. It is not clear whether such rumors are based on locally available information or on newspaper reports. For examples of the latter, see: *Ta Nea* (Athens), July 10, 1981, p. 11, article by An. Koumandos; news item reported from Iraklio in *Ta Nea* (Athens), July 28, 1981, p. 3. The PA.SO.K. party newspaper for the nome of Rethimni, *Allayi*, carried a lengthy descriptive and analytical article on July 2, 1981 (pp. 1, 5).

A noteworthy exception to the general pattern of journalistic reporting on the subject is provided by Dafermos (1984), who, while highly critical of the ethical position represented by animal theft and of the political interests supporting it, nevertheless sensitively acknowledges its ideological and social basis.

11. For a more detailed discussion, see Herzfeld 1982a.

12. This may be a "learnedism" introduced through the influence of a schoolteacher or some other representative of the official culture, and in any case is unlikely to represent a "folk memory" of the legend of Minos.

13. *Dios genos* in Greek; hence the spurious etymology that makes *Digenes* a corrupted title of Herakles.

14. As far as I could ascertain during a brief visit to some villages in Sitia, the normative practice is in fact virtually the same as in Glendi. Apparently, however, a Sitian employer might, on entering the coffeehouse, treat those of his laborers who were already assembled there; but this could perhaps be explained on the grounds that, since treating normally indicates a kind of contextual superiority, it would be inappropriate for the laborers to treat their boss. This is a situation unlikely to arise in Glendi, where the degree of social stratification found in Sitia is virtually unknown. When questioned about their alleged reversal of the Glendiot treating pattern, Sitians seemed somewhat embarrassed, as though I had attributed something discreditable to them. This may sug-

gest that they share the Glendiots' view of the importance of correct coffeehouse etiquette, but are aware of violating it more frequently.

15. This term is apparently derived from Classical *knisa*, a term meaning the layer of fat used to wrap sacrificial offerings, as well as the smell emanating from the burnt sacrifice (see Liddell and Scott, s.v.). If so, it suggests that the demonstrative consumption of this fat entails an arrogation to the human shepherd of divine prerogatives—a progression that is also suggested by the practice of scapulomancy (see chapter 8). While such speculative uses of etymology are extremely tendentious, what they suggest is certainly in harmony with the social ideology discussed here.

16. Cf. pp. 130-135 for a further discussion of food symbolism.

17. The very phrasing of this account is suggestive of the Glendiots' poetic ability to invert the conventions of ideological discourse. In a description of Turkish rule, for example, we read: "For such men, for reasons of 'personal bravery,' the Sultan had set aside olive-groves and hamlets, even in other districts where they were worked by Christians and [']eaten['] by the 'Braves' . . ." (Marnieros 1984:106). If we recall that the Greek term for "brave" (*andhrios*) more specifically means "manly," we can all the more readily appreciate how pregnant with subversion the Glendiot tale really is: *andrismos*, "manliness," is above all a virtue that Glendiot men deny both the lowlanders and the island's rulers, past and present. Such linkages with the rhetoric of local scholarship are not merely fanciful; on the contrary, they illustrate how essential to an understanding of local values such connections are.

A further transformation of the same set was offered in gnomic form by a hard-working Glendiot entrepreneur and middleman: "If you don't work, you don't eat [*ama dhe dhoulepsis dhe tros*]."

18. The *rebetika* are a distinctive song group, once associated with the urban underworld, and widely fashionable today (often in modified form). A detailed study by Petropoulos (1968) seems to have played some part in creating this vogue, as did the attentions of the composers Manos Hadjidakis and Mikis Theodorakis, among others. Nikos Xylouris was a Cretan singer, born in the Mylopotamos district, who achieved fame throughout Greece for his passionate renditions of Cretan folksongs and instrumental music.

19. Cf. Danforth 1983 for a careful ethnographic analysis of the sources of women's power over men in a Greek village.

20. For this reason, the approach also helps to emphasize the problems of analyzing moral-value terminology as though it were semantically uniform throughout the country.

CHAPTER TWO

1. In the Rhodian village I had studied earlier ("Pefko"), a population of 160 was served by only three coffeehouses. While this represents approximately the same ratio of coffeehouses to population, the Pefko figure represents the results of depopulation; the same number of coffeehouses had served the village before World War II, when its population was about 480. In terms of rural Greece generally, the Glendi figure is extremely high.

For additional comparative data on Pefko and Glendi, see Herzfeld 1980a, 1980b.

2. Like all such statements, this one should be read as ideal and symbolic, although everyday actuality comes close to it. Women may enter the coffeehouses if there are no men present; this often happens when a proprietor leaves his wife in charge. They do not tarry long, however, since to do so might invite critical attention. When the proprietor returns, his wife may continue to run the actual business of preparing and serving the drinks, or she may assist him. Some proprietors' wives spend a good deal of time in the coffeehouses, quietly doing needlework or knitting in the the background, and occasionally volunteering a contribution to the discussion if the customers present are sufficiently close to her husband. Women may also sit quietly in the coffeehouse if they are waiting for a bus, and the wives and daughters of visitors—especially urban ones—can sit with the company. But women never play cards in the coffeehouse or anywhere else. They do not drink alcohol there, even though they may touch a drop of wine or beer at home and entertain each other formally with sweet liqueurs. Above all, they conduct themselves with a quiet reserve that may be very different from the way they behave in the intimacy of their homes. Any exception to this pattern immediately provokes a challenge to their womanhood.

3. This system has been formalized by Andromedas 1957. Its general applicability to Greece has been challenged by Bialor 1973, and differences in consanguineous terminology are to be found on Rhodes; in Pefko, *aksadherfia* [all gender forms] include "first cousins once removed" [*protodheftera*] and "second cousins once removed" [*tritodheftera*]—forms *not* found in Glendi, where the more usual *thios/thia* and *anipsi* [all gender forms] are employed. Also, note the older forms *ablos* (B), *abla* (Z), *čiris* (F), *thighatera* (D), as well as the use of *papous* (MF and FF) for MFB and FFB. *Mami* (MM and FM) may similarly be used of MMZ and FMZ.

The cognatic character of the terminology does not appear to be compromised by any of these variations. On the other hand, there is some difficulty regarding the interpretation of *group* terms, among which the most problematical is *soi*. Campbell (1964) accords it an unequivocally cognatic significance, and du Boulay (1974:144) follows him on this point. Bialor (1973), on the other hand, argues that it is a "minimal lineage" analogous to those reported for some Turkish and Arab communities. In Pefko, I found some ambivalence as to its correct interpretation, but the weight of evidence (e.g., rhyming couplets celebrating particular groups, informant responses to specific questions about the uses of the term) suggests that it is *primarily* an agnatic unit, though not one that plays any very significant political or social role today. Much more research is needed to determine the exact semantic range of the term. Meanwhile, I suggest that it is best treated as the designation of a *moral community*—that of one's closest and most reliable kin (see also an extended discussion in Herzfeld 1983c). This interpretation has the advantage that it encompasses a measure of slippage in the exact range of meanings: in Pefko, for instance, a shift in emphasis away from agnatic and toward bilateral preferences would produce the terminological ambiguity of *soi* just mentioned. It may well prove to be the case that concern with "kinship" as a domain of anthropological inquiry and its heavy reliance upon the evidence of formal terminological analysis have thwarted understanding of the moral and political uses to which ostensibly kinship-based terms are put in social life (see Needham 1971; Karp 1978).

4. The term *fara*, associated in the educated Greek imagination with the great "families" of Revolutionary klefts, enjoys wide currency in Glendi for all levels of segmentation of the agnatic group, and as such is synonymous with *soi*. *Yenia*, another term sometimes encountered in the literature about the War of Independence, seems to be applied more nearly exclusively to the total surname group. Further data from the area, as well as detailed case studies of patrigroup history, can be found in Saulnier 1980:101-128.

5. Bialor (1973) suggests the term "minimal lineage" on the basis of analogies with Near Eastern parallels. The question of whether these groups "are" lineages or not can all too easily degenerate into mere nominalism. Saulnier (1980) classifies them unequivocally as *lignages*. Certainly they are not prescriptively exogamous, as much of the Africanist use of the term would require, but then neither are the segmentary lineages of Arab groups. Calling the Glendiot groups "lineages" might also provoke the objection that they are not technically corporate: they do not own land or livestock as groups. To this, one might respond that they are *conceptually* and *ideologically* corporate, as is shown by the naming of whole neighborhoods after such groups and by the fact that

the groups ideally vote in solidary blocs in local (and sometimes also in national) elections. Although I would be comfortable with the term "lineages" on this basis, it does entail a measure of special pleading. A possible alternative is to speak of "surname groups." This works well for the largest level of segmentation: each *soi* at this level is defined by a common surname, legally recognized. It does not work at all, however, for the subsidiary groupings, which are defined by what eventually became the surname of the encompassing unit—in other words, a *paratsoukli*, or nickname. In the end, it seemed simplest to adopt the unambiguous neologism "patrigroup." Each patrigroup, in this sense, is defined by possession of a group name, derived from the baptismal name or *paratsoukli* of an apical ancestor; each *soi*, at whatever level of segmentation, is bound by ties of corporate solidarity, revealed with particular clarity in the conduct of local elections; and each patrigroup is liable to segment into subsidiary units *in each generation*. No currently existing Glendiot patrigroup exceeds a nominal depth of five generations, each one marked by segmentation of this kind. There seems, however, to have been some telescoping of generations, so that the oldest patrigroups cannot always specify the genealogical relationship between outlying branches.

6. The incest rules of the village forbade marriage between kin up to the distance of third cousins. The church, however, permits second-cousin marriage (*In Trullo* LIV; see Alivizatos 1949:99-100, 531, 721). First-cousin marriage is regarded as totally incestuous, especially if the parties are the children of brothers, in which case their relationship confuses the categories of relationship within the patrigroup, and threatens agnatic unity by setting two brothers (i.e., their fathers) at each other's throats.

7. < *timi*, glossed (e.g., by Campbell [1964:268] and du Boulay [1974:107]) as "social worth."

8. See pp. 152-155 on the uses of coffeehouse space.

9. The term *ghamos* is used particularly of the *secular* celebration of marriage, as opposed to the liturgical *stefanosi* ("crowning"). Given this significance and the fact that betrothal is also celebrated with merrymaking at a special gathering (*arravoniasi*), it is easy to see how the term *ghamos* has come to be used informally for the engagement celebration as well. The usage has been reinforced by the practice of allowing young couples to sleep together from this point on, and perhaps also by the cognate verb for the sexual act. For a more detailed analysis of these terminological vagaries, see Herzfeld 1983b.

10. One of the songs on this occasion, as on many others of a similar nature, was *Pote tha kami ksasteria*, a famous *rizitiko* celebrating revolt

against the foreign oppressor and adapted in recent times to meet the exigencies of political oppression (e.g., under the junta, in Athens). The song is usually assumed to have originated with the Cretans' resistance to Turkish rule, although Morgan (1960:26) has suggested that it may in fact have originated earlier, as a localized vendetta song under the scarcely gentler rule of the Venetians.

11. See especially pp. 142-143 and 144-146.

12. See especially Galaty 1981:78-89. Galaty's argument for a semiotic interpretation of segmentary political action disposes at a stroke of the awkward dichotomy between the "ideal" character of the segmentary model and the "reality" of observed political action. Actions are given meanings by the actors and those with whom they deal. Any description of these actions that fails to present them in terms of these indigenous interpretations must be ethnographically suspect. When a small group acts *as the representative of a larger group*, this does not necessarily entail a violation of the segmentary model *as far as the actors themselves are concerned*.

13. Etymologically cognate with *sazo*, "to pull taut [e.g., a string]" (standard Greek *siazo*). Note that this derivation does *not* imply that tension has been banished through the act of *sasmos*. On the contrary, tension is a definitive trait of friendship and alliance in Glendi as much as it is of enmity; alliance is ideally the transform of a previously hostile relationship.

14. I had expressed the view that the garbage collection was a remarkable display of village unity, and that it deserved to be recorded photographically—a view that the village president and the president of Glendi's intermittently active Cultural Society both enthusiastically endorsed. (Note, too, that they were also both Skoufades.) The other man's objection seemed to rest on the idea that dirty clothes and a filthy job hardly made for a dignified view of village life. Others thought he might have minded less had more of the villagers actually joined in, having put himself out to initiate the whole undertaking. A recent returnee from Germany, he was clearly upset by the failure of his native village to measure up to what he, like so many former *Gastarbeiter*, had come to regard as civilized standards of hygiene and civic responsibility.

15. On the other hand, they did not intervene when a senior clergyman made arrangements for two of her children to be admitted to an orphanage. It was generally felt that she was too poor to be able to support seven children on her own, and the two who went to the orphanage would continue to bear the patrigroup name.

16. For an excellent discussion of male and female attributes, see du Boulay 1974:100-120. This analysis builds, in part, on the earlier work

of Campbell (1964:274-291); cf. also Friedl (1962:89-91). Detailed re-
finements of these insights are contained in some of the essays in vol.
1 (1983) of the *Journal of Modern Greek Studies*. Some suggestive discussion of the negotiation of female identity, especially in connection
with death rituals, is to be found in Caraveli-Chaves 1980 and Danforth
1982.

17. On the symbolism of food consumption in Glendi, see pp. 130-
135.

18. I borrow this term from Ardener 1975. It may seem incongruous
to use a term specifically devised for the description of female ideology
in order to characterize an androcentric ideology of this sort. Glendiot
men, however, while aggressive in their opposition to bureaucratic values, accept the need to dissemble when dealing directly with the official
system. In those situations, their ideology is "muted" in that there is no
effective way of verbalizing it without inviting criticism or repression.
Their view of the situation underlines a central theme of this ethnography:
that the various, hierarchically ordered levels of social-group opposition
reproduce each other's salient characteristics as *moral boundaries*. In
this case, the subordination of Glendiot women to Glendiot men resembles that of Glendiots in general to the political authorities. Given that
Glendiots reject the latter subordination *when speaking among themselves*, further research on Cretan women may reveal similarly disemic
distinctions between what women are prepared to say about their own
role in public and what their private demeanor suggests. As it is, there
are strong hints in the narratives of sheep theft that women treat their
constant need to guard their husbands and sons against the consequences
of foolish masculinity as an imposition that enhances rather than undermines their own feeling of moral superiority. See especially pp. 169-
170.

Chapter Three

1. This may be a calumny, but it enjoys wide currency, and villagers
tell of frequent experiences that appear to bear it out. In Greece a trainee
doctor must do a period of rural service in order to qualify for a full
position. This means that some of the village doctors seem more like
reluctant conscripts than dedicated physicians, although there have been
many praiseworthy exceptions in Glendi and elsewhere. A further difficulty is raised by the villagers' normative suspicion of the young expert,
something of a contradiction in terms from their point of view, and this
is further compounded when the current doctor is a woman.

2. *Sandolos*, < Venetian Italian *santolo*, cognate with *santo*, "saint,
sacred." The reciprocal term is *filiotsos*, < Venet. It. *figliozzo*, "godson,"

< *figlio*, "son." Fem. forms: *sandola*, *filiotsa*. The "standard Greek" equivalents, rarely used in Glendi except in conversation with non-Cretan outsiders, are, respectively: *no(u)nos* and *vaftistikos*. All these terms are used in both address (in vocative form where applicable) and reference.

3. The ordinary demotic form is *kaka*, but this would have been less readily understood since a tone of moral disapprobation almost automatically demands the *katharevousa* form here. Note especially that Mitsos is trying to distance himself *in this instance* from the imputation of *eghoismos*, a "village" or "rustic" value that should not be allowed to intrude upon the modern notions implied by adherence to the Socialist ideology. Mitsos was not lacking in *eghoismos* in *other* situations, however; as this book is intended to demonstrate, *eghoismos* is nothing if it is not actively *performed*, but this condition also gives the individual the possibility of choosing when and under what circumstances to perform it.

4. Cf. Herzfeld 1980a:346-347. "Conscience," *sinidhisi*, conflated with *sinithio/sinithia*, "custom," and the verb *sinithizo*, "become accustomed to," to produce the form *sinithisi*. Villagers also say *dhen ekhi sinithio*, "he doesn't have *sinithio*," to indicate someone's lack of social responsibility, a concept in which a sound knowledge of village norms is virtually inseparable from the question of inner motivations. Since villagers claim that it is impossible to penetrate another person's innermost thoughts and feelings, moreover, the analytical separation between "custom" and "conscience" has little meaning for them.

5. In doing this, he was foregrounding a popular assumption—namely, that the party his patrigroup supported was essentially that of the deposed military junta—in a way that effectively precluded any serious discussion. At the same time, he suggested that he could not be deflected from his primary, agnatic loyalty, however much his previous political associations in the village might have inclined him to place his vote elsewhere. Thus, his performance presented him as a good patrigroup member, therefore also as a good Glendiot and Cretan, but also as a man of sound judgment who had been dragged into a political obligation not of his own choosing.

6. As a Macedonian, Karamanlis hails from a part of Greece that Glendiots associate with "exile"—banishment to Macedonia having been a much favored form of punishment for suspected animal thieves in former years. Cretans who fought in Macedonia in earlier generations reinforced the prejudice that these people represent an ethnically mixed heritage; there are indeed several significant, non-Greek-speaking minorities there. Finally, the *Karamanlidhes* were Turkish-speaking, Orthodox Christians, who used Greek instead of Arabic script. While Glen-

diots may not have been thinking specifically of any of these particulars, some of which they are indeed unlikely even to have known, the general aura of "foreignness" that they attribute to Macedonians seems to have affected the image of Karamanlis held by some.

7. Note that a favorite curse consists in "screwing *your/their/his/her* Virgin Mary/Cross/Christ." The segmentation of divine personae is perhaps less surprising when it occurs in blasphemous utterances than when we encounter it in political propaganda, but the idiom is so common that its theological implications were probably never noted.

8. Mavrakakis (1983:249) reports this verse as a traditional wedding response to the groom's party, which has come to "capture" the bride. It thus has associations—not necessarily entertained by those who heard it on this occasion but nevertheless potentially present—with Cretan traditions of bride theft and with the distinctiveness of Cretan weddings.

9. The decision of the Skoufas candidate not to run released many of his agnates' votes to PA.SO.K., which received an impressive absolute majority in the 1981 national elections in Glendi. The Communists obtained eighteen votes on that occasion. The death of Pavlos Vardinoyannis just before the 1984 Euro-elections appears to have halved the liberal vote, while allowing the New Democracy Party to close in on PA.SO.K. without, however, catching up with the latter. On this occasion, too, the extreme right (EPEN) party polled eighteen votes, presumably through the usual agnatic connections of this group.

Municipal elections were held in 1982. Initially four Skoufas candidates wanted to contest the village presidency. Two, including the incumbent, dropped out for lack of support; the remaining two, clearly identified with PA.SO.K. and New Democracy, respectively, were thus engaged in a municipal electoral battle in which party allegiance began to take precedence over agnatic loyalties. The PA.SO.K. candidate and slate won.

Chapter Four

1. The meaning of *skoutelovarikhno* is unclear. Many Cretans derive it from *koutelo,* "forehead," but Kriaris (1979:66-67) suggests that it comes from *skouteli,* a large clay vessel that could be used for drinking. I offer "mug" as a suitably ambiguous translation.

2. See Danforth 1982 for extensive treatment of this theme and full bibliographical references, and Alexiou 1974 for a detailed historical and philological treatment of the lament tradition in Greece.

Such imagery is by no means confined to Greece, but it is extensively elaborated there and has consequently attracted scholarly attention from an early date (e.g., Zambelios 1859).

3. On the reproduction of social structure in the performance of bibulous conviviality, see especially Karp 1980.

4. This term is often glossed as "honor." As I have tried to show elsewhere (Herzfeld 1980a), however, this gloss ignores some important components of the use of the term. In general, monolithic "translations" of indigenous moral terms, while perhaps acceptable for the sake of convenience in a fully documented ethnography, become dangerously counterproductive when they are used as the basis of comparative analyses. I would therefore *not* want to suggest that "social excellence" should replace "honor" as a translation of *filotimo*; indeed, that would subvert the point of my argument. Glendi may be rather unusual among present-day rural Greek communities in the extent to which its ideology exalts *eghoismos* and equates it with *filotimo*, and any attempt to reduce either term to a convenient translation would thwart recognition of this diacritical feature.

5. See, for example, N. G. Politis 1874:272.

6. This term is derived from Classical Greek *hetoimos*, "ready," and should not be confused with the homophonic term for "etymology" (Class., *etymologia*).

7. A similar convention obtains on Rhodes, where the villagers of Pefko use *mesa* ("inside") to refer to the direction of the town of Rhodes (in a northeastern direction from them) and *ekso* ("outside") to refer to their own area. They also claim to live "on the edge of the world" (*stin akria tou kosmou*).

CHAPTER FIVE

1. The form *klari*, familiar from the descriptions of mainland kleftism, is replaced in Glendi by the more everyday *kladhi*.

2. *Stefana*, "crowns," are placed by the marriage sponsor (*koumbaros*) on the heads of the marrying couple, as a symbol of their becoming rulers of a new household.

3. This incident recalls both the moral and the style of a cautionary tale, in which a passer-by regrets his initial refusal of meat and asks where it came from in the hope of getting a second chance; he is rebuffed (Mavrakakis 1983: 118, no. 58; provenance not given).

CHAPTER SIX

1. When we invited some of our friends to sample curry, the men professed great enjoyment of the "peppery" food. One woman who tasted it was less impressed!

2. For a discussion of disemia, see chapter 1, note 5.

3. Slaughtered animals must be inspected by the village president, who certifies that the animal came from the flock of the owner and stamps an official paper to that effect. This measure is part of the provisions for the prevention and punishment of animal theft originally drawn up in a national law (#2836, July 23-25, 1911). See also Anagnostopoulos 1955:63.

4. On the complex relationship between the dominant male ideology of oppression and the self-view of women, see chapter 1, note 19, and chapter 2, note 18.

5. The people of Aghora are locally known for their inhospitability, which has earned them the pejorative sobriquet of *ghaidhouria* ("donkeys")—i.e., people without a sense of social obligation. On my first visit to the village, I was struck by the lack of warmth or curiosity on the part of the men sitting in the coffeehouse we entered with our Glendiot companion, an indifference that contrasted sharply with our first experiences in Glendi and with what we encountered in other visits in the region. It is difficult for an ethnographer not to be beguiled by the local stereotypes, and our reception on this occasion may have been due to causes beyond our immediate knowledge. Nevertheless, patterns of reciprocity and hospitality may differ sufficiently from village to village for some of these local stereotypes to have a basis in social fact.

6. The *adynaton* is discussed extensively in Tuffin 1972-73. A more specialized case is documented in meticulous ethnographic detail by Danforth (1982).

7. This remark illustrates the embarrassment that Glendiots, and many Greeks, feel when admitting to the presence of Turkish (or "non-European") elements in Greek culture. The speaker might have preferred to give me a figure in kilos, but he was aware of my interest in historical detail, and evidently felt that we had achieved sufficient intimacy for this slightly hesitant Turkism to be acceptable. The moment illustrates the social negotiation of disemia very clearly.

CHAPTER SEVEN

1. See also Herzfeld 1982b for a fuller discussion of this rhetoric.

2. I borrow this term from a significantly different context. Lewis (1961:101) applies it to the progressive omission of intermediate and relatively insignificant names from the genealogy of a lineage, whereas there is no question here that the present bearer of a *paratsoukli* would literally have forgotten his own father! On the other hand, it is possible that such consistent re-use might eventually lead, in some cases, to the

"loss" of some of the earlier bearers of the nickname from the genealogical memory.

3. On another occasion, I heard the same expression addressed during a card game to a bystander whose insistent commentary threatened to spoil everything. Again, the "sin" being committed is a social rather than a theological one. Given the relationship between card games and animal theft, the equation between "confession" and "betrayal" is especially suggestive here.

4. Many Cretans are familiar with Kazantzakis' epitaph, a quotation from his own writings: "I hope for nothing, I fear nothing—I am free!"

5. The most detailed information available is still that provided in Megas 1926. Some variation is also encountered within a given community. One striking variation, for which Megas provides some analogues, is that the "bad weather cloud" (see fig. 8) may prove opaque against the light, and this is taken to mean the imminence of war—specifically of "guerrilla warfare" (*andartika*), a suggestive reading in view of the Glendiots' attitude toward authority.

CHAPTER EIGHT

1. The tension between "Greek" and "un-Greek" views of animal theft is nicely captured in the headlining of an article in *Ta Nea* (Athens) (July 10, 1981, p. 11). In thin capitals at the top of the page, all the way across, we read: "Organized networks are active and . . . ruling (*vasilevoun*) in parts of Crete." The phrasing is nicely allusive: it parodies the reply that sailors are supposed to give the mermaid who asks them about her beloved Alexander (*zi ke vasilevi*, "he lives and rules"); it suggests that there may be something familiar to any Greek in what is happening in Crete. This is then contradicted by the next line, in heavier and larger lower-case letters: "Now the thefts of animals recall the Mafia."

In another item in *Ta Nea* (July 18, 1981, p. 1), we read of "*Far West* scenes with a wild chase after a gang of animal thieves." Shortly thereafter, the same newspaper (July 20, 1981, p. 1) reported, "The whole village hunts for the *gangsters*." In both cases, the English words were transliterated, rather than replaced by Greek glosses—an effective way of alienating the concepts they represent.

For a detailed report on the trial of modern animal-theft operators, see *Ta Nea* (Athens), July 28, 1981, p. 3.

The preferred local rhetoric, which may be derived from more official models, has animal theft as a "scourge" (*mastigha*) of Cretan pastoralism (e.g., *Eleftheri Ghnomi* [Rethimno], July 7, 1981, p. 4). This rhetoric was much in evidence at the meeting in the district capital. It is customary for the formal representatives of villages in the area to deny the endemic character of animal theft (e.g., *Kritiki Andilali* ["Cretan Echoes," a monthly Athens newspaper for Cretan migrants], July 27, 1981, pp. 1-2). The success of the PA.SO.K. representatives in capitalizing on the issue may well have influenced their 1981 victory (officially reported as 56.65 percent of the Glendi vote, as compared with New Democracy's 24.49 percent and the New Liberals' 17.29 percent [provisional figures]).

2. An estimated 90 percent of the adult male population was engaged in pastoralism until about 1960. In 1981 the proportion was approximately 30 percent and still declining. The last semiofficial local estimate put the number of households primarily involved in animal husbandry at not more than 240.

REFERENCES

Alexiou, Margaret B. 1974. *The Ritual Lament in Greek Tradition*. Cambridge, Eng.: Cambridge University Press.

Alivizatos, Amilkas S. 1949. Οἱ ἱεροὶ κανόνες καὶ οἱ ἐκκλησιαστικοὶ νόμοι. Athens: Βιλιοθήκη 'Αποστολικῆς Διακονίας, 19.

Allbaugh, Leland G. 1953. *Crete: A Case Study of an Underdeveloped Area*. Princeton, N.J.: Princeton University Press.

Allen, Peter S. 1976. "Aspida: A Depopulated Community." In Dimen Friedl 1976:168-198.

Anagnostopoulos, Xenophon. 1955. Λαογραφικὰ Ρούμελης. Athens: n.p.

Andromedas, John. 1957. "Greek Kinship Terms in Everyday Use." *American Anthropologist* 59:1086-1088.

Ardener, Edwin. 1975. "Belief and the Problem of Women" *and* "The Problem Revisited." In S. Ardener, ed., *Perceiving Women*, pp. 1-27. London: Malaby.

Bauman, Richard. 1977. *Verbal Art as Performance*. Rowley, Mass.: Newbury House.

Berks, Bradley. 1982. *Tragic Thought and the Grammar of Tragic Myth*. Bloomington, Ind.: Indiana University Press.

Bialor, Perry A. 1973. "A Century and a Half of Change: Transformations of a Greek Farming Community in the Northwestern Peloponessos." Ph.D. dissertation, Department of Anthropology, University of Chicago.

Blok, Anton. 1983. "On Negative Reciprocity among Sicilian Pastoralists." In Di Bella 1983:43-46.

Bourdieu, Pierre. 1977. *Outline of a Theory of Practice*. Cambridge, Eng.: Cambridge University Press.

Brandes, Stanley. 1980. *Metaphors of Masculinity: Sex and Status in Andalusian Folklore*. Publications of the American Folklore Society, n.s., 1. Philadelphia: University of Pennsylvania Press.

Brown, Richard Harvey. 1977. *A Poetic for Sociology: Toward a Logic of Discovery for the Human Sciences*. New York and London: Cambridge University Press.

Burgel, Guy. 1965. *Pobia: Étude géographique d'un village crétois*. Athens: Centre des Sciences Sociales d'Athènes.

Burke, Kenneth. 1954. *Permanence and Change: An Anatomy of Purpose*. 2nd rev. ed. Indianapolis: Bobbs-Merrill.

Campbell, J. K. 1964. *Honour, Family, and Patronage: A Study of Institutions and Moral Values in a Greek Mountain Community*. Oxford: Clarendon Press.

Caraveli-Chaves, Anna. 1980. "Bridge Between Worlds: The Greek Women's Lament as Communicative Event." *Journal of American Folklore* 93:129-157.

Couloumbis, Theodore A., and Iatrides, John O. 1980. *Greek American Relations: A Critical Review*. New York: Pella.

Couloumbis, T. A., Petropulos, John A., and Psomiades, H. J. 1976. *Foreign Interference in Greek Politics: An Historical Perspective*. New York: Pella.

Crick, Malcolm. 1976. *Explorations in Language and Meaning: Towards a Semantic Anthropology*. New York: John Wiley (Halsted).

Dafermos, Olimbios. 1984. Ζωοκλοπή—Κοινωνική μάστιγα και "καπετανιλίκι," Αντί (Περίοδος Β'), issue no. 267 (Aug. 3, 1984), p. 33.

Danforth, Loring M. 1976. "Humour and Status Reversal in Greek Shadow Theatre." *Byzantine and Modern Greek Studies* 2:99-111.

———. 1982. *The Death Rituals of Modern Greece*. Princeton, N.J.: Princeton University Press.

———. 1983. "Power through Submission in the Anastenaria." *Journal of Modern Greek Studies* 1:203-223.

Davis, John. 1977. *People of the Mediterranean: An Essay in Comparative Social Anthropology*. London: Routledge & Kegan Paul.

Di Bella, Maria Pia, ed. 1983. "Dossier: Les représentations du vol du bétail dans les sociétés meditérranéennes." In *Production Pastorale et Société: Bulletin de l'Équipe Écologie et Anthropologie des Sociétés Pastorales* 13:4-83.

Dimen, Muriel, and Friedl, Ernestine, eds. 1976. *Regional Variation in Greece and Cyprus: Towards a Comparative Perspective on the Ethnography of Greece*. Annals of the New York Academy of Sciences 268:1-465.

Douglas, Mary. 1975. *Implicit Meanings: Essays in Anthropology*. London: Routledge & Kegan Paul.

du Boulay, Juliet. 1974. *Portrait of a Greek Mountain Village*. Oxford: Clarendon.

Evans-Pritchard, E. E. 1940. *The Nuer: A Description of the Modes of Livelihood and Political Institutions of a Nilotic People*. Oxford: Clarendon.

Fernandez, James W. 1976-77. "Poetry in Motion: Being Moved by

Amusement, by Mockery, and by Mortality in the Asturian Countryside." *New Literary History* 8:459-483.

Frangaki, Evangelia K. 1949. Συμβολή στα λαογραφικά της Κρήτης. Athens: Ioann. G. Goufa.

Freeman, John, ed. 1975. Ξενοκρατία· το αποκαλυπτικό χρονικό των ξένων επεμβάσεων στην Ελλάδα (1944-1974). Athens: Viper-Papyros (originally published in serial form by Επίκαιρα).

Friedl, Ernestine. 1962. *Vasilika: A Village in Modern Greece*. New York: Holt, Rinehart & Winston.

Galaty, John G. 1981. "Models and Metaphors: On the Semiotic Explanation of Segmentary Systems." In L. Holy and M. Stuchlik, eds., *The Structure of Folk Models*, pp. 83-121. ASA Monographs 20. New York: Academic Press.

————. 1983. "Ceremony and Society: The Poetics of Maasai Ritual." *Man* (n.s.) 18:361-382.

Geertz, Clifford. 1973. *The Interpretation of Cultures*. New York: Basic Books.

Gerola, Giuseppe. 1961. Τοπογραφικὸς κατάλογος τῶν τοιχογραφημένων ἐκκλησιῶν τῆς Κρήτης. Iraklio: Society for Cretan Historical Studies (Ἑταιρεία Κρητικῶν Ἱστορικῶν Μελετῶν). Originally published as *Elenco topografico delle chiese affrescate di Creta*.

Goffman, Erving. 1959. *The Presentation of Self in Everyday Life*. New York: Doubleday.

Goldschläger, Alain. 1982. "Towards a Semiotics of Authoritarian Discourse." *Poetics Today* 3:11-20.

Goodman, Nelson. 1981. "Twisted Talk; or, Story, Study, and Symphony." In Mitchell 1981:99-115.

Grodzynski, Denise. 1974. "Par la bouche de l'empereur (Rome IVe siècle)." In J. P. Vernant et al., *Divination et Rationalité*, pp. 267-294. Paris: Seuil.

Hadjidakis, G[eorgios] I. 1958. Κρητικὴ Μουσική. Athens: n.p.

Herrnstein-Smith, Barbara. 1981. "Narrative Version, Narrative Theories." In Mitchell 1981:209-232.

Halpern, Joel M. 1967. *A Serbian Village*. Revised edition. New York: Harper & Row.

Herzfeld, Michael. 1977. "Ritual and Textual Structures: The Advent of Spring in Rural Greece." In Ravindra K. Jain, ed., *Text and Context: The Social Anthropology of Tradition*, pp. 29-50. ASA Essays 2. Philadelphia: Institute for the Study of Human Issues.

————. 1979. "Exploring a Metaphor of Exposure." *Journal of American Folklore* 92:285-301.

Herzfeld, Michael. 1980a. "Honour and Shame: Problems in the Comparative Analysis of Moral Systems." *Man* (n.s.) 15:339-351.

————. 1980b. "Social Tension and Inheritance by Lot in Three Greek Villages." *Anthropological Quarterly* 53:91-100.

————. 1981. "An Indigenous Theory of Meaning and its Elicitation in Performative Context." *Semiotica* 34:113-141.

————. 1982a. *Ours Once More: Folklore, Ideology, and the Making of Modern Greece*. Austin: University of Texas Press.

————. 1982b. "The Etymology of Excuses: Aspects of Rhetorical Performance in Greece." *American Ethnologist* 9:644-663.

————. 1982c. "Disemia." In Michael Herzfeld and Margot D. Lenhart, comps., *Semiotics 1980*, pp. 205-215. New York: Plenum.

————. 1983a. "Signs in the Field: Prospects and Issues for Semiotic Ethnography." *Semiotica* 46:99-106.

————. 1983b. "Semantic Slippage and Moral Fall: The Rhetoric of Chastity in Rural Greek Society." *Journal of Modern Greek Studies* 1:161-172.

————. 1983c. "Interpreting Kinship Terminology: The Problem of Patriliny in Rural Greece." *Anthropological Quarterly* 56:157-166.

————. 1983d. "Reciprocal Animal-Theft in Crete: At the Intersection of Ideologies." In Di Bella 1983:47-54.

Hobsbawm, Eric. 1959. *Primitive Rebels: Studies in Archaic Forms of Social Movement in the 19th and 20th Centuries*. Manchester, Eng.: Manchester University Press.

Jakobson, Roman. 1960. "Linguistics and Poetics." In Thomas A. Sebeok, ed., *Style in Language*, pp. 350-377. Cambridge, Mass.: MIT Press.

————. 1980. "On Poetic Intentions and Linguistic Devices in Poetry: A Discussion with Professors and Students at the University of Cologne." *Poetics Today* 2:87-96.

Kapsomenos, Eratosthenis G. 1980. Η αντίθεση φύση vs κουλτούρα στο ελληνικό δημοτικό τραγούδι. In Karin Boklund-Lagopoulou, ed., Σημειωτική και Κοινωνία, pp. 227-232. Athens: Odisseas.

Karp, Ivan. 1978. "New Guinea Models in the African Savannah." *Africa* 48:1-17.

————. 1980. "Beer Drinking and Social Experience in an African Society." In Ivan Karp and Charles S. Bird, eds., *Explorations in African Systems of Thought*, pp. 83-119. Bloomington, Ind.: Indiana University Press.

Kevelson, Roberta. 1977. *Inlaws/Outlaws: A Semiotics of Systemic Interaction*. Lisse: Peter de Ridder, and Bloomington, Ind.: Research Center for Language and Semiotic Studies (Indiana University).

Koliopoulos, John. 1979. Λῃστές: Η κεντρική Ελλάδα στα μέσα του 19ου αιώνα. Athens: Ermis.

————. 1982. " 'Enemy of the Nation': Attitude Towards Brigandage in Nineteenth-Century Greece." In A. Lily Macrakis and P. Nikiforos Diamandouros, eds., *New Trends in Modern Greek Historiography*, pp. 39-51. Modern Greek Studies Association *Occasional Papers*, 1.

Kondoyoryis, Y. D. 1980. Η ελλαδική λαϊκή ιδεολογία. Athens: Nea Sinora.

Kriaris, Arist. I. 1979. Αθιβολές. Vol. 1, 2nd edition. Athens: Knossos.

Lambithianaki-Papadaki, Evangelia. 1972. Ο σεβντάς του ντελικανή· το προξενειό, ο αρραβώνας και ο γάμος σ[']ένα χωριό τση Κρήτης. Iraklio: n.p.

Lévi-Strauss, Claude. 1968. *L'Origine des Manières de Table*. (*Mythologiques*, 3.) Paris: Plon.

Lewis, I. M. 1961. "Force and Fission in Northern Somali Lineage Structure." *American Anthropologist* 63:94-112.

Liddell, Henry George, and Scott, Robert, 1968. *A Greek-English Lexicon*. Oxford: Clarendon.

Loizos, Peter. 1975. *The Greek Gift: Politics in a Cypriot Village*. Oxford: Blackwell.

Marnieros, Spiros Ap. 1984. Η αντίσταση στο Αμάρι· Ενθυμήματα Αλέξανδρου Κοκονά. Athens: n.p.

Mauss, Marcel. 1968. "Essai sur le Don." In *Sociologie et Anthropologie*. pp. 143-279. *Année sociologique*, 2ᵉ série I (1923-24). Paris: Presses Universitaires de France.

Mavrakakis, Yannis. 1983. Λαογραφικά Κρήτης. Athens: Stef. Vasilopoulos Historical Editions.

Meeker, Michael E. 1979. *Literature and Violence in North Arabia*. Cambridge: Cambridge University Press.

Megas, G. A. 1926. Βιβλίον Ὠμοπλατοσκοπίας ἐκ κώδικος τῆς Ἐθν. Βιβλιοθήκης Ἀθηνῶν. Λαογραφία 8:3-51.

Mintz, Jerome R. 1982. *The Anarchists of Casas Viejas*. Chicago: University of Chicago Press.

Mitchell, W.J.T., ed. 1981. *On Narrative*. Chicago: University of Chicago Press.

Molfese, Franco. 1964. *Storia del Brigantaggio dopo l'Unità*. Milan: Feltrinelli.

Morgan, Gareth. 1960. *Cretan Poetry: Sources and Inspiration*. Iraklio: A. Kalokerinos. Originally published as Κρητικὰ Χρονικὰ 14:4-68, 203-270, 379-434.

Moss, David. 1979. "Bandits and Boundaries in Sardinia." *Man* (n.s.) 14:477-496.

Mouzelis, Nicos P. 1978. *Modern Greece: Facets of Underdevelopment*. London: Macmillan.

Needham, Rodney. 1971. "Introduction." In Rodney Needham, ed., *Rethinking Kinship and Marriage*, pp. xiii-cxvii. ASA Monographs 11. London: Tavistock.

Papamanousakis, Stratis G. 1979. Ἡ Ξενοκρατία στην Κρήτη. Athens: Kalvos.

Peristiany, J. G. 1965. "Honour and Shame in a Cypriot Highland Village." In J. G. Peristiany, ed., *Honour and Shame: The Values of Mediterranean Society*, pp. 171-190. London: Weidenfeld & Nicolson.

Pashley, Robert. 1837. *Travels in Crete*. Vol. 1. London: John Murray.

Petropoulos, Ilias, Ριζίτικα τραγούδια, Athens: n.p.

Politis, Alexis. 1973. Το δημοτικό τραγούδι: Κλέφτικα. Athens: Ermis.

Politis, N. G. 1874. Νεοελληνικὴ Μυθολογία. Vol. 2, pp. 205-end. Athens: Karl Wilberg and N. A. Nakis.

Ricoeur, Paul. 1981. "Narrative Time." In Mitchell 1981:165-186.

Romanias, Alekos. 1965. Η Λεβεντογέννα: Ηθογραφικά Κρήτης. Iraklio: n.p.

Rosaldo, Michelle Z. 1980. *Knowledge and Passion: Ilongot Notions of Self and Social Life*. Cambridge, Eng.: Cambridge University Press.

St. Clair, William. 1972. *That Greece Might Still Be Free: The Philhellenes in the War of Independence*. London: Oxford University Press.

Saulnier, Françoise. 1980. *Anoya, Un Village de Montagne Crétois*. Paris: P. H. Stahl/Laboratoire d'Anthropologie Sociale.

Spyridonidis, K.-V. 1980. Εφαρμογές των αρχών της σημειωτικής στο πολεοδομικό σχεδιασμό. In Karin Boklund-Lagopoulou, ed., Σημειωτική καὶ Κοινωνία, pp. 131-156. Athens: Odisseas.

Tanner, Adrian. 1978. "Divinations and Decisions: Multiple Explanations for Algonkian Scapulimancy [*sic*]." In Erik Schwimmer, ed., *The Yearbook of Symbolic Anthropology*, 1, pp. 89-101. Montreal: McGill-Queen's; London: C. Hurst.

Tuffin, Paul G. 1972-73. "The Whitening Crow: Some *Adynata* in the Greek Tradition." Ἐπετηρίς, Κέντρον Ἐπιστημονικῶν Ἐρευνῶν [Nicosia] 6:79-92.

Turner, Victor. 1974. *Fields and Metaphors: Symbolic Action in Human Society*. Ithaca: Cornell University Press.

Vasdravellis, John K. 1975. *Klephts, Armatoles and Pirates in Macedonia during the Rule of the Turks, 1627-1821*. Scientific Treatises, Philological and Theological Series, no. 43. Thessaloniki: Society for Macedonian Studies (Ἑταιρεία Μακεδονικῶν Σπουδῶν).

Vlastos, Pavlos. 1909. Ὁ Διγενής: Ἀρχαῖος Γίγας καὶ Μέγας Ἥρως τῆς Κρήτης. Iraklio, fascicle of Ὁ Κρητικὸς Λαός.

Waugh, Linda. 1980. "The Poetic Function in the Theory of Roman Jakobson." *Poetics Today* 2:57-82.

Xenos, Stefanos. 1865. *East and West: A Diplomatic History of the Ionian Islands to the Kingdom of Greece*. London: Trübner.

Zambelios, Spyridon. 1859. Πόθεν ἡ κοινὴ λέξις Τραγουδῶ; Σκέψεις περὶ Ἑλληνικῆς Ποιήσεως. Athens: P. Sousas & A. Ktenas.

INDEX

abduction. *See* bride theft

action, as basis of meaning, xiv, 16, 18, 140

adynaton, figure of speech, 224, 290n

affines, 54, 58, 59, 60, 70, 76, 88, 96, 101, 103, 105, 117, 118, 161, 162

agnosticism. *See* belief

Agricultural and Pastoral Cooperative, 270

Agricultural Bank, 270

agriculture, 4, 6, 55, 95, 111, 229, 262, 264, 266, 268. *See also* farmers, attitudes toward

Alexander the Great, 291n

Alexiou, Margaret B., 288n

Alivizatos, Amilkas S., 68, 284n

Allayi (Rethimno), 280n

Allbaugh, Leland G., 131

Allen, Peter S., 23

alliances, allies, 55-56, 126, 157, 162, 166, 184, 185, 190, 193, 194, 215, 285n

Anagnostopoulos, Xenophon, 280n

androcentrism, 52, 100, 286n

Andromedas, John, 282n

animals, male competition over, 52

aorites (mountain people), 38, 39, 40, 69, 81, 259

"apostasy," phase in Greek parliamentary history (1963-67), 97, 118

Arab society, kinship in, 283n

archaeology of Crete, 8

Ardener, Edwin, 286n

Aristotle, 10

Arkadi monastery, burning of in 1866, 7, 9-10

arotikhtadhes, 32, 74, 99, 175, 189, 197

Asia Minor disaster of 1922, 93; refugees on Crete, 31

Assyria, 34

Athens, Athenians, xvi, 19, 24, 34, 37, 93, 97, 98, 100, 106, 117, 118, 215, 261, 266, 285n, 292n

avoidance, 61, 62, 74, 80

Axos, 280n

backgrounding, 97, 206

Balkans, little, as metaphor for small patrigroups, 67, 84

banditry, 29, 279-280n. *See also* brigandage

baptism, celebrations of, 20, 68-69, 212-213; rite of, parodied, 242; used as basis of local alliances, 55-56, 157, 219, 220; to resolve quarrels, 74, 82-83; used to resolve raiding cycles, 174, 191, 219, 220; as basis of patronage, 20, 98, 106; providing context for arranging patronage, 107; as trope for adherence to ideology, 98, 117. See also *sindeknia*

barbarism, as concept, 73

Bauman, Richard, 18, 25

belief, religious, 201-202, 241, 248-249n

belly, folds of, as metaphor for cunning, 196-197

Berks, Bradley, 215

Bialor, Perry A., 282n, 283n

Blok, Anton, 231

blood, as symbol, 10, 77, 81, 157

boasting, consequences of, 207

boundaries, property, 56

Bounialis, Marinos Tzane, 277n

Bourdieu, Pierre, 139-140, 173

Brandes, Stanley, 148

Brandt, Willy, 94

bride theft, 20, 25, 52, 152, 162, 180, 288n